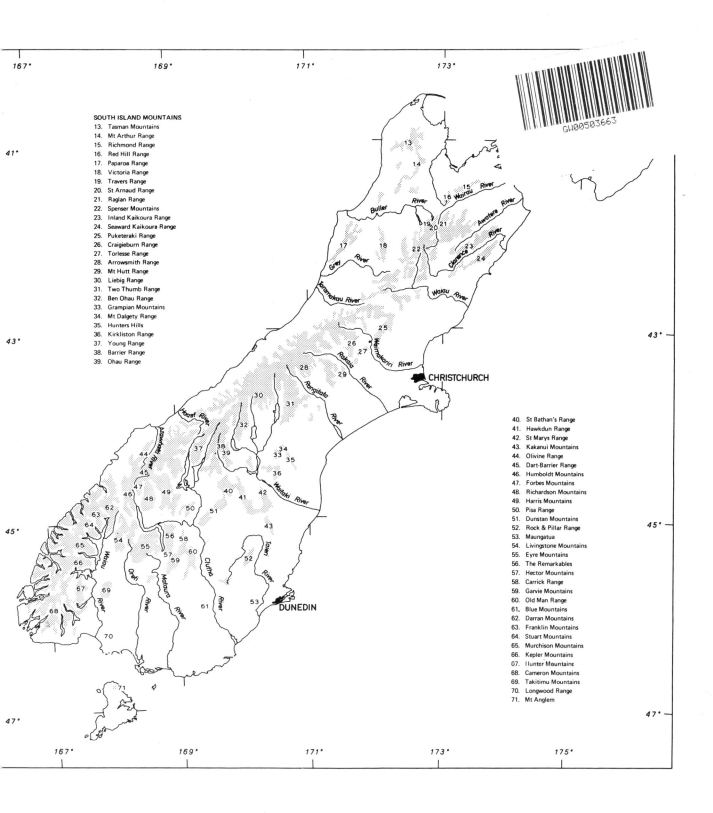

SOUTH ISLAND MOUNTAINS

13. Tasman Mountains
14. Mt Arthur Range
15. Richmond Range
16. Red Hill Range
17. Paparoa Range
18. Victoria Range
19. Travers Range
20. St Arnaud Range
21. Raglan Range
22. Spenser Mountains
23. Inland Kaikoura Range
24. Seaward Kaikoura Range
25. Puketeraki Range
26. Craigieburn Range
27. Torlesse Range
28. Arrowsmith Range
29. Mt Hutt Range
30. Liebig Range
31. Two Thumb Range
32. Ben Ohau Range
33. Grampian Mountains
34. Mt Dalgety Range
35. Hunters Hills
36. Kirkliston Range
37. Young Range
38. Barrier Range
39. Ohau Range

40. St Bathan's Range
41. Hawkdun Range
42. St Marys Range
43. Kakanui Mountains
44. Olivine Range
45. Dart-Barrier Range
46. Humboldt Mountains
47. Forbes Mountains
48. Richardson Mountains
49. Harris Mountains
50. Pisa Range
51. Dunstan Mountains
52. Rock & Pillar Range
53. Maungatua
54. Livingstone Mountains
55. Eyre Mountains
56. The Remarkables
57. Hector Mountains
58. Carrick Range
59. Garvie Mountains
60. Old Man Range
61. Blue Mountains
62. Darran Mountains
63. Franklin Mountains
64. Stuart Mountains
65. Murchison Mountains
66. Kepler Mountains
67. Hunter Mountains
68. Cameron Mountains
69. Takitimu Mountains
70. Longwood Range
71. Mt Anglem

CHRISTCHURCH

DUNEDIN

New Zealand
alpine plants

New Zealand
alpine plants

A. F. Mark and
Nancy M. Adams

GODWIT

DEDICATION

To Professor G. T. S. Baylis
a friend and teacher to us both.

When the idea of producing this book became a reality we knew that we should need to rely on the help of botanical friends and colleagues to augment our own efforts.

Much of the collecting and describing of the alpine vegetation was done in National Parks and to the Boards who gave us permission to gather plants we express our thanks for this privilege. These collections are now in the Herbarium of the Department of Botany, University of Otago.

We received many courtesies from the National Park rangers; in particular we should like to thank the Chief Rangers of Mt Aspiring (R. W. Cleland), Fiordland (H. A. Jacobs), Nelson Lakes (G. Lyons), Mt Egmont (G. G. Atkinson in 1967) and Tongariro (J. Mazey) for their help and hospitality.

Many of our plants have been examined by specialists in certain groups. We should like to thank Dr Lucy B. Moore (*Myosotis* etc.), Dr Elizabeth Edgar (Juncaceae, Cyperaceae), Dr David Given (*Celmisia*), Dr David Drury (Asteraceae) and Mrs M. J. Bulfin (*Raoulia*), all of the Botany Division, Department of Scientific and Industrial Research, Lincoln, as well as Dr Peter Raven, Stanford University, California (*Epilobium*) and Dr John Dawson, Victoria University, Wellington (Apiaceae), Mr A. P. Druce of the Botany Division, who has made a number of important observations in the North Island and Nelson mountains, made many useful comments on the illustrations and offered additional plant material.

Much of the field work, including provision of a utility vehicle, was generously supported by the Miss E. L. Hellaby, Indigenous Grasslands Research Trust.

Professor G. T. S. Baylis, Botany Department, University of Otago has from the first given generous support to this project. To him and his department, in particular Mrs D. E. Mills who tirelessly and accurately typed the manuscript and Mrs Trish Fleming who handled the reviews, we are greatly indebted.

We thank Mr G. A. H. Kidd of the Geography Department, University of Otago for preparing the maps and diagrams. We also thank Dr Elizabeth Edgar and Mr D. A. Little (Classics Department, University of Otago) for their help in complementing the booklet by Arnold Wall and H. H. Allan on 'The Botanical Names of the Flora of New Zealand' (1945), with the derivation of scientific names. Dr Edgar and Dr Henry Connor commented on the keys for *Poa* and *Chionochloa*, respectively, for this revision.

It is impossible to undertake a book of this size, involving as it has a very large proportion of our leisure and holiday time, without its having an effect on our respective families. The artist has many reasons for thanking Patricia Mark for her generous acceptance of a frequent guest.

A.F.M., N.M.A.

First published 1973
Reprinted with revisions 1979, 1986
This fully revised and updated edition published 1995 by

Godwit Publishing Ltd
15 Rawene Road, P.O. Box 34-683
Birkenhead, Auckland, New Zealand

ISBN 0 908877 83 8

Cover design by Marie Low
Cover illustrations by Nancy M. Adams
Printed in Singapore

CONTENTS

PART 1

PART 2

THE PLANTS

INTRODUCTION

To the ever-growing numbers of biologists and naturalists the mountains have much to offer. Especially interesting is the changing pattern of life that is associated with increasing altitude. For naturalists the alpine zone is perhaps the most exciting. It begins at the tree line—the upper limit reached by trees or large shrubs, and continues upwards to the nival zone—the region of permanent ice and snow.

Except in the subpolar regions, alpine plants are dependent on mountains for their very existence. Yet because of variation in the shape, size, geographic location and parent material of mountains, their vegetation is highly variable throughout the world. Mountain climates may be quite different from place to place, making them difficult to characterise, although one over-riding climatic feature is the very short growing season. Adaptation to this highly demanding environment is perhaps the most unifying feature of all alpine plants because in order to survive here, all organisms have to complete their seasonal growth and reproduction during the short alpine summer.

This book presents some of the more important features of the New Zealand mountains: their origin and structure, environment, flora and vegetation. The main section deals with most of the 600 or so vascular plants found beyond the tree line; the plants are arranged systematically more or less as in the technical books dealing with the floras. *Flora of New Zealand* Volume I, 1961, by Dr H. H. Allan (Government Printer, Wellington), covers the pteridophytes, conifers and dicotyledonous flowering plants, while Volume II, 1970, by Dr Lucy B. Moore and Dr Elizabeth Edgar, deals with the monocotyledons except for the grasses and Volume IV, 1988, by Dr Colin Webb and others deals mainly with naturalised pteridophytes, conifers and dicotyledons but also includes some recent revisions of indigenous members of these groups. In these works, the order of the plant families and their genera is based upon the vegetative and especially floral features that best demonstrate evolutionary patterns and relationships. This system seems preferable to an ecological arrangement because such classifications of plant communities are more subjective and less precise than a systematic classification. Also, many alpine plants have very wide environmental tolerances, allowing them to grow in a range of habitats and hence in more than one plant community. Moreover, anomalous patterns of geographical distribution in many New Zealand alpine plants mean that association between such species and certain plant communities is likely to be only partial.

Nevertheless, we have tried to emphasise the ecological aspects in the descriptions accompanying each species. Brief plant descriptions are given together with geographical and altitudinal distributions. The six altitudinal zones recognised on the basis of climate, type of plant cover and changes in the flora are: lowland, montane, subalpine, low-alpine, high-alpine and nival. Each zone occupies 300-500 m (1,000-1,500 ft) but their exact elevations vary; they decrease as the latitude increases.

In most species, flowering occurs in December-January but those with a wide altitudinal range have a more extended flowering period. An increase in elevation of about 120 m (400 ft) tends to delay flowering in a species by about four days.

Scientific names of plants are used throughout and the author of each name is also given. At first sight these names and their authorities may seem formidable and discouraging as they are often long and unfamiliar, but they are indispensable for precision. Popular names, which to the beginner are more encouraging, are unsatisfactory mainly because no rules have been laid down for their use and it is possible to have the same name applied to two or more unrelated plants, or different names to the same species in the same or different localities. Moreover, relatively few alpine species have an approved common name. Common names are included only where they are in general use or where they seem particularly appropriate, but a note of explanation follows each scientific name to indicate its relevance. In those cases where scientific names have changed since publication of the last (revised) edition of this book in 1986 and therefore may not yet be generally known, the earlier name is included in brackets. Varieties have been described in several alpine species, but in four genera (*Chionochloa, Leptinella (Cotula), Epilobium, Ranunculus*), which have been revised recently, subspecies rather than varieties have been recognised where the variation is reinforced by a difference in geographical distribution. Keys and technical terms are kept to a minimum and for terms used there is a glossary.

The drawings are from fresh plants, many, as the locality notes indicate, collected from National Parks. Plants that were drawn and described were collected with the permission of the respective Park Boards. After pressing and drying they have been added to the herbarium at Otago University as a permanent record. Species not illustrated in Part 2 have an asterisk before their name.

Metric units are used throughout but for convenience we have included equivalent values in feet (in most cases rounded off).

We trust that this book will assist with one of the main purposes of National Parks and other protected natural areas—to improve the knowledge of and increase the general interest in the many splendid natural features which these areas contain. If we may achieve this for alpine vegetation and its plants then, hopefully, we may also justify our claim for the need to conserve our alpine vegetation everywhere as close to its natural state as possible. We owe this to future generations. In addition it will provide the best safeguard for conservation of the alpine soils and the maximum control and yield of water, potentially the most valuable usable product from the mountains.

IN THIS 1995 reprinting the several changes in plant names made since the book was last revised have been incorporated. There have been several new species described in this period and a number of important genera have been revised. Notable here have been several grass genera: *Agrostis, Deyeuxia, Lachnagrostis, Poa* and *Chionochloa*, the last two being both large and important. For them as well as *Kelleria* (*Drapetes*) keys to aid identification have been included. Some additional illustrations are also included in this substantially revised and updated (to August 1995) edition.

Chapter 1
ORIGIN AND STRUCTURE OF THE MOUNTAINS

THE MOUNTAINS in New Zealand that support alpine plants begin in the north with Te Moehau and the Raukumara Range, and continue to Stewart Island (see map). These mountains differ considerably in their parent materials, present and past climates and degree of isolation. All of these are important factors in determining distribution of the alpine plants.

Geologists tell us that the present topography in New Zealand only began to develop about 20 million years ago. The main mountain ranges providing an alpine environment are probably no more than two million years old.

Apart from the volcanic mountains in the North Island, all of the New Zealand mountains which today support alpine vegetation arose about the same time, as a result of earth movements along a belt extending from Gisborne south-westward down the North Island and through the Southern Alps along the Alpine Fault to Fiordland. These movements of the Kaikoura Orogeny were, in fact, responsible for the present shape, size and general relief of New Zealand. The Alpine Fault which separates two of the world's major tectonic plates, the Indian-Australian Plate to the west and the Pacific Plate to the east, remains relatively active. One of the few faults visible from space, the Alpine Fault extends in virtually a straight line from Milford Sound to the Spencer Mountains in Nelson. The collision of these two crustal plates has not only thrust up the Southern Alps at a rate which currently averages about 10 mm annually, but has also resulted in the lateral displacement of the rocks on either side of the fault by some 450 km. This is revealed most dramatically by the distinctive, mostly barren reddish ultramafic or ultrabasic rocks or Red Hills on the eastern side of the fault in Nelson being exactly matched by the Red Mountain area in northwest Otago. The uplift has amounted to at least 18,600 m, and the rate measured in south Westland (ca 107 m for the last 10,000 years or about 11 mm a year) has been about balanced by extremely active erosion, largely by water but in the alpine regions also by ice, wind and freeze-thaw action. The interactions of these opposing forces has been largely responsible for the detailed relief patterns we see today. The magnitude of these erosive agents is indicated by the relatively modest elevation of the Southern Alps today, with Mt Cook, the highest peak, some 3,764 m above sea level. The products of this erosion are widespread on both sides of the Alps.

The rocks that were uplifted differ from place to place and these differences can affect their present erodibility and hence vegetation. Notable here is the metamorphosed sedimentary rock, greywacke, extending down the North Island mountain chain (Kaweka, Kaimanawa, Ruahine, Tararua Ranges) and continuing in the South Island from Marlborough (Kaikoura Ranges) and south-east Nelson (Spenser Mountains, St Arnaud Range) along the Southern Alps and including the several outlying ranges in central Canterbury (Two Thumb, Ben Ohau, Torlesse, Craigieburn, Puketeraki Ranges) to north Otago (St Bathans, Hawkdun Ranges). Here it merges with the more highly metamorphosed schist from western Otago (Humboldt, Richardson, Harris, Eyre Mountains; Young Range) which extends eastwards towards the coast through Central Otago (Pisa, Old Man, Carrick, Rock & Pillar Ranges; Hector, Garvie, Dunstan Mountains and The Remarkables) and also northwards as a narrow strip on the western flank of the Southern Alps. The mountains of Fiordland and Stewart Island (Mt Anglem) are formed of very much harder, less erodible metamorphosed rocks, mostly gneiss and granite, as are most of the mountains in northern Westland (Victoria and Paparoa Ranges). The Tasman Mountains in north-west Nelson are a mixture of sedimentary, metamorphic and granitic rocks.

Greywacke is particularly prone to frost shattering and is eroding rapidly, resulting in the development of talus slopes or screes, whereas schist is relatively stable. Granite weathers very slowly into a sparse, sandy soil. Apart from this and the striking effect of the ultrabasic rocks in the mineral belt adjacent to the Alpine Fault in Nelson-Marlborough and north-western Otago, the different materials seem to have little effect on the distribution of alpine plants.

In the North Island the most spectacular mountains are of volcanic origin. The highest, Ruapehu, 2,796 m (9,175 ft) rises at the south of the central volcanic plateau and nearby are the other active volcanoes of Tongariro National Park, Ngauruhoe 2,290 m (7,515 ft) and Tongariro 1,986 m (6,517 ft). Close to the west coast is the isolated cone of Mt Egmont, 2,518 m (8,260 ft) high. These volcanic mountains are even more recent in origin than the others and reached their present height only during the last ice age of the Pleistocene, except for Ngauruhoe which is younger still. Since then, there has been some slight modification by erosion and continuing activity.

The highly porous lava and loose scoria, together with the vulnerability of the scoria and ash to erosion, adds to the problems with which alpine plants must contend and is one reason for the rather limited alpine flora and vegetation on these mountains: but their youth also means that there has been less time for plants to colonise them than on the main alpine ranges.

Chapter 2
THE ALPINE ZONE

IN MANY PARTS of New Zealand the lower limit of the alpine zone, marked by the tree line, is a conspicuous feature of the mountain landscape. Here, a continuous subalpine hardwood forest of dark evergreen trees up to 6 m (20 ft) tall, gives way abruptly, usually to a mixture of shrubs, large snow tussocks and herbs in which, from a distance, the straw colour of the tussocks predominates. The line is usually sharp, regular and strikingly horizontal when seen from a distance. This is the situation where some type of beech forest forms the tree line. Usually it is silver beech with small toothed leaves but in the drier areas, especially Canterbury, eastern Nelson and Marlborough in the South Island and on the highly porous soils of the volcanic plateau in the North Island, silver beech is replaced by mountain beech with small, smooth-edged leaves (Fig. 1)

For information on the important species involved here see Poole & Adams *Trees and Shrubs of New Zealand.* DSIR Publishing, Wellington, 1990.

The altitude of the beech tree line is about 1,500 m (4,900 ft) on Mt Ruapehu and the Kaweka Range in the north and it decreases fairly steadily southwards to be about 1,200 m (4,000 ft) on the Tararua Range in the southern North Island and 900 m (3,000 ft) on the mountains of Fiordland in the far south. This decrease reflects the reduction in temperatures with increasing latitude. But superimposed on this pattern is one of a rising tree line according to the distance from the coast at a particular latitude. At about 42°S the tree line is about 1,100 m (3,700 ft) on the Paparoa Range near the west coast, 1,400 m (4,600 ft) at Nelson Lakes near the centre and about 1,200 m (4,000 ft) on the Seaward Kaikoura Range near the east coast.

There are two important exceptions to this pattern of abrupt tree lines of beech, and with both of these the subalpine-alpine boundary is not at all obvious; in fact it may be quite difficult to recognise. The first of these situations occurs in areas lacking beech, apparently because the beeches have not yet

Fig. 1. Silver beech, *Nothofagus menziesii.*

Mountain beech, *Nothofagus solandri* var. *cliffortioides.*

9

returned since the last glacial period drove forest from many areas. In the absence of beech forest there is a subalpine coniferous-hardwood forest as on Mt Egmont, in central Westland, on Stewart Island and other smaller areas. Because the dominant trees in this forest are less cold-tolerant than either silver or mountain beech they do not extend as high on the mountain sides. Tall subalpine shrubs, especially those of *Olearia, Brachyglottis* (*Senecio*) and *Dracophyllum*, which occur within the forest, also gradually replace it as the main cover. They usually form a dense, almost impenetrable tangle before being in turn replaced gradually by typical alpine species at an elevation close to that of the regional tree line.

The second occurs in the drier central and eastern areas of the South Island where many of the mountain ranges carry no forests today. Various types of tussock grassland usually occur from the lowlands to at least 1,500 m (5,000 ft) although remains of sub-fossil forest—surface logs, buried charcoals, forest dimples, fossil soils and isolated trees or small relic stands of forest—indicate that forest was once widespread up to about 1,200 m (4,000 ft). Radiocarbon dating of several wood and charcoal fragments indicates extensive destruction of these forests, almost certainly by Maori fires, some time about the twelfth century. However, treeless grasslands or mixed shrub-grasslands have persisted during the post-glacial period above the climatic treeline and in the drier basins of the central South Island, particularly Central Otago, in isolated frost hollows in the central North Island, and also on riverbeds. Between 2,500 and 1,500 years ago, or at least 500 years before recorded human habitation, many parts of the South and North Island were swept by natural fires. These destroyed the drier forests over large areas in both Central Otago and the Mackenzie basin of inland South Canterbury, as well as locally elsewhere. Both the frequency and extent of fires increased in the central and eastern South Island from about 1000 AD, coinciding with human settlement. This resulted in extension of the grasslands, often preceded by bracken fern, through the invasion of fire-tolerant plants from either the alpine zone or from lower elevations where grasslands had previously been established. As a result of this, the alpine-subalpine boundary has virtually disappeared today. Usually the level of the ancient tree line is not easy to determine, but those relic patches of forest that persist in some areas may be a useful guide. Most of the conspicuous grassland species cross this line today, but one of them, the common hard tussock, *Festuca novae-zelandiae*, reaches its upper altitudinal limit in many areas close to the natural tree line.

So much for the lower limits of the alpine zone. Its upper limit is at the summer snow line—the level to which snow thaws during most summers. This line, of course, is not at all regular but varies with topographical features, especially steepness and direction of slope. These affect both snow-lie patterns and rates of thaw. In general the permanent snow line, like the tree line, falls with latitude, from 2,400 m (7,800 ft) on Mt Ruapehu to about 2,000 m (6,500 ft) in Fiordland. Above it is the permanent ice and snow of the nival zone. This is limited to Mt Ruapehu and perhaps Mt Egmont in the North Island, but in the South Island it is very extensive, especially along the Southern Alps where Mt Cook, near the centre, rises to 3,764 m (12,349 ft). In the nival zone only a few alpine plants, mostly lichens, can survive on rocks that are either too steep or too exposed to be permanently snow-covered. Nevertheless, there are a few flowering plants (*Ranunculus grahamii, Parahebe birleyi*) that are essentially confined to crevices in such places. The *Ranunculus* reaches its upper limit at about 2,830 m (9,300 ft) but the *Parahebe*, together with *Hebe haastii*, extend a further 100 m, to 2,930 m (9,600 ft), in the Mt Cook region.

Chapter 3
THE ALPINE ENVIRONMENT

GENERAL: Probably the most distinctive feature of the mountain environment in New Zealand is the erratic and changeable weather that can virtually bring all seasons within the compass of one day. This comes from our latitude being close to the low pressure belt in the southern ocean, with strong westerly winds and the frequent alternation of eastward-moving depressions and anticyclones at all times of the year. In addition, the general climate of New Zealand is influenced by its small size in a vast ocean and by its shape and relief. The Southern Alps are a major barrier to the prevailing moist westerly wind and create a sharp contrast in climate between the western and eastern slopes. This contrast, though less obvious in the alpine zone than in the lowlands, nevertheless has an important effect on the vegetation.

Though New Zealand is a mountainous country and has been settled by Europeans for more than a century, there is still limited information on our mountain climate, especially from alpine areas. This merely reflects the absence of habitation in these often inhospitable regions. The severe conditions and difficulties of access in winter greatly increase the problems and cost of obtaining precise and reliable records. So, apart from two official stations close to the alpine zone, Chateau Tongariro, 1,119 m (3,670 ft), on the slopes of Mt Ruapehu and The Hermitage, 765 m (2,510 ft), under Mt Cook, climatic measurements from high altitudes have been obtained from just a few areas, notably the Black Birch Range in Marlborough, Cupola Basin in Nelson Lakes National Park, the Craigieburn Range in Canterbury and the Old Man and Rock & Pillar Ranges in Central Otago.

TEMPERATURE: Temperatures from one lowland and four alpine sites (Fig. 2) give some idea of the range that alpine plants must tolerate from season to season and with increasing altitude above the tree line. Comparisons with many alpine areas abroad emphasise the oceanic effects here which produce relatively mild winters and cool summers. Mid-summer temperatures for tree line on the Craigieburn Range and at Chateau Tongariro,

Fig. 2. Air temperature values for five sites; one lowland, one tree line, one low-alpine and two high-alpine. Christchurch records are for a 56-year period (1905–60); Craigieburn Range for an 8-year period (1961–68) and Old Man Range for 6 years (1963–68).

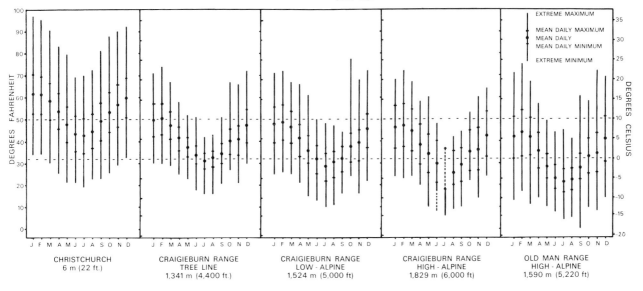

which is about 380 m (1,250 ft) below the tree line on Mt Ruapehu, indicate that in New Zealand, as in many other parts of the world, the lower limit of the alpine zone, i.e. the tree line, occurs where the mean air temperature for the warmest month is about 10 degrees C. In some way, probably by a temperature limitation of photosynthesis, leaf growth and wood production, this mean temperature value appears to reflect the limit for tree growth. Wood production is quite wasteful in the economy of a plant and this probably explains the reduction in both size and number of woody plants with increasing altitude that we see in the alpine zone. While the mean summer isotherm is about 10°C at tree line or the lower limit of the alpine zone it is reduced by five degrees to about 5°C at the upper limit of the low-alpine zone and by another five degrees to about 0°C at the upper limit of the high-alpine zone or the permanent snow line (see Chapter 5). Temperatures are highest close to the ground surface and many alpine plants are adapted in their size and form to make the maximum use of the available heat. On the coldest, most exposed sites, extremely dwarfed cushion plants predominate.

Even though we can enjoy warm days in the mountains, temperatures recorded at the three alpine sites shown in Figure 2 indicate an overall severity. At the highest altitudes, in fellfield and cushion vegetation, the cold is especially harsh. The mean annual air temperature at the two sites shown in Figure 2 between 1,500 and 1,800 m (5,000-6,000 ft) is close to freezing, as it is in many alpine areas abroad. A five-year continuous record of air temperatures made at 1,590 m (5,200 ft) in Central Otago emphasises the prevailing cold even during the growing season. The longest period without frost varied, over five summers, only from eight to thirteen days! Away from the equatorial mountains, where summers come by day and winters by night, this seems to be about the shortest frost-free period so far recorded in an alpine zone. During a full year only about 20 per cent of the days, extending over a nine-month period, are free of frost (Fig. 3) During the warmest month, February, freezing occurs on about 40 per cent of the days. About half of the days in a year fluctuate across freezing point while about 30 per cent never thaw.

Even though temperatures in the soil are much less severe, those of bare soil or rock, as on a scree, experience even more violent temperature variation. It is not unusual in some regions to find bare rocks too hot for a comfortable seat. At the coldest alpine sites the soil usually remains unfrozen during the warmest four months and, in winter, the insulating cover of snow will prevent deep freezing and also hold the temperatures of the rooting zone within just a few degrees of freezing. But on very exposed sites where snow does not persist, freezing may occur at least down to 50 cm (20 in).

PRECIPITATION: Measurements of precipitation from most alpine areas may not be very reliable because of the difficulties of high winds and of coping with snow. Amounts may vary enormously

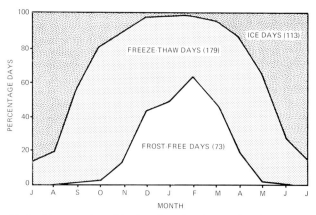

Fig. 3. **Mean percentage of ice days, freeze-thaw days and frost-free days per month in air temperatures in the high-alpine zone (1,590 m: 5,220 ft) of the Old Man Range, Central Otago for a 5-year period (1963–68).**

over quite small distances. Even so, it is obvious that precipitation is very high on all the mountains that first intercept the westerly winds—731 cm (or 288 in) a year on Mt Egmont; 709 cm (279 in) at Homer Tunnel in Fiordland; over 500 cm (200 in) above the tree line in the central Tararua Range; 439 cm (173 in) at The Hermitage; 290 cm (114 in) at Chateau Tongariro; 396 cm (156 in) at Arthurs Pass township. Greater amounts than these (up to 1,200 cm: 472 in) have been estimated for some more remote western areas, but east of the main ranges there is a striking decrease, even in the mountains. On the Craigieburn Range in mid-Canterbury, just 32 km (20 miles) east of Arthurs Pass, the yearly average is no more than about 200 cm (80 in), while less than half this distance further east, on the Torlesse Range, it is reduced to about 100 cm (40 in). The top of the Old Man Range in Central Otago receives about 165 cm (65 in) while only 16 km (10 miles) away, Alexandra, about 1,500 m (5,000 ft) below, in the valley, gets only one fifth as much. Everywhere in the mountains the precipitation is well distributed throughout the year but with increasing altitude a greater proportion of it falls as snow.

SNOW: In the alpine zone snow may fall during any month. The depth and duration of snow in the mountains are both variable, but only exceptionally does a continuous cover persist at the tree line for more than a month or two. Avalanche damage to tree-line forests is not uncommon. At higher altitudes there are much greater amounts of snow that reduce the length of the growing season. Very few plants survive at altitudes above the permanent snow line, but even for a considerable distance below it there are cirques and other large depressions where snow accumulates and persists into late summer. Only the plants that can cope with a very short growing season occupy these snowbank areas.

WIND: New Zealand is a windy country and the mountains especially so, though there are few actual records. The estimated average wind speed 4.6 m (15 ft) above ground level in the alpine zone of the Black Birch Range, Marlborough, based on a thirteen-month record, is about 6m/sec (14 mph). On top of the Old Man Range in Central Otago, the average wind speed over two years just 1.2 m (4 ft) off the ground was only slightly less, with little seasonal variation. The violence of the wind often makes the mountains unpleasant to visit. Measurement for one growing season on the summit of the Rock & Pillar Range in Central Otago showed wind speeds even greater than those recorded during the growing season on the notoriously windy Mt Washington in north-eastern USA. But wind speed usually declines sharply on the more sheltered leeward slopes: on the Rock & Pillar it is almost halved, less than 500 m (1,650 ft) below the summit.

HUMIDITY: In the high rainfall areas along and west of the main mountain chain the air is usually humid. But after having shed much of its moisture load as it cools on being forced over the mountains, the air becomes much drier as it reaches the leeward eastern sides. This pattern is pronounced in Canterbury where, at lower altitudes, the blustery, hot, dry nor'wester is an important climatic feature. In the mountains to the east of the main divide, the nor'wester is cooler, but still relatively dry—humidity often falls below 40 per cent, occasionally below 30 per cent, during the warmest part of the day. Low night temperatures, however, usually bring the humidity up close to saturation.

EVAPORATION AND SOIL MOISTURE: High winds and low humidities by day mean that evaporation rates during summer can be quite high in the mountains to the east of the main divide, but the lower temperatures and, in many areas, frequent fog, keep the rates lower than in the adjacent lowlands. This means that in the soil, moisture is freely available for the plants, even on the apparently desiccated screes in Canterbury. In this feature alpine areas in New Zealand are unlike many alpine regions abroad where droughts in summer are common.

FOG: The very few records of fog incidence are not entirely accurate because they have been made from a distance, but they indicate that this is probably an important climatic factor in most alpine areas in New Zealand. Fog not only reduces sunshine and evaporation and raises the humidity, but in addition it can contribute significantly to the soil water through condensation and fog drip. The notoriously foggy Tararua Range and the southern Ruahine Range may be partially fog-bound along their higher crests for more than 250 days a year. Even in the drier regions—the Old Man Range in Central Otago, the Torlesse Range in mid-Canterbury and the Black Birch Range in Marlborough—the incidence of fog is still high (175-200 days a year) and here it often occurs without general rain.

MICROCLIMATE: It is important to realise that alpine environments can change drastically over quite short distances. In fact local climates are more important in the alpine than in any other zone. Differences in steepness of slope and direction of exposure in particular, can alter the intensity and duration of sunshine, and hence also the temperature, evaporation rate, persistence of snow and soil moisture, while variations in wind speed and direction can affect accumulation and persistence of snow. The wide range of local or micro-environments so produced is reflected in an equally wide range of local alpine communities. Where the ground surface is patterned into stripes or hummocks as in parts of the Central Otago high-alpine cushionfield, differential freezing over winter between the crests (where the soil is usually frozen) and adjacent depressions (where it may remain unfrozen) appears to be responsible for the maintenance of the microtopography.

SOILS: In the alpine zone soils like microclimates form complex patterns because of the interplay of several factors — parent material, topography, climate, vegetation and time. Within short distances soils may be developed on intact weathered rock, solifluction debris, scree, fan material, moraine or on wind-borne loess. Mobility of soils on steep slopes prevents them maturing into a series of well defined horizons — they remain permanently young and are called skeletal or steepland soils. Localised slumping or landslides on otherwise stable mountain slopes can similarly rejuvenate soils, thereby improving drainage and fertility, that results in changes in composition of the plant community. Temperature and effective precipitation are also important. Low temperatures reduce rates of chemical weathering so that the fine colloidal fraction is small and soil texture becomes coarser with altitude. Soil moisture is never limiting for plant growth in the alpine zone — except when frozen, as it may be for up to six months. Excess moisture causes leaching of nutrients over time. Leaching, then, increases with rainfall, causing soil acidity also to increase, so that at high altitudes soils are both more highly leached and strongly acid while an increasing proportion of the nutrients, especially phosphorus, become tied up in undecayed organic matter.

Under moderate rainfalls, mature soils of the low-alpine zone generally have a thin, brownish, friable and structureless topsoil overlying a yellow-brown subsoil. High rainfalls produce strongly leached or podzolised yellow-brown earths. Where impeded drainage creates permanent waterlogging, decay is incomplete and organic matter accumulates on the surface as peat. Since plants are essential for soil development, the thin or patchy vegetation of the high-alpine zone is associated with equally sparse soil. Removal of the insulation provided by a plant cover anywhere in the alpine zone usually initiates erosion by allowing frost action, often associated with needle ice, throughout the snow-free season. Such mobility seriously retards seedling establishment and hence revegetation.

Chapter 4
THE ALPINE FLORA

THERE are certain general features of the New Zealand alpine flora that are sufficiently important and striking to be mentioned here.

Questions about Origin of the Alpine Flora

One feature which our alpine plants share with the rest of the native flora is the very high proportion which are confined to New Zealand. About 93 per cent of the alpine species are endemic to the New Zealand Biological Region (which includes the Subantarctic Islands), compared with about 80 per cent for the whole vascular flora.

Among the many alpine genera, however, the number confined to New Zealand is quite small. Moreover, they tend to be the less significant members[1] in terms of plant cover. Also, there are several, including some of the most conspicuous genera, that are represented outside New Zealand by just one or a few species[2], or by only a small proportion of their total species[3]. All of these genera, being centred in New Zealand, are considered to have originated either here or perhaps on the Antarctic continent.

Other alpine genera are well represented in Australia[4], or South America[5], or South Africa[6]. Unlike the lowland flora, there is only a slight relationship among our alpines with the subtropical Malaysian region[7]. There are many of our alpine genera that have a wide distribution outside New Zealand[8].

The very high degree of endemism among the alpine species here, suggests in itself a relatively long history of evolution under alpine conditions. Yet geologists claim, as mentioned earlier, that alpine environments have been present for only about two million years. This implies a quite recent development of our alpine plants. There have been attempts to explain this rather puzzling situation of how so many plants developed here in virtual isolation and in such a relatively short time. Dr Peter Raven has argued that many New Zealand plants of alpine and sub-alpine habitats arrived here via Australia through long distance dispersal, following the creation of mountains there and in Malaysia and New Guinea. By claiming unusual opportunities for rapid evolution and adaptive radiation of New Zealand's mountain flora, particularly through hybridisation, he even included some of the largest and most important New Zealand mountain genera, with few representatives in Australia (e.g. *Celmisia, Hebe, Ourisia, Chionochloa, Aciphylla*) in this interpretation. An important issue with these latter, largely alpine genera, is whether their few lower elevation species represent ancestral or derived members. Dr Peter Wardle rejected Raven's

case for this latter group of plants, given their centre of distribution in New Zealand. Rather, he claimed for them a dispersal centre in New Zealand while accepting that some other genera on Raven's list — *Epilobium, Olearia* and certain epacrids, may well have reached New Zealand via Australia. Wardle earlier suggested that several mountain groups e.g. species of *Donatia, Phyllachne, Forstera, Oreostylidium, Herpolirion, Rostkovia, Carpha, Gaimardia, Oreobolus, Haastia* and *Hectorella*, could have had a greater antiquity in New Zealand through occupation of cold, wet, infertile soils on peneplained uplands in a generally forested landscape here or perhaps on a southern extension of the country. Such habitats might have been adequate for a cold region flora which later developed into our present alpine flora when mountain building and climatic cooling greatly extended suitable environments. This certainly seems plausible for those genera (and many species) that occur below treeline in New Zealand today which is most of the above plus *Coprosma, Hebe, Raoulia, Poa, Polystichum* and others. *Haastia* and *Hectorella*, however, are not in this category, being strictly alpine genera. Indeed *Hectorella* is a special case, being a strictly high-alpine endemic and monotypic genus with just the single species *H. caespitosa*, along with a species of *Lyallia* on Kerguelen Island, in the family Hectorellaceae. The possible role of Antarctica as a source for this and perhaps other alpine elements of our flora has been heightened by the recent discovery there of beech (*Nothofagus*) remains of late Pliocene age (2.8 million y BP), some 200 km from the South Pole. Prior to this significant find, Antarctica was considered not to have been directly involved in the origin and distribution of southern hemisphere alpine floras since it was assumed to have been entirely ice covered prior to alpine environments being available in New Zealand and other southern hemisphere countries.

It is also possible that much of our alpine flora has developed in New Zealand only within the last two million years or so, by evolution from certain members of a pre-existing non-alpine flora, together with occasional chance immigrations from some other areas that supported alpine plants, notably Antarctica and, more recently, Australia. The very rapid development and evolution in our alpine flora, which this suggestion implies, is supported by the widespread occurrence of hybridism and the variation or polymorphism in many of the alpine plant groups. Natural crosses or hybrids occur in many of our alpine genera[10]. There are certain pairs of genera where hybridism may occur: *Leucogenes* and *Raoulia, Gnaphalium* and *Helichrysum*; *Helichrysum* and

Ewartia: *Aciphylla* and *Gingidia*; *Forstera* and *Phyllachne*; *Gaultheria* and *Pernettya* — in this latter case all species of *Pernettya* have recently been placed in *Gaultheria*.

Such hybridism suggests that the diversification and evolution necessary to adapt to the variety of alpine environments has been too recent and explosive to allow evolution of the usual genetic barriers to interbreeding in many groups. However, another reason that has been suggested to account for the unusually high incidence of hybridism is the general simplicity of structure and colour in the flowers which thereby attract an unusually wide range of pollinating insects (see p. 16).

The presence of several highly variable and intergrading plant groups or complexes within the alpine flora, which so far have proved difficult to resolve, may be a further indication of recent rapid evolution. Such complexes resulting from variation or polymorphism occur in many groups[11]. Further studies should indicate whether this variation is caused merely by differences in the habitats they occupy or whether it can be attributed to innate genetical variability between one population and another, or to a combination of these effects. Such a detailed study has been made of the indigenous alpine species of *Ranunculus*.

1. *Corallospartium, Dolicoglottis, Gingidia, Hectorella, Notothlaspi, Leucogenes, Lignocarpa, Oreostylidium, Pachycladon, Parahebe.*
2. *Aciphylla, Celmisia, Chionochloa, Chionohebe, Hebe.*
3. *Abrotanella, Anisotome, Astelia, Brachyglottis, Carmichaelia, Cheesemania, Coprosma, Dracophyllum, Helichrysum, Lagenifera, Myosotis, Schizeilema.*
4. *Brachyscome, Caladenia, Craspedia, Cyathodes, Empodisma, Epacris, Leucopogon, Lyperanthus, Pentachondra, Pimelea, Prasophyllum, Stackhousia, Swainsona, Thelymitra.*
5. *Acaena, Donatia, Forstera, Gunnera, Marsippospermum, Oreomyrrhis, Ourisia, Phyllachne, Uncinia.*
6. *Bulbinella, Geranium, Oxalis, Wahlenbergia.*
7. *Coprosma, Coriaria, Mazus, Melicytus, Nertera.*
8. *Agrostis, Anemone, Carex, Cardamine, Drosera, Epilobium, Euphrasia, Gaultheria, Gentiana, Geranium, Geum, Hydrocotyle, Juncus, Lobelia, Luzula, Myrsine, Oxalis, Plantago, Poa, Psychrophila (Caltha), Ranunculus, Schoenus, Scleranthus, Stellaria, Trisetum, Utricularia, Viola.*
9. *Actinotus novae-zelandiae, Astelia nervosa, Carpha alpina, Cassinia leptophylla, Celmisia gracilenta, Centrolepis ciliata, Chionochloa rubra, C. rigida, Cyathodes pumila, C. empetrifolia, Donatia novae-zelandiae, Drosera spathulata, D. arcturi, Gaultheria macrostigma, G. depressa, Gentiana lineata, Helichrysum filicaule, Herpolirion novae-zelandiae, Lagenifera pumila, Leucopogon fraseri, Microlaena thomsonii, Nertera balfouriana, Oreobolus strictus, O. pectinatus, Oreomyrrhis colensoi, Oreostylidium subulatum, Pentachondra pumila, Phyllachne colensoi, Prasophyllum colensoi, Pseudognaphalium luteo-album, Schoenus pauciflorus, Utricularia monanthos, Viola cunninghamii.*
10. *Aciphylla, Anisotome, Brachyglottis, Celmisia, Chionochloa, Chionohebe, Coriaria, Craspedia, Dolicoglottis, Dracophyllum, Epilobium, Gaultheria, Gingidia, Hebe, Helichrysum, Ourisia, Pimelea, Ranunculus.*
11. *Brachyscome sinclairii, Aciphylla lyallii, Dracophyllum recurvum, Celmisia dureitzii, Myosotis australis, Pimelea oreophila, Pratia angulata, Wahlenbergia albomarginata, Plantago langera,* in several species of *Gentiana, Euphrasia, Pratia* and *Parahebe* and a number of other groups.

Present Distribution Patterns

Several species are widely distributed throughout the alpine regions of New Zealand. Others are quite restricted, either to particular habitats, e.g. screes (*Ranunculus haastii*), or to natural regions, e.g. Central Otago (*R. pachyrrhizus*), the volcanic plateau (*Ourisia vulcanica*), where some regional feature of the environment probably is important. Much more puzzling are patterns that are discontinuous because of the wide gaps in distribution despite apparently favourable habitats in the interven-

ing areas. This pattern involves a number of alpine plant species from a range of habitats (*Celmisia traversii, C. petriei, Kelleria laxus, Actinotus suffocata, Microlaena thomsonii, Mitrasacme novae-zelandiae* — as well as pairs or groups of closely related species — *Raoulia rubra* in the north and *R. buchananii* in the south, *Brachyglottis adamsii* and *B. revolutus, Celmisia dallii, C. hieraciifolia* and *C. holosericea, Dracophyllum densa* and *D. politum*) that occur in these two areas yet are absent from the intervening extensive alpine region with apparently suitable habitats.

These anomalies in distribution are probably the result of glaciations during the Pleistocene. The most recent glaciation produced a very extensive ice sheet right across central and south Westland. This probably eliminated all vegetation from the region. To the north and south, as well as in the east, glaciation was less complete. In the east it was rather light, being confined to the mountains and some main river valleys, but the intervening ridges in an area of reduced precipitation were subject to a severe periglacial (frost) climate. In Nelson, glaciers seem to have descended only a small distance below the present tree line. Fiordland obviously was much more heavily glaciated, yet here, steep headlands along the present coastline and extensive submarine shelves then laid bare by low sea levels (Puysegur Bank), probably remained ice-free and vegetated, as in parts of Greenland today.

Fiordland and Nelson were important refuges for plants, particularly alpines, during this period. The effects are seen today, not only in these disjunctive distributions, but also in the large numbers of species which now are confined to either of these areas. It is perhaps surprising that these species have not spread further in the 15,000 years or so of post-glacial time. Some species appear to be progressing faster than others. Migration can be a very slow process when growth is slow and seed production somewhat precarious, especially with unhelpful prevailing winds, alpine seed-eating birds relatively rare, and when encroaching seedlings must compete with a cover of established vegetation. In fact about 6 per cent of the alpine flora is restricted to the northern end of the South Island while another 8 per cent is limited to western Otago and Fiordland in the south. This compares with less than 2 per cent confined to the very extensive alpine regions of Canterbury and Westland, and among these few species are some (*Ranunculus grahamii* and *R. godleyanus*) that favour extremely cold sites in or close to the nival zone.

Flower Colour

One of the most obvious yet perhaps disappointing features of our alpine plants is the very limited range of flower colour. The range of attractive colours that occur in alpine areas abroad is curiously missing here. The larger more conspicuous flowers, or clusters of small flowers, are frequently white, less commonly cream or yellow. These shades also predominate among the many small and inconspicuous flowers. There are some which are brightly coloured even if too minute to be appreciated, for example the crimson flowers in a few of the cushion species of *Raoulia*.

The predominance of white flowers is even more curious when we see bright colours in some closely related species outside New Zealand. On the Subantarctic Islands there are *Hebe benthamii*, *Myosotis capitata* and *M. antarctica* with vivid blue flowers, *Gentiana concinna* whose flowers range to rich crimson, and *Anisotome latifolia* and *A. antipoda*, which are rosy-red. The florets are purple in *Damnamenia vernicosa* (related to *Celmisia*) and in the three species of the allied genus *Pleurophyllum*.

Closer inspection, however, often reveals flushes of colour or tinted veins in otherwise white petals of many New Zealand alpine species among several families: Orchidaceae (*Aporostylis*), Fabaceae (*Carmichaelia, Chordospartium*). Violaceae (*Viola*), Scrophulariaceae (*Ourisia, Euphrasia, Chionohebe, Parahebe*), Gentianaceae (*Gentiana*), Portulacaceae (*Neopaxia*), Lobeliaceae (*Pratia, Lobelia*), Stylidiaceae (*Forstera*). In addition, coloured forms are often seen, particularly blue in such genera as *Herpolirion* (Liliaceae) and *Wahlenbergia* (Campanulaceae), and occasionally in *Myosotis* (Boraginaceae), while pink is not infrequent in *Geranium* (Geraniaceae), *Drosera* (Droseraceae), *Epilobium* (Onagraceae), *Pimelea* (Thymelaeaceae), *Myosotis* (Boraginaceae), *Celmisia* (Asteraceae), *Gaultheria* (Ericaceae), and *Lobelia* (Lobeliaceae). In other alpines the underside of petals may be coloured (usually pink) so that the unopened flower buds are bright but the flowers open white. *Celmisia viscosa, C. hectorii, C. sessiliflora, Parahebe trifida, Chionohebe densifolia* and *Ourisia* spp. are in this group.

These features all suggest that in the New Zealand alpine flora bright colours, especially reds, blues and purples, and other types of flower specialisation, offer no advantage. Indeed they may be a disadvantage. A likely explanation is the lack of specialised pollinating insects, especially long-tongued bees and perhaps also the scarcity of butterflies among our native insects. Insect pollination here appears to be carried out largely and quite efficiently by flies, with beetles, moths and short-tongued bees playing smaller roles. The flowers are in fact well adapted for pollination by these types of insects. White petals are usually associated with short-tubed flowers and these seem best suited to the insects available. Yellow flowers seem best adapted for flies and short-tongued bees, although they are often visited by beetles also. Thus, the colours which predominate among our alpine plants appear to be those which attract the greatest number of native pollinating insects. In *Epilobium* it was found that white flowers occur in 34 of the 37 species, some of which originated from outside New Zealand. In addition, the more brightly coloured flowers were considered to be the more primitive.

There appears to be no one explanation for the evolution of white flowers in New Zealand's indigenous plants since they occur in genera with different origins, histories, distributions and breeding systems.

There is no lack of scent in flowers of the alpine plants, although with the usual windy conditions we may overlook it. Probably scent is a more effective lure for the natural pollinaters than bright colours although there has been no systematic study of fragance in New Zealand plants.

There is compensation for the lack of flower colour in the variety to be seen in the fleshy fruits produced by several genera. Red predominates (*Leucopogon, Pimelea, Astelia, Pentachondra, Cyathodes, Gaultheria, Lepidothamnus*) but pink (*Gaultheria, Pratia*) and orange (*Leucopogon, Nertera, Astelia, Podocarpus*) and purple (*Myrsine*) also occur with a wide variety in *Coprosma* even within certain species (*C. cheesemanii*). In *Myrsine* and *Pentachondra* fruits usually take two years to ripen. The general association between fleshy fruits and separate sexes, which has been noted for the seed plants generally, also applies in New Zealand, including its alpine flora, although there is no clear explanation for it either here or abroad. According to Dr David Lloyd about half of the genera in New Zealand with separate sexes also have fleshy fruits or seeds. This also appears to be true for the alpine plants.

Unisexual Plants

Most flowering plants have male and female parts that are both functional contained within each flower, or at least on each plant if in separate flowers. In the New Zealand flora, however, there is a high incidence of species with separate plants of each sex.

Among the total flora they amount to about 18 per cent of the genera and 13 per cent of the species, and for the alpine species the incidence is only slightly less. It has been suggested that the high proportion of unisexual species in New Zealand is correlated with the unspecialised promiscuously pollinated flowers and maybe an adaptation to ensure cross-pollination in the absence of specialised pollinating insects. It has also been noted that the scarcity of bright flowers is specially evident in genera that frequently have brightly coloured flowers in other parts of the world, e.g. notably *Myosotis* and *Gentiana*.

Alpine genera in which unisexuality is a feature include *Coprosma, Aciphylla, Anisotome, Gingidia, Halocarpus, Lepidothamnus, Melicytus, Hectorella, Astelia, Pimelea*, while it occurs less frequently in *Leptinella* (*Cotula*), *Bulbinella, Cyathodes* and *Poa*. In some of these, flower parts of only one sex are present on each plant, e.g. *Halocarpus, Lepidothamnus* and *Coprosma*, whereas in others, parts of both sexes are present but only one is functional, e.g. *Aciphylla, Anisotome, Melicytus, Pimelea, Myrsine*.

In some genera, such as *Aciphylla*, the separate sexes are generally obvious from a distance when plants are flowering, but

16

most require much closer inspection to distinguish the sexes, e.g. *Anisotome, Astelia, Coprosma, Gingidia, Hectorella, Melicytus, Myrsine, Pimelea,* and some species of *Bulbinella,* or even between individual florets within the flower head (capitulum) of some *Leptinella (Cotula)* species.

Although this separation of the sexes has the advantage that crossing is compulsory and hence maximum genetic variability is retained, the system is obviously highly wasteful since only about half the population can produce seeds. There are a few cases where bisexual and female plants are present, e.g. some species of *Gaultheria, Cyathodes, Pimelea,* and *Gentiana.* This also promotes crossing, yet all plants are able to produce seed.

Despite the occurrence of some plant groups that have unisexual plants only in New Zealand, notably members of the Apiaceae, it appears that most of the selection for unisexuality in New Zealand plants occurred elsewhere, prior to their migration to New Zealand.

Flowering Behaviour

Most of our alpine plants flower annually but there are several that are quite irregular. Notable here are the several alpine species of snow tussock (*Chionochloa*) and speargrass (*Aciphylla*), also the mountain flax (*Phormium cookianum*). In these there are flowering and non-flowering years: with abundant and widespread flowering, or without it. Flowering years do not necessarily coincide between these genera but species within a genus usually behave alike. We do not have many records for the speargrasses or mountain flax but in the narrow-leaved snow tussock there have been 16 flowering years in the 38 following 1947-48, with zero to three non-flowering years separating the seed years.

Such mast flowering (heavy synchronous flowering only in some years) is not uncommon, particularly in wind pollinated plants, where it may confer advantages in energy conservation, as well as in reducing the incidence of seed eaters, both birds and specialised insects (predator satiation), or by increasing the efficiency of pollination.

Even in the species which flower regularly there may be a large variation in flower numbers from year to year. This is true in several of the *Celmisia* species, at least in Otago, where the variation appears to be at least partly dependent upon the rate of thaw in spring.

Experimental work on snow tussocks has shown that their flowering years depend on high summer temperatures in the season before actual flowering occurs. This is when the flower development begins. In most of the New Zealand alpine plants, as in those from abroad, partly developed flower buds are present in autumn and these overwinter in a fairly advanced state. This is an obvious adaptation to cope with the short growing season. In *Psychrophila (Caltha) obtusa*, a plant from snowbank areas, the flowers are fully formed in the buds by autumn. This allows *Psychrophila* to be among the first alpines to flower in spring, even though they do not usually emerge from snow until November or later. The flowers are often open within a week of snow melt. They may even open under the edge of a melting snowbank or under a stream of ice-cold water from the melt. The flowers of *Psychrophila* appear to have a low-temperature requirement to safeguard against premature opening in late autumn, but the many alpines that will flower in a lowland garden within a few months of being collected in the field in late summer or autumn, obviously do not have such a control mechanism.

Chapter 5
THE ALPINE VEGETATION

IN THE 1,000 m (3,300 ft) or so between the tree line and snow line in New Zealand there is a greater range of alpine vegetation than occurs in most parts of the world. At the lower levels one or more of the several species of snow tussock (*Chionochloa*) is dominant. Close to the tree line these may be more than 1 m tall forming, unless they have been damaged by fire or by heavy grazing of introduced animals such as deer, an almost complete cover of tussocks. Large bunch grasses like the snow tussock are uncommon in alpine vegetation outside the tropics. They may reflect the unusually low tree line in New Zealand, or the relatively mild winters (also a feature of tropical mountains), or some other factor. At the other extreme, close to the snow line, plants are quite dwarfed; many are cushions or mats less than 2 cm high, while much of the ground is rocky or stony and bare.

Because of this wide range in vegetation, two belts have been recognised. Low-alpine embraces the vegetation dominated by the snow tussocks; high-alpine includes those types with a shorter and less complete plant cover. Distinction in the field is not always clear since the transition may be gradual. In most places it occurs about halfway between tree line and snow line.

Introduced plants are relatively unimportant in the alpine zone. Two grasses, browntop *(Agrostis capillaris)* and sweet vernal *(Anthoxanthum odoratum)*, as well as sheep sorrel *(Rumex acetosella)* and catsear *(Hypochoeris radicata)* are widespread in the less remote areas and heather *(Calluna vulgaris)* is a serious threat on the central North Island volcanic mountains up to ca. 1,500 m. Within the last two decades several hawkweeds *(Hieracium spp.)* have become aggressive and also extended their ranges upwards into the alpine zone in many of the drier and more accessible mountains where they threaten conservation values in several regions. Mouse ear hawkweed *(H. pilosella)* is widespread in the central North Island and most of the central-eastern South Island mountains while king devil *(H. praealtum)* is of only slightly less extent. Tussock hawkweed *(H. lepidulum)* and field hawkweed *(H. caespitosum)* are less extensive but no less threatening, in western Otago and Marlborough, respectively.

THE LOW-ALPINE VEGETATION TYPES

1. MIXED SNOW TUSSOCK-SCRUB: In the first 100 m (300 ft) or so above a beech forest tree line there is often a mixture of the tallest snow tussocks, in the wetter areas usually the narrow-leaved snow tussock (*Chionochloa rigida*) in the far south and broad-leaved snow tussock (*Chionochloa flavescens*) from central Westland northward with a variety of large herbs and the tallest of the alpine shrubs (Fig. 4). These shrubs, often no higher than the tussocks, vary somewhat from place to place but snow totara (*Podocarpus nivalis*), mountain toatoa (*Phyllocladus alpinus*) and some of the mid-sized species of *Dracophyllum* (*D. uniflorum, D. longifolium*), *Hebe* (*H. odora*) and *Coprosma* (*C. pseudocuneata*) are widespread.

In addition there may be a few subalpine shrubs more characteristic of the nearby forest. Usually there are some large and prominent herbs, particularly mountain flax, speargrasses, buttercups, astelias and celmisias. Under this mixed cover there is usually a great variety of smaller herbs and shrubs.

A similar low-alpine community takes over gradually from the subalpine scrub that substitutes for beech forest at tree-line altitudes in forested areas from which beech is absent.

2. SNOW TUSSOCK-HERBFIELD: This occurs as an upward extension of the mixed snow tussock-scrub, but only in the wetter, more western regions. The tall tussocks are usually dominant with large herbs important and conspicuous, especially species of *Celmisia, Ranunculus, Gentiana, Aciphylla, Anisotome, Astelia,* and *Ourisia.* There may also be occasional shrubs of *Hebe* and *Dracophyllum.*

Fig. 4. Tall snow tussock, *Dracophyllum, Astelia* **and** *Ranunculus,* **Westland.**

Fig. 5.   Red tussock herbfield, Mt Egmont.

Again the most important and widespread tussock is the broad-leaved snow tussock, with narrow-leaved snow tussock replacing it in the southern South Island. On the volcanic mountains of the North Island its place is taken by a subspecies of the red tussock, *Chionochloa rubra* (Fig. 5). Broad-leaved snow tussock is often mixed with midribbed snow tussock (*C. pallens*), which may dominate extensively in some areas (north-west Nelson and Fiordland) yet be rather insignificant in others (Tararua Range, and western Otago).

In the North Island these large tussocks usually extend to the limit of the low-alpine belt but in the South Island there are some smaller, more cold-tolerant species that replace the larger ones as altitude increases. One of these, carpet grass (*C. australis*), which is confined to the north-west (Nelson and north-west Canterbury), forms a short, extremely dense turf only about 10 cm high. Carpet grass has a wide altitudinal range, occurring throughout the low-alpine and extending into the high-alpine belt. It often forms very extensive carpets with only a few other plants amongst it, especially at higher altitudes. It may also be present in small patches among the tall snow tussock at lower altitudes as on Mt Robert in Nelson Lakes National Park (Fig. 6).

The curled snow tussock (*C. crassiuscula*), with three sub-species, occurs to the south of the Spenser Mountains in Nelson although only in the wetter regions. It is of medium height (about 30 cm) and may cover extensive areas, especially towards the southern South Island. Here it usually occupies a distinct zone on the mountainsides, extending to the upper limit of the low-alpine belt. In Fiordland and on Stewart Island there are also local species of snow tussock (see p. 252 – 256), some of which are important in vegetation.

In high rainfall regions snow tussock community patterns have been related to both winter snow lie, as affected by topography, such as at Arthur's Pass and Lewis Pass on the Southern Alps, or to the soil factors affected by differences in site stability. Both in Fiordland and on the Tararua Range snow tussock grassland communities have been shown to relate to local differences in landscape stability. Here more recently disturbed sites with immature, well drained relatively fertile soils are usually dominated by midribbed snow tussock *Chionochloa pallens*, often in association with the larger species of *Ranunculus, Anisotome, Celmisia, Ourisia,* and/or *Astelia*, while nearby stable sites with more mature, fine textured, poorly drained often peaty acidic and less fertile soils are dominated by broad-leaved or narrow-leaved snow tussock often associated with sedges and rushes and other species more typical of poorly drained sites — *Oreobolus, Carpha, Astelia linearis, Schoenus, Psychrophila (Caltha), Abrotanella, Isolepis, Deschampsia, Plantago, Drosera, Phyllachne, Forstera* and/or *Donatia*. Intermediate or more extreme sites in the vicinity may have different associations, related mainly to physical and chemical properties of the soil.

Fig. 6. Carpet grass, Mt Robert.

20

Fig. 7. Herbfield, Fiordland.

3. HERBFIELD: Low-alpine herbfield is characterised by large or medium herbs such as the taller species of *Celmisia, Ranunculus, Aciphylla, Astelia, Anisotome, Gingidia,* and *Ourisia* (Fig. 7). Snow tussocks are sparse either because of some special site conditions or because of heavy but selective grazing by deer of the more palatable plants, including snow tussocks. In the latter case celmisias, astelias and speargrasses are the usual dominants since the large buttercups, ourisias, gingidiums and anisotomes are more often eaten than the snow tussocks.

4. SNOW TUSSOCK GRASSLAND: In the drier alpine regions of central and eastern parts of the South Island, large herbs and shrubs are not usually conspicuous. The most important plant in this alpine grassland is the narrow-leaved snow tussock (*Chionochloa rigida*) which extends from the Rakaia Valley to northern and western Southland and from the east coast to the main divide (and west of it in Otago and Southland) where it merges, as rainfall increases to the west, with the plants typical of snow tussock-herbfield. Throughout much of this grassland there is a smaller slim snow tussock (*C. macra*) which usually replaces the narrow-leaved snow tussock at higher altitudes and north of the Rakaia Valley.

In the few areas where this alpine grassland has been but slightly modified, snow tussocks are the only important and conspicuous plants. The dense, tall cover and thick litter beneath them discourage the growth of many small plants.

Many alpine grassland communities in the South Island rain-shadow region have been transformed from their natural state through more than a century of extensive pastoral farming. This has been associated with managed or accidental fires which have substantially modified many communities. Furthermore, composition of the vegetation has been affected by the differential palatability of plant species to a new environmental factor, introduced mammalian herbivores both domestic (sheep, cattle) and feral (deer, hares, etc.). In the more remote alpine regions, beyond the pastoral run country and particularly along and west of the Southern Alps red deer had increased to the stage of seriously depleting most communities. The more palatable species

21

of snow tussock and other large herbs had been greatly reduced but since the early 1970s they have substantially recovered in response to a drastic reduction in animal numbers through very effective aerial hunting, using helicopters, to supply a lucrative overseas, mostly European market. The combined effect of these factors has been to reduce the size and cover of tussocks and to eliminate the leaf litter. Therefore, on the more stable sites at least, the plants which sheep ignore have increased in numbers.

On the unstable greywacke slopes in Marlborough, Canterbury and north Otago, erosion and frost have not only weakened the tussocks but have also prevented the increases of most other plants. Today, many of these areas have deteriorated into active scree with little or no vegetation and land degradation has become a major concern.

In some other areas a few unpalatable species have increased to the extent that snow tussocks have been superseded by an induced vegetation. Some of the smaller tussocks, blue tussock (*Poa colensoi*), alpine fescue tussock (*Festuca matthewsii*) and bristle tussock (*Rytidosperma setifolium*), have become aggressive in this way. Bristle tussock now dominates in parts of Marlborough and north Canterbury while the other two are more important in inland areas of south Canterbury and Otago.

Some of the species of *Celmisia* have similarly increased in certain areas of the eastern grasslands. The common cotton daisy (*C. spectabilis*) has become important over much of its range, more especially in parts of Marlborough and Canterbury. The false spaniard (*C. lyallii*) dominates more locally in Canterbury and Central Otago, as does the loose-cushion forming *C. viscosa*. A larger celmisia (*C. semicordata*) now forms extensive herbfields, especially on the Garvie Mountains in northern Southland. The golden spaniard (*Aciphylla aurea*) is another of these unpalatable aggressive herbs. In Central Otago and parts of Canterbury and northern Southland are areas where this handsome but dagger-leaved plant has increased, often with alpine fescue tussock and blue tussock, to replace the natural snow tussock grassland with an induced cover of very low grazing value. With the golden spaniard, however, grazing by hares may reduce numbers of seedlings.

5. BOGS: These are depressions with poor drainage where the turf is soft and the water table never far from the surface. Bogs occur locally throughout the alpine regions, more commonly in the low-alpine zone and in the high rainfall regions. They vary in their plant cover because of such factors as altitude, height above the average water table, slope and acidity. Bogs are characterised by plants that are tolerant of a permanently high water table. Usually there is a gradual change from the slightly better drained (and aerated) margins of a bog where, at moderate altitude, the red tussock (*Chionochloa rubra*) may be common, to the lowest parts where bog moss (*Sphagnum* spp.) and small open pools or tarns may be present (Fig. 8).

Sedges (*Carex* species) and rushes (*Carpha alpina*, *Schoenus pauciflorus*, *Juncus* species) usually reach their greatest importance in bogs. Like many bog plants they also extend on to seepage areas within other types of low-alpine vegetation.

Several species are virtually confined to peat bogs – the wire rush (*Empodisma minus*) and the tangle fern (*Gleichenia dicarpa*). More characteristic perhaps are some of the cushion plants – the comb sedge (*Oreobolus pectinatus*) and those of the much softer *Gaimardia* and *Centrolepis* species, plus *Donatia*, *Phyllachne colensoi*, *Mitrasacme*, *Actinotus* and *Celmisia argentea*. Small trailing shrubs – the pygmy pine (*Lepidothamnus laxifolius*), creeping heath plants – dracophyllums (*D. prostratum*, *D. politum*), *Pentachondra pumila*, *Cyathodes pumila* and *C. empetrifolia*, also *Coprosma perpusilla* and *C. niphophila* are typical of peat bogs. Probably the most fascinating members of alpine bogs are the small insectivorous plants – bladderworts (*Utricularia*) and sundews (*Drosera* species).

Peat bogs in which cushions predominate are usually called cushion bogs or herb moor. These are quite distinct from the high-alpine cushion vegetation on mineral soil. Herb moor is best developed in the cool, moist, cloudy regions of southeastern (Maungatua, Blue Mountains) and southern (Longwood Range, Key Summit) South Island and Stewart Island (Mt Anglem). Here the flattish mountain summits have extensive areas of peat which is covered with cushion bog. In other parts of New Zealand bogs occur most commonly in depressions on alpine passes, e.g. Arthurs Pass, and in cirque basins.

THE HIGH-ALPINE VEGETATION TYPES

1. FELLFIELD: The high-alpine belt in most areas has only a sparse plant cover. In fellfield there is very little soil, most of the plants being wedged among more or less stable rocks. Some of these plants will be found in the low-alpine belt but in addition there are many that typify fellfield. Among these are the several species of vegetable sheep, perhaps the most unusual of our alpine plants. Two related species (*Raoulia rubra* and *R. buchananii*), which are green, occur with many other alpines in the wet fellfields of the north-west and south-west areas, respectively, of the South Island. On the mountains of Stewart Island there are similar cushions of *R. goyenii*. To the east of the Southern Alps, between north Otago and southern Nelson-Marlborough, there are very much drier fellfields in which the light-coloured cushions of the true vegetable sheep (*R. eximia*) are common. In Canterbury it is accompanied by the smaller cushions of *R. mammillaris*. Further north are found the similar *R. bryoides* and the much larger and coarser *Haastia pulvinaris*. Among the few other plants that occur in these dry fellfields, some of the smaller hebes are usually present, and towards the south one of the cushion speargrasses (*Aciphylla dobsonii*) becomes common.

In wet fellfields of the western mountains there is a great variety of smaller alpine plants. Among the important genera are some that are also represented in the low-alpine zone (*Celmisia*,

Fig. 8. Bog at Arthurs Pass with red tussock.

Ranunculus, Brachyglottis, Gentiana, Aciphylla) with the significant additions of *Chionohebe* and *Hectorella*.

2. SCREE: Dry fellfield is usually associated with an even more austere habitat in which the surface stones are loose and sometimes quite mobile, on uniformly steep slopes of 30-35 degrees. These talus slopes or screes characterise the steep greywacke mountains of north Otago, Canterbury, southern Nelson and Marlborough. Screes may span a wide altitude, running from the snow line down to subalpine or even montane levels, but their extremely sparse plant cover makes them more akin to the high-alpine vegetation.

Although the stones of a scree slide easily, it is usually only a surface layer of 10-20 cm that will run. Beneath this is a compact, permanently moist soil which may be quite deep. From the head of a scree there is usually a continuous supply of frost-shattered rock fragments which maintains it. Measurements have shown that the stone movement tends to be least during the growing season and greatest after heavy snowfalls or during very wet weather.

Screes seem to be quite bare, yet they support a number of the most specialised plants (Fig. 9). There are about twenty five alpine species essentially confined to screes with some remarkable modifications that allow them to live in this extremely demanding habitat. These are the very extensive underground stems and root systems that penetrate deep into the soil layer and in most, their leaves are succulent, blue-grey or glaucous,

Fig. 9. Canterbury mountainside showing *Ranunculus haastii* on the scree slope with *Raoulia* and *Haastia* on more stable fellfield.

24

glabrous and deeply cut, with a waxy bloom. Highly adapted and successful are the plants with large fleshy taproots (*Lignocarpa carnosula*) or rhizomes (*Ranunculus haastii*) buried in the stable soil beneath the mobile stony layer. The leaves of these plants do not persist over winter and, moreover, they are very delicately attached to the stem so that they break off easily without damaging it. All underground parts of scree plants will be found trailing upslope, showing the continuing influence of gravity on the steep slopes.

This unique flora in itself suggests that screes certainly are not a recent habitat in New Zealand. But not all screes support these specialised plants. Those that have developed through recent degradation of other types of vegetation, and even recent extensions of natural screes, usually lack these plants. The underlying mantle of soil that appears necessary for the scree plants to establish themselves is usually missing from such areas.

3. CUSHION VEGETATION: An extremely dwarfed, tundra-like cushionfield covers the extensive plateau summits of the several mountain ranges in Central Otago. The dwarfishness of this vegetation is even further accentuated by the massive rock tors that dot the landscape.

Wind-blown material (loess) has produced an abundance of soil on these mountain tops but the persistent strong winds, cold summers and frequent freeze-thaw cycles keep plants close to the ground. About eighteen different genera have developed cushion, mat or low creeping species that can survive in this most severe environment. Even though quite unrelated, many of these plants may look remarkably alike. Lichens are also significant among the cushions.

The importance of shelter is obvious from the mosaic of vegetation associated with the patterned ground, namely solifluction terraces, soil hummocks and soil stripes that are common on these mountains.

4. SNOWBANK VEGETATION: For some distance below the snow line snow will accumulate and persist until late summer where cirques or other large depressions are sheltered from prevailing winds. The snow pattern here is not haphazard. Indeed it is repeated each year although the amount of snowfall and rate of thaw can affect the time of melt. In late-snow areas the thaw in some years may be incomplete.

Plants are usually arranged in bands in a snowbank depression, according to the length of growing season they need successfully to complete reproduction and annual growth (Fig. 10). At the upper edge are plants that can tolerate only slightly prolonged snow-lie while at the base of the depression will be those that can manage with a short period of activity. Here we see important differences in micro-environments.

Apart from very late sites with near-permanent snow there is usually a good cover of plants in a snowbank. This probably reflects the greater amounts of soil and the increased shelter and warmth that such depressions usually experience at the height of the growing season.

Like most other alpines, snowbank plants vary from place to place. Most of them will be found in nearby fellfield but often at much higher altitudes. Along the Southern Alps the most important snowbank plant is the snow-patch grass (*Chionochloa oreophila*), the smallest of the snow tussocks, which forms a dense, even turf only 5-10 cm high. Other characteristic snowbank plants in various parts of the country are *Psychrophila* (*Caltha*) species; *Celmisia haastii* and the semi-cushion *C. hectorii;* the very fine-textured cushion *Kelleria croizatii; Gaultheria nubicola;* the sedge *Carex pyrenaica;* two buttercups *Ranunculus sericophyllus*, in Central Otago the related *R. pachyrrhizus*, and one of the most versatile of all alpines, *Neopaxia australasica*. In sites with very late snow melt, where snow may persist for several years, only non-flowering plants such as mosses and lichens are usually present.

Fig. 10. Snowbank, Old Man Range.

THE FERNS AND FERN ALLIES

THE FERNS and fern allies are typically plants of moist and warm lowland regions,
but among them are a few that tolerate the rigours of the alpine zone,

Genus LYCOPODIUM

"Wolf foot"—roots of the European *L. clavatum* resemble a wolf's paw.

The club-mosses are almost worldwide with more than 150 species.
Of the 12 native club-mosses three reach the alpine zone.

Lycopodium australianum (Herter) Allan
"Southern".

Plants vary with the habitat from 5–20 cm tall. The sporangia are
not in cones but scattered in the axils of normal leaves towards the
branch tip. Towards the tips are small bulbils which shed easily to
propagate vegetatively.
DISTRIBUTION North, South and Stewart Islands: throughout most
of the mountain regions.

Subalpine to low-alpine: 600–1,700 m (2,000–5,500 ft).
HABITAT Usually common but rarely abundant. In open, often rocky
areas of snow tussock grassland and herbfield of the higher rainfall
regions. It also occurs on well-lit rock outcrops in subalpine forest
and scrub.
COLLECTED Whakapapanui Valley, Mt Ruapehu, Tongariro National
Park, 1,160 m (3,800 ft). November 1968.

Lycopodium scariosum Forst.f.
"Scarious"—thin chaffy and dry.

The main creeping stems are branched and up to 1 m or more
long. They produce at intervals erect, branched, tufted stems up to
30 cm tall.
Cones develop in early summer and persist into winter.
DISTRIBUTION North, South and Stewart Islands: widespread except
north of Rotorua, but often rather local.

Coastal to low-alpine: to 1,200 m (4,000 ft).
HABITAT Usually the least important club-moss in the alpine zone yet
it may be common locally on open sites—rock outcrops or depleted
areas—in both red tussock and snow tussock grasslands and mixed
snow tussock-scrub. Below the alpine zone it also favours well-lit
sites, especially rock outcrops, and tolerates the ultrabasic rocks of
the mineral belts in Nelson and north-western Otago.
COLLECTED Whakapapanui Valley, Mt Ruapehu, Tongariro National
Park, 1,160 m (3,800 ft). November 1968.

Lycopodium fastigiatum R.Br.
"Fastigiate"—branches close together, parallel and erect.

The stout creeping rhizome is branched and usually buried, up
to 50 cm or more long, with erect tufted branches 5–25 cm tall.

Stalked cones develop much as for *L. scariosum* and when mature
may be bright orange.
DISTRIBUTION North, South and Stewart Islands: in hilly and
mountain regions throughout.

Montane to high-alpine: 200–2,000 m (500–6,500 ft).
HABITAT Common throughout the low-alpine zone in most areas,
especially on open ground, depleted sites and rock outcrops. It is
less common, often quite dwarfed and rather inconspicuous, in
high-alpine fellfield, herbfield and cushion vegetation. In the subalpine and montane zones it is in tussock grassland, open scrub
and pasture, where it sometimes produces "fairy rings".
COLLECTED Rock and Pillar Range, Central Otago, 1,370 m (4,500 ft).
December 1969.

Genus OPHIOGLOSSUM

"Adder's Tongue"—referring to the spike.

A widespread genus of primitive ferns in which the species are not
well understood. Of the two native ophioglossums recognised, one
reaches the alpine zone.

Ophioglossum coriaceum A. Cunn.
"Leathery".

A variable summer-green herb: the sterile leaf may be narrow or
broad, 1–5 cm long, and its veins indistinct or obvious. The fertile
spike is < 2 cm long and in alpine areas plants seldom exceed 4 cm.
DISTRIBUTION North and South Islands: apparently widespread
throughout but in mountainous regions it is more common in the
South Island.

Lowland to low-alpine: to 1,300 m (4,500 ft).
HABITAT In open tussock grassland on gravel or other well-drained
material. It is common in valley-floor grasslands of South Westland
and western Otago but in the eastern tussock grasslands its occurrence is rather erratic, perhaps only because, being so inconspicuous
it is easily overlooked.
COLLECTED Hawkdun Range, north Otago, 1,310 m (4,300 ft).
December 1969.

Lycopodium scariosum

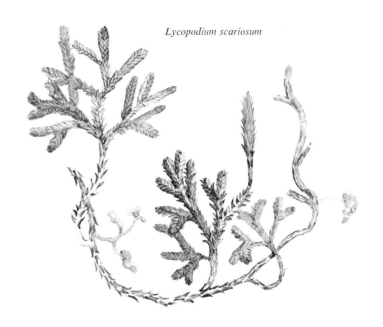

Lycopodium australianum

Lycopodium fastiglatum

Ophioglossum coriaceum

PLATE 1

Genus **BLECHNUM**
"Blekhnon"—the Greek name of a fern.

A genus of more than 200 species, mostly from the southern hemisphere. Of the 15 native blechnums only one is strictly alpine.

Blechnum pennamarina (Poir.) Kuhn.
"Sea-pen"—from its resemblance to this marine polyp.

The creeping wiry rhizomes may be up to 50 cm or more long but are only occasionally branched, so that the fronds usually appear in distinct lines. Newly-developed sterile fronds are bronze rather than dark-green. Frond height decreases with altitude to only a few cm near their upper limit.
DISTRIBUTION North, South and Stewart Islands: widespread except for North Auckland.
Lowland to high-alpine: to 2,000 m (6,500 ft).
HABITAT Although rarely of much importance this versatile plant extends from open forest and scrub to moraine, tussock grassland, herbfield, fellfield and even to early snowbanks. In the subalpine and low-alpine zones of the drier mountains it is usually confined to the shade of rock outcrops.
COLLECTED Hooker Valley, Mt Cook National Park, 910 m (3,000 ft). January 1969.

Genus **GRAMMITIS**
"Lines"—referring to distribution of the sori.

A large and widespread genus. Only the smallest of the five native species is an alpine.

Grammitis poepiggiana (Mett.) Pichi Germ.
After Poepiggi, German botanist.

Our smallest fern, usually forming loose tufts or mats up to 5 cm or more across.
DISTRIBUTION North, South and Stewart Islands: occurs in most of the mountain regions but is less common in the North Island.
Subalpine to high-alpine: 800–2,000 m (2,500–6,500 ft).
HABITAT Typically an insignificant plant of shady rock ledges and clefts where it may easily be overlooked. Sometimes it occurs on steep, usually mossy banks in snow tussock grassland and herbfield, and also below the tree line on rock outcrops in well-lit areas such as avalanche chutes or open subalpine forest or scrub.
COLLECTED Pisa Range, Central Otago, 1,770 m (5,800 ft). December 1968.

**Grammitis givenii* Parris
After Dr D.R. Given, botanist.

Altogether larger than *G. poepiggiana*, with creeping rhizomes covered in pale brown scales and dull-green leathery, spatula-shaped fronds 2–6 cm x 4–8 mm with hairs towards the base and up to

ten pairs of obviously elongated sori towards the tip. It is confined to New Zealand and some sub-Antarctic islands. Rare in the North Island, but locally common in the higher rainfall regions further south, particularly on shaded rocks in scrub and snow tussock grassland up to the low-alpine zone; to 1,400 m (4,500 ft).

Genus **POLYSTICHUM**
"Many rows"—referring to the sori.

A widespread genus containing some 180 species. Only one of the four native polystichums is truly alpine.

Polystichum cystostegia (Hook.) Cheesem. MOUNTAIN SHIELDFERN
"Bladder cover"—referring to the swollen indusium.

The short, erect, scaly rhizome produces a dense cluster of distinctive, summer-green fronds with conspicuous round sori on their lower surface.
DISTRIBUTION North, South and Stewart Islands: widespread in alpine regions but restricted in the North Island — only Mt Egmont.
Low- to high-alpine: 900–2,000 m (3,000–6,500 ft).
HABITAT Usually on rocky sites. In the low-alpine zone it is virtually confined to shady crevices and ledges on rock outcrops but in high-alpine areas it also occurs among stable rock debris in sheltered fellfields and early snowbanks.
COLLECTED Ohau Range, north-western Otago, 1,520 m (5,000 ft). January 1969.

Genus **CYSTOPTERIS**
"Bladder-fern"—referring to the inflated indusium.

A small but rather widespread genus. The only native species reaches the alpine zone.

Cystopteris tasmanica Hook. BLADDER FERN
"Tasmanian"

Rather variable with a short creeping rhizome and semi-erect branches covered by pale red-brown scales. The branches end in clusters of delicate summer-green fronds, usually <15 cm tall in alpine regions. Southern forms are somewhat smaller, with the fronds less membranous and less finely divided than in the north.
DISTRIBUTION North and South Islands: widespread on the South Island mountains but more local in the North Island—recorded from Mt Egmont, Kaimanawa and Tararua Ranges.
Montane to low-alpine: 300–1,200 m (1,000–4,000 ft).
HABITAT A plant of rock outcrops, in shady clefts and crevices, but in the low-alpine zone it may also inhabit damp, shady, overhung banks. It is rarely abundant and conspicuous.
COLLECTED Mt Gladstone, Inland Kaikoura Range, Marlborough, 1,740 m (5,700 ft). January 1970.

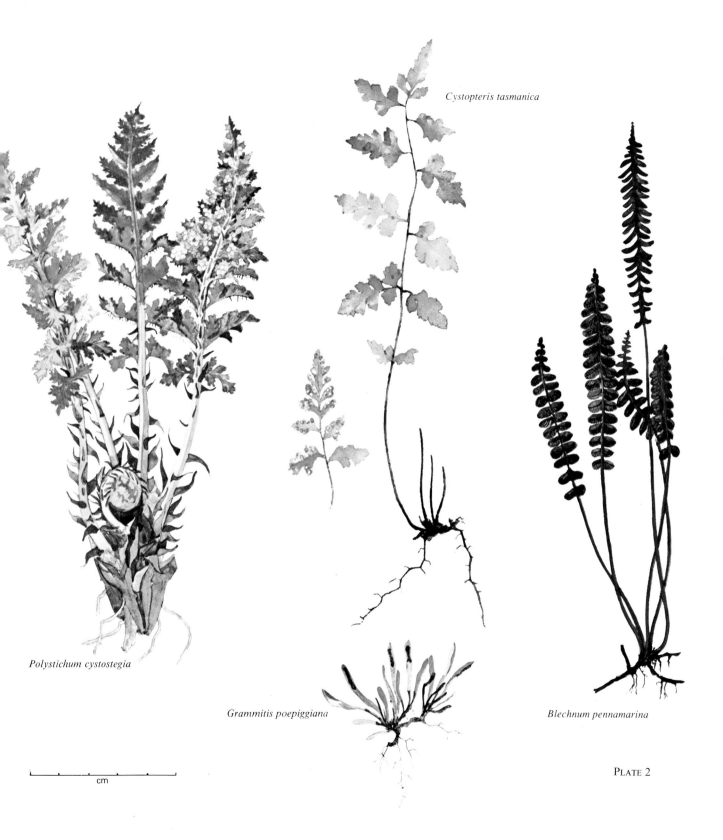

Cystopteris tasmanica

Polystichum cystostegia

Grammitis poepiggiana

Blechnum pennamarina

cm

PLATE 2

Genus **HYPOLEPIS**

"Under scale"—referring to the modified leaf margin protecting the sorus.

Contains about 45 species, mainly tropical and subtropical. One of the 5 native species reaches the alpine zone.

Hypolepis millefolium Hook.
THOUSAND-LEAVED FERN

"Many-leaved".

A rather delicate and fragile fern with an extensive creeping rhizome that produces numerous summer-green fronds. In alpine areas they are usually < 30 cm tall.

DISTRIBUTION North, South and Stewart Islands: widespread in the mountains of the South Island but more local in the North Island— Mt Ruapehu, Mt Egmont, Ruahine and Tararua Ranges.

Lowland to low-alpine: to 1,400 m (4,500 ft).

HABITAT Typically a plant of forest openings but in the subalpine and low-alpine zones it may cover snow-slide areas and avalanche chutes. The summer-green habit and extensive network of rhizomes adapt it to this precarious habitat. In mid-summer the characteristic bright-green colour of hypolepis patches at and near the tree line is usually an indication of such sites.

COLLECTED Rock & Pillar Range, Central Otago, 1,250 m (4,100 ft). January 1971.

Genus **GLEICHENIA**

After a German botanist, Baron von Gleichen.

A large, tropical and south-temperate genus. Of the five native umbrella ferns only one reaches the alpine zone.

Gleichenia dicarpa R. Br.
TANGLE FERN

"Two-seeded".

The alpine form is relatively small, usually < 30 cm tall. It has been suggested as a distinct variety, but the species requires further study. Erect fronds, as shown, are abundant along the length of the extensive branched rhizomes.

DISTRIBUTION North, South and Stewart Islands: occurs almost wherever a suitable habitat is present.

Lowland to low-alpine: to 1,400 m (4,500 ft).

HABITAT Restricted in the alpine zone to flushed but poorly-drained peaty areas or wet depressions in snow tussock grassland or herbfield close to the tree line. It may occupy similar sites in subalpine scrub, red tussock grassland, or on ultrabasic rocks of the mineral belt.

COLLECTED Whakapapanui Valley, Mt Ruapehu, Tongariro National Park, 1,370 m (4,500 ft). November 1968.

Genus **HYMENOPHYLLUM**

"Membranous leaf".

A large and widespread genus. At least four of the 22 native filmy ferns extend well into the low-alpine zone and may occasionally reach the high-alpine. Even though they are dwarfed here, the species can usually be separated on the following characters (for use of key see Glossary):

A	Margins of leaves very finely toothed	B
AA	Margins of leaves smooth	C
B	Sori large (*ca* 3 mm long), near base of leaflets close to centre of leaf, not immersed in leaf	

Hymenophyllum multifidum (Forst.f.) Swartz
"Much divided".

BB	Sori smaller (1–1.5 mm long), scattered over the leaf, partly immersed	

*****Hymenophyllum bivalve*** (Forst.f.) Swartz
"Two-valved"—referring to the indusium.

C	Fronds dark green; few hairs on stalk; sori mostly on lateral segments	

Hymenophyllum sanguinolentum (Forst.f.) Swartz
"Smelling like blood".

CC	Fronds dull green; many hairs on stalk; sori mostly on terminal segments	

Hymenophyllum villosum Col.
"Shaggy-hairy".

DISTRIBUTION North, South and Stewart Islands: all four species occur throughout the mountain regions but are more common in high rainfall areas. They have a wide altitudinal range.

HABITAT In the alpine zone filmy ferns are often found in shady clefts of rock outcrops or on steep or overhanging banks in tussock grassland or herbfield.

COLLECTED *H. multifidum:* Temple Basin, Arthurs Pass National Park, 1,310 m (4,300 ft). January 1971.

H. villosum: Excelsior Peak, Takitimu Mountains, western Southland, 1,370 m (4,500 ft). February 1971.

H. sanguinolentum: Stratford Plateau, Mt Egmont National Park, *ca* 1,300 m (4,300 ft). March 1964.

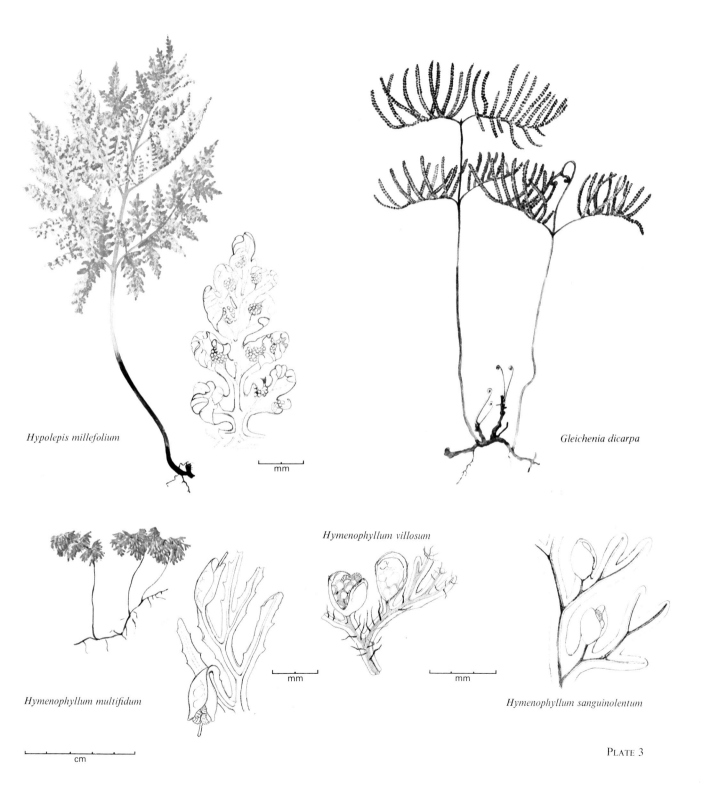

Hypolepis millefolium

mm

Gleichenia dicarpa

Hymenophyllum villosum

Hymenophyllum multifidum

mm

mm

Hymenophyllum sanguinolentum

cm

PLATE 3

THE CONIFERS

Alpine conifers in New Zealand all belong to the Podocarp family in which only the pollen is produced in typical cones. The seed is either surrounded by a cup-shaped aril or seated on a fleshy scale or stalk.

Genus **PODOCARPUS**

"Seed with a foot"—referring to the stalked seed.

A very large southern hemisphere genus. Of the seven native species only one is an alpine.

Podocarpus nivalis Hook.   SNOW TOTARA
"From high altitudes".

A prostrate or sprawling to semi-erect, highly aromatic shrub up to 2 m tall, usually without a main trunk. Plants are unisexual; male cones ripen in early summer while the fruits mature in autumn and if uneaten may persist on the shrubs into winter.
Var. ***erectus*** Ckn., is altogether larger (to 3 m) and more erect; possibly a hybrid with *P. hallii* (thin-barked totara).
DISTRIBUTION North and South Islands: throughout most mountainous areas of the South Island but more local in the North Island, from Te Moehau in the northern Coromandel Range to the central volcanic mountains and the Ruahine Range.
Var. *erectus* occurs in parts of Nelson and Canterbury.
Mostly subalpine to low-alpine: 700–1,500 m (2,500–5,000 ft).
HABITAT Over much of the South Island snow totara is important in subalpine scrub and mixed snow tussock-scrub. On the greywacke mountains east of the main divide it often occurs in extensive patches on scree margins and partly stable rock-debris slopes where its spreading and rooting habit provides further stability. It is also important among the woody vegetation that eventually develops on the moraine of receding glaciers, as in the Hooker Valley under Mt Cook.
COLLECTED The female plant from Mt Ruapehu, Tongariro National Park, *ca.* 1,220 m (4,000 ft). March 1963. The male plant is from the Ohau Range, north-western Otago, 1,310 m (4,300 ft). January 1969.

Genus **LEPIDOTHAMNUS**

"Scale (leaved) bushes".
Contains three species, one in Chile and two in New Zealand, one of which reaches the alpine zone.

Lepidothamnus laxifolius (Hook.f.) Quin   PYGMY PINE
"Loose-leaved".

A scrambling, usually prostrate, slender shrub with branches up to 1 m or more long. The leaves are often glaucous and rather variable; up to 5 mm long in the juvenile stage but reduced to 1–2 mm in the adult. Most plants are unisexual; male cones shed their pollen in early summer while the bright crimson fruits ripen in late autumn and may persist into winter.
DISTRIBUTION North, South and Stewart Islands: widespread to the south of the volcanic plateau.
Lowland to low-alpine: 100–1,500 m (500–5,000 ft).
HABITAT A characteristic plant of poorly-drained or boggy, but well-lit sites. It is common in most sphagnum and cushion bogs, in red tussock grassland and poorly-drained snow tussock-herbfield not far beyond the tree line.
COLLECTED Waihohonu, Mt Ruapehu, Tongariro National Park, *ca* 1,220 m (4,000 ft). April 1963.

Genus **PHYLLOCLADUS**

"Leaf-branches"—referring to the flattened leaf-like branches.

A small genus of the Pacific region. Among the three native species only one reaches the alpine zone.

Phyllocladus alpinus Hook.f.   MOUNTAIN TOATOA
"Alpine".   MOUNTAIN CELERY PINE

A highly aromatic shrub or small tree, reaching 8 m but < 2 m in the alpine zone. Juvenile leaves of seedlings are deeply divided with narrow segments. Plants are unisexual and in the alpine zone male plants shed their pollen about December. Seeds ripen on female plants in autumn.
DISTRIBUTION North and South Islands: widespread in mountainous regions from the northern Coromandel Range to Foveaux Strait, but absent from Mt Egmont.
Lowland to low-alpine: to 1,500 m (5,000 ft).
HABITAT Usually present in subalpine forest and scrub, and in mixed snow tussock-scrub. In the south and west of the South Island it may extend as a minor species to sea level.
COLLECTED The male plant from the Ohau Range, north-western Otago, 1,220 m (4,000 ft). January 1969. The female plant is from Whakapapanui Valley, Mt Ruapehu, Tongariro National Park, *ca.* 1,220 m (4,000 ft). April 1963.

Podocarpus nivalis

Phyllocladus alpinus

Lepidothamnus laxifolius

mm

cm

mm

PLATE 4

FLOWERING PLANTS

THE DICOTYLEDONS

The Buttercup Family: **RANUNCULACEAE**

Genus **RANUNCULUS**

"Small frog"—referring probably to the swampy habitat of some species.

A large genus, widespread in temperate regions of the world.

In a recent revision of the native alpine buttercups by Dr Fulton Fisher, several former species have been merged. Extensive collecting, combined with cultivation and crossing experiments, revealed some intergrading and interbreeding complexes among species previously considered distinct.

Of the 32 native buttercups, at least 17 reach the alpine zone. Redundant species names are given in brackets.

Ranunculus lyallii Hook.f.   GREAT MOUNTAIN BUTTERCUP

After Dr Lyall, surgeon-naturalist on the HMS *Terror* and *Acheron* in 1840–60.

A magnificent, glabrous, summer-green buttercup, reaching 1 m high, often wrongly referred to as a lily. The leaves are most distinctive, but seedling plants can be misleading by having leaves of a different shape, as shown.

The tall, branched flowering stems usually have many large white or rarely cream flowers, each with many (10–25) overlapping petals. Flowering may begin in October at lower altitudes and persist until January at the higher sites.

DISTRIBUTION South and Stewart Islands: only in the higher rainfall areas throughout most of the length of the South Island but rare on Mt Anglem, Stewart Island.

Subalpine to low-alpine: 700–1,500 m (2,500–5,000 ft).

HABITAT Once prominent throughout the snow tussock-herbfields, especially along stream banks or in wet hollows and flushes, it is much less important today. Introduced game animals have caused its decline so that large plants now tend to be restricted either to inaccessible bluffs or to areas where heavy human traffic discourages the animals. Much-visited areas such as Temple Basin above Arthurs Pass, the Hooker Valley under Mt Cook and the upper Hollyford Valley in Fiordland have a luxuriant alpine vegetation in which the great mountain buttercup is one of the outstanding features during spring and early summer.

COLLECTED Hooker Valley, Mt Cook National Park, 910 m (3,000 ft). November 1967. The seedling leaf is from Mt Brewster, Haast Pass, Mt Aspiring National Park, 1,280 m (4,300 ft).

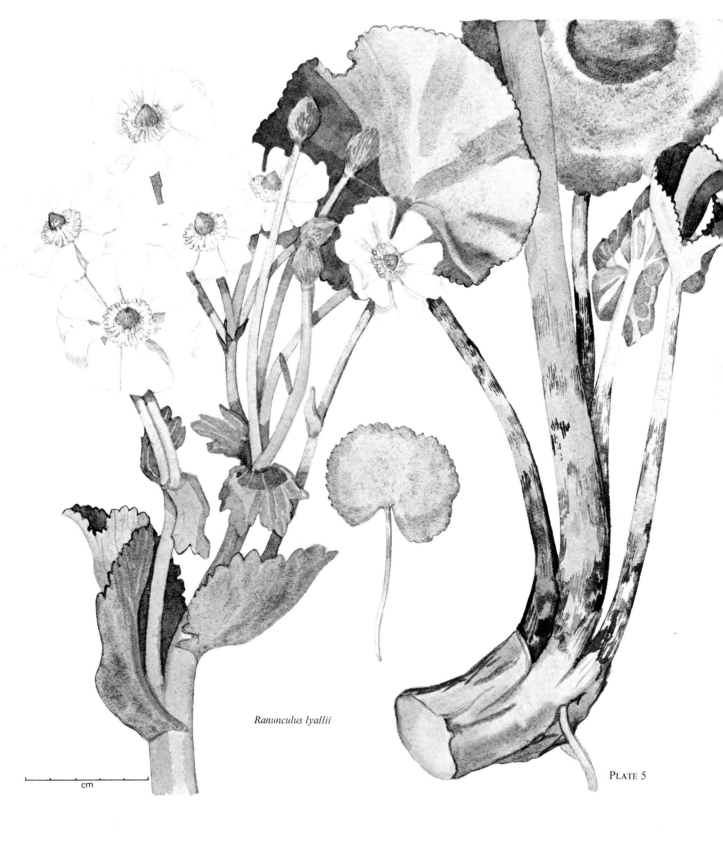

Ranunculus lyallii

PLATE 5

cm

Ranunculus buchananii Hook.f.

After Mr J. Buchanan, early New Zealand botanist.

A pale, summer-green, partly-hairy herb, usually 10–20 cm tall, often with several branches arising from the crown. The prominent and spectacular white flowers may occur singly or up to four per stem, each with many (15–25) overlapping petals. The pale-green fruiting heads (1–2 cm across) turn brown as they ripen.

DISTRIBUTION South Island: South Westland, Fiordland and western Otago–Southland, extending eastwards to the Lakes district (The Remarkables and Hector mountains).

High-alpine: 1,500–2,400 m (5,000–8,000 ft).

HABITAT Confined to fellfield and rock, especially in cirques but, being highly palatable, it is now almost restricted to inaccessible ledges and bluffs. As one of the most cold-tolerant alpines, it is among the highest flowering plants on Mt Aspiring.

COLLECTED Mt Burns, Hunter Mountains, Fiordland National Park, 1,580 m (5,200 ft). January 1968.

Ranunculus sericophyllus Hook.f.

"Silky-leaved".

A small silky-hairy herb that forms evergreen rosettes, often in loose patches. The pale-green trifoliate blades have their leaflets very deeply cut into many narrow pointed segments that are conspicuously fringed by hairs. Plants are smaller and the leaves rather less dissected towards the southern end of its range.

Usually single flowers with 5–10 petals appear soon after the winter snow has melted. The fruiting head is *ca* 1 cm across and, like the flower, appears large for the size of the plant.

DISTRIBUTION South Island: on the higher mountains of the Southern Alps from Lewis Pass southwards.

High-alpine: 1,400–2,100 m (4,500–7,000 ft).

HABITAT It occupies snowbanks and sheltered fellfields because of its tolerance of a short growing season and the chilled flow of melt water. Here it may be one of the most conspicuous plants.

COLLECTED B'limit Col, Temple Basin, Arthurs Pass National Park, 1,830 m (6,000 ft). December 1967.

Ranunculus pachyrrhizus Hook.f.

"Thick-rooted"—referring to the creeping stems.

A matted very hairy herb with creeping ropelike stems that are only partly buried. The fleshy leaves have a 3-lobed blade and the single leaf shows how 2 (or 3) of the lobes may be deeply or shallowly cut into broad segments. Towards the west, where it meets the related *R. sericophyllus*, leaf dissection increases.

Single flowers reach just beyond the leaves and have 5–15 broad overlapping petals, more than in most flowers of *R. sericophyllus*.

DISTRIBUTION South Island: rather local, being confined to the higher mountains of Central Otago and the Lakes district. It extends into western Otago along the ranges between the Rees and Matukituki Valleys beyond Lakes Wakatipu and Wanaka, to overlap locally with *R. sericophyllus*.

High-alpine: 1,600–2,300 m (5,300–7,500 ft).

HABITAT Confined to late-melt areas of snowbanks on the schistose mountains. Towards the west of its range it also occupies sheltered fellfield and rock crevices where snow or melt water persist well into summer.

COLLECTED Old Man Range, Central Otago, 1,650 m (5,400 ft). December 1968.

Ranunculus buchananii

Ranunculus pachyrrhizus

Ranunculus sericophyllus

cm

PLATE 6

Ranunculus insignis Hook.f.
"Striking".

It varies from a robust herb up to 50 cm tall down to a short tufted plant < 10 cm high. Thick, basal, evergreen leaves vary in colour, shape and size but they are typically undivided and have a conspicuous fringe of brown hairs around their coarsely-toothed margins. The range of this variation is shown.

Flowering stems are usually branched and multiflowered but in small forms they may be unbranched with just a single flower. Their flowers are 1–5 cm across with 5–7 (or in Marlborough populations occasionally up to 12), bright-yellow petals.

DISTRIBUTION North and South Islands: on the eastern, central and southern mountains of the North Island; Nelson, Marlborough and the more eastern mountains in Canterbury, southwards to about the Two Thumb Range. The smaller forms tend to occur in the southern part of the range and at higher elevations, but even single populations can be variable.

Mostly subalpine to low-alpine: 700–1,800 m (2,500–6,000 ft). Along the Kaikoura coast it occurs locally on limestone even closer to sea level.

HABITAT Usually common in shady areas of subalpine scrub, in snow tussock grassland or herbfield where it is often conspicuous on sheltered bluffs and rock outcrops. The smaller forms are much less prominent even though often common, as in the depleted snow tussock grassland at Porter's Pass, Canterbury. Where small forms replace larger ones as a result of increasing altitude or exposure to wind, as on Mt Ruapehu, in north-west Nelson and on the St Arnaud Range at Nelson Lakes, they usually remain conspicuous throughout their total habitat range.

COLLECTED The large plant from above Lake Sylvester, Cobb Valley, north-west Nelson, 1,500 m (5,000 ft). December 1967. The smaller high-altitude form is from Mt Ruapehu, Tongariro National Park, 1,830 m (6,000 ft). January 1958. The small southern form ("R. monroi") is from Porters Pass, Torlesse Range, Canterbury, 1,300 m (4,300 ft). January 1968. The leaf of "R. lobulatus" is from the Inland Kaikoura Range, 1,520 m (5,000 ft).

*Ranunculus godleyanus Hook.f.
From the Godley District.

A rather rare plant, restricted to high altitudes. It is a handsome, evergreen, yellow-flowered herb up to 60 cm tall, with large, broad, wavy, bright-green, leathery leaves. A plant of fellfield, it occurs on loose rocky debris or cliffs that are saturated with melt water. It grows between 1,200–2,100 m (4,000–7,000 ft) in the central Southern Alps.

Ranunculus haastii Hook.f.
After Sir Julius von Haast, famous geologist and explorer.

A fleshy, glabrous, summer-green herb with waxy glaucous leaves arising from a stout rhizome.

Flowers often occur singly but there may be up to 6 per stem, each with many (5–20) waxy-yellow petals which contrast strikingly with the dull leaves and rocky background.

Subspecies piliferus Fisher, "Hairy", has less dissected leaves with white hairs on their lower surfaces and larger flowers (to 5 cm across).

DISTRIBUTION South Island: confined to the highly-erodible grey-wacke mountains of central and eastern areas of the South Island from the Seaward Kaikoura Range in Marlborough to the Takitimu Mountains in western Southland. Ssp. piliferus is confined to the Eyre Mountains in northern Southland.

Low- to high-alpine: 1,000–2,000 m (3,500–6,500 ft).

HABITAT Restricted to debris slopes and screes, being one of the most characteristic and widespread species of these highly-demanding habitats. With its stout underground rhizome embedded in the moist stable soil layer, and the delicately attached leaves projecting through the surface layer of unstable stones, plants can tolerate movement of the scree even in midsummer. Although one of the more common scree plants, its sparse cover, together with a colour that matches its rocky background, means that it is obvious only when in flower.

COLLECTED Fog Peak, Torlesse Range, Canterbury, 1,650 m (5,400 ft). The flowering plant November 1968, the fruiting one February 1969.

Ranunculus insignis

Ranunculus insignis

"*Ranunculus lobulatus*" *(leaf)*

"*Ranunculus monroi*"

cm

PLATE 7

Ranunculus scrithalis Garnock-Jones   EYRE MOUNTAINS BUTTERCUP
"Scritha" — referring to its scree habitat.

An inconspicuous mostly submerged and strongly rhizomatous herb with dark greenish-grey silky hairy leaves that are finely divided into many linear pointed segments. Its small size and distinctive colour, leaf dissection and extremely short, almost buried single flower stem with lemon yellow petals distinguish it from *R. haastii* with which it occurs but in adjoining habitats.

DISTRIBUTION   South Island: confined to the Eyre Mountains in northern Southland.

Low- to high-alpine: 1,200–1,800 m (4,000–6,000 ft).

HABITAT   Confined to localised areas of brownish clayey rock debris on relatively gentle slopes. With only the dark leaf tips and small flowers showing, plants are most inconspicuous.

COLLECTED   The flowering plant was collected from upper Eyre Creek, Eyre Mountains, northern Southland, 1,250 m (4,100 ft). November 1970. The fruiting plant came from nearby Hummock Peak, 1,430 m (4,700 ft). December 1969

Ranunculus crithmifolius Hook.f.
"Crithmum" (Samphire)-leaved.

Small, glabrous, debris plants with two subspecies, both characterised by mottled, greyish-brown, fleshy leaves. Of the two subspecies, only the summer-green ssp. *crithmifolius* is alpine. Size, shape and dissection of the leaves all vary with location, but the one shown here is a common form.

The short flowering stem carries but a single flower. When ripe, the brownish fruiting head may be almost hidden among the leaf bases or surrounding stones by a curious bending of the stalk as the fruits ripen.

DISTRIBUTION   South Island: from the upper Wairau Gorge in south-east Nelson there is a gap in the distribution of ssp. *crithmifolius* until it reappears in central Canterbury (Craigieburn Range). From here it is fairly common southwards to north Otago, on the drier greywacke mountains.

Low- to high-alpine: 1,000–2,000 m (3,500–6,500 ft).

HABITAT   Another alpine of loose rock debris, the ssp. *crithmifolius* is more common on gentle, recently-formed debris slopes or small terraces where both eroding soil and loose stones are exposed. Such recently-formed screes are usually indicated by the brown colour of the rocks which contrasts with the much darker colour of the lichen-covered ones from older screes. There is a remarkable similarity between the colour of these plants and their background.

COLLECTED   Mt Richmond, Two Thumb Range, South Canterbury, 1,460 m (4,800 ft). The flowering plant was collected in November 1968, the fruiting one in January 1969.

Ranunculus grahamii Petrie
After Mr Peter Graham, who first collected it while Chief Guide at the Hermitage.

A stout probably summer-green plant up to 15 cm tall. The rather slender flower stems carry usually one but up to 4 large flowers with 5–10 petals. Considering their very high-altitude habitat they flower remarkably early, beginning about November.

DISTRIBUTION   South Island: confined to a small area, Mt Cook to D'Archiac in the central Southern Alps.

Nival: 2,400–2,800 m (8,000–9,300 ft).

HABITAT   A plant of inaccessible sites—clefts on rock faces, ice-free ledges and fine loose debris, all above the snow line. Although at least two other species of flowering plants (*Parahebe birleyi* and *Hebe haastii*) extend 100 m higher, this buttercup probably has the highest overall distribution.

COLLECTED   Messrs H. Wilson and A. M. Buchanan collected it from the north face of the Aiguilles Rouges, Mt Cook National Park, 2,840 m (9,300 ft). January 1970.

Ranunculus nivicola Hook. f.
"Inhabiting high altitudes".

A sparingly-branched herb 5–30 cm tall, with a short rootstock enclosed by blackened old leaf bases. The edges of the leaves are often red-tinted.

Flowering stems vary from short and unbranched on exposed sites, to up to 30 cm long and branched in sheltered areas.

DISTRIBUTION   North Island: a curious pattern across the centre of the island—from Mt Egmont to the volcanic plateau and nearby Kaweka and Kaimanawa Ranges, with a north-eastern outlier on the Rau-kumara Range. On the Tararua Range occasional plants that resemble *R. nivicola* are considered by Dr Fisher as possible sterile hybrids between *R. insignis* and *R. verticillatus*.

Subalpine to high-alpine: 1,200–1,800 m (4,000–6,000 ft).

HABITAT   Common on moist sites in herbfield, especially on stable scoria at Mt Egmont. On the volcanic plateau it is common on fine scoria, especially in seepage areas.

COLLECTED   North slope, Mt Egmont National Park, 1,460 m (4,800 ft). November 1967.

Ranunculus enysii Kirk
After Mr J. D. Enys, early Canterbury botanist.

A somewhat variable group of small, glabrous, bright-green herbs, 5–30 cm tall, with a short rootstock that form small patches up to 10 cm across. The numerous basal leaves vary in shape but often have red veins and margins. On the Carrick Range and Hector Mountains in Central Otago they are usually roundish and shallowly 3-lobed, on short petioles ("*R. berggrenii*" type). In most other areas the leaves are 3–5-foliate on longer petioles (to 12 cm), with the leaflets deeply 3-lobed and the lobes irregularly cut. Around some margins of its range, e.g. parts of Fiordland and the Kakanui Range in north-east Otago, highly dissected leaf forms are common.

Ranunculus haastii

Ranunculus crithmifolius

Ranunculus scrithalis

cm

PLATE 8

A plant may have up to five unbranched flowering stems reaching to 20 cm, each with a single small flower of 5–10 waxy bright-yellow petals. Fruiting heads are *ca* 6 mm in diameter.

DISTRIBUTION South Island: a wide but rather sporadic occurrence chiefly along the interior ranges, but curiously with some large gaps—its northern limit is between Lake Sumner and the Lewis Pass highway in northern Canterbury and it occurs on and near the Craigieburn Range in mid Canterbury. Further south it is common on most of the mountains of Central and North Otago and again in south-eastern Fiordland near Lake Monowai.

Low- to high-alpine: 900–1,500 m (3,000–5,000 ft).

HABITAT Its usual habitat is moist, sheltered sites among snow tussocks, not far above the limits of subalpine scrub. Here it may be inconspicuous, but on the Central Otago mountains it is usually plentiful and much more obvious, especially around rock outcrops and other sheltered sites in the high-alpine zone.

COLLECTED The flowering plant is from Rock & Pillar Range, Central Otago, 1,310 m (4,300 ft). December 1964. The single leaf shows the "*berggrenii*" type from the Hector Mountains, Otago Lakes district, 1,520 m (5,000 ft).

Ranunculus multiscapus Hook.f.
"With several leafless flower stalks".

(= *R. lappaceus* Smith)

A tufted usually hairy herb, up to 15 cm tall, with a rosette of evergreen leaves. It is about the most variable of the alpine buttercups and several varieties are recognised. Forms with broad, coarsely-toothed to 3-lobed or 3-foliate leaves on thin petioles up to 10 cm long, as shown, are the most common.

There may be several flowering stems that usually exceed the leaves but in some plants they are very short. Each stem carries a single flower (1–2.5 cm across) with 5 non-overlapping petals. The fruits are strongly hooked.

DISTRIBUTION North, South and Stewart Islands: widespread in areas of tussock grassland and alpine vegetation throughout.

Lowland to high-alpine: to 1,800 m (6,000 ft).

HABITAT Common as a minor species in most areas of tussock grassland, occasionally in early snowbanks and extending into other types along streamsides. In the wetter western regions, although still widespread, it is altogether less important.

COLLECTED The larger form shown is smaller than many in the field. It came from Rock & Pillar Range, Central Otago, 1,280 m (4,200 ft). November 1967. The small form with very short flower stems is also from Rock & Pillar Range, 1,370 m (4,500 ft). December 1964.

Ranunculus verticillatus Kirk
"Whorled"—referring to the appearance of the stem leaves.

A delicate herb which varies in habit both within an area and throughout its range. The one to few basal leaves may vary from relatively large (10 × 6 cm), broadly and deeply trilobed especially at lower altitudes, to smaller (7 × 4 cm) and finely dissected with narrow segments especially at higher altitudes, as shown. Stem leaves are equally variable, the lower ones usually resembling the basal leaves except in being sessile; the upper ones are long and narrow.

Flower stems vary from 10 to 60 cm, mostly with habitat. The larger stems are branched above. Flowers have 10–12 narrow, non-overlapping petals which are strikingly different in the colour of their upper and lower surfaces.

DISTRIBUTION North and South Islands: from Mt Hauhungatahi in the central volcanic mountains of the North Island, southwards to the Ruahine and Tararua Ranges. In the South Island it occurs throughout Nelson and in western Marlborough (west of the Wairau Valley).

Low- to high-alpine: 1,100–1,800 m (3,500–6,000 ft).

HABITAT Usually on permanently wet sites in low-alpine vegetation. Plants often emerge out of low shrubs or snow tussocks which support the delicate stems. On exposed sites at higher altitudes plants may be more conspicuous, occurring as small rosettes with short erect flowering stems in dwarf carpet grassland, as in north-west Nelson.

COLLECTED Above Lake Sylvester, Cobb Valley, north-west Nelson, 1,460 m (4,800 ft). December 1967.

Ranunculus gracilipes Hook.f.
"Slender".

A small, partly hairy, evergreen herb, 5–15 cm tall, with a distinctive rosette of pinnate leaves. The leaves are quite variable with 2–6 pairs of leaflets that may be 3–5-lobed or irregularly and deeply cut into a few or many narrow, pointed segments. The degree of leaf dissection decreases from north to south.

Several unbranched flower stems may be produced successively during the flowering season. They usually exceed the leaves and carry a single small flower with 5–10 petals.

DISTRIBUTION South and Stewart Islands: widespread south of central Nelson-Marlborough but absent from the Kaikoura Ranges and western Fiordland.

Subalpine to high-alpine: 700–1,800 m (2,000–6,000 ft).

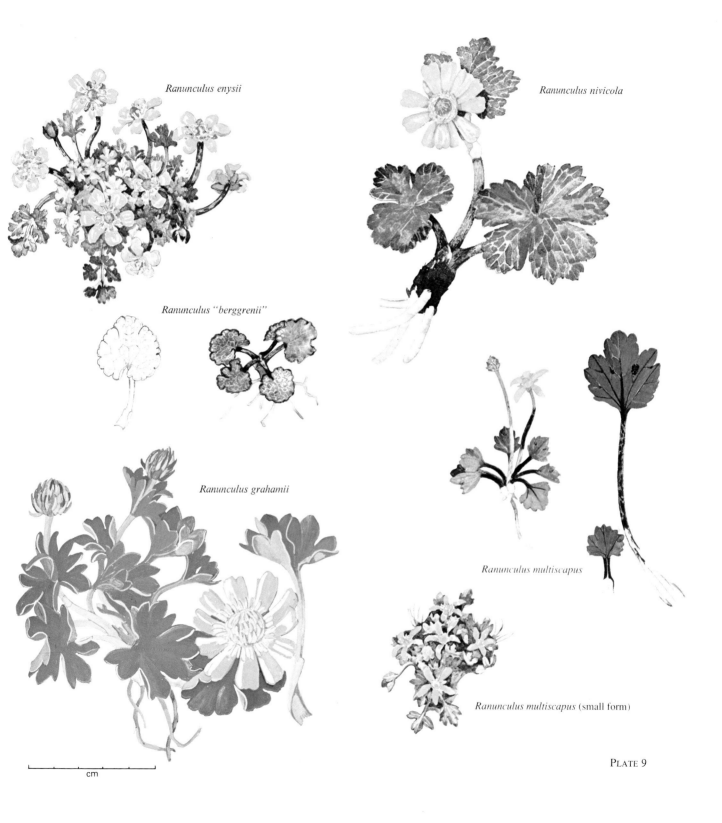

Ranunculus enysii

Ranunculus nivicola

Ranunculus "berggrenii"

Ranunculus grahamii

Ranunculus multiscapus

Ranunculus multiscapus (small form)

cm

Plate 9

HABITAT Apart from a requirement for abundant soil water it has a wide temperature tolerance and so extends from moist hollows, flushes and streamsides in the subalpine and low-alpine zones up to late snowbanks in the high-alpine.

COLLECTED Rock & Pillar Range, Central Otago, 1,280 m (4,200 ft). December 1969. This plant shows the smaller form and less dissected leaves, typical of most Central Otago populations.

Ranunculus foliosus Kirk is widespread and highly variable. It often reaches the alpine zone as a trifoliate tufted herb with dense rosettes of hairy leaves and flower stems, each with up to three sometimes apetalous flowers. Six other alpine buttercups are not shown. They are either very local or quite insignificant in the vegetation, or both. *R. carsei* Petrie, from flushes on the volcanic plateau Kaimanawa, Kaweka and Ruahine Ranges; *R. mirus* Garnock-Jones in north-west Nelson on limestone and marble; *R. royi* Simpson, on the Kaimanawa, Kaweka and Ruahine Ranges and southern South Island mountains; *R. maculatus* Ckn. & Allan, in bogs and flushes in south Canterbury and Otago; *R. cheesemanii* Kirk, from stream banks in Nelson, Marlborough and Canterbury.

Genus PSYCHROPHILA
"Cold-loving".

Recently separated from *Caltha* on the basis of both flower and leaf features as well as ecology, being essentially confined to snowbanks. Contains only a few species from North and South America, Australia and New Zealand.

Psychrophila obtusa (Cheesem.) W.A. Weber
"Blunt"—referring to the petals.

(= *Caltha obtusa* Cheesem.)

A low-growing herb with stout, branched, whitish rhizomes that form diffuse bright-green carpets up to 50 cm or more across.

The sweet-scented flowers usually appear during or soon after the winter snow has thawed.

DISTRIBUTION South Island: from Canterbury to Central and western Otago and eastern Fiordland, but rather erratic in the west and north.

Low- to high-alpine: 1,200–1,800 m (4,000–6,000 ft).

HABITAT Common along streamsides and in permanently wet hollows, especially snowbanks. It is one of the first alpines to flower in spring, despite a habitat where snow persists.

COLLECTED Rock & Pillar Range, Central Otago, 1,280 m (4,200 ft). December 1967.

Psychrophila novae-zelandiae (Hook.f.) W.A. Weber
"Of New Zealand"

(= *Caltha novae-zelandiae* Hook.f.)

Vegetatively similar to *P. obtusa* except that the rhizomes are usually longer and thinner and the leaf margins less wavy. With their narrow, pointed, pale-yellow petals the flowers are quite distinct but the flowering period, scent and fruits are generally similar to *P. obtusa*.

DISTRIBUTION North, South and Stewart Islands: widespread throughout the alpine zone but absent from many areas in the region occupied by *P. obtusa*: the two species only rarely occur together even though they occupy similar habitats.

Low- to high-alpine; 1,200–1,800 m (4,000–6,000 ft).

COLLECTED Both the flowering and fruiting plants are from Mt Brewster, Mt Aspiring National Park, 1,460 m (4,800 ft). February 1967.

Genus CLEMATIS
"A vine-branch".

A cosmopolitan mostly temperate genus of some 250 species of climbing plants. Of the eight native species an unusual one is localised in the alpine zone.

Clematis marmoraria Sneddon
"Of or belonging to marble" — referring to its habitat.

A low-growing suckering subshrub with slender spreading stems up to 50 cm long and almost glabrous, thick, 3-foliate leaves that are usually deeply divided.

Separate male and female plants both have prominent flowers 2-5 cm across with usually six white sepals and either numerous stamens or carpels.

DISTRIBUTION South Island: confined to north-west Nelson, on the Arthur Range, Mt Crusader and Hoary Head.

Low-alpine: 1,280–1,460 m (4,200–4,800 ft).

HABITAT Confined to rock crevices and other rocky sites in open herbfield on marble.

COLLECTED A cultivated plant collected from Mt Hoary Head. October 1982.

Genus ANEMONE
"Wind flower"—some species are reputed to open their flowers only in the wind.

A large and widespread genus. The one native anemone is an alpine.

Anemone tenuicaulis (Cheesem.) Parkin & Sledge NATIVE ANEMONE
"Thin-stemmed".

A slender delicate herb, up to 50 cm tall when growing among tussocks, but usually 10–20 cm tall. There is usually only one

Cont. on page 46

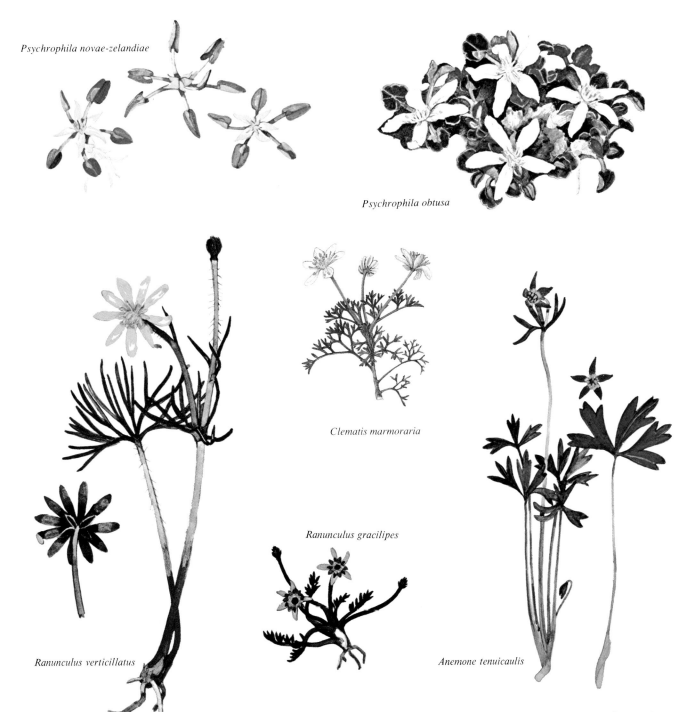

Psychrophila novae-zelandiae

Psychrophila obtusa

Clematis marmoraria

Ranunculus gracilipes

Ranunculus verticillatus

Anemone tenuicaulis

cm

PLATE 10

flowering stem with a single or rarely 2 flowers that may vary from pinkish- to reddish-brown.

DISTRIBUTION North and South Islands: from the Tararua Range southwards, throughout much of the wetter South Island mountain regions, but apparently rather erratic.

Subalpine to low-alpine: 600–1,500 m (2,000–5,000 ft).

HABITAT Usually confined to damp sites in snow tussock grassland and herbfield. Being an insignificant plant with small dull flowers it is often overlooked, especially among tall snow tussocks.

COLLECTED Eyre Mountains, northern Southland, 1,070 m (3,500 ft). November 1969.

The Mustard Family: BRASSICACEAE

Genus NOTOTHLASPI
"Southern *Thlaspi* or Penny cress".

The genus is endemic and both species are alpine.

Notothlaspi rosulatum Hook.f. PENWIPER PLANT
"Rosulate"—referring to the closely overlapping leaves.

A fleshy taprooted herb, usually forming a single rosette up to 8 cm across.

The stout, tapered flower head may reach 25 cm, smothered with fragrant cream flowers. They mature from the base upwards so that when the terminal ones are open the large flattened fruits are almost mature at the base. Only the larger plants normally flower and these die before winter.

DISTRIBUTION South Island: confined to the drier greywacke mountains east of the Southern Alps from Marlborough and eastern Nelson to North Otago.

Subalpine to high-alpine: 800–1,800 m (2,500–6,000 ft).

HABITAT Penwiper plants occupy loose stony sites such as the finer or mixed debris of screes or frost-sorted stony areas among fellfield. Like most scree plants their colour blends closely with the rocky background.

COLLECTED The flowering plant from the Craigieburn Range, Canterbury, 1,650 m (5,400 ft). January 1968. The fruiting plant is from the very extensive screes on Shingle Peak, upper Awatere Valley, Marlborough, 1,220 m (4,000 ft). January 1970.

Notothlaspi australe Hook.f.
"Southern".

It differs from *N. rosulatum* in that the stem is usually branched, each branch having a smaller rosette of quite glabrous leaves, so that plants may form loose patches up to 20 cm across.

Flowers are in flattish terminal heads that are smaller, looser and altogether less spectacular than in the penwiper plant. Individual flowers and fruits are also smaller but the style is more prominent and distinctly longer (2–5 mm) than in *N. rosulatum* (<1 mm).

DISTRIBUTION South Island: Nelson and Marlborough only, but including the mineral belt.

Subalpine to high-alpine: 700–1,700 m (2,500–5,500 ft).

HABITAT Generally similar to the penwiper plant—they occur together on the Travers and St Arnaud Ranges in Nelson Lakes National Park.

COLLECTED The flowering mat from above Lake Sylvester, Cobb Valley, north-west Nelson, 1,460 m (4,800 ft). December 1967.

Genus PACHYCLADON
"Thick shoot".

Another endemic genus with two species, both alpine.

Pachycladon novae-zelandiae Hook.f.
"Of New Zealand".

A small strongly-taprooted herb forming flat, usually single rosettes up to 8 cm across.

Several flower stems radiate from among the older leaves and carry 2–6 small, sweet-scented flowers. Fruits are larger (up to 1 cm long), more conspicuous and light-brown when ripe.

DISTRIBUTION South Island: on the schistose mountains from Central to western Otago–Southland.

High-alpine: 1,300–2,000 m (4,500–6,500 ft).

HABITAT In rock crevices and exposed fellfield or cushion vegetation where the plant cover is thin and frost activates the soil. The deep, stout taproot is an obvious adaptation to these severe conditions.

COLLECTED Rock & Pillar Range, Central Otago, 1,310 m (4,300 ft). December 1965.

Pachycladon crenatus Philipson
"Crenate"—referring to the shallow rounded teeth of the leaf margins.

A recently described species that occupies similar habitats but at somewhat lower altitudes in Fiordland. It is usually more robust than *P. novae-zelandiae*, with brighter green leaves that have coarse rounded teeth rather than deeply cut margins. Also, plants of *P. crenata* may be less hairy, but more distinctive, microscopic examination will show that any leaf hairs are simple rather than star-shaped or forked as in *P. novae-zelandiae*.

Genus CARDAMINE
From a Greek name for "cress".

A large genus of about 120 species, mostly from temperate regions. Of the 200 cardamines presently in New Zealand, only four have been named and three of these reach the alpine zone.

Cardamine corymbosa Hook.f.
"With corymbs"–referring to the type of flower head.

A rather delicate but variable glabrous herb, up to 15 cm tall, that forms either a single rosette or several intertwined ones. Leaves are all basal and usually thin and delicate, with slender petioles up to 4 cm long and a small blade that may be bilobed at the base.

Notothlaspi rosulatum

Notothlaspi australe

Cardamine corymbosa

Pachycladon novae-zelandiae

Cardamine bilobata

PLATE 11

Slender flower stalks often exceed the leaves and carry a single, or if branched up to 5 white flowers. Fruits are very narrow and up to 2 cm long.

DISTRIBUTION North, South and Stewart Islands: throughout much of New Zealand.

Lowland to low-alpine: to 1,600 m (5,000 ft).

HABITAT Occurs chiefly on permanently wet sites such as bogs or along streamsides, but sometimes on rock outcrops in wet regions.

COLLECTED The small single-flowered form shown is from the Old Man Range, Central Otago; 1,550 m (5,100 ft). December 1968

Cardamine bilobata Kirk *(See plate 11)*
"Two-lobed"–referring to the leaves.

Another variable species not always easily distinguished from *C. corymbifera*. However, it is separated by its rather stout rootstock, deeply trilobed to trifoliate leaves which sometimes have an additional pair of leaflets, somewhat larger flowers (*ca.* 8 mm across) on a sparsely branched flowering stem, and slightly longer fruits (to 2.5 cm).

DISTRIBUTION South Island: its more restricted distribution is mostly east of the main divide but it also occurs in northwest Nelson.

Mainly low-alpine: 900–1,500 m (3,000–5,000 ft).

HABITAT It usually occupies stable or semi-stable rock debris such as fellfield, moraine or scree edges, but like *C. corymbosa* it may also occupy rock crevices.

COLLECTED Mt Richmond, Two Thumb Range, South Canterbury, 1,520 m (5,000 ft). January 1969.

**Cardamine depressa* Hook.f.
"Low-growing".

Another alpine species from the South and Stewart Islands which, like the others, is variable, especially in its vegetative parts. It is distinguished chiefly by its rather stout, usually branched flowering stem bearing single, very small flowers *ca* 3 mm across.

Moist habitats are preferred but they may range from the coast to high-alpine snowbanks.

Genus **CHEESEMANIA**
After Mr T. F. Cheeseman, well-known New Zealand botanist.

An endemic genus; all five species are alpine.

Cheesemania latisiliqua (Cheesem.) Schulz
"With broad fruits".

A robust partly-hairy herb with a dense rosette of leathery basal leaves and a deep stout taproot.

The erect, branched flower stem, up to 50 cm tall, carries smaller leaves that are not always serrated, and has crowded white flowers *ca* 1 cm across. Ripe fruits are quite large (*ca* 4 × 0.5 cm) and prominent.

DISTRIBUTION South Island: confined to the mountains of north-west Nelson.

Low- to high-alpine: 1,200–1,800 m (4,000–6,000 ft).

HABITAT Like all cheesemanias this one is practically confined to ledges and crevices of large rock outcrops. Here it may be conspicuous among the thin plant cover.

COLLECTED Mt Peel, Cobb Valley, north-west Nelson, 1,520 m (5,000 ft). January 1969.

Cheesemania wallii (Carse) Allan
After Professor Arnold Wall, collector of alpine plants.

It differs from *C. latesiliqua* in leaf shape, size of fruit which here is much smaller, and in having an unbranched flowering stem.

DISTRIBUTION South Island: on the mountains immediately west of Lake Wakatipu, Otago.

Low- to high-alpine: 1,000–1,800 m (3,500–6,000 ft).

HABITAT Ledges and crevices of rock outcrops, mostly in fellfield.

COLLECTED Eyre Mountains, northern Southland, 1,370 m (4,500 ft). The flowering plant was collected in November 1969, the fruiting stem in December 1969.

Three cheesemanias are not illustrated. All occupy ledges and crevices of rock outcrops and are similar in habit to those shown.
* *C. gibbsii* (Cheesem.) Schulz, differs from *C. latesiliqua* chiefly in having uniformly narrow and glabrous leaves. It is also confined to the mountains of north-west Nelson.
* *C. enysii* (Cheesem.) Schulz, is a low herb, <10 cm tall, with toothed leaves and a very dense, branched flowering stem. It occurs sporadically on the drier mountains to the north and east of the Southern Alps.
* *C. fastigiata* (Hook. f.) Schulz, is the most widespread species, inhabiting the drier interior mountains from Marlborough to northern Southland, but rather local in its occurrence. It has quite narrow fruits (<3 mm wide) and deeply lobed leaves which extend up the tall flower stem.

The Viola Family: **VIOLACEAE**

Genus **VIOLA**
"Violet".

An almost worldwide genus of about 400 species. Of the three native violets one reaches the alpine zone.

Viola cunninghamii Hook.f. *(See plate 13)*   MOUNTAIN VIOLET
After Mr A. Cunningham, Australian botanist who visited New Zealand in the 1830s.

A glabrous summer-green herb, often with several tufts arising close together from a branched stock. Leaves have a pair of small tapered and undivided stipules at their base.

These violets are white, usually with lilac or yellow veins. They have a long flowering period beginning about October. Fruits are triangular capsules almost 1 cm long.

DISTRIBUTION North, South and Stewart Islands: occurs almost throughout.

Lowland to high-alpine: to 1,800 m (6,000 ft).

HABITAT The mountain violet has a wide range. Below the alpine zone it is usually confined to moist sites, but with soil moisture freely available in most alpine situations it is much less restricted

Cont. on page 50

Cheesemania wallii

Cheesemania latisiliqua

cm

Plate 12

here. Indeed, it may be present in most alpine vegetation, including unstable rocky sites approaching scree. In the high-alpine zone it is rare except for some early snowbanks.

COLLECTED Manganui Valley, Mt Egmont National Park, 1,310 m (4,300 ft). November 1967.

Genus **MELICYTUS**

"Honey cup" — referring to the nectaries in the flowers.

A small woody genus from Australasia, Norfolk, Tonga and Fiji Islands. Four of the species, including the one which reaches the alpine zone, were recently transferred from *Hymenanthera*.

Melicytus alpinus (Kirk) Garnock-Jones
"Alpine"
(= *Hymenanthera alpina* (Kirk) W.R.B. Oliver

A low rigid shrub, up to 50 cm tall, with short, stout, whitish or pale grey (rarely dark-grey), interlacing branches that have tapered spinous ends. Leaves are few and generally sparse on shrubs from exposed sites but more plentiful in sheltered areas.

Minute bell-shaped flowers are easily overlooked but the single-seeded berries are more obvious, being white or dull-blue, somewhat larger than the flowers and usually abundant along the stems.

DISTRIBUTION South Island: generally widespread along and east of the main divide.

Montane to high-alpine: 200–1,800 m (500–6,000 ft).

HABITAT On rocky outcrops almost regardless of altitude and often hugging the surface on the most exposed parts. Shrubs may also occur sporadically through snow tussock grassland or herbfield and even on the almost bare areas of serpentine in the mineral belt.

COLLECTED Rock & Pillar Range, Central Otago, 1,370 m (4,500 ft). December 1969.

The Sundew Family: **DROSERACEAE**

Genus **DROSERA**

"Dewy"—referring to the secretions from the leaves.

The only native genus, *Drosera*, is characterised by glandular hairs on the leaves, an insectivorous habit and a bog habitat. A widespread genus of about 100 species, many of them Australian. Of the six native sundews, three are alpine.

Drosera arcturi Hook.f.
"Of Arcturus, i.e. of Arthur"—Mt Arthur, Tasmania, is the type locality.

A small summer-green herb with strap-shaped leaves and persistent, dark, sheathing bases.

One to few flower stalks usually exceed the leaves and their single flowers have prominent dark-green sepals alternating with the white petals. The black capsule is *ca* 1 cm long.

DISTRIBUTION North, South and Stewart Islands: widespread from the central North Island southwards.

Montane (in the south) to low-alpine: 300–1,500 m (1,000–5,000 ft).

HABITAT In acid peat bogs, both of sphagnum and cushions, and around the edges of tarns.

COLLECTED Key Summit, Fiordland National Park, 910 m (3,000 ft). January 1968.

Drosera stenopetala Hook.f.
"With narrow petals".

Dark-green or reddish-green, similar in size to *D. arcturi* and likewise without stipules, but differing in the shape of the leaves and the sepals which are rounded and much shorter. The capsule is also somewhat shorter, *ca* 7 mm long.

DISTRIBUTION North, South and Stewart Islands: similar to *D. arcturi*.

HABITAT Also in bogs of various types, often with other sundews. In addition, it occupies permanently wet depressions or flushed areas in most types of low-alpine vegetation, and on wet avalanche chutes below the tree line.

COLLECTED Key Summit, Fiordland National Park, 910 m (3,000 ft). January 1968.

Drosera spathulata Labill.
"Spathulate"—referring to the leaf shape.

Usually smaller than the other two alpine sundews but best distinguished from them by a pair of very small, brown, papery stipules up to 7 mm long at the leaf base.

The one to few flower stalks may, as in the other two alpine sundews, carry only a single flower each, especially at higher altitudes, but usually there are several arranged along one side of the stalk. The capsule is quite small, only 1–2 mm long.

DISTRIBUTION North, South and Stewart Islands: the total extent in New Zealand is wide but it is more local than the other alpine sundews.

Lowland (in the far south) to low-alpine: to 1,400 m (4,500 ft).

HABITAT On thin acid soils and peat, here often with other sundews.

COLLECTED Key Summit, Fiordland National Park, 910 m (3,000 ft). January 1968.

The Chickweed Family: **CARYOPHYLLACEAE**

Genus **COLOBANTHUS**

"Imperfect flower"—referring to the absence of petals.

A southern hemisphere genus of more than 20 species. Nine of the 11 mainland New Zealand ones reach the alpine zone.

These can be separated into two habit groups, cushion and tufted, and within each group, flower characters and leaf tips are most useful in recognising the species as follows (for use of key see Glossary):

A	Forms brownish-green moss-like cushions; intertwining branches are much longer than the short (<7 mm) overlapping leaves	B
AA	Forms small tufts or rosettes with short stems and long (>10 mm) overtopping leaves	G
B	Flower parts in fours	C
BB	Flower parts in fives	D

Cont. on page 52

50

Viola cunninghamii

Melicytus alpinus

Drosera arcturi

Drosera stenopetala

Drosera spathulata

cm

PLATE 13

C   Leaves with long hair tips; sepals sharp-pointed
            C. monticola

CC   Leaves without hair tips; sepals blunt; Nelson
            C. wallii

D   Leaves pointed but without hair tips; West Nelson
            C. masonae

DD   Leaves with pronounced hair tips   E

E   Sepals distinctly wider than leaves, not longer than
       the mature capsule   *C. canaliculatus*

EE   Sepals not wider than leaves; longer than the mature
       capsule   F

F   Leaves incurved against the stem, with very long hair
       tips and margins not thickened when dry   *C. acicularis*

FF   Leaves spreading, with short hair tips and margins
       obviously thickened when dry   *C. buchananii*

G   Sepals broad and blunt-tipped, much shorter than
       the capsule   *C. affinis*

GG   Sepals narrow and sharp-tipped, at least as long as
       the capsule   H

H   Sepals about same length as capsule; leaves with
       short pointed tips   *C. apetalus*

HH   Sepals longer than capsule; leaves with long hair tips
            C. strictus

DISTRIBUTIONS

*C. monticola Petrie
"Growing in mountains".

    South Island: the Mt Cook district and for some distance southwards along the Southern Alps.

C. wallii Petrie
After Professor Arnold Wall, collector of plants.

    South Island: confined to the mountains of Nelson.

*C. masoniae L. B. Moore
After Miss R. Mason, botanist.

    South Island: on the mountains of western Nelson.

C. canaliculatus Kirk
"Channelled"—referring to the leaves.

    ?North and South Islands: Nelson and Otago, especially Central and western Otago. Cushions common on Mt Egmont, less so on several other North Island mountains—Mt Hikurangi; Kaimanawa, Ruahine and Tararua Ranges—may be a form of this species, or possibly *C. buchananii* with shorter than normal sepals.

C. acicularis Hook.f.
"Needle-shaped"—referring to the leaves.

    North and South Islands: Ruahine Range; in the South Island similar to *C. buchananii* but often more common.

C. buchananii Kirk
After Mr J. Buchanan, early botanist.

    ?North and South Islands: Nelson and the drier mountains east of the main divide. (See under *C. canaliculatus* for possible occurrence in the North Island).

C. affinis (Hook.) Hook.f.
"Related"—referring to its resemblance to a Falkland Island species.

    North, South and Stewart Islands: Mt Egmont, Ruahine and Tararua Ranges; Nelson, Westland, western Otago, Fiordland; Mt Anglem.

*C. apetalus (Labill.) Druce
"Without petals".

    North and South Islands: Mt Hikurangi, Kaimanawa, Ruahine and Tararua Ranges; more widespread in the South Island but mostly east of the main divide, extending into Fiordland.

C. strictus Cheesem.
"Erect and straight"—referring to the leaves.

    North and South Islands: Ruahine Range; east of the main divide in the South Island.

HABITATS

    The cushion species generally are on exposed, rocky but fairly stable, well-drained, open sites in snow tussock grassland, herbfield or high-alpine vegetation, including rock outcrops, but may extend into snowbanks. They may easily pass for small clumps of moss.

    Most are low- to high-alpine, but *C. buchananii* extends down to montane levels (500 m) in Central Otago.

    By contrast, two of the tufted alpine species (*C. affinis*, *C. apetalus*) prefer moist sites such as streamsides, flushes, wet depressions and snowbanks, but *C. strictus*, while occasionally in moist grassland, is more common in depleted tussock grassland on gravelly or other well-drained sites and in rock crevices.

    C. affinis is strictly alpine but the other two may extend to sea level.
COLLECTED *C. wallii*: Red Hill Range, Wairau Valley, Marlborough, 1,340 m (4,400 ft). January 1971.

C. canaliculatus: Mt Peel, Cobb Valley, north-west Nelson, 1,520 m (5,000 ft). January 1971.

C. buchananii: Old Man Range, Central Otago, 1,580 m (5,200 ft). April 1968.

C. acicularis: Hawkdun Range, North Otago, 1,220 m (4,000 ft). December 1969.

C. affinis: Mt Mytton, Cobb Valley, north-west Nelson, 1,460 m (4,800 ft). January 1971.

C. apetalus: Old Man Range, Central Otago, 1,430 m (4,700 ft). February 1969.

C. strictus: Hawkdun Range, North Otago, 1,070 m (3,500 ft). December 1969.

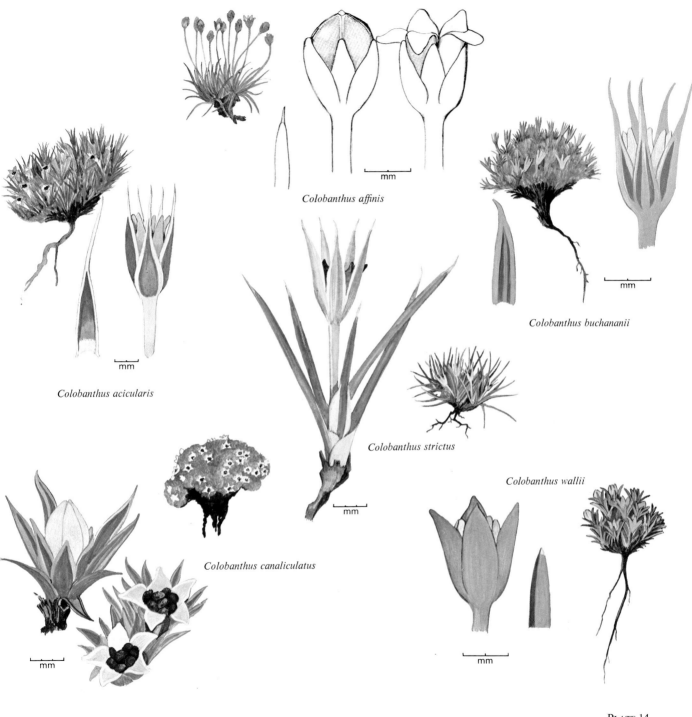

Colobanthus affinis

Colobanthus buchananii

Colobanthus acicularis

Colobanthus strictus

Colobanthus wallii

Colobanthus canaliculatus

PLATE 14

Genus SCLERANTHUS

"Hard flower".

A widespread genus in which the total number of species is still uncertain. Two of the three native ones reach the alpine zone.

Scleranthus brockiei P. A. Williamson
After Mr W. B. Brockie, botanist and alpine gardener.

Scleranthus uniflorus P. A. Williamson
"Single-flowered".

Both species form mosslike mats up to 10 cm or more across, but with a single central root system. Mats are bright green in *S. brockiei*, golden- to orange-green in *S. uniflorus*. Leaves are very small, strongly overlapping and persistent along the stem. In both species the flowers are minute.

The clearest distinction between them is in the very small dry fruits which occur either singly (*S. uniflorus*) or paired on the short flower stalk. Another distinction, to be seen with a good lens, is in the number of sepals: 4 in *S. uniflorus*, 5 in *S. brockiei*. They persist in the fruit. After the fruit falls, 2 bracts remain on the flower stalk in *S. uniflorus* and 4 in *S. brockiei*.

DISTRIBUTIONS

S. brockiei: South Island; occurs sporadically from Nelson through Canterbury, Otago and into Fiordland.

S. uniflorus: South Island; only on the drier mountains east of the main divide.

Both are coastal to high-alpine: to 1,700 m (5,500 ft).

HABITAT In alpine areas both species occupy well-drained sites in open snow tussock grassland and herbfield, but may be more conspicuous on rock outcrops.

COLLECTED The mat of *S. uniflorus* from Old Man Range, Central Otago, 1,520 m (5,000 ft). February 1969.

Genus STELLARIA
"Star-like"—referring to the flowers.

A world-wide genus of about 85 species. Of the six native ones two reach the alpine zone.

Stellaria roughii Hook.f.
After Captain Rough, early collector, especially in the Nelson mountains.

A highly-branched and rather delicate, fleshy, summer-green herb that forms open patches up to 20 cm across from a much-branched pale rhizome. The narrow pointed leaves are smaller near the tips of the branches.

Flowers occur singly on the ends of many branches. Each one has rather leaflike sepals that tend to conceal the much shorter deeply-bilobed petals. Mature capsules are also much shorter than the sepals and also tend to be concealed by them.

DISTRIBUTION South Island: from Nelson southwards to the Takitimu Mountains in western Southland but its occurrence is erratic, determined largely by the availability of its habitat.

Low- to high-alpine: 1,000–2,000 m (3,500–6,500 ft).

HABITAT Confined to screes and other sites with loose rocky debris such as on the Nelson mineral belt. Like most other scree plants there is a remarkable similarity in colour with the surrounding stones.

COLLECTED Fog Peak, Torlesse Range, Canterbury, 1,680 m (5,500 ft). January 1968.

Stellaria gracilenta Hook.f.
"Slender".

A small erect herb with wiry, often tangled branches up to 10 cm high. Paired leaves clasp the stem and are concave above. In the axil of just one of each pair there is a short leafy shoot.

Single flowers are on delicate erect stalks at the branch tips. Five pointed sepals are usually exceeded by the 5 white petals which are deeply split and hence look double. Mature capsules slightly exceed the persistent calyx.

DISTRIBUTION North and South Islands: uncommon in the North Island—the Ruahine Range and Mt Hikurangi; but widespread in the drier interior and eastern regions of the South Island.

Montane to high-alpine: 500–1,800 m (1,500–6,000 ft).

HABITAT Prefers rocky and other well-drained, fairly stable sites in the tussock grasslands, but it also occurs sporadically in herbfield and fellfield. In the wetter regions it is practically confined to recent moraine.

COLLECTED Rock & Pillar Range, Central Otago, 1,220 m (4,000 ft). January 1971.

The Hectorella Family: HECTORELLACEAE

Genus HECTORELLA
After Sir James Hector, geologist and explorer.

Contains but a single endemic alpine species.

Hectorella caespitosa Hook.f.
"Turf-forming".

Forms cushions up to 20 cm or more across. Many short, vertical, fleshy branches arise from deep swollen taproots and each ends in a small, glabrous, leafy rosette.

Up to a dozen flowers develop in each rosette, among the older leaves. Even though the individual flowers are small and almost sessile, they project beyond the leaves and together may almost mask the foliage when fully open. Plants are unisexual; the bright orange stamens in male flowers, as shown, make them more colourful than the female.

DISTRIBUTION South Island: southwards from Arthurs Pass along

Cont. on page 56

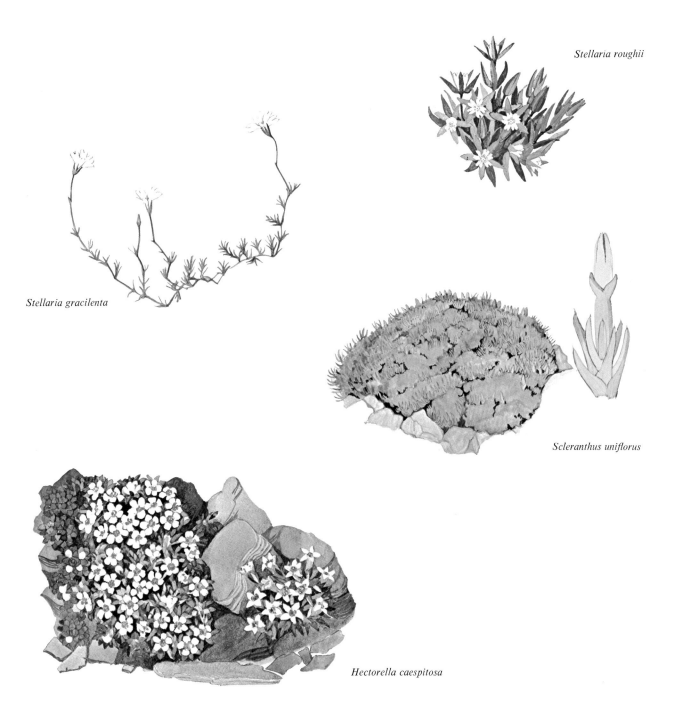

Stellaria roughii

Stellaria gracilenta

Scleranthus uniflorus

Hectorella caespitosa

cm

PLATE 15

the Southern Alps to Fiordland, but extending eastwards into Central Otago.

Mostly high-alpine: 1,300–2,000 m (4,500–6,500 ft).

HABITAT One of the most characteristic plants of fellfield and cushion vegetation in the southern South Island, both on soil and in rock crevices.

COLLECTED Rock & Pillar Range, Central Otago, 1,370 m (4,500 ft). December 1964.

The Geranium Family: **GERANIACEAE**

Genus **GERANIUM**
"Cranesbill"—referring to the beak-like fruit.

A widespread genus of some 300 species. Of the six native geraniums, three reach the alpine zone.

Geranium microphyllum Hook.f.
"Small-leaved".

A small, trailing, partly hairy herb with several slender, straggling, usually branched stems arising from a woody taproot. Leaves typically have a long slender petiole, a pair of small brown stipules at their base and a thin, sometimes reddish blade with 3, 5 or 7 broad lobes that are shallowly lobed or toothed.

Flower stems are also slender with one or occasionally 2 white flowers. Their 5 small narrow sepals have a characteristic bristlelike tip and the ripe fruits opens, as in all geraniums, by each of the 5 sections curling upwards and remaining attached at the tip of the long beak.

DISTRIBUTION North, South and Stewart Islands: occurs almost throughout.

Lowland to high-alpine: to 1,500 m (5,000 ft).

HABITAT Usually present as a minor plant on open, well-drained or rocky sites in the tussock grasslands and herbfields, especially east of the main divide. Because of its straggling habit it is often overlooked among the tussocks. In the high-alpine zone small forms may be present in the more sheltered sites, including early snowbanks.

COLLECTED Rock & Pillar Range, Central Otago, 1,220 m (4,000 ft). January 1969.

Geranium potentilloides DC.
Like "*Potentilla*" — widespread genus in the rose family.

Previously included within *G. microphyllum* but distinguished from it by the more slender rootstock, less straggling habit, more deeply lobed leaves and pink as distinct from white flowers.

The two species may occur together but *G. potentilloides* is more common in disturbed or modified habitats.

Geranium sessiliflorum Cav.
"With sessile flowers".

Much more compact than the other two species with a stout woody rootstock and short stems. It is rather variable; three lowland varieties are recognised. The leaves form basal rosettes and have somewhat thicker, often mottled blades that may be more obviously hairy than in either of the other two species.

Flower stalks are very hairy but quite short with a single, small, white or pink flower. Conspicuous hairs on the calyx and fruit is another feature distinguishing it from the other species.

DISTRIBUTION North, South and Stewart Islands: throughout, but as an alpine only on the drier interior and eastern South Island mountains.

Coastal to high-alpine: to 1,700 m (5,500 ft).

HABITAT Much more common in lowland to subalpine grasslands and coastal areas than in the alpine zone where it is almost restricted to well-drained, usually open, stony sites in snow tussock grassland, induced herbfield, or even on semi-stable scree.

COLLECTED Old Man Range, Central Otago, 1,070 m (3,500 ft). December 1970.

The Buckwheat Family: **POLYGONACEAE**

Genus **MUEHLENBECKIA**
After the Alsatian botanist and physician, Muehlenbeck.

Contains about 20 species from South America and Australasia. Of the five native muehlenbeckias, one reaches the alpine zone.

Muehlenbeckia axillaris (Hook.f.) Walp.
Flowers develop in the axils of leaves.

A creeping or straggling shrub with dark wiry branches above or below ground that form mats or loose patches up to 1 m or more across. Thick dark-green leaves are paler and broad to almost round (3–8 mm long).

Small male and female flowers occur singly or paired in the leaf axils, but the small black fruits are more prominent, attached to the petals which usually enlarge to become succulent and glassy.

DISTRIBUTION North and South Islands: widespread in mountain regions from the central North Island southwards.

Mostly montane to low-alpine: 300–1,500 m (1,000–5,000 ft).

HABITAT Often common on damp stony sites, especially as a pioneer on gravel of riverbeds or moraine. Also found on open or rocky areas of tussock grassland and herbfield and on the ultrabasic soils of the mineral belts.

COLLECTED A fruiting plant from Waihohonu, Tongariro National Park, *ca* 1,400 m (4,600 ft). February 1971.

The Portulaca Family: **PORTULACACEAE**

Genus **NEOPAXIA**
"A new Paxia".

Contains only a single Australasian species.

Neopaxia australasica (Hook.f.) Ö. Nilsson
"Australasian".
(= *Claytonia australasica* Hook.f.; *Montia australasica* (Hook.f.) Pax and Hoffm.)

Geranium microphyllum

Geranium sessiliflorum

Oxalis magellanica

Neopaxia australasica

Muehlenbeckia axillaris

cm

PLATE 16

A rather variable, glabrous, semi-succulent, creeping herb that usually forms diffuse mats up to 20 cm or more across. The pale, branched, creeping stems may be thin or fleshy, with roots confined to the prominent nodes. Leaves are arranged singly or in clusters and have a papery sheath clasping the stem.

Flowers are usually single with 2 prominent and persistent green sepals that enclose the bud, and 5 white or pale-pink petals that open into a characteristic star-shaped flower. The rounded capsule about equals the sepals and contains usually 3 glossy black seeds.

DISTRIBUTION   North, South and Stewart Islands: apart from the northern half of the North Island it occurs almost throughout.

Lowland to high-alpine: 100–2,000 m (500–6,500 ft).

HABITAT   It is among the most versatile of our native plants, extending from lowland areas to the latest snowbanks, at least in the southern South Island. Only on damp sites that are thinly vegetated is it common and aggressive — presumably it cannot tolerate strong competition. Gravel creek beds subject to flooding, mossy stream-banks and flushed or eroding areas of tussock grassland, herbfield, fellfield, fine scree, loose scoria, rock debris on serpentine or late snowbanks are all colonised.

COLLECTED   Rock & Pillar Range, Central Otago, 1,070 m (3,500 ft). December 1969.

The Oxalis Family: **OXALIDACEAE**

Genus **OXALIS**
"Sharp, acid" — referring to the taste.

A widespread genus of about 800 species. Two of the three native oxalis extend to the alpine zone.

Oxalis magellanica Forst.f. *(See plate 16)*
From southern South America.

A creeping rhizomatous herb with many small leafy tufts that form open patches up to 30 cm or more across. The distinctive leaves are whitish below and often purple-margined.

Each tuft may produce a slender flower stalk with a single flower that may be coiled shut.

DISTRIBUTION   North and South Islands: occurs throughout except for North Auckland.

Lowland to low-alpine: 700–1,400 m (2,500–4,500 ft).

HABITAT   On damp but well-lit sites, including open scrub and forest. In alpine areas it occurs chiefly on avalanche chutes close to the tree line, in sphagnum bogs and along streamsides, in flushed areas, or wet depressions in snow tussock grassland or herbfield, and occasionally in early snowbanks.

COLLECTED   Rock & Pillar Range, Central Otago, 1,220 m (4,000 ft). December 1969.

Oxalis exilis A. Cunn.
"Acid" — referring to the juice.

Highly variable, with slender, creeping, almost wiry stems. The typical oxalis leaves are often glaucous or reddish, especially beneath,

but the most distinctive feature is the yellow flowers. In the alpine zone I have seen it only as an occasional plant on screes in the upper Awatere Valley, Marlborough and on the Hawkdun Range in North Otago at *ca* 1,200 m (4,000 ft).

The Marestail Family: **HALORAGACEAE**

Genus **GONOCARPUS**
"Angled fruit".

Contains about 70 species, mostly Southern Hemisphere, but extending into South-east Asia. Of the four native species, one reaches the alpine zone.

Gonocarpus micranthus Thunb.
"Small-flowered".

A small wiry herb with highly branched creeping stems, both below and above ground, the latter usually < 10 cm long. Most of the leaves are opposite with up to 4 shallow nicks on each side.

Minute dark-red flowers occur singly in the leaf axils or in small plants often only at the stem tips. Flower details are shown. When mature, the square fruit is dark-brown and shining, *ca* 2 mm long.

DISTRIBUTION   North, South and Stewart Islands: widespread almost throughout.

Lowland to low-alpine: to 1,200 m (4,000 ft).

HABITAT   Occupies a wide range of moist open sites from sand or gravel of river flats or fine scree to snow tussock grassland and herbfield. It is small and wiry and easily overlooked.

COLLECTED   Mt Burns, Hunter Mountains, Fiordland National Park, 1,110 m (3,600 ft). January 1968.

The Gunnera Family: **GUNNERACEAE**

Genus **GUNNERA**
After Dr Gunner, Norwegian Bishop and botanist.

Contains about 40 species, mostly from South America, South Africa, East Indies, New Guinea, Tasmania and New Zealand. Of the five native gunneras at least three may reach the alpine zone.

Gunnera monoica Raoul
"Monoecious"—having separate male and female flowers on the same plant.

A rather variable usually dark green herb, creeping by runners and with thick leaves ranging in shape from heart-shaped to rounded, deeply lobed to unlobed, and with margins pointed to rounded. Male flowers develop on prominent erect stems, as shown, but the female ones are on much shorter branches, usually concealed by the leaves. The tight or elongated clusters of small, round, fleshy fruits are usually white and often concealed.

DISTRIBUTION   North, South and Stewart Islands: widespread south of the Auckland Isthmus.

Lowland to low-alpine: to 1,500 m (5,000 ft).

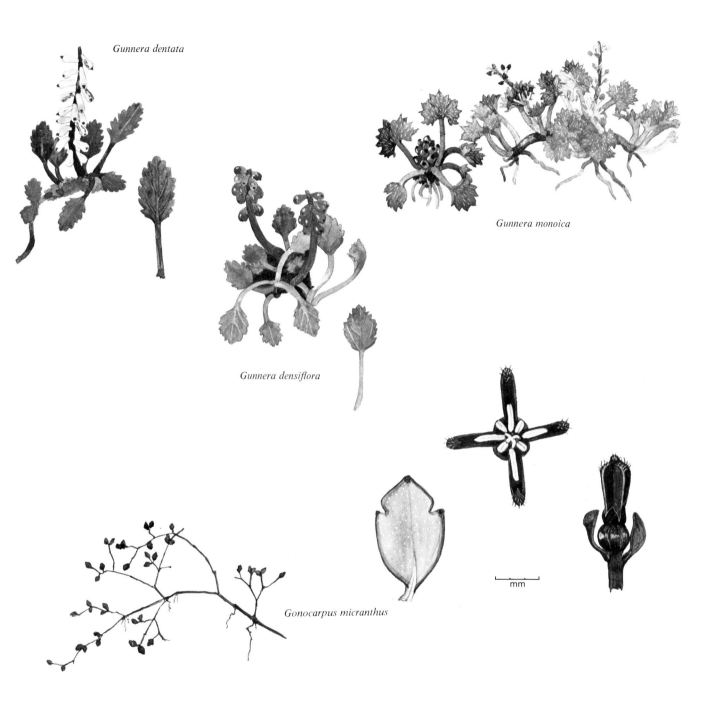

Gunnera dentata

Gunnera monoica

Gunnera densiflora

Gonocarpus micranthus

mm

cm

PLATE 17

HABITAT Most commonly found on permanently wet or shady faces, especially stream banks and waterfalls, where it often forms extensive carpets.

COLLECTED The plant in flower is from Manganui, Stratford Plateau, Mt Egmont National Park, 1,280 m (4,200 ft). November 1967. Fruits are from the same area, in March.

Gunnera densiflora Hook.f. *(See plate 17)*
"With crowded flowers".

A creeping herb with stems mostly underground. The typical habit and shape of the dark-green usually heart-shaped leaves are shown, together with the pear-shaped fleshy fruits which are orange or more often dark red.

DISTRIBUTION   South Island: Nelson, southern Marlborough and Canterbury.

Montane to low-alpine: 600–1,200 m (2,000–4,000 ft).

HABITAT   Permanently damp grasslands and bogs, especially of sphagnum.

COLLECTED By Dr I. Morice from the Waimakariri River near Bealey, Canterbury, *ca* 730 m (2,400 ft). April 1968.

Gunnera dentata Kirk *(See plate 17)*
"Dentate" — referring to the leaf margins.

The habit is similar to *G. densiflora* but the leaves are narrower. Its fleshy club-shaped fruits become widely spaced as they mature. They vary in colour from red to orange or cream.

DISTRIBUTION North and South Islands: rather widespread to the south of the central North Island, but rare or absent from the drier regions of the South Island.

Montane to low-alpine: 100–1,400 m (500–4,500 ft).

HABITAT   Confined to bogs and other permanently wet sites in open grassland, especially stream banks and sandy river beds.

COLLECTED By Dr I. Morice at the Hohonu River, Westland. April 1968.

The Evening Primrose Family: **ONAGRACEAE**

Genus **EPILOBIUM**
"Flower on top of the pod" — referring to the attachment of the petals at the end of the long ovary.

A large genus of about 200 species, mostly from temperate regions. The many native willow herbs have recently been revised by Dr Peter Raven who has recognised 18 species that reach the alpine zone; 14 are treated here. Among these are several that are quite distinct but there are also some that may be difficult to identify.

The genus is easily recognised from foliage, flowers and fruits although the habit may vary. Leaves are opposite, at least near the base, frequently reddish- or purplish-green, and often bluntly toothed.

Flowers usually occur singly with the individual parts in fours and the petals white or pink and generally 2-lobed. Fruits are long, narrow, often red capsules that curl on opening to release many small fluffy seeds.

Epilobium tasmanicum Hausskn.
"Tasmanian".

A small glabrous herb with branched, creeping and rooting stems that ascend near their tips to form open patches up to 10 cm across. The leaves are rather thick but not fleshy.

Flowers are almost sessile but, as shown, the stalks elongate somewhat as the capsules mature.

DISTRIBUTION South Island: widespread, but appears to be rare or absent from the wettest areas along and west of the main divide.

Subalpine to high-alpine: 800–2,100 m (2,500–7,000 ft).

HABITAT In permanently moist hollows with thin open vegetation of a wide variety—snow tussock grassland, herbfield, fellfield, early snowbanks.

COLLECTED Old Man Range, Central Otago, 1,660 m (5,450 ft). January 1970.

Epilobium alsinoides A. Cunn.
"Resembling Alsine"—Chickweed.

Two of the three subspecies reach the alpine zone.

Ssp. *atriplicifolium* (A. Cunn.) Raven & Engelhorn
"*Atriplex*-like leaf".

A variable, small, tufted plant, up to 15 cm tall in the alpine zone, with several usually branched stems radiating from the small woody rootstock. Often plants grow together with their stems intertwined. Leaves are thin but their shape is rather variable; the one shown is typical of many populations.

Small flowers develop near the tips of the branches. Fruits are often pale and densely hairy when young, becoming dark-red and almost glabrous when mature, as do their prominent stalks.

DISTRIBUTION North, South and Stewart Islands: occurs almost throughout.

Lowland to low-alpine: to 1,700 m (5,500 ft).

HABITAT Widespread in tussock grasslands, herbfields, riverbeds and other open, usually well-drained sites.

COLLECTED Old Man Range, Central Otago, 1,400 m (4,600 ft). January 1970.

*Ssp. *tenuipes* (Hook.f.) Raven & Engelhorn
"Thin"—referring to the plant as a whole, but especially to the flower stalk.

Somewhat more slender and less branched than the other subspecies, with the leaves narrower and often erect.

Very small white flowers usually occur singly at the branch tips and the long, slender, almost glabrous capsules develop on slender stalks that are characteristically whitish from the dense cover of fine hairs.

DISTRIBUTION North and South Islands: widespread to the south of the central North Island.

Lowland to low-alpine: to 1,700 m (5,500 ft).

HABITAT Prefers open but permanently wet sites in tussock grasslands and herbfields.

Epilobium pernitens Ckn. & Allan
"Shining"—referring to the leaves.

A branching, creeping and rooting herb forming small loose patches. The glossy leaves have somewhat thickened, down-turned margins.

Epilobium tasmanicum

Epilobium porphyrium

Epilobium purpuratum

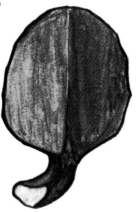

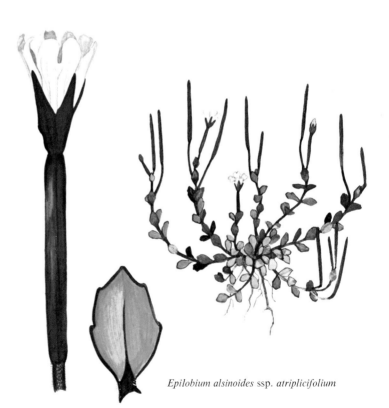

Epilobium alsinoides ssp. *atriplicifolium*

cm

Plate 18

Prominent white flowers (*ca* 1 cm across) with characteristic purple veins are produced on very long delicate stalks which also support the slender capsules.

DISTRIBUTION North and South Islands: widespread, but often local in mountain regions south of the Ruahine Range.

Subalpine to low-alpine: 900–1,600 m (3,000–5,500 ft).

HABITAT On permanently wet rather open sites, especially stream banks and edges of tarns, but it may also occur in open depleted snow tussock grassland.

Epilobium brunnescens (Ckn.) Raven & Engelhorn
"Pale brown".

Rather variable, with two subspecies. Both reach the alpine zone:
Ssp. *brunnescens*
Ssp. *minutiflorum* (Ckn.) Raven & Engelhorn
"Minute flowers".

Both are generally similar to *E. pernitens* but lack its shining leaves and relatively large, purple-veined flowers (here white or pale-pink and <5 mm across). The two subspecies are separated on leaf colour (pale-brown vs. dark-green to reddish-purple) and on the minute flowers and smaller, almost round leaves (<5 mm long) of ssp. *minutiflorum*.

DISTRIBUTION North and South Islands: both subspecies are widespread and extend from lowland to low-alpine: to 1,200 m (4,000 ft).

HABITAT They occupy similar sites—open, permanently wet areas near tarns or streams, and on raw gravel of river beds or recent moraine.

Epilobium porphyrium Simpson   (*See plate 18*)
"Dark purplish-red"—referring probably to the colour of the stems and capsules.

A small plant, usually <10 cm tall, with several to many weakly-erect or spreading stems that are often branched near the base from a small woody rootstock. Leaves are rather crowded and usually pale coloured, especially below, where also the midrib is prominent.

Small flowers develop close to the stem tips and the prominent dark-reddish-purple capsules are produced on very short stalks.

DISTRIBUTION South Island: on the higher mountains of Fiordland, central and western Otago, extending into Canterbury, Marlborough and Nelson.

High-alpine: 1,200–2,000 m (4,000–6,500 ft).

HABITAT Apparently confined to permanently moist sites, especially debris slopes and rock crevices, in snowbanks and fellfield.

COLLECTED Old Man Range, Central Otago, 1,630 m (5,350 ft). January 1970.

Epilobium purpuratum Hook.f.
"Purple"—referring in particular to the stems and fruits.

A low glabrous plant with creeping and rooting, sparingly-branched stems that form open patches up to 15 cm across. The rather thick leaves have a distinctive shape and are usually purplish, at least beneath.

Small white flowers are scattered along the branches and very dark capsules are produced on equally dark stalks of similar length.

DISTRIBUTION South Island: apparently quite sporadic between the Mt Cook and Mt Aspiring regions, extending eastwards to a few of the Central Otago ranges.

High-alpine: 1,200–1,800 m (4,000–6,000 ft).

HABITAT On rocky ledges and loose rubble slopes where snow persists.

COLLECTED Hector's Col, west Matukituki Valley, Mt Aspiring National Park, 1,520 m (5,000 ft). January 1970.

Epilobium macropus Hook.
"Large-stemmed".

A slender low-growing herb. Dark-purple stems, up to 25 cm long, are branched, creeping and rooting near the base but more erect above.

The few usually white flowers are produced along the stem, followed by very long (to 5 cm) glabrous fruits on even longer stalks.

DISTRIBUTION North and South Islands: fairly widespread in mountain regions to the south of central North Island.

Montane to low-alpine: 600–1,500 m (2,000–5,000 ft).

HABITAT In slow, shallow streams and other permanently wet sites.

COLLECTED Island Pass, upper Wairau Valley, south-eastern Nelson, 1,430 m (4,700 ft). January 1971.

Epilobium chlorifolium Hausskn.
"Pale-yellow-green leaved".

A semi-woody often pale plant, up to 40 cm tall (but usually <20 cm in alpine areas), with a small woody rootstock and one to several erect or straggling stems that are usually unbranched above. The leaf shape and arrangement is characteristic.

A few rather large white flowers (8–12 mm across) develop near the stem tips, to be followed by prominent, usually greenish, partly hairy capsules on obvious though much shorter stalks.

DISTRIBUTION North and South Islands: widespread south of the central North Island, but rare in the driest regions of inland South Island.

Lowland to low-alpine: to 1,700 m (5,500 ft).

HABITAT Prefers open, rather damp sites ranging from forest, scrub, tussock grasslands and herbfield to the gravel of river beds and moraine.

COLLECTED Upper West Matukituki Valley, Mt Aspiring National Park, 1,070 m (3,500 ft). January 1970.

Epilobium glabellum Forst.f.
"Almost glabrous".

A rather variable sub-shrub up to 35 cm tall (but usually <10 cm near its upper limit), with several to many erect, sparingly-branched stems radiating from a small woody rootstock. The glabrous leaves are thin, glossy and rather widely spaced.

Several quite large flowers are produced towards the tips of the branches and the slender, glabrous, pale brown to purplish fruits develop on short stalks.

Cont. on page 64

62

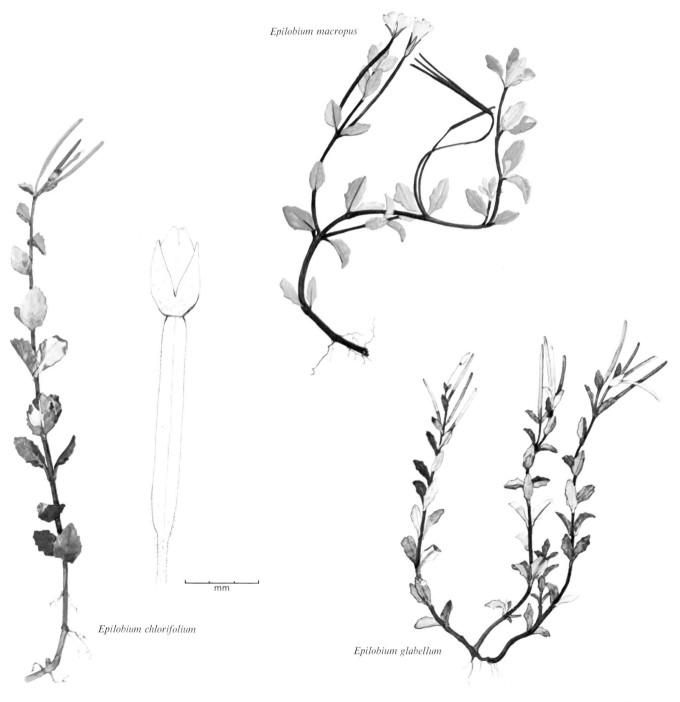

Epilobium macropus

Epilobium chlorifolium

mm

Epilobium glabellum

cm

PLATE 19

DISTRIBUTION North and South Islands: widespread south of the latitude of East Cape but rare or absent from the driest regions of the South Island interior.

Lowland to high-alpine: 700–2,100 m (2,500–7,000 ft).

HABITAT Usually this is the most common and widespread willow herb in alpine areas since it has a very wide habitat range—gravel river beds and moraines, avalanche chutes, tussock grasslands, herbfield, fellfield, rubble slopes and in the wetter regions, even scree.

COLLECTED Upper West Matukituki Valley, Mt Aspiring National Park 1,160 m (3,800 ft). January 1970.

Epilobium crassum Hook.f.
"Thick, stout"—referring to both stems and leaves.

Stout and glabrous with creeping and rooting, occasionally-branched stems that are semi-woody near the base. The stem tips and crowded leaves are quite thick and fleshy, their margins especially so.

White or reddish flowers have petals split about one-third their length. Long stout capsules mature on stout rigid stalks of about similar length.

DISTRIBUTION South Island: on the drier greywacke mountains of Nelson, Marlborough and Canterbury but reaching the St Mary's Range in North Otago and even the Livingstone Mountains in northern Southland.

Low- to high-alpine: 1,000–1,800 m (3,500–6,000 ft).

HABITAT This most distinctive species occupies screes and broken rock in fellfield but is seldom important.

COLLECTED Fog Peak, Torlesse Range, Canterbury, 1,520 m (5,000 ft). January 1968.

Epilobium margaretiae W. B. Brockie
After Mrs M. J. A. Bulfin, who first collected it.

A small glabrous herb with short, usually unbranched creeping and rooting stems. Crowded fleshy leaves are arranged on the top side of the reddish stems. Dead leaves persist at the base.

One or two white flowers develop among the upper leaves and later the short stout capsules partly project beyond the leaves on very short stalks.

DISTRIBUTION South Island: confined to the mountains of Nelson.

High-alpine: 1,300–1,700 m (4,500–5,500 ft).

HABITAT A plant of flattish, stony, frost-activated sites, chiefly in fellfield.

COLLECTED Iron Hill, Cobb Valley, north-west Nelson, 1,650 m (5,400 ft). January 1971.

Epilobium pycnostachyum Hausskn.
"Thick-stemmed".

A semi-woody plant with a small, woody, highly-branched root-stock that produces an extensive root system and usually numerous, semi-erect, unbranched but intertwined stems. Below the ground surface the glabrous leaves are small and distant but above they are thick but not fleshy, larger and crowded.

White flowers are usually numerous near the branch tips, while the capsules are slightly curved on very short stalks, almost hidden by the leaves.

DISTRIBUTION North and South Islands: Ruahine Range, widespread on the greywacke mountains of the South Island as far south as the Hawkdun Range in North Otago.

Low- to high-alpine: 800–1,800 m (2,500–6,000 ft).

HABITAT One of the most characteristic, conspicuous and important plants of screes. It may also occur on unstable rocky sites among fellfield.

COLLECTED Shingle Peak, upper Awatere Valley, Marlborough, 1,310 m (4,300 ft). January 1970.

Epilobium forbesii Allan
After Mr J. K. Forbes, plant collector from north Canterbury.

A semi-fleshy plant about 10 cm tall with a thick rootstock, extensive root system, and rather few partly-trailing to upright stems. Dead leaves persist near the base of the stems which usually branch before ending in a cluster of overlapping leaves with sticky, glandular hairs.

Pinkish flowers develop only among the upper leaves, followed by green sticky capsules on very short stalks.

DISTRIBUTION South Island: rather local in south-east Nelson–Marlborough—on the southern end of the Inland Kaikoura Range, extending to the upper Wairau Valley.

Low- to high-alpine: 1,200–1,700 m (4,000–5,500 ft).

HABITAT Almost confined to scree, where it is usually much less common and on finer material than E. pycnostachyum.

COLLECTED Mt Balaclava, upper Wairau Valley, south-eastern Nelson, 1,680 m (5,500 ft). January 1971.

* Epilobium hectorii Hausskn.
After Sir James Hector, geologist and explorer.

A clumped slender herb up to 25 cm tall and usually multi-branched and spreading from the base, with elongated narrow leaves that have up to ten very shallow teeth on each side. Although not unlike E. alsinoides ssp. atriplicifolium, with which it often occurs, it can be readily distinguished from it by the obviously hairy mature capsules and short stalks (up to 2 cm long).

DISTRIBUTION North and South Islands: Volcanic Plateau, Kaimanawa and northern Ruahine Ranges; east of the main divide in the South Island.

Montane to low-alpine: to 1,600 m (5,200 ft).

HABITAT Widespread on open slopes, mostly in tussock grassland.

Epilobium crassum

Epilobium forbesii

Epilobium pycnostachyum

Epilobium margaretiae

cm

PLATE 20

The Daphne Family: **THYMELAEACEAE**

Genus **KELLERIA**

After Engelhardt Keller, German author of an 1838 book on wine.

A small genus from open uplands of the south-western Pacific, recently separated from the genus *Drapetes* which now becomes restricted to a single South American species. Of the 11 species nine are New Zealand alpines and all but one of these is endemic.

A mixture of low trailing and cushion-forming species, the following key should allow recognition of the nine indigenous members (for use of key see Glossary):

A	More or less prostrate subshrub with creeping branches forming at most a loose mat	B
AA	Stems erect to creeping and forming a dense mat or cushion	F
B	Plants glabrous, leaves pale green to glaucous, young stems light brown	*K. paludosa*
BB	Plants hairy, not as above	C
C	Young branches pale due to a dense cover of white hairs	D
CC	Young branches light to dark brown with few hairs	E
D	Leaves short, 3–4 mm long; only 3–4 flowers per head	*K. villosa*
DD	Leaves longer, 4–6 mm; more flowers (5–15) per head	*K. multiflora*
E	Leaves 4–7 mm long and flattened	*K. laxa*
EE	Leaves usually <4 mm long, canoe-shaped	*K. dieffenbachii*
F	Leaves narrow and grey-green (Stewart Island and Bluff Hill)	*K. lyallii*
FF	Plants not as above	G
G	Stems with dense hairs, 1 mm long, that are shed with the leaves as they age; mostly W. Nelson	*K. tessellata*
GG	Plants not as above	H
H	Leaves grey-green or glaucous; widespread in South Island	*K. croizatii*
HH	Leaves bright olive- or yellowish-green; Central Otago	*K. childii*

DISTRIBUTIONS, HABITATS AND COLLECTIONS

K. paludosa Heads
"swampy or marshy" — referring to its habitat.
DISTRIBUTION   South and Stewart Islands: eastern Fiordland, western and Central Otago and mid Canterbury.
Low- to high-alpine: 950–2,000 m (3,200–6,500 ft).
HABITAT Alpine bogs, flushes and snowbanks.
COLLECTED Hector Mountains, Otago Lakes District, 1,520 m (5,000 ft). February 1965.

K. villosa Berggren
"With long soft hairs".
(= *Drapetes villosus* (Bergg.) Cheesem.)
DISTRIBUTION   South Island: Widespread but more common on the drier mountains. Variety *barbata* Heads, with a dense tuft of hairs at the leaf tip, is confined to the Rock and Pillar Range, Central Otago.
Subalpine to high-alpine: 500–1,800 m (1,600–6,000 ft).
HABITAT Snow tussock grassland, herbfield, cushionfield, fellfield and early snowbanks.
COLLECTED var. *barbata* is from the Rock and Pillar Range, Central Otago, 1,310 m (4,300 ft). November 1967.

K. multiflora (Cheesem.) Heads
"Many-flowered".
(= *Drapetes multiflorus* (Cheesem.) Allan)
South Island: in the wetter areas from Nelson and western Marlborough, southwards along and east of the main divide as far as the Cascade Valley in south Westland.
Subalpine to low-alpine: 900–1,500 m (3,000–5,000 ft).
COLLECTED St Arnaud Range, Nelson Lakes National Park, 1,610 m (5,300 ft). December 1967.

K. laxa (Cheesem.) Heads
"Loose" — referring to the habit of the plant.
(= *Drapetes laxus* (Cheesem.) Allan)
DISTRIBUTION   North and South Islands: Volcanic Plateau, Kaimanawa and Ruahine Ranges; Nelson and north Westland.
Subalpine to high-alpine: 900–1,700 m (3,000–5,500 ft).
COLLECTED Above Lake Sylvester, Cobb Valley, north-west Nelson, 1,430 m (4,700 ft). December 1967.

K. dieffenbachii (Hook.) Endl.
After Dr Dieffenbach, early naturalist with the New Zealand Company.
(= *Drapetes dieffenbachii* Hook.)
DISTRIBUTION   North, South and Stewart Islands: the most widespread species, being present in mountain regions almost throughout.
Subalpine to low-alpine: 600–1,500 m (2,000–5,000 ft).
COLLECTED North slope, Mt Egmont National Park, 1,460 m (4,800 ft). November 1967.

**K. lyallii* (Hook. f.) Bergg.
After Dr Lyall, surgeon-naturalist on the HMS *Terror* in the 1840s.
(= *Drapetes lyallii* Hook.f)
DISTRIBUTION   South and Stewart Islands: Bluff Hill, widespread on Stewart Island and some nearby islands.
Lowland to low-alpine: to 930 m (3,050 ft).
HABITAT From permanently wet to well drained open sites.

**K. tessellata* Heads
Refers to the distinctive pattern of their dried leaves against the whitish hairy stems.
DISTRIBUTION   South Island: West Nelson south to Arthurs Pass.
Low- to high-alpine: 1,380–1,680 m (4,500–5,500 ft)
HABITAT On fine debris and gravel fields in snow tussock grassland and herbfield.

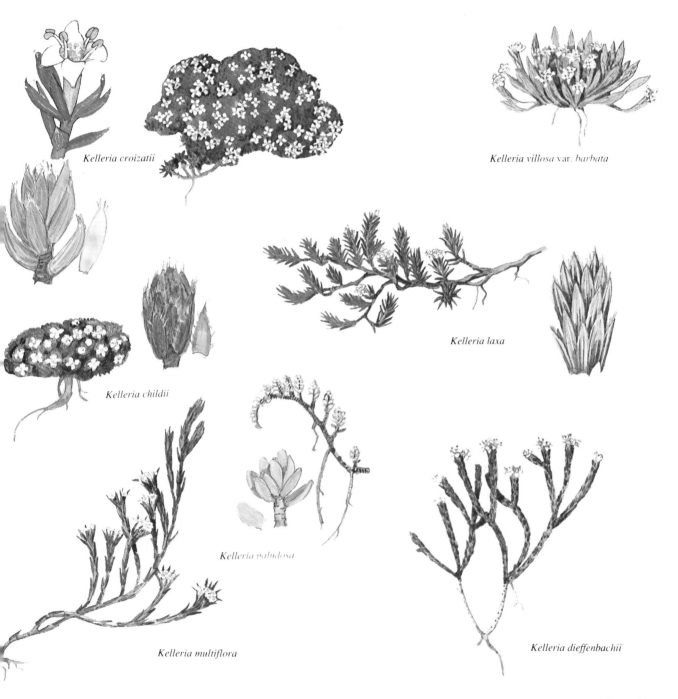

Kelleria croizatii

Kelleria villosa var. *barbata*

Kelleria laxa

Kelleria childii

Kelleria paludosa

Kelleria multiflora

Kelleria dieffenbachii

cm

PLATE 21

K. croizatii Heads

After Leon Croizat, biogeographer.

DISTRIBUTION South Island: From Nelson to southern Fiordland, along and east of the main divide.

Low- to high-alpine: 1,000–2,000 m (3,350–6,500 ft).

HABITAT Snow tussock grassland, herbfield, fellfield and rocky sites.

COLLECTED Mt Brewster, Mt Aspiring National Park, 1,830 m (6,000 ft). March 1968.

K. childii Heads

After Dr John Child, natural and economic historian.

DISTRIBUTION South Island: Confined to central Otago and the Lakes District of Otago.

Low- to high-alpine: 1,200–1,800 m (4,000–5,000 ft).

HABITAT Snowbanks and damp areas of cushionfield.

COLLECTED Old Man Range, Central Otago, 1,580 m (5,200 ft). December 1963.

Genus PIMELEA

"Fat"—referring to the oily seeds.

A group of about 80 shrub or semi-woody species, chiefly Australasian. Of the 17 native pimeleas about nine reach the alpine zone.

They all have grey or dark stems with prominent leaf scars, palegreenish-grey leaves and terminal, white to pinkish, 4-lobed, silkyhairy, tubular flowers. Most plants are functionally unisexual so that not all bear fruit.

The alpine species can be distinguished on vegetative and floral features, though with considerable variation in a few and some hybridism, positive identification may be difficult (for use of key see Glossary):

A	Leaf blade hairy, at least when young	B
AA	Leaf blade quite glabrous	E
B	Stems almost black; leaves very narrow, needlelike	*P. suteri*
BB	Stems grey; leaves wider, not needlelike	C
C	Leaves very close set and distinctly hairy; plant a low compact shrub	*P. sericeovillosa*
CC	Leaves not very close set, only slightly hairy; plant not very compact	D
D	Branches usually 20–50 cm long	*P. pseudolyallii*
DD	Branches <20 cm long in alpine areas	*P. oreophila*
E	Leaves inflated, <1 cm long; young stems glabrous; South Island only	*P. traversii*
EE	Leaves usually 1 cm or more in length; young stems hairy; North Island only	*P. buxifolia*

DISTRIBUTIONS AND HABITATS

P. oreophila Burrows

"Mountain-loving".

North and South Islands: on the volcanic plateau and the mountains between the Kaweka and Ruahine Ranges in the North Island; throughout most mountain regions of the South Island.

Montane to high-alpine: 500–2,000 m (1,500–6,500 ft).

Common and generally the most important pimelea throughout the tussock grasslands and herbfields, extending into fellfield on sheltered sites and occasionally into early snowbanks.

COLLECTED Pisa Range, Central Otago, 1,460 m (4,800 ft). February 1970.

P. pseudolyallii Allan *(See plate 23)*

"Resembling (*Pimelea*) *Lyalli*".

South Island: on the eastern mountains of Marlborough, Canterbury and Otago, extending inland in mid-Canterbury and North Otago.

Lowland to low-alpine: to 1,500 m (5,000 ft).

Grows in closed vegetation near the tree line, including scrub and tussock grasslands, or vegetation induced from them.

COLLECTED Hawkdun Range, North Otago, 1,100 m (3,600 ft). December 1969.

P. sericeovillosa Hook.f.

"With long silky hairs".

South Island: the drier greywacke mountains east of the main divide from Marlborough to mid-Canterbury.

Subalpine to high-alpine: 500–1,700 m (1,500–5,500 ft).

On well-drained sites (moraine, riverflats and terraces) in tussock grasslands and fellfield.

COLLECTED Above Island Pass, upper Wairau Valley, south-eastern Nelson, 1,670 m (5,500 ft). January 1971.

P. suteri Kirk

After the Right Rev. Dr Suter, early collector of New Zealand plants.

South Island: eastern Nelson and western Marlborough.

Low-alpine: 900–1,400 m (3,000–4,500 ft).

Essentially confined to the ultra-basic rock of the mineral belt.

COLLECTED Red Hill Range, Wairau Valley, Marlborough, 1,070 m (3,500 ft). January 1971.

P. traversii Hook.f.

After Mr W. T. L. Travers, early collector of northern South Island plants.

South Island: widespread, but common only on the drier greywacke mountains east of the main divide.

Lowland to high-alpine: 100–1,800 m (500–6,000 ft).

Usually on rock outcrops or partly stable rock debris. Also on shingle river terraces and in well-drained areas of tussock grassland, especially on depleted stony sites.

COLLECTED Mt Dalgety, Dalgety Range, South Canterbury, 1,220 m (4,000 ft). January 1969.

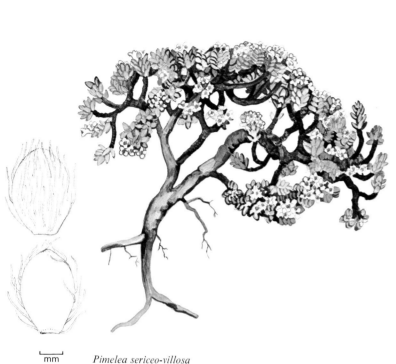

Pimelea sericeo-villosa

mm

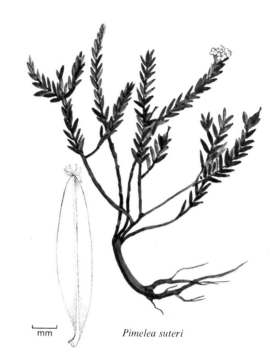

mm

Pimelea suteri

Pimelea oreophila

Pimelea traversii

PLATE 22

P. buxifolia Hook.f.
"Box-leaved".

North Island: on most of the North Island mountains except Egmont and the Tararuas.

Subalpine to low-alpine: 500–1,400 m (1,500–4,500 ft).

Usually a minor species in snow tussock grassland, herbfield and fellfield.

COLLECTED Whakapapanui Valley, Mt Ruapehu, Tongariro National Park, 1,070 m (3,500 ft). January 1958.

Of the remaining alpine pimeleas, two, *P. crosby-smithiana* and *P. poppelwellii* have glabrous leaves. They are quite local in the southern South Island: Hump Ridge in western Southland and the Garvie Mountains in northern Southland, respectively. Another, *P. concinna*, forms ball-like clumps up to 80 cm across with very dark brown bark and dense silvery-white hairs on the leaves and young branches. It occurs in tussock grasslands and fellfield in southern Marlborough—North Canterbury.

The Tutu Family: **CORIARIACEAE**

Genus **CORIARIA**
"Leather"–some species abroad are used for tanning leather.

A genus of poisonous plants, widely distributed in warm to temperate regions. Most of the seven native tutus are variable, partly due to hybridism, and at least two reach the alpine zone.

Coriaria plumosa W. R. B. Oliver   MOUNTAIN TUTU
"Feathery"—referring to the leaves.

A summer-green sub-shrub up to 40 cm high, with erect, squarish, often purplish stems arising in tufts from a stout, branched rhizome. The erect stems have many slender branches, closely set with leaves. The lower leaves on the branches are usually broader.

From 15 to 30 inconspicuous flowers develop on each of several small partly-leafy stems near the middle of the main stem. The purplish fruits enlarge when ripe and become succulent.

DISTRIBUTION North and South Islands: widespread in mountain regions as far north as Mt Egmont and Mt Hikurangi.

Lowland to low-alpine: 300–1,500 m (1,000–5,000 ft).

HABITAT On moist open sites, often locally important on avalanche chutes near the tree line and along stream banks in open forest, scrub or tussock grassland. It also occurs in damp rocky sites in snow tussock grassland and herbfield, and on moraine, as in the Hooker Valley under Mt Cook. Fixation of atmospheric nitrogen in the root nodules probably assists this species to grow on the infertile moraine.

COLLECTED Flowering plant from Eyre Mountains, northern Southland, 1,070 m (3,500 ft). November 1970. Fruits are from a Hooker Valley plant, Mt Cook National Park, 1,100 m (3,600 ft). March 1968.

*Coriaria pteridoides W. R. B. Oliver
"Fernlike"—referring to the leaves.

A much larger erect shrub, up to 1 m tall, with several tufted stems arising from a branched rhizome. Branchlets are very slender, squarish and partly hairy, and the leaves are similar in shape to those of *C. plumosa* but about twice as large. Flowers and fruits are also generally similar to *C. plumosa*.

DISTRIBUTION North Island: the volcanic plateau and Mt Egmont.

Montane to low-alpine: 800–1,400 m (2,500–4,500 ft).

HABITAT On permanently moist but well-lit sites, chiefly along stream banks and on wet rocky bluffs in open forest, subalpine scrub and mixed red tussock-scrub.

The Euphorbia Family: **EUPHORBIACEAE**

Genus **OREOPORANTHERA**
"Mountain plant having anthers with pores".

A small Australasian genus. One of the two native species is an alpine.

---

*Oreoporanthera alpina (Cheesem.) Hutch.
"Alpine".

A straggling, wiry, glabrous, sub-shrub with many branches, up to 10 cm tall. Thick, close-set, opposite leaves are broad-triangular in shape, up to 5 mm long and rolled under almost to the midrib.

Inconspicuous flowers develop on short stalks in the axils of the upper leaves. They have 5 white to greenish sepals but no petals. Fruits ripen into 3 dry sections *ca* 2 mm across.

DISTRIBUTION South Island: north-west Nelson.

Mostly subalpine to low-alpine: to 1,800 m (6,000 ft).

HABITAT Apparently confined to rock outcrops in well-lit areas, but I have not seen it in the field.

Pimelea pseudolyallii

Pimelea buxifolia

Coriaria plumosa

cm

PLATE 23

The Rose Family: ROSACEAE

Genus ACAENA
"Thorn"—referring to the spines on both flowers and fruits of most species.

A large, predominantly southern hemisphere genus. Most of the 16 native bidibidis are variable and varieties have been described for several. These distinctive-looking herbs or sub-shrubs usually have creeping stems with erect leafy branches. Leaves have a characteristic shape and prominent stipules at their base. Minute flowers are tightly clustered into balls at the end of erect stems. These balls break up when ripe, especially when the spiny hooked fruits become firmly attached to clothing or fleeces.

At least eight bidibidis reach the alpine zone.

Acaena glabra Buchan.
"Without hairs".

Plants form loose patches, up to 30 cm or more across. Leafy, upright, pale-brownish- to purplish-green branches arise from stout, creeping and rooting, brown or grey, woody stems. Leaves are almost glaucous, *ca* 3 cm long, with prominent cut stipules and 7–11 leaflets.

Purplish-green flower heads, 1–2 cm across, develop on stalks up to 10 cm long. Each flower is flattened and carries 4 very short spines without hooks, and 2 white stamens.

DISTRIBUTION South Island: widespread on the greywacke mountains along and east of the main divide.

Subalpine to low-alpine: 600–1,400 m (2,000–4,500 ft).

HABITAT On open, rocky, rather unstable sites such as scree edges, eroding snow tussock grassland and river beds.

COLLECTED Porters Pass, Torlesse Range, Canterbury, 1,110 m (3,600 ft). February 1969.

Acaena saccaticupula Bitter
"With a pouched cupule or calyx".

A dull, slaty- or reddish-green, creeping and rooting, glabrous sub-shrub. The narrow leaves have 9–15 leaflets and usually un-divided stipules.

Stout, reddish-purple flower stalks carry a few small bracts and a purplish head. Each flower has 4 hooked purple spines, 2–4 purple stamens and a purple feathery stigma.

DISTRIBUTION South Island: east of the main divide from southern Marlborough to central and western Otago.

Subalpine to high-alpine: 900–1,900 m (3,000–6,000 ft).

HABITAT On open but rather sheltered areas, especially in fellfield, herbfield and early snowbanks, but also in open snow tussock grassland and subalpine scrub.

COLLECTED Coronet Peak, Otago Lakes district, 1,370 m (4,500 ft). December 1969.

Acaena fissistipula Bitter
"With divided stipules".

A dull, greyish- or slaty-green to reddish-brown, creeping and rooting herb. Leaves have 7–11 leaflets with the lower ones small and widely spaced. At least the veins on the undersurface and usually the tips of the leaflets are hairy. The prominent stipules are deeply cut into 3–5 narrow teeth.

Slender, brownish, somewhat hairy flower stalks have a purplish-green head. The flowers have long hairs at the base, 4 brownish-red hooked spines, with stamens and stigma as in *A. saccaticupula*.

DISTRIBUTION South Island: widespread.

Montane to low-alpine: 300–1,500 m (1,000–5,000 ft).

HABITAT On moist open sites, especially streamsides in forest, scrub and tussock grassland or wet depressions in tussock grassland and herbfield.

COLLECTED Island Pass, upper Wairau Valley, south-eastern Nelson, 1,280 m (4,200 ft). December 1967.

Acaena caesiiglauca (Bitter) Bergmans
"Bluish-grey, glaucous"—referring to the leaves.

A spreading and rooting, densely-hairy plant with ascending branches about 5 cm long. Its leaves are less hairy above, up to 5 cm long with 7–9 leaflets, the lower ones much smaller. Stipules are usually simple.

The hairy brownish-green flower stalk usually has a few bracts and the flowers are hairy with 4 brown, barbed, spines, 2 white stamens and a white feathery style.

Variety *pilosa* (Kirk) Allan, is distinguished by its leaves—divided stipules and 11–13 leaflets that are equally hairy above.

DISTRIBUTION South Island: both the species and its variety are equally widespread, but chiefly east of the main divide.

Montane to low-alpine: 600–1,500 m (2,000–5,000 ft).

HABITAT A plant of tussock grasslands, both the montane short tussock and higher altitude snow tussock grasslands.

COLLECTED Rock & Pillar Range, Central Otago, 910 m (3,000 ft). December 1969.

Acaena pusilla (Bitter) Allan
"Very small, insignificant".

A brownish or pale green, creeping and rooting plant with ascending branches 3–5 cm long. Leaves are 2.5–3.5 cm long with 9–11 leaflets, the upper ones larger. Hairs occur at least on the veins of the lower surface and on the pointed tips of the leaflets.

The hairy greenish-brown flowering stalks usually have few very small bracts and each flower in the head has 4 hooked, yellowish-green, often unequal spines, 2 white stamens and a white feathery style.

DISTRIBUTION South Island: on the mountains of Canterbury.

Lowland to low-alpine: to 1,500 m (5,000 ft).

HABITAT Common in areas of open tussock grassland and herbfield. Also on moraine of the Hooker Glacier under Mt Cook.

Acaena saccaticupula

Acaena glabra

Acaena fissistipula

Acaena caesiiglauca

mm

cm

PLATE 24

* *Acaena profundeincisa* (Bitter) B.Macmillan
"Deeply incised" — referring to the leaflets.

Somewhat similar to *A. caesiiglauca* but leaves are subglaucous to ash grey and smooth above and glaucous below with the margins deeply toothed. The lower leaflets and teeth are often red.

The hairy flower stalks are shorter (4–12 cm) while the style and anthers are red.

DISTRIBUTION North and South Island: Widespread on the higher mountain ranges south of the Raukumara Range.

Subalpine to high-alpine: 900–1,900 m (2,950–6,200 ft).

HABITAT A plant of shady moist sites in snow tussock grassland, shrubland and rocky herbfields, particularly in later snow-lie areas.

* *Acaena rorida* B. Macmillan
"Bedewed" – with water droplets on the leaflet teeth; a common feature early in the day.

A low-growing dull apple- or olive-green or pale purple creeping plant with dark brown buried stems and small leaves 2–3 cm long with 4–5 pairs of rounded glabrous leaflets that are paler and glaucous beneath with distinct veins and have 7–12 teeth. The very short (0.6-1.5 cm) densely hairy flower stalks carry 10–12 florets that mature among the foliage and have up to four pale red spines without hooks.

It is confined to the Ruahine Range of the North Island in low-alpine (*ca* 1,130 m; 3,700 ft) moist hollows in tussock grassland, sometimes on limestone.

* *Acaena tesca* B. Macmillan
"Wild region" — remote and often desolate, referring to its habitat.

A low-growing often mat-forming pale brown plant, leaflets 3–5 pairs, glaucous with sparse flattened hairs and dull red teeth. Flowering stems are short with about 10 florets, anthers are white and fruits have 4 fine red spines.

It is confined to the Central Otago region of the South Island, in low- to high-alpine zones, often depleted tussock grassland and herbfield at 1,150 –1,750 m (3,800–5,750 ft).

Genus **GEUM**

Perhaps from Greek *geuo*—"to give pleasant flavour to". Some species are aromatic.

A widespread genus of about 60 species. Four of the five mainland geums are alpine.

Geum uniflorum Buchan.
"Single-flowered".

A branched, creeping and rooting plant with a stout woody base, each branch ending in a leafy rosette, as shown. There are prominent, brown, papery stipules at the base of the leaves.

Hairy flower stalks usually occur singly and carry one large white flower. The green or reddish-green calyx surrounds the cluster of dry hairy fruits in which the persistent styles usually redden.

DISTRIBUTION South Island: widespread in the higher rainfall areas.

Low-alpine: 900–1,700 m (3,000–5,500 ft).

HABITAT Characteristic of steep shady banks, moist hollows and streamsides in snow tussock-herbfield.

COLLECTED Temple Basin, Arthurs Pass National Park, 1,310 m (4,300 ft). December 1967.

Geum parviflorum Smith
"Small-flowered".

Forms bright-green rosettes or tufts, often with several arising from the woody base.

Several branched hairy flower stalks may reach 30 cm. The long hooked styles persist and often redden as the partly-hairy fruits mature.

DISTRIBUTION North and South Islands: with a few exceptions (volcanic plateau, Mt Egmont, Central Otago) it occurs throughout most of the mountain regions.

Subalpine to low-alpine: 800–1,700 m (2,500–5,500 ft).

HABITAT In snow tussock grassland and herbfield, usually on moist sites, including shady rock crevices and ledges. It extends into the subalpine zone along open streambanks.

COLLECTED Hooker Valley, Mt Cook National Park, 910 m (3,000 ft). January 1969.

Geum leiospermum Petrie
"Smooth-seeded".

Forms small brownish-green or green rosettes, often with several arising from the short woody base.

Several hairy flower stalks develop. They are often unbranched, up to 15 cm tall, and with a cluster of a few small flowers. Small brown fruits are quite glabrous with short hooked styles.

DISTRIBUTION North, South and Stewart Islands: local in the North Island—Mt Egmont, Ruahine Range; but more widespread in mountain regions of the South Island.

Subalpine to high-alpine: 800–2,000 m (2,500–6,500 ft).

HABITAT In the North Island it occurs in bogs but southwards it has a much wider range—tussock grasslands, herbfield, fellfield and early snowbanks.

COLLECTED Coronet Peak, Otago Lakes district, 1,460 m (4,800 ft). December 1968.

Geum pusillum Petrie
"Very small".

Its habit, colour and leaves are like a miniature *G. leiospermum*, but the flowers are minute and occur singly on a short stalk. Fruits are small and glabrous as in *G. leiospermum*.

DISTRIBUTION South Island: confined to Central Otago.

High-alpine: 1,500–1,700 m (5,000–5,500 ft).

HABITAT Restricted to snowbanks.

COLLECTED Old Man Range, Central Otago, 1,610 m (5,300 ft). December 1969.

Geum pusillum

Geum uniflorum

Geum leiospermum

Geum parviflorum

cm

Plate 25

The Pea Family: FABACEAE

Genus SWAINSONA

After Mr W. G. Swainson, English botanist.

Contains about 50 species of rhizomatous herbs or sub-shrubs. Except for the single native species, all are Australian.

Swainsona novae-zelandiae Hook.f.
"Of New Zealand".

A rather exotic-looking summer-green herb with dull green leafy tufts arising from buried, thin, branched stems that extend to the surface from a deeply buried stout rootstock. The leaves have stipules at the base and 6–10 pairs of leaflets.

Flower stalks develop in the axils of older leaves and carry 3–5 purplish flowers. The pods enlarge and darken when mature.

Variety *glabra* Simpson, "Glabrous" differs in being brighter green, since it lacks the scattered, fine, white hairs.

DISTRIBUTION South Island: on the greywacke mountains east of the main divide from Marlborough to North Otago. Var. *glabra* is in the south.

Subalpine to low-alpine: 800–1,500 m (2,500–5,000 ft).

HABITAT Rather rare on screes and mobile rocky slopes in eroding snow tussock grassland.

COLLECTED Both flowering and fruiting plants are var. *glabra* from the Hawkdun Range, North Otago, 1,070 m (3,500 ft). December 1969.

Genus CORALLOSPARTIUM

"Coral Broom"—referring to the stems.

Consists of a single species, confined to the South Island.

Corallospartium crassicaule (Hook.f.) J. B. Armst.   CORAL BROOM
"Thick-stemmed".

A very stiff, leafless, erect shrub up to 2m tall. Branches are stout and almost cylindrical with notches alternating at 1–2 cm intervals.

Cream flowers, sometimes with purple veins, develop in dense clusters of up to 20 at the notches. The pods are < 1 cm long and pale due to a covering of whitish hairs.

Variety *racemosum* Kirk, has finer, more spreading and less rigid branches and fewer flowers in the clusters.

DISTRIBUTION South Island: on the drier mountains east of the main divide between mid-Canterbury and Central Otago. Var. *racemosum* is confined to Otago.

Montane to low-alpine: 600–1,300 m (2,000–4,000 ft).

HABITAT Occurs sporadically on well-drained open sites, including rock outcrops, in the drier parts of the tussock grassland region.

COLLECTED Hawkdun Range, North Otago, 850 m (2,800 ft). December 1969.

Genus CARMICHAELIA

After Captain D. Carmichael, a Scottish botanist.

Contains 38 species, almost all from New Zealand. At least one of these extends into the alpine zone.

Carmichaelia monroi Hook.f.
After Sir D. Monro, early New Zealand botanist.

A dwarfed, much-branched, taprooted shrub which forms dense flat patches up to 30 cm across. Their stout rigid branches are short, erect and flattened.

Clusters of 2–5 flowers develop on slender stems to be followed by almost black curved pods *ca* 1.5 cm long.

DISTRIBUTION South Island: east of the main divide from Marlborough to North Otago.

Montane to low-alpine: 800–1,500 m (2,500–5,000 ft).

HABITAT Typically on open, stony or rocky, well-drained sites in depleted tussock grassland. Its dwarfness is often accentuated by close-grazing.

COLLECTED Mt Richmond, Two Thumb Range, South Canterbury, 1,430 m (4,700 ft). January 1970.

The Stackhousia Family: STACKHOUSIACEAE

Genus STACKHOUSIA

After John Stackhouse, early English botanist.

A small genus, chiefly Australian. The only New Zealand species occasionally reaches the alpine zone.

Stackhousia minima Hook.f.
"Very small".

An insignificant, glabrous, almost fleshy herb with pale branched rhizomes, producing numerous, small, erect branches that form loose mats up to 1 m or more across.

The small fragrant flowers develop into equally small, yellow to brown, dry fruits.

DISTRIBUTION North and South Islands: from the central North Island southwards. Collections to date suggest it is somewhat local in occurrence.

Lowland to low-alpine: to 1,400 m (4,500 ft).

HABITAT On rather open sites where competition is slight, but these may range from permanently wet flushed areas, to well-drained bare soil or fine gravel of depleted tussock grasslands.

COLLECTED Old Man Range, Central Otago, 1,400 m (4,600 ft). January 1970.

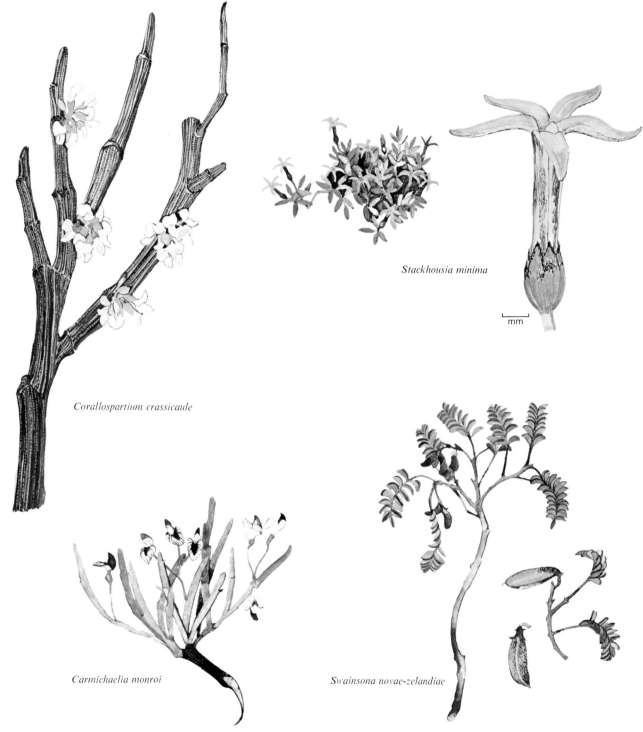

Corallospartium crassicaule

Stackhousia minima

mm

Carmichaelia monroi

Swainsona novae-zelandiae

cm

PLATE 26

The Carrot Family: APIACEAE

Genus ACTINOTUS

"Radiating" — referring to the floral bracts.

A small Australasian genus of some 14 species with only one in New Zealand.

Actinotus novaezelandiae (Petrie) Petrie

"Of New Zealand".

A dwarfed, creeping and rooting, bright-green herb, forming mats up to 30 cm across or tangled among other cushion plants. The almost fleshy leaves may be glabrous but often they have a terminal tuft of hairs and sometimes there are long white hairs scattered along their margins.

The hairy flower stalks end in an unbranched head of 5 bracts surrounding 4–5 minute flowers without petals. The pair of prominent tapered styles persist in the fruit.

DISTRIBUTION South and Stewart Islands: in the wetter areas although rather sporadic in the South Island.

Coastal to low-alpine: to 1,100 m (3,500 ft).

HABITAT In cushion bogs and open flushed areas in forest, scrub or low-alpine vegetation. When growing as a mat it is usually conspicuous, but not so when intertwined among other bog plants.

COLLECTED Key Summit, Fiordland National Park, 910 m (3,000 ft). January 1968.

Genus SCHIZEILEMA

"Split cover"—referring apparently to the deeply divided floral bracts of a non-alpine species, *S. trifoliolatum*.

A small genus of about 15 species, concentrated in New Zealand. Of the ten mainland schizeilemas, five reach the alpine zone.

Schizeilema exiguum (Hook.f.) Domin

"Small".

A minute tufted herb with a deep stout rootstock. Leaves may be slightly 3–5 lobed.

The 1–3 inconspicuous flower heads barely emerge beyond the leaves. There are up to 8 minute flowers or fruits in each head.

DISTRIBUTION South Island: confined to the higher mountains of Central and western Otago.

High-alpine: 1,500–2,100 m (5,000–7,000 ft).

HABITAT Sometimes common but quite insignificant among cushion plants on exposed sites. Larger plants than the one shown may occur in fellfield and early snowbanks.

COLLECTED Pisa Range, Central Otago, 1,900 m (6,250 ft). March 1968.

Schizeilema hydrocotyloides (Hook.f.) Domin

"Resembling *Hydrocotyle*".

A bright- or yellowish-green herb with rosettes at the nodes of short stout runners which often intertwine to form patches up to 10 cm or more across. Leaves have simple stipules and thick blades with 3–5 lobes and thickened margins.

Up to 4 flower stalks per rosette arise together, each with a single head of up to 10 minute flowers. The pedicels elongate to be slightly longer than the squarish, pale, greenish-brown fruits.

DISTRIBUTION North and South Islands: Tararua Range; in the South Island mostly east of the main divide on the greywacke mountains.

Subalpine to low-alpine: 800–1,800 m (2,500–6,000 ft).

HABITAT Usually on open, rather unstable, stony sites such as eroding snow tussock grassland or scree edges; occasionally in more stable habitats—along stream banks or forest and scrub margins.

COLLECTED Porters Pass, Torlesse Range, Canterbury, 1,160 m (3,800 ft). January 1970.

Schizeilema haastii (Hook.f.) Domin

After Sir Julius von Haast, famous geologist and explorer.

A shining, glabrous, tufted herb, 5–15 cm tall, that creeps by runners or rhizomes and forms loose patches up to 10 cm or more across. The single leaf shows the delicate stipules (sometimes more deeply cut than this), long petioles and almost fleshy blade.

Flower stems are usually branched and have a few leafy bracts. There are several crowded flowers (up to 50) surrounded by bracts. A single flower is shown in detail. Fruits are squarish and much shorter than their stalks.

Var. *haastii* is a relatively large plant, with leaves at least 2 cm across.

Var. *cyanopetalum* (Domin) Cheesem., "Blue-petalled", is somewhat smaller, with the leaves no more than 2 cm across, but the flower heads are not reduced. The petals, when dry, are bluish in both varieties.

DISTRIBUTION North and South Islands: widespread from the Ruahine Range southwards. Var. *cyanopetalum* is absent from the southern South Island.

Subalpine to low-alpine: 800–1,800 m (2,500–6,000 ft).

HABITAT Usually on moist, rocky or stony sites, especially shady ledges and crevices. It may also occur in damp hollows of fine scree or as a minor plant in snow tussock-herbfield.

COLLECTED Homer Tunnel, Fiordland National Park, 1,070 m (3,500 ft). January 1968.

Schizeilema roughii (Hook.f.) Domin

After Captain Rough, early collector, especially in the Nelson mountains.

Its habit is similar to *S. haastii*, the distinctive features being the leaves that have thin, deeply-cut stipules and dark-green blades deeply divided into 3–5 lobes.

DISTRIBUTION South Island: confined to Nelson and western Marlborough.

Cont. on page 80

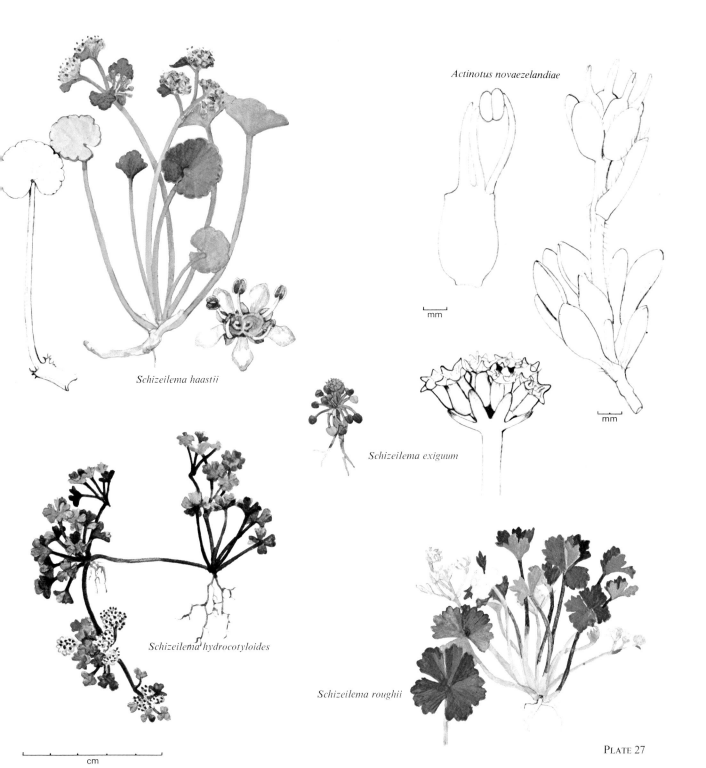

Actinotus novaezelandiae

mm

Schizeilema haastii

Schizeilema exiguum

mm

Schizeilema hydrocotyloides

Schizeilema roughii

cm

PLATE 27

Subalpine to low-alpine: 800–1,700 m (2,500–5,500 ft).
HABITAT Usually in clefts and on ledges of rock outcrops among snow tussock-herbfield.
COLLECTED Mt Robert, Travers Range, Nelson Lakes National Park, 1,400 m (4,600 ft). December 1967.

Schizeilema pallidum (Kirk) Domin
"Pale".

A tufted plant with creeping stolons, similar in habit to *S. roughii* but distinguished by its thin pale-green leaves that are deeply 3-lobed.

Flower stems are usually unbranched with 4–12 flowers surrounded by narrow bracts, while the fruits are *ca* 2 mm long, much shorter than their pedicels.
DISTRIBUTION South Island: Nelson and North Canterbury.
Montane to low-alpine: 400–1,200 m (1,500–4,000 ft).
HABITAT In damp, open areas under forest or scrub and moist hollows in snow tussock grassland and herbfield.

Genus OREOMYRRHIS
"Mountain Myrrh".

A predominantly southern-hemisphere genus of about 20 species. The three native species intergrade to some extent. One of the four varieties of the most variable species reach the alpine zone.

Oreomyrrhis colensoi Hook.f.
After the Rev. W. Colenso, early New Zealand botanist.

Var. *colensoi* A small, dull or dark green, sometimes glaucous herb with glabrous to hairy rosettes and a small fleshy taproot. Sometimes there are several tufts from a branched rootstock.

A few slender hairy flower stalks radiate among the leaves and end in simple heads. There are 5–8 small sessile flowers in each head but later their pedicels elongate to be longer than the glabrous dark-brown fruit.
DISTRIBUTION North, South and Stewart Islands: widespread, apart from the northern half of the North Island.
Coastal to high-alpine: to 1,800 m (6,000 ft).
HABITAT Usually present but rarely abundant or conspicuous on open well-lit sites in most types of alpine vegetation except unstable or highly exposed areas.
COLLECTED Old Man Range, Central Otago, 1,070 m (3,500 ft). January 1970.

Genus ANISOTOME
"Unequally cut"—referring to the unequal carpels.

A recent revision of this genus by Dr John Dawson recognises 15 species from New Zealand and the Subantarctic Islands. 11 of the 12 mainland anisotomes are alpines.

Anisotome aromatica Hook.f.
"Aromatic"—referring particularly to the roots.

Small rosette herbs with leaves 3–12 cm long, a deep stout rootstock and prominent erect flower stem with a compound head.

In male plants the flower stems are branched and up to 10 cm high. The uppermost heads are 3–4 cm across with many small white flowers. Female plants usually have smaller and shorter heads with fewer flowers and only these bear the brown fruits.

Three varieties reach the alpine zone:

Var. *aromatica* has its 4–9 pairs of leaflets crowded or partly overlapping, with shallow teeth that have short hair tips.

Var. *major* Allan, is altogether larger with leaves and leaflets about twice the size of those shown for var. *aromatica*.

Var. *obtusa* Allan, differs from var. *aromatica* in that the teeth on the leaflets are blunt.
DISTRIBUTION North, South and Stewart Islands: the var. *aromatica* is widespread in mountain regions throughout.
Montane to low-alpine: 600–1,700 m (2,000–5,500 ft).
Var. *major* is absent from Stewart Island and the west and south of the South Island, while var. *obtusa* extends southwards only to the northern South Island.
HABITAT It may be common but rarely conspicuous in a wide range of moist, open, low-alpine habitats. Also on rock outcrops and in the North Island in alpine bogs and on scoria of the volcanic mountains.
COLLECTED Var. *aromatica* from the north slope, Mt Egmont National Park, 1,460 m (4,800 ft). November 1967. Var. *obtusa* is from above Lake Sylvester, Cobb Valley, north-west Nelson, 1,460 m (4,800 ft). December 1967.

Anisotome flexuosa Dawson
"Flexuous, wavy"—referring particularly to the flowering stems.

Its habit is similar to *A. aromatica*, but petioles are virtually absent, hair tips are prominent on the divided leaflets and male flower stems remain short. Female plants have erect flowering stems that may reach 20 cm. Plant size, shape of leaflets and the length of the hair tips are all variable.
DISTRIBUTION South and Stewart Islands: widespread in the mountain regions except for Marlborough and northern Nelson.
Montane to high-alpine: 500–1,800 m (1,500–6,000 ft).
HABITAT In rather severe, open or exposed habitats, ranging from depleted and eroding tussock grassland to herbfield, fellfield, rock crevices and the stony debris of moraines and scree edges. The deep stout taproot is an obvious adaption to these severe sites.
COLLECTED Old Man Range, Central Otago, 1,460 m (4,800 ft). November 1967.

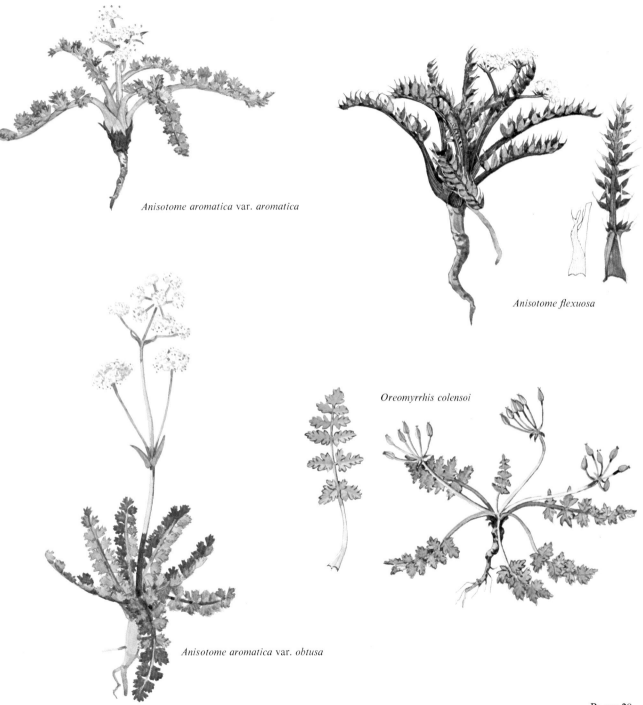

Anisotome aromatica var. *aromatica*

Anisotome flexuosa

Oreomyrrhis colensoi

Anisotome aromatica var. *obtusa*

cm

Plate 28

Anisotome lanuginosa (Kirk) Dawson
"Woolly, downy".

A very small rosette herb with a deep taproot that sometimes branches above to produce a cluster of rosettes. The characteristic colour is produced by a dense covering of long silvery hairs on the ends of the infolded leaflets. These, and the absence of a distinct petiole can be seen on the enlarged single leaf.

Flower stalks are erect with male ones much shorter than female which may reach 5 cm.

DISTRIBUTION South Island: confined to the higher ranges of Central Otago except for an isolated occurrence on the Two Thumb Range in South Canterbury.

High-alpine: 1,400–1,800 m (4,500–6,000 ft).

HABITAT In cushion vegetation of exposed sites but sometimes extending into early snowbanks and exposed herbfield.

COLLECTED Old Man Range, Central Otago, 1,650 m (5,400 ft). February 1968.

Anisotome imbricata (Hook.f.) Ckn.
"Overlapping"—referring to the leaves.

Small rosette herbs with milky sap; stout, highly-branched, prostrate stems and very small leaves in which the infolded leaflets have prominent silvery or light brown hair tips.

Male and female flower stems are equally short, hardly emerging above the leaves. There are two varieties:

Var. *imbricata* forms low, dense, dull-green cushions up to 30 cm or more across, due to the highly intertwined stems which end in small compact rosettes. Leaves have silvery or occasionally brownish hairs.

Var. *prostrata* Dawson, "prostrate" , has longer, more creeping stems so that plants form loose, usually open, brighter green mats or even intertwine among other plants. Both leaves and flower stems are somewhat larger than in var. *imbricata* and the leaf hairs are brownish.

DISTRIBUTION South Island: var. *imbricata* is in Central and western Otago.

High-alpine: 1,200–2,000 m (4,000–6,500 ft).

Var. *prostrata* is somewhat erratic but extends from Marlborough–Nelson to Otago. Here both varieties may be present in the same locality.

Low- to high-alpine: 1,200–1,800 m (4,000–6,000 ft).

HABITAT Var. *imbricata* is important in the cushion vegetation of Central Otago. Further west it occurs locally in fellfield and on exposed ridges near the upper limit of snow tussock-herbfield.

Var. *prostrata* occupies rather similar habitats north of Otago but in Central Otago it is in alpine bogs or wet depressions in snowbanks.

COLLECTED Both varieties from Rock & Pillar Range, Central Otago, 1,370 m (4,500 ft). December 1969.

Anisotome pilifera (Hook.f.) Ckn. & Laing
"Hairy,"—referring to the tips of the leaf segments.

A stout, usually glaucous herb with a large taproot and persistent dead flower stems and leaf bases. Although the leathery leaves are distinctive they are quite variable, with the leaflets ranging from broad lobed ones in some localities, as shown, to quite highly divided ones in other areas. Prominence of the hair tip on the leaf segments also varies.

The robust flower stems may have 1–2 leafy bracts below the large compound head.

DISTRIBUTION South Island: widespread throughout most of the higher mountain regions, but absent from all but the more westerly ranges of Central Otago.

Low- to high-alpine: 1,100–2,100 m (3,500–7,000 ft).

HABITAT Almost restricted to rocky sites, especially ledges and crevices on rock faces and bluffs in fellfield and near the upper limit of snow tussock-herbfield. Introduced animals have now virtually eliminated it from accessible sites in herbfield and fellfield.

COLLECTED Pisa Range, Central Otago, 1,770 m (5,800 ft). December 1968.

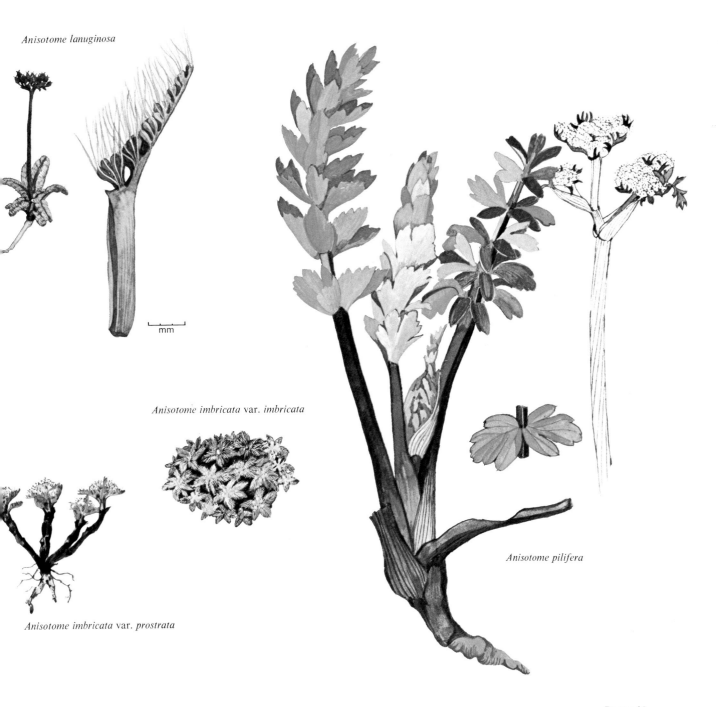

Anisotome lanuginosa

mm

Anisotome imbricata var. *imbricata*

Anisotome imbricata var. *prostrata*

Anisotome pilifera

cm

PLATE 29

Anisotome capillifolia (Cheesem.) Ckn.
"Hair-leaved".

A tufted herb, similar to *A. haastii* but smaller and with much finer, hairlike leaves (<0.5 mm wide), the divisions not all in one plane and with very long hair tips.

The one or more flower stems have 1–2 small leafy bracts where they branch near the top into a compound head.

DISTRIBUTION South Island: western Otago and northern Southland, with occasional plants in Fiordland.

Low- to high-alpine: 1,200–2,000 m (4,000–6,500 ft).

HABITAT On shady ledges and crevices of rock outcrops, usually in fellfield. On sites inaccessible to animals it may be one of the most prominent plants.

COLLECTED Mt Burns, Hunter Mountains, Fiordland National Park, 1,580 m (5,200 ft). January 1968.

Anisotome haastii (F. Muell. ex Hook.f.) Ckn. & Laing
After Sir Julius von Haast, famous geologist and explorer.

A large tufted herb with a stout taproot and leaves highly divided in one plane. Their segments are narrow yet not hairlike, but they end in fine hair tips.

The prominent flower stems have large compound heads. They are distinctly leafy and generally similar in male and female plants but only the female ones persist and produce fruit.

DISTRIBUTION South Island: throughout most mountain regions but more common in the central and southern high-rainfall areas, rare in the drier areas such as Marlborough, and absent from Central Otago.

Subalpine to low-alpine: 600–1,500 m (2,000–5,000 ft).

HABITAT Once a conspicuous plant in the snow tussock-herbfields and scrub of wet regions, it has been heavily grazed by animals and is now much less prominent. Mature plants that persist on inaccessible bluffs provide a valuable seed supply for its re-establishment so that young plants may be quite common.

COLLECTED Borland Saddle, Hunter Mountains, Fiordland National Park, 970 m (3,200 ft). January 1968.

Anisotome brevistylis (Hook.f.) Poppelwell
"Short-styled".

A taprooted or sometimes rhizomatous herb, usually smaller than *A. haastii* but 15–50 cm tall, with its leaves narrower in outline and less highly divided (2- or 3–pinnate). The final leaf segments are also narrower (0.5–1 mm wide) and distinctly grooved on their upper surface. Their tips, although pointed, usually lack hair processes.

Flower stems are quite narrow and the compound heads are smaller and much less compact than in *A. haastii*.

DISTRIBUTION South Island: Central Otago, extending westwards to the Lakes district.

Montane to low-alpine: 500–1,500 m (1,500–5,000 ft).

HABITAT Even though rather uncommon, plants occupy a range of habitats from open tussock grassland to scrub and occasionally rock outcrops.

COLLECTED Mt Ida, Hawkdun Range, North Otago, 1,460 m (4,800 ft). December 1969.

Anisotome cauticola Dawson
"Rock-dwelling".

Similar to *A. brevistylis* and sometimes growing in its vicinity. Best recognised by the obvious joints on the petiole, one at or near the top of the sheath and usually a second near the first pair of leaflets.

It is confined to rock outcrops in the subalpine and low-alpine zones; 500–1,500 m (1,500–5,000 ft) in Central Otago and the Lakes district.

Anisotome filifolia (Hook.f.) Ckn. & Laing
"Slender-leaved".

A distinctive slender herb with a deep taproot, persistent papery leaf bases and leaves divided into very narrow segments up to 4 cm long. Occasional plants have much shorter and broader leaves.

The one to few flower stems have leafy bracts and compound heads.

DISTRIBUTION South Island: widespread but often local, as far south as Canterbury.

Montane to low-alpine: 300–1,500 m (1,000–5,000 ft).

HABITAT Frequent but often overlooked in tussock grasslands and herbfield. It persists and sometimes increases on open stony sites in eroding areas and may occasionally be found on screes.

COLLECTED Both the flowering and fruiting plants are from Porters Pass, Torlesse Range, Canterbury, 1,220 m (4,000 ft). January 1970.

Anisotome deltoidea Cheesem.
"Deltoid; broadly triangular" — referring to the leaf outline.

A slender herb, usually < 10 cm tall, with the base thickened by many persistent papery leaf bases. The delicate leaves are triangular in outline and deeply cut into small, narrow, pointed lobes.

The one to few short flower stems have minute bracts where they branch and several, small, compound heads. The minute male and female flowers each have 5 pale-pink petals.

DISTRIBUTION South Island: northern Nelson and western Marlborough.

Low-alpine: 1,200–1,700 m (4,000–5,500 ft).

HABITAT Usually common in snow tussock-herbfield, especially on poorly drained sites, but easily overlooked because of the sparse finely-divided leaves. Also extends into early snowbanks where, amongst the much shorter vegetation, it is more prominent.

COLLECTED Near Lake Sylvester, Cobb Valley, north-west Nelson, 1,400 m (4,600 ft). December 1967.

Anisotome capillifolia

Anisotome brevistylis

Anisotome haastii

cm

PLATE 30

Genus **GINGIDIA**

From the vernacular name of a Syrian species of carrot.
A small predominantly New Zealand genus. Four native species reach the alpine zone. All smell strongly of aniseed when their leaves are crushed.

Gingidia montana (J.R. & G. Forst.) Dawson

"Growing in mountains".

A highly aromatic tufted herb with a deep fleshy taproot and old leaf remains.

Compound flower heads are up to 10 cm across. The 2 prominent styles persist on the flattened fruits, as shown.

DISTRIBUTION North and South Islands: rather sporadic south of Lake Taupo in the North Island and apparently absent from alpine areas. But in the South Island it is in all mountain areas except South Canterbury, North and Central Otago, western Southland and southern Fiordland.

Lowland to low-alpine: to 1,500 m (5,000 ft).

HABITAT In moist open sites in forest, scrub and snow tussock-herbfield. Being one of the most palatable native plants it is now found mainly on inaccessible rocky bluffs, except for areas such as the Hooker Valley under Mt Cook where people discourage deer and other grazing animals.

COLLECTED Hooker Valley, Mt Cook National Park, 910 m (3,000 ft). January 1969.

Gingidia decipiens (Hook.f.) Dawson

"Misleading" — often mistaken for *Anisotome aromatica*.

A bright or dark green, strongly aromatic, glabrous, rosette herb with numerous old-leaf remains and a stout fleshy taproot. The 5–10 pairs of sub-fleshy leaflets have a characteristic shape and sometimes a glaucous bloom.

Either one or several erect flower stalks, up to 10 cm long, are rather stout and usually without bracts. They end in a compound head up to 4 cm across. The 2 prominent styles persist in the brown fruits.

DISTRIBUTION South Island: widespread yet rather sporadic in the mountain regions, but rare or absent from South Canterbury, Central and North Otago.

Montane to low-alpine: 300–1,800 m (1,000–6,000 ft).

HABITAT Usually on rock debris, especially raw moraine and fine scree, but it also occurs in rock crevices, in stony eroding snow tussock grassland occasionally in less damaged grassland and herbfield.

COLLECTED Mt Richmond, Two Thumb Range, South Canterbury, 1,220 m (4,000 ft). January 1969.

Gingidia enysii (Kirk) Dawson

After Mr J.D. Enys, early New Zealand naturalist.

A glaucous, aniseed-scented, fleshy, rosette herb with a stout taproot, leaves have 2–10 pairs of partly overlapping leaflets.

The equally glaucous, compound flower heads exceed the leaves.

DISTRIBUTION South Island: mid- and North Canterbury, but as an alpine plant, apparently only from the frost-shattered outcrops of greywacke on the Hawkdun Range, North Otago.

Montane to low-alpine: 300–1,400 m (1,000–4,500 ft).

COLLECTED Above Dansey Pass, Hawkdun Range, North Otago, 1,310 m (4,300 ft). December 1969.

Gingidia baxterae (Dawson) Webb

After Mrs M. Baxter, Dunedin naturalist.

A small delicate herb, not unlike *Anisotome aromatica* but the thin leaflets are glaucous, at least below, with the terminal one similar in size to the 3–7 pairs of laterals. Unlike *A. aromatica*, bruised leaves are strongly aniseed-scented.

DISTRIBUTION South Island: Gouland Downs, Nelson, with a large gap to Central and eastern Otago and northern Southland.

Montane to low-alpine: 600–1,300 m (2,000–4,000 ft).

HABITAT A minor species of moist, sometimes peaty sites in snow or blue tussock grassland and subalpine scrub.

COLLECTED Rock & Pillar Range, Central Otago, 1,130 m (3,700 ft). November 1970.

Gingidia decipiens

Gingidia enysii

Gingidia baxterae

Gingidia montana

cm

PLATE 31

Genus **LIGNOCARPA**
"Woody seed".

An endemic genus with two species, both alpines.

They are easily distinguished by the type of bracts associated with each of the small simple heads; they also differ in distribution.

Lignocarpa carnosula (Hook.f.) Dawson
"Rather fleshy".

Fleshy, glabrous and glaucous, summer-green herbs with much-divided leaves and deep taproots.

Either all female flowers or both male and bisexual ones are arranged in compound heads. The minute flowers have white or occasionally pink petals that, together with the stamens, are hardly developed in the female flowers. The flower heads have deeply divided bracts associated with each of the small flower heads. Moreover, these bracts extend well beyond the flowers and tend to conceal them.

DISTRIBUTION South Island: east of the main divide on the greywacke mountains of southern Nelson–Marlborough, southwards to the Rangitata Valley in Canterbury.

Low- to high-alpine: 900–2,100 m (3,000–7,000 ft).

HABITAT Confined to screes but one of their less common plants. Because of their colour they are easily overlooked, even in flower.

As Philipson & Hearn have noted in their book (*Rock Garden Plants of the Southern Alps*, Caxton Press, 1962), seeds often disperse across the scree slopes when the stem breaks at its delicate connection with the rootstock, dries out, and becomes a tumbleweed in the wind.

COLLECTED Fog Peak, Torlesse Range, Canterbury, 1,520 m (5,000 ft). January 1967.

Lignocarpa diversifolia (Cheesem.) Dawson
"With differing leaves".

Its habit and colour are very like *L. carnosula* but the floral bracts are undivided and quite short so that the flowers are much more conspicuous. Also, many plants have only male flowers rather than both bisexual and male ones, and therefore set no seed.

DISTRIBUTION South Island: to the north of *L. carnosula*, found rather locally on the greywacke mountains in the northeast—Travers, St Arnaud and Gordon Ranges in eastern Nelson; Inland Kaikoura Range and west of the Awatere Valley in Marlborough.

Low- to high-alpine: 1,200–1,800 m (4,000–6,000 ft).

HABITAT As for *L. carnosula* except that the surface material of the scree where it grows is often much finer than of those occupied by *L. carnosula*.

COLLECTED Mt Robert, Travers Range, Nelson Lakes National Park, 1,370 m (4,500 ft). December 1967.

Lignocarpa diversifolia

Lignocarpa carnosula

Anisotome filifolia

Anisotome deltoidea

cm

Plate 32

Genus ACIPHYLLA
"Sharp leaf".

One of the most distinctive and important alpine genera, with 38 species. Apart from one each in Australia and the Chatham Islands the rest are confined to New Zealand, where almost all reach the alpine zone. Several are quite restricted in distribution and a few of these are possibly hybrids. Some of the more local ones (*A. flexuosa, A. hookerii, A. inermis, A. latibracteata*) are omitted but others are mentioned briefly with their related species.

Many aciphyllas are quite distinctive while others are much more difficult to identify. Plant size and habit, leaf size and shape especially the stipules, size and shape of the flower head including their leafy bracts, and to some extent the locality are all useful for identification. Since most of the species flower irregularly, identification sometimes has to be made on the vegetative parts alone.

All of the larger aciphyllas are commonly referred to as speargrass or spaniard.

Aciphylla horrida W. R. B. Oliver
"Horrid"—referring to its piercing leaves.

A massive plant growing as single clumps or in small groups from a divided crown of the large taproot. The stipules are leaflike, *ca* 15 cm long and rather flexible but sharp-pointed, while the leaflets are often curved.

The spectacular flower stems are *ca* 1.5 m tall and very broad at the base, to be almost triangular in outline, especially in female plants. Only the extreme basal part of the stem lacks flowers, so that they occur well below the level of the foliage. The middle sections of female and male flower stems, together with a single leafy bract from the base of each, is shown.

DISTRIBUTION South Island: throughout the higher rainfall areas along and near the main divide but apparently more common towards the south where it extends eastward into the lakes district of Otago.

Subalpine to low-alpine: 600–1,400 m (2,000–4,500 ft).

HABITAT Conspicuous and sometimes abundant in short subalpine scrub, mixed snow tussock-scrub and occasionally higher up, in snow tussock-herbfield.

COLLECTED Near Homer Tunnel, upper Hollyford Valley, Fiordland National Park, 850 m (2,800 ft). January 1969.

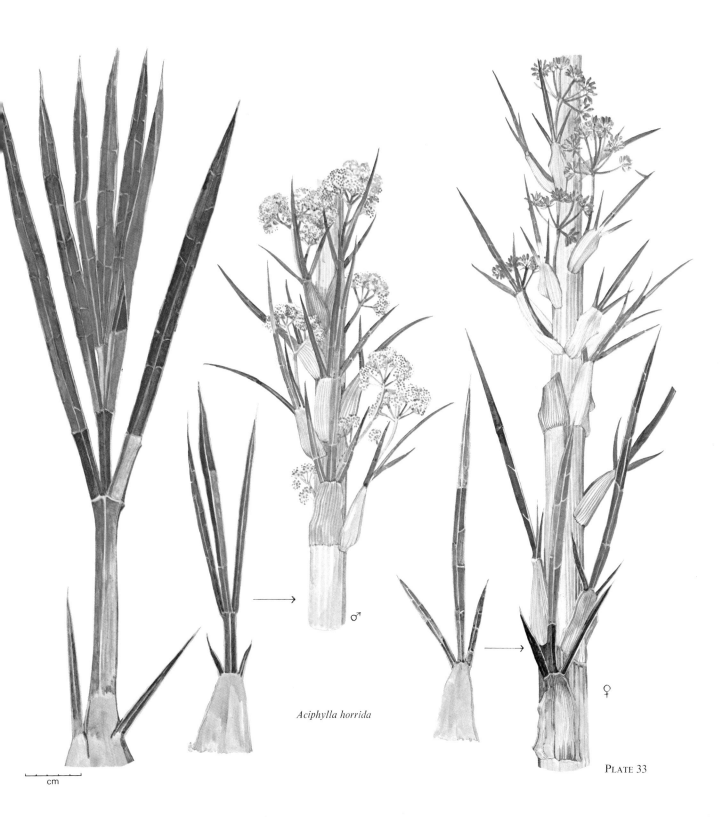

♂

Aciphylla horrida

♀

cm

PLATE 33

Aciphylla scott-thomsonii Ckn. & Allan
After Mr J. Scott-Thomson, Otago botanist.

Another spectacular plant, the tallest in the genus, with a habit similar to *A. horrida*. It differs in having distinctly glaucous leaves that are longer (up to 1 m or more), usually more highly divided and with shorter stipules. The yellowish margins are very finely serrated.

Flower stems are up to 3 m tall and rather narrow throughout, with flowers mostly above the level of the leaves—a basal sterile part is shown. Male heads are distinctly broader and more colourful than female ones.

DISTRIBUTION South Island: rather widespread in the wetter regions but to the east of the main divide, as far north as Arthurs Pass.

Subalpine to low-alpine: 600–1,200 m (2,000–4,000 ft).

HABITAT Often conspicuous in subalpine scrub, mixed snow tussock-scrub, herbfield or grassland on permanently moist sites. They are an outstanding feature, especially when flowering, of the snow tussock-herbfield in the Hooker Valley under Mt Cook.

COLLECTED Hooker Valley, Mt Cook National Park, 910 m (3,000 ft). January 1969.

Aciphylla scott-thomsonii

♀

♂

♀

♂

♂

cm

PLATE 34

Aciphylla colensoi Hook.f.

After the Rev. W. Colenso, early New Zealand botanist.

Rather similar to *A. scott-thomsonii* but differs in being smaller in all its parts. In addition, the leaflet margins are more strongly serrated, their midribs reddish to orange and prominent, while the leaflets are much closer together. Stipules are longer and more daggerlike.

Flower stems are similarly narrow but their leafy bracts have prominent red to yellow midribs.

DISTRIBUTION North and South Islands: widespread in mountain regions from Mt Hikurangi southwards to mid-Canterbury.

Subalpine to low-alpine: 900–1,500 m (3,000–5,000 ft).

HABITAT Similar to *A. scott-thomsonii*.

COLLECTED Field Peak, Tararua Range, 1,220 m (4,000 ft). November 1968.

Aciphylla aurea W. R. B. Oliver   GOLDEN SPANIARD

"Golden".

Similar in habit to the previous ones but distinctly golden. Leaves may have 1–2 of the lower leaflets divided. The leaflike stipules are very long and the yellowish edges of the leaflets, being finely serrated, are rough to feel.

Flower stems usually reach *ca* 1 m with the paler male stems distinctly broader than the female ones, especially at the base.

DISTRIBUTION South Island: from Marlborough and Nelson southwards to northern Southland, mostly east of the main divide.

Montane to low-alpine: 300–1,500 m (1,000–5,000 ft).

HABITAT On well-drained sites, including rock outcrops, in mixed snow tussock-scrub or tussock grassland. It may overlap with *A. scott-thomsonii* in higher rainfall regions, but here it selects the best-drained sites. A tolerance of fire and resistance to sheep has resulted in its replacement of snow tussocks in many areas of run country.

COLLECTED Pisa Range, Central Otago, 1,280 m (4,200 ft). December 1968.

Aciphylla ferox W. R. B. Oliver

"Fierce, dangerous".

The habit is similar to *A. horrida* but it has very much shorter stipules, as shown, that are quite rigid and taper to very sharp tips.

It occurs to the north of *A. horrida* in Nelson and Marlborough, where its altitudinal range and habitat are similar to those of *A. horrida* further south.

COLLECTED Mt Peel, Cobb Valley, north-west Nelson, 1,460 m (4,800 ft).

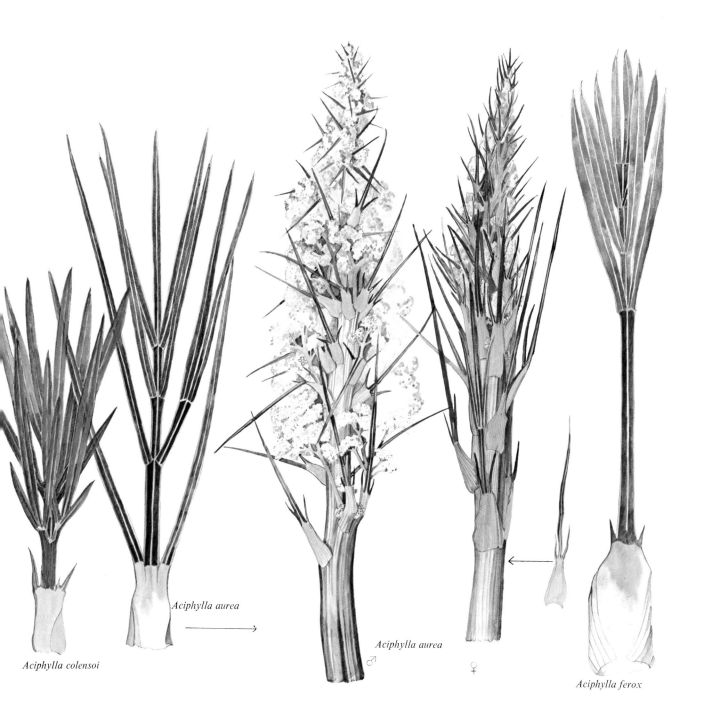

Aciphylla colensoi

Aciphylla aurea

Aciphylla aurea
♂

♀

Aciphylla ferox

cm

PLATE 35

Aciphylla squarrosa J. R. & G. Forst.
"Rough, with spreading processes"—referring to the leaflets.

Plants occur as single tufts or a few together. Their leaves are highly divided and glaucous, but rather soft or flaccid, and the leaflets are narrow (<5 mm) and quite divergent. Midribs are very prominent and, together with the margins, are finely serrated. Stipules are trifoliate with the central segment very much shorter than the other two.

Flower stems are usually <1 m tall, with many very narrow leafy bracts that are crowded above, but wide apart near the base. The central leaflet of these bracts is turned down.

DISTRIBUTION North and South Islands: from Mt Hikurangi at least as far south as central Canterbury but rare and local to the south of northern Marlborough and Nelson.

Coastal to low-alpine: to 1,400 m (4,500 ft).

HABITAT In the alpine zone it occurs along streamsides and on wet or shady banks or depressions in mixed tussock-scrub and snow tussock grassland.

COLLECTED Mt Richmond, Two Thumb Range, South Canterbury, 1,310 m (4,300 ft). January 1969.

*Aciphylla glaucescens W. R. B. Oliver
"Bluish-green".

Superficially it resembles an overgrown *A. squarrosa* but there are some differences—the usually trifoliate stipules have a relatively long stout central leaflet, while the central leaflet of the floral bracts is not turned down but remains erect.

It is more widespread than *A. squarrosa* extending southwards from Mt Hikurangi almost to Foveaux Strait. Their altitudinal ranges and habitats are similar.

Aciphylla takahea W. R. B. Oliver
After Takahe Valley—its type locality in Fiordland.

It resembles *A. squarrosa* but the leaves (25–45 cm long), are dark-green rather than glaucous and only 2-pinnate, with sharp tips, prominent pale midribs, rough edges and usually 3-foliate stipules in which the central segment is quite long (8–15 cm).

Female flower stems are much more robust and longer (*ca* 1 m) than the male stems (60 cm) but in both, the leafy bracts are much as in *A. squarrosa* except that their central leaflet is not turned down.

DISTRIBUTION South Island: almost confined to central Fiordland.

Subalpine to low-alpine: 900–1,300 m (3,000–4,500 ft).

HABITAT Often prominent on damp sites in mixed tussock-scrub and snow tussock-herbfield, especially among large boulders.

COLLECTED Above Lake Wapiti, upper Doon Valley, Fiordland National Park, 1,220 m (4,000 ft). December 1970.

Aciphylla dissecta (Kirk) W. R. B. Oliver
"Divided"—referring to the leaves.

A rather stout, dark-green, tufted herb with highly divided, rather flexible but sharp-pointed leaves. There are 9–10 pairs of leaflets which are further divided (3-pinnate). The leaves bear some resemblance to *Anisotome haastii* (it was once included in this genus), but the stipules are typical of the aciphyllas. They are fine, almost hairlike, and usually divided.

Stout flower stems are *ca* 30 cm tall with a broad, rounded but rather loose head and leafy bracts.

DISTRIBUTION North Island: Tararua Range only.

Low-alpine: 1,000–1,600 m (3,500–5,500 ft).

HABITAT Common, and when in flower quite conspicuous throughout the snow tussock-herbfield.

COLLECTED By Mr A. P. Druce. A rather small female plant from Marchant Ridge, Tararua Range, *ca* 1,040 m (3,400 ft). December 1965.

*Aciphylla intermedia Petrie
"Intermediate"—between *A. dissecta* and *A. monroi*.

Altogether larger than *A. dissecta* but with leaves almost as much dissected and stipules also divided.

Flower stems reach 60 cm and both male and female heads are broad but less congested than in *A. dissecta*.

Although its distribution is as for *A. dissecta* it is much less common. Mr A. P. Druce, with a knowledge of the Tararua flora, has suggested that it may be a hybrid between *A. dissecta* and the much larger *A. colensoi*.

Aciphylla polita (Kirk) Cheesem.
"Smooth, polished"—referring to the leaves.

One of the smallest species, occurring as single tufts or small clumps. Their dark green leaves are rather soft and highly divided (2–3-pinnate) with very narrow (*ca* 1 mm wide), sharp-pointed leaflets and fine stipules (*ca* 1 cm long).

The slender flower stems have fairly loose heads in both male and female plants, and their leafy bracts are quite small.

DISTRIBUTION North and South Islands: Tararua Range; northern Marlborough–Nelson.

Low-alpine: 900–1,700 m (3,000–5,500 ft).

HABITAT Rather insignificant yet sometimes common in snow tussock-herbfield; less common in the drier tussock grasslands of Marlborough.

COLLECTED Mt Peel, Cobb Valley, north-west Nelson, 1,520 m (5,000 ft). February 1969.

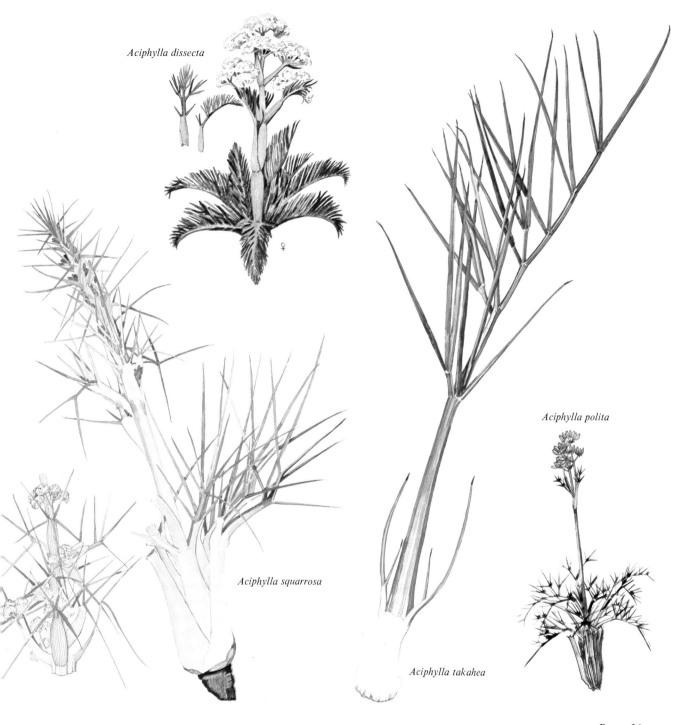

Aciphylla dissecta

Aciphylla squarrosa

Aciphylla polita

Aciphylla takahea

♀

cm

PLATE 36

Aciphylla anomala Allan
"Anomalous".

A slender, tufted, rather flaccid herb with only a few leaves that may vary from simple to trifoliate. Leaflets have finely serrated margins while the stipules are very small or absent.

Flower stems of male plants are slender, as shown. Their leafy bracts are mostly simple with very small stipules and the flower heads are relatively small. Female stems are stouter but their flower heads are hidden by the bracts.

DISTRIBUTION South Island: confined to north-west Nelson.
Low-alpine: 1,400–1,700 m (4,500–5,500 ft).

HABITAT Rather uncommon in snow tussock-herbfield.

COLLECTED Above Lake Sylvester, Cobb Valley, north-west Nelson, 1,520 m (5,000 ft). December 1967.

*Aciphylla hookerii Kirk
After Sir J. D. Hooker, famous early botanist.

Now merged with *A. townsonii*, its habit is similar to *A. anomala* but differences include shorter, narrower petioles (*ca* 4 cm x 1 mm vs 8 cm x 2 mm) and leaflets (*ca* 7.5 cm x 1.5 mm vs 10 cm x 2.5 mm), with smooth margins. Also, the bracts on the flower stems have longer stipules (10 mm vs 5 mm).

It extends south and west of the area occupied by *A. anomala*, from north-west Nelson through north Westland to about Arthurs Pass, chiefly on the western side of the main divide. Like *A. anomala* it is a low-alpine species with an altitudinal range of 900–1,400 m (3,000–4,500 ft).

Aciphylla crenulata J. B. Armst.
"With minute, shallow, rounded teeth"—on the leaf margins.

A slender tufted herb with soft flexible leaves and small stipules. Leaflets have prominent, often reddish midribs and thickened, finely-serrated margins.

Flower stems are slender and carry rather small heads on their upper half. Male heads are somewhat broader and more lax than female ones, shown here in fruit.

DISTRIBUTION South Island: widespread in the high rainfall areas close to and west of the main divide.
Low-alpine: 900–1,700 m (3,000–5,500 ft).

HABITAT Often common in snow tussock-herbfield, but because of its lax tussocklike habit, it is easily overlooked among the snow tussocks, except when in flower.

COLLECTED Mt Brewster, Haast Pass, Mt Aspiring National Park, 1,220 m (4,000 ft). March 1968.

*Aciphylla indurata Cheesem.
"Hard"—referring to the leaves.

Its habit is similar to *A. crenulata* but plants are more robust, up to 60 cm tall, and their leaves harder, shorter (to *ca* 30 cm) and 2-pinnate with a reddish to yellow midrib and thickened rough edges.

They occur from south-west Nelson through Westland, in the subalpine and low-alpine zones: 900–1,300 m (3,000–4,000 ft).

Aciphylla lyallii Hook.f.
After Dr Lyall, surgeon-naturalist on HMS *Terror* in the 1840s.

A tufted herb that is highly variable even in one area. Leaves are thick, yet rather flaccid, and vary from simple to divided, with up to 5 or occasionally more leaflets. A key feature is the irregularly spaced joints on the leaves, even the undivided ones. Stipules are usually small and narrow (2 cm x 2 mm), leaflets are usually *ca* 3 mm wide but sometimes narrower, their midribs are prominent and edges thickened but smooth.

Flower stems are 10–50 cm tall with very broad sheaths to the leafy bracts, especially in female stems where they conceal the small flower heads and later, the fruits.

DISTRIBUTION South Island: through most of the wetter mountain regions but it seems to be common only in parts of Fiordland.
Low-alpine: 1,100–1,400 m (3,500–4,500 ft).

HABITAT On permanently wet sites in snow tussock-herbfield. Here it may be common yet usually quite inconspicuous among the tussocks except when flowering.

COLLECTED Mt Burns, Hunter Mountains, Fiordland National Park, 1,110 m (3,600 ft). January 1969.

Aciphylla kirkii Buchan.
After Mr T. Kirk, eminent New Zealand botanist.

Easily distinguished by its 1–3-foliate leaves with very thick harsh leaflets, similar in length and abruptly narrowed to sharp points. The leaflets have thickened smooth margins and midribs, and prominent veins.

Both male and female heads are elongated on the stout flower stems. All but the upper bracts are trifoliate with the central blade much longer than the pair of stipules; the upper bracts lack stipules.

DISTRIBUTION South Island: Central and western Otago but east of the main divide.
Low- to high-alpine: 1,300–2,000 m (4,500–6,500 ft).

HABITAT In high-altitude snow tussock grassland and herbfield, extending into the high-alpine zone in fellfield and cushion vegetation where plants may be reduced almost to the size of *A. hectori*.

COLLECTED Relatively large plants from Coronet Peak, Otago Lakes district, 1,220 m (4,000 ft). December 1968.

Aciphylla crenulata

Aciphylla lyallii

Aciphylla anomala

Aciphylla kirkii

cm

PLATE 37

Aciphylla divisa Cheesem.
"Divided" — referring to the leaves.

Occurs as single golden-green tufts or more usually as clumps or small loose cushions of several tufts. The single leaf shows its distinct petiole that is often channelled, with 4 (but up to 8) pairs of primary leaflets, the lower ones of which are further divided (= 2-pinnate). Most of the leaflets are *ca* 3 mm wide with slightly thickened yellow margins and sharp points. The slender stipules are *ca* 2 cm long.

Flower stems may reach 40 cm and end in a large, pale-yellow, almost globose head up to 10 cm across. The leafy bracts have stipules, large papery sheaths, but small divided blades.

DISTRIBUTION South Island: from central Canterbury southwards, close to the main divide. It is rare and apparently local in the northern half of the island, but common towards the south, especially in south Westland and western Otago.

Low-alpine: 1,100–1,700 m (3,500–5,500 ft).

HABITAT Most common in the higher elevation snow tussock-herbfield where it may be one of the most conspicuous herbs. In heavily grazed areas it has become restricted to inaccessible bluffs and large outcrops.

COLLECTED French Ridge, west Matukituki Valley, Mt Aspiring National Park, 1,580 m (5,200 ft). December 1968.

Aciphylla multisecta W. R. B. Oliver
"Much-divided" — referring to the leaves.

Its habit, colour and flower heads resemble *A. divisa* but the leaves are usually longer (to 40 cm) and more divided (3-pinnate) with narrower segments (1.5 vs 3 mm).

It occurs in the low- and high-alpine zones along the main divide south of about Hokitika, in similar habitats to *A. divisa* but appears to be generally less common except locally, as in parts of central Fiordland.

Aciphylla hectori Buchan.
After Sir James Hector, geologist and explorer.

Small and rather rigid, occurring as single tufts or in small clumps. Leaves vary from 7-foliate (2 leaf-like stipules, the terminal and 2 pairs of leaflets) to simple, with 5-foliate forms (less 1 pair of leaflets) most common. Even single plants may be variable but western populations tend to have more leaflets than eastern ones—the single leaf shown is 3-foliate.

Both male and female heads are somewhat elongated on the flower stems, but more so in male plants and in western populations. Their bracts are uniformly trifoliate with the central leaflet longer than the pair of stipules.

DISTRIBUTION South Island: on the schistose mountains of Central and western Otago and South Westland.

Low- to high-alpine: 1,000–1,800 m (3,500–6,000 ft).

HABITAT In Central Otago it is usually common in dwarfed herbfield but further west it occurs in short snow tussock-herbfield and may extend into fellfield, especially in rock crevices.

COLLECTED Rock & Pillar Range, Central Otago, 1,400 m (4,600 ft). February 1969.

Aciphylla verticillata W. R. B. Oliver
"Whorled"—referring to the lowest floral bracts.

Its habit is similar to *A. hectori* but with somewhat longer 5-foliate leaves (including the pair of leaf-like stipules). Flower stems reach 25 cm and have their lowest bracts (up to 12) in a distinctive whorl that is quite separate from the remaining bracts above.

It is found along and west of the main divide for some distance south of Amuri Pass and again in the low-alpine zone on the Hawkdun Range, North Otago.

Aciphylla lecomtei Dawson
After Mr J. Le Comte, amateur botanist.

Plants are generally similar to *A. montana* var. *montana*, but their leaves usually have four rather than three pairs of leaflets and the rosettes are tighter and more definite. Male inflorescences are almost spherical in *A. lecomtei* but narrower and more elongated in *A. montana*. Female heads are somewhat less distinct. The species is restricted to the Otago Lakes District (Garvies, Eyres, Remarkables) where it occurs in fellfield and snow tussock grassland of the low- and high-alpine zones. 1,400–1,900 m (4,600–6,200 ft).

Aciphylla trifoliolata Petrie
"With trifoliate leaves".

Yellow to orange plants up to 40 cm tall, occurring as single or several tufts with slender trifoliate leaves plus a pair of long narrow stipules. The narrow flower stems are reddish-brown and extend somewhat above the leaves.

It is known only from the Lyall Range, north of the Buller Gorge, where it grows on and around rock outcrops in snow tussock grassland down to *ca* 1,300 m.

Aciphylla stannensis Dawson
From the Tin Range.

Generally similar to *A. trifoliolata* but restricted to the Tin Range in southern Stewart Island, at 550–760 m, among tussocks and shrubs on exposed sites.

Aciphylla hectori

Aciphylla traillii

Aciphylla divisa

cm

PLATE 38

Aciphylla similis Cheesem.
"Resembling" – *A. monroi.*

A rather variable tufted herb with a habit and colour similar to *A. divisa*, but it differs in having only once-pinnate leaves. The single leaf shows the typical fine stipules, long, slender, flattened petiole and 7 (range 4–10) pairs of undivided leaflets, 2–4 mm wide with thickened yellow margins.

Flower stems may reach 40 cm and the heads may be either loosely clustered near the top or, more usually, distributed along much of the stem, especially in male plants and in the more southern populations. The leafy bracts have prominent sheaths, >5 mm wide, and small divided blades. However, in male plants and the upper bracts on female plants, the blades may be simple.

DISTRIBUTION South Island: a rather erratic occurrence between Lewis Pass and the mountains of south Canterbury.

Low-alpine: 900–1,400 m (3,000–4,600 ft)

HABITAT Ranging from wet, mixed snow tussock-scrub and snow tussock-herbfield as at Arthurs Pass (where it is common) and south Canterbury (Ohau Range) where it is in open, often depleted snow tussock grassland and on rock outcrops.

COLLECTED Temple Basin, Arthurs Pass National Park, 1,430 m (4,700 ft). December 1967.

* Aciphylla montana J.F. Armstrong
"Growing in mountains".

Occurs usually in golden green rather loose clumps of up to 25 rosettes or more, each one up to 25 cm across. Leaves have 2–3 pairs of leaflets (1-pinnate) with a prominent sheath and very slender stipules of variable length.

Flower stems are long (to 60 cm) and with rather narrow, tapered yellow-orange heads.

DISTRIBUTION South Island: East of the main divide from central Canterbury to the Otago Lakes District.

Low- to high-alpine 1,400–2,000 m (4,600–6,500 ft).

HABITAT Often common and prominent in snow tussock grassland including rock outcrops and stabilised screes.

Aciphylla montana var. *gracilis* (Oliver) Dawson
"Slender".

Occurs usually as small single tufts with many persistent dead leaf bases and only a few (< 15) living leaves which have just two pairs of leaflets.

The slender flower stems have 6–12 bracts that are much more widely spaced in male plants. Apart from the lower few bracts which have 3 (or 5) leaflets, the rest are simple.

DISTRIBUTION South Island: from South Canterbury (Two Thumb-Kirkliston Ranges) into North Otago (St Bathans–Hawkdun Ranges).

Low-alpine: 1,100–1,700 m (3,500–5,500 ft).

HABITAT In open, depleted snow tussock grassland on the greywacke mountains.

COLLECTED Mt Dalgety, Dalgety Range, South Canterbury, 1,220 m (4,000 ft). January 1967.

Aciphylla traillii Kirk (*See plate 38*)
After Mr A. W. Traill, of Stewart Island.

Occurs as small single tufts or in small clumps, with leaf-like stipules and 1–3-foliate leaves. Their leaflets have obvious midribs and thickened, smooth, yellow margins.

Female heads are more compact than male ones and the bracts in both have prominent broad sheaths and usually a simple leaflet.

Variety **cartilaginea** (Petrie) Cheesem., differs in having 3–5-foliate leaves with broad yellow midribs and thicker, yellow, cartilaginous margins to the leaflets.

DISTRIBUTION Stewart Island: both the species and its variety are the only aciphyllas on Stewart Island—Mt Anglem, Mt Rakiahua, Table Hill, Frazer Peaks.

Subalpine to low-alpine: 600–970 m (2,000–3,200 ft).

HABITAT Common and usually prominent in wet meadow grassland and herb moor.

COLLECTED By Mr G. C. Baker from Mt Anglem, 940 m (3,100 ft). March 1969.

Aciphylla monroi Hook.f.
After Sir D. Monro, early collector of South Island alpine plants.

The habit resembles *A. similis* but there are fewer (2–8) pairs of leaflets in each leaf.

Flower stems never have their heads congested; they are distributed along much of the stem. Moreover, the leafy bracts have smaller sheaths (*ca* 3 cm x 3 mm) and simple blades.

However, the distinction between these two species is not clear, especially in eastern populations (see under *A. similis*). Bracts on the male and female stems from South Canterbury, shown here, have simple blades but their sheaths are wider than described for *A. monroi*, as shown in the plant from Nelson Lakes.

DISTRIBUTION South Island: widespread in the north and extending southwards along and east of the main divide at least to mid-Canterbury.

Low-alpine: to 1,100–1,700 m (3,500–5,500 ft).

HABITAT Generally similar to that of *A. similis* except that it increases in the open, partly eroding snow tussock grassland of the drier eastern mountains.

COLLECTED St Arnaud Range, Nelson Lakes National Park, 1,610 m (5,300 ft). December 1967. Plants from Mt Richmond, Two Thumb Range, South Canterbury, 1,610 m (5,300 ft), January 1969, have some features of *A. similis*.

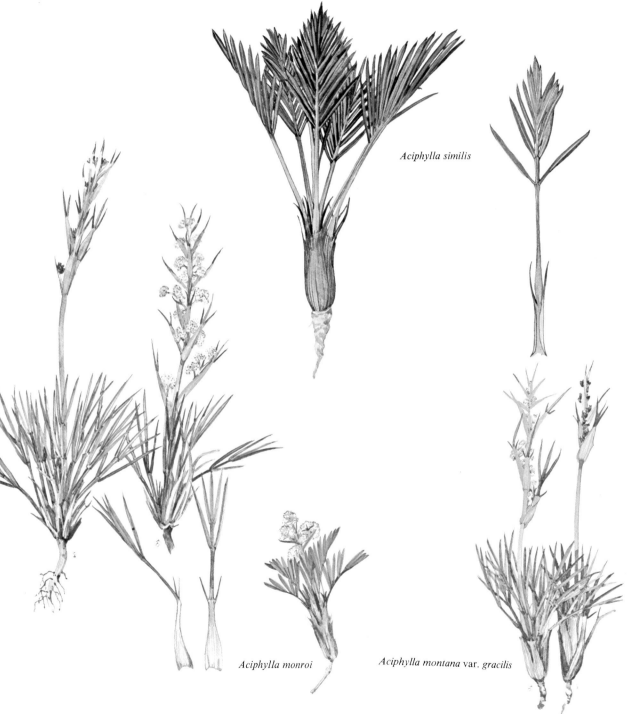

Aciphylla similis

Aciphylla monroi

Aciphylla montana var. *gracilis*

cm

PLATE 39

Aciphylla congesta Cheesem.
"Crowded"—referring to the flower heads.

A tufted herb, usually occurring as loose cushions up to 60 cm across. The dark-green leaves are rather thin and flexible, with leaf-like stipules plus 3–6 leaflets, all reaching a similar level, and large thin sheaths.

The stout, almost fleshy flower stems end in a crowded globose head in both male (shown) and female plants.

DISTRIBUTION South Island: in the high rainfall region of the south-west—south Westland, western Otago, north-western Southland, Fiordland.

Low- to high-alpine: 1,200–2,000 m (4,000–6,500 ft).

HABITAT Often one of the most important species in fellfield, especially where snow accumulates and persists. It also occurs with snow-patch grass (*Chionochloa oreophila*) in snowbank depressions, and on the more exposed sites in short snow tussock-herbfield.

COLLECTED Mt Burns, Hunter Mountains, Fiordland National Park, 1,680 m (5,500 ft). January 1969.

Aciphylla spedenii Cheesem.
After Mr J. Speden, of Gore, who discovered it.

Very similar to, but slightly smaller in all its parts, than *A. congesta*. It differs mainly in leaf shape—here the stipules and 5 leaflets fan out from the top of the sheath and are often red-tipped.

DISTRIBUTION South Island: confined to the Eyre Mountains in northern Southland apart from one record further west, in Fiordland (Gertrude Saddle).

High-alpine: 1,700–1,900 m (5,500–6,000 ft).

HABITAT Almost restricted to fellfield where it may be quite prominent.

COLLECTED Hummock Peak, Eyre Mountains, northern Southland, 1,830 m (6,000 ft). December 1969.

Aciphylla crosby-smithii Petrie
After Mr J. Crosby-Smith, who first collected it.

A rigid herb, usually forming cushions up to 60 cm across. The leaf-like stipules plus 7 (or 8) pairs of leaflets are thick and rigid with prominent but smooth margins and midribs, and their tips rather abruptly narrowed into sharp points.

The stout flower stems end in a fairly broad head with leafy bracts.

DISTRIBUTION South Island: confined to southern Fiordland.

Low-alpine: 1,400–1,600 m (4,500–5,500 ft).

HABITAT I have seen it only at one site where the cushions are locally common on fairly exposed rocky slopes in short snow tussock-herbfield.

COLLECTED Mt Burns, Hunter Mountains, Fiordland National Park, 1,520 m (5,000 ft). January 1969.

Aciphylla spedenii

Aciphylla crosby-smithii

Aciphylla congesta

cm

PLATE 40

Aciphylla pinnatifida Petrie
"Pinnately cut"—referring to the leaves.

A very distinctive rosette herb, with leaves deeply divided to the prominent yellow midrib, and a pair of quite leaf-like stipules on each.

Large orange sheaths on the bracts of both male and female flower stems make plants conspicuous and colourful when in flower.

DISTRIBUTION South Island: south-west Otago, northern Southland and Fiordland.

Low- to high-alpine: 1,100–1,700 m (3,500–5,500 ft).

HABITAT A plant of stream sides, wet depressions and snowbanks where it may be locally abundant. When not in flower, plants can be overlooked because their leaves tend to be pressed against the ground.

COLLECTED Mt Burns, Hunter Mountains, Fiordland National Park, 1,460 m (4,800 ft). January 1969.

Aciphylla leighii Allan
After Mr D. Leigh, who first collected it.

Similar to, but smaller than A. dobsonii, except that the cushions may be more extensive. The leaves are softer and their tips quite blunt.

DISTRIBUTION South Island: Fiordland—on the Darran Mountains.

High-alpine: 1,800–2,000 m (6,000–6,500 ft).

HABITAT Confined to fellfield.

COLLECTED By Mr D. J. Lyttle, a female plant from the head of the Toaka Icefall in the central Darrans, 1,830 m (6,000 ft). December 1969.

Aciphylla dobsonii Hook.f.
After Mt Dobson, near Lake Tekapo, where it was first collected.

A very distinctive tufted herb, with deep stout taproots, that forms hard cushions up to 60 cm across. The thick rigid leaves have two leaf-like stipules and a single blade.

The spectacular globose flower heads are on short stout stems.

DISTRIBUTION South Island: the higher mountains of south Canterbury, north and north-west Otago.

High-alpine: 1,500–2,200 m (5,000–7,500 ft).

HABITAT Confined to fellfield, especially along exposed ridge crests, where it is often the most important plant.

COLLECTED A male plant from Mt Richmond, Two Thumb Range, south Canterbury, 2,130 m (7,000 ft). January 1969.

Aciphylla simplex Petrie
"Undivided"—referring to the leaves.

The cushions and their individual tufts are similar to those of A. dobsonii. There are no stipules so that the leaves are simple, but in some western populations (The Remarkables, Eyre Mountains) plants may have a few 2- and 3-foliate leaves.

The smaller, more compact flower heads of female plants are shown.

DISTRIBUTION South Island: the higher mountains of Central Otago and northern Southland.

High-alpine: 1,500–2,000 m (5,000–6,500 ft).

HABITAT Confined to fellfield, including ledges and crevices of rocky bluffs where it is often prominent.

COLLECTED Pisa Range, Central Otago, 1,740 m (5,700 ft). December 1968.

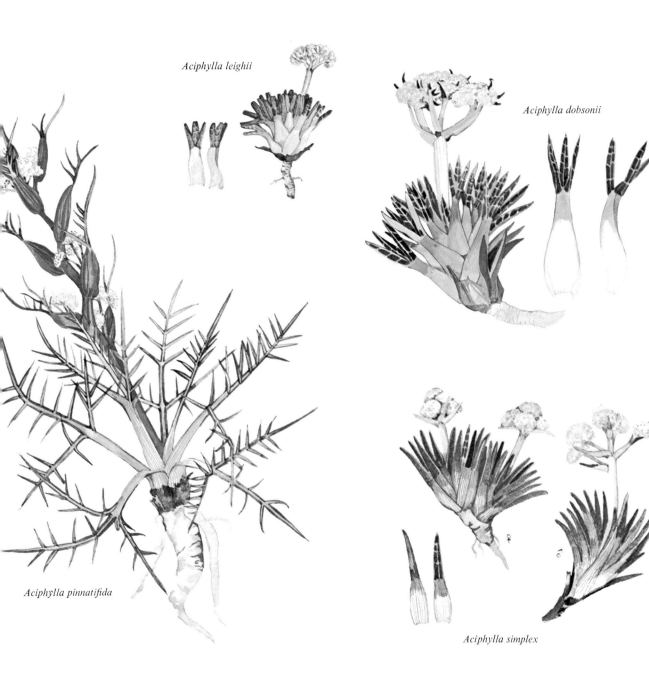

Aciphylla leighii

Aciphylla dobsonii

Aciphylla pinnatifida

Aciphylla simplex

cm

PLATE 41

The Heath Family: **ERICACEAE**

Genus **GAULTHERIA**
After Dr Gaulthier, a physician from Quebec.

A large and widespread genus which now includes all species previously in *Pernettya*. Of the ten native gaultherias six reach the alpine zone.

Gaultheria depressa Hook.f.
"Low growing".   SNOWBERRY

A small low-growing shrub with branches up to 20 cm long; only their ends are leafy. There are two varieties; in both the small white flowers occur singly and are quite inconspicuous. The fleshy fruits are large and brightly coloured; red, pink or white on different plants.

Var. *depressa* has trailing branches and almost round leaves which have prominent bristles along their margins.

Var. *novae-zelandiae* Franklin, tends to be matted and the leaves are more narrow and pointed, more obviously toothed and without persistent bristles.

DISTRIBUTION North and South Islands: var. *depressa*: southern Tararuas; along the main divide and in the Dunedin district in the South Island.

    Montane to low-alpine: 500–1,500 m (1,500–5,000 ft).

    Var. *novae-zelandiae*: widespread in mountain regions from the volcanic plateau southwards.

    Lowland to low-alpine: to 1,500 m (5,000 ft).

HABITAT Both varieties occupy similar sites in open subalpine forest or scrub and the more open areas in snow tussock grassland and herbfield, including rock outcrops.

COLLECTED The three colour forms of var. *novae-zelandiae* from Mt Ruapehu, Tongariro National Park, 1,370 m (4,500 ft). The red-fruited var. *depressa* is from Fiordland. May 1964.

Gaultheria colensoi Hook.f.
After Rev. W. Colenso, early New Zealand botanist.

A low-growing or sprawling shrub which becomes more erect, up to 1 m tall, at lower altitudes. Leaves are very thick and stiff with prominent veins on their lower surface and the flowers are characteristically in short compact spikes at the branch tips.

DISTRIBUTION North Island: around the base of the central volcanic mountains and on the northern Ruahine Range.

    Subalpine to low-alpine: 900–1,700 m (3,000–5,500 ft).

HABITAT Occurs from the subalpine scrub almost to the upper limit of the red tussock grassland, but it is more important and prominent as a small ground shrub on open rocky sites.

COLLECTED Whakapapanui Valley, Mt Ruapehu, Tongariro National Park, 1,650 m (5,400 ft). November 1968.

Gaultheria crassa Allan
"Stout, thick"—referring to the habit and leaves.

A stout, much branched shrub up to 1 m tall but often dwarfed near its upper limit. The leaves are very thick and rigid. Clusters of up to 4 spikes near the branch tips make the small white flowers quite prominent and these are followed by dry brown capsules.

DISTRIBUTION North and South Islands: widespread throughout the mountain regions from the Ruahine Range southwards.

    Subalpine to low-alpine: 700–1,700 m (2,500–5,500 ft).

HABITAT One of the most versatile low-alpine species, being present in both high- and low-rainfall regions and in most plant communities.

COLLECTED Above Lake Lyndon, Torlesse Range, Canterbury, 910 m (3,000 ft). December 1966.

Gaultheria depressa var. *novae-zelandiae*

Gaultheria depressa var. *depressa*

Gaultheria crassa

Gaultheria colensoi

cm

PLATE 42

Gaultheria parvula Middleton
"Very small".

(= *Pernettya nana* Col.)

A very low shrub with slender, creeping and rooting branches that form mats up to 30 cm or more across. White or pink (sometimes red) flowers occur singly along the short ascending branches. They are large for the rest of the plant and often so numerous as to form an almost complete cover. The large, round, fleshy fruits, surrounded by the persistent, often succulent calyx are even more conspicuous than the flowers.

DISTRIBUTION South Island: east of the main divide from mid-Canterbury to Central and western Otago.

Subalpine to low-alpine: 600–1,400 m (2,000–4,500 ft).

HABITAT On rather open, sparsely vegetated, usually damp sites on river beds, in tussock grasslands and bogs. Because of its extremely small size it is easily overlooked unless in flower or fruit.

COLLECTED Flowering mat from Mt Richmond, Two Thumb Range, south Canterbury, 1,340 m (4,400 ft). January 1969. Dr I. Morice collected the fruiting plant from bogs on the terraces of Broken River, Canterbury, *ca* 800 m (2,500 ft). April 1968.

Gaultheria macrostigma (Col.) Middleton
"Large stigma".   PINK SNOWBERRY

(= *Pernettya macrostigma* Col.)

A freely branched, straggling shrub with interlacing wiry stems. Their thick, hard, shiny leaves are widely spaced and mostly confined to the younger branches.

Small white to pink flowers occur singly in the axils of the leaves. The style and large stigma usually persist in the pink fleshy fruits which are partly enclosed by the persistent fleshy calyx.

Because it crosses with some other species of *Gaultheria*, many populations of *G. macrostigma* show a range of leaf shapes and sometimes also of fruit colour. Only plants with narrow leaves and pink fruits are likely to be the true species.

DISTRIBUTION North, South and Stewart Islands: in the mountain regions from about Lake Taupo southwards. Mostly east of the main divide in the South Island but somewhat local in occurrence.

Montane to low-alpine: 500–1,500 m (1,500–5,000 ft).

HABITAT Rather inconspicuous on poorly drained even peaty areas of open scrub, tussock grasslands and bogs. In some areas it is quite abundant and when in fruit, one of the more colourful features of the vegetation.

COLLECTED Waihohonu, east Ruapehu, Tongariro National Park, *ca* 1,220 m (4,000 ft). March 1963. There is also a pink-fruited hybrid with *Gaultheria depressa* from Te Anau Downs, Eglinton Valley, Fiordland, *ca* 300 m (900 ft). May 1964.

Gaultheria nubicola Middleton
"Living in the clouds".

(= *Pernettya alpina* Franklin)

A creeping highly-branched shrub, usually with underground stems and small leafy tufts that form loose mats up to 1 m or more across. As in the other pernettyas, its leaves are thick, hard and shiny but their shape is distinctive.

Relatively large single flowers at or near the branch tips are white except for their pink lobes. Fruits remain small (3–4 mm across), green, and inconspicuous, at least until late autumn.

DISTRIBUTION South Island: widespread in the higher mountains.

Low- to high-alpine: 1,100–2,000 m (3,500–6,500 ft).

HABITAT Usually common in snowbank depressions and on exposed sites in fellfield. It descends into the low-alpine zone only on highly-exposed sites such as ridge crests where the tussock cover is usually short and thin.

COLLECTED Flowering plant from Rock & Pillar Range, Central Otago, 1,250 m (4,100 ft). December 1964. The fruiting plant is from Mt Brewster, Mt Aspiring National Park, 1,680 m (5,500 ft). March 1967.

The Epacris Family: EPACRIDACEAE

Genus EPACRIS
"On the top"—most species grow on mountain tops.

Contains about 50 species, chiefly Australian but also in Tasmania and New Caledonia.

Of the two native species, one reaches the alpine zone.

Epacris alpina Hook.f.
"Alpine".

A spreading or erect, slender, prickly shrub up to 1 m tall. The small, hard, pointed leaves are close-set and erect when young but become more distant and horizontal when older. They have a distinct midrib and thickened keel on the lower surface.

Small white flowers with 5 bright-red stamens occur singly in the axils of leaves and are usually abundant near the branch tips.

DISTRIBUTION North and South Islands: from Mt Tauhara (north end of Lake Taupo), southwards through the central volcanic mountains, the Kaimanawa and Ruahine Ranges. In the South Island its occurrence is quite scattered in the high rainfall north-western region, as far south as the Buller Valley.

Subalpine to low-alpine: 800–1,500 m (2,500–5,000 ft).

HABITAT It appears to require seasonally wet sites with very thin, acid or impoverished soil associated with granite, gneiss or pumice. At lower altitudes it occurs in open scrub or dwarf forest, but elsewhere it may be an important plant in mixed tussock-scrub.

COLLECTED Mt Ruapehu, Tongariro National Park, *ca* 910 m (3,000 ft). December.

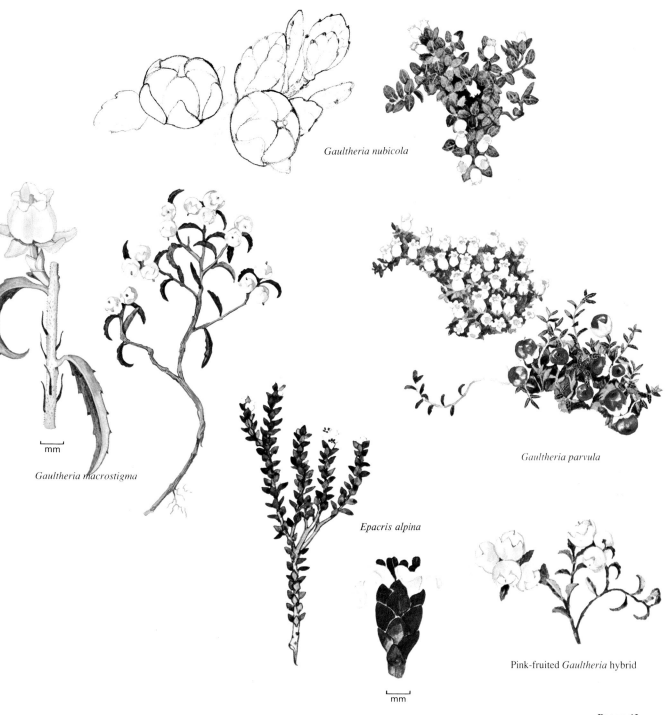

Gaultheria nubicola

Gaultheria macrostigma

Gaultheria parvula

Epacris alpina

Pink-fruited *Gaultheria* hybrid

mm

mm

cm

PLATE 43

Genus PENTACHONDRA

"Five seeds".

A small Australian genus. The single native species reaches the alpine zone.

Pentachondra pumila (J. R. & G. Forst.) R.Br.

"Very small".

A slender, much branched, creeping shrub that forms dark purplish patches 2–4 cm thick and up to 50 cm or more across. The small hard leaves are crowded on the branches and similar in colour above and below.

Very small tubular flowers occur singly near the branch tips and usually persist, somewhat withered, as the fruit develops. The lobes of the corolla are obviously furry as in *Cyathodes pumila*. By late autumn the fruits are only small, green and immature but in the following season they mature into prominent, bright-red, oval fruits which look deceptively fleshy but instead are rather thin-skinned and dry. Five (to 10) small hard seeds are loose inside.

DISTRIBUTION North, South and Stewart Islands: from the Coromandel Peninsula southwards, but rare to the north of East Cape. Common on the volcanic plateau and in most mountain regions further south.

Mostly subalpine to low-alpine: 600–1,500 m (2,000–5,000 ft).

HABITAT Often important in cushion bog (herb moor) and open snow tussock grassland or herbfield, either on exposed or rocky sites where the soil is thin, or on poorly drained, even peaty sites. It may be present under open subalpine scrub as in the mineral belt of Nelson and north-western Otago.

COLLECTED Rock & Pillar Range, Central Otago, 1,220 m (4,000 ft). December 1969.

Genus CYATHODES

"Cup-like"—referring to the disc in which the flower sits.

Contains numerous species from Malaysia and Australasia. Four of the eight native ones reach the alpine zone.

Cyathodes pumila Hook.f.

"Very small".

The habit is quite similar to *Pentachondra pumila*; the two are often confused, yet are easily distinguished since the leaves of *Cyathodes* are distinctly whitish beneath except for their margins and midrib.

The single tubular flower shows the many small, overlapping, leafy bracts around the base and the obviously furry lobes of the corolla. Unlike *Pentachondra*, the bright-red fruits are quite fleshy and smaller.

DISTRIBUTION North and South Islands: Kaimanawa and Ruahine Ranges; widespread in mountain regions of the South Island.

Subalpine to low-alpine: 800–1,600 m (2,500–5,500 ft).

HABITAT Generally very similar to *Pentachondra*; the two often occur together, but because of their similar appearance from above they are not always distinguished by the casual observer.

COLLECTED Flowering plant from Mt Brewster, Haast Pass, Mt Aspiring National Park, 1,310 m (4,300 ft). March 1968. The fruiting plant came from Arthurs Pass, Arthurs Pass National Park, 910 m (3,000 ft). April 1962.

Cyathodes empetrifolia Hook.f.

"With leaves like *Empetrum*"—Crow Berry, a Northern Hemisphere and Andean moorland shrub.

A creeping or trailing, almost prickly shrub with long (to 40 cm), slender, wiry branches. The small, narrow, hard leaves have down-turned margins and are pale to glaucous beneath.

Minute white flowers occur along the branches and/or at the tips, either singly or in clusters of 2–4. Developing fruits are green and inconspicuous but when ripe are red and fleshy.

DISTRIBUTION North, South and Stewart Islands: widespread in mountain regions but its habitat preference restricts the occurrence.

Mostly subalpine to low-alpine: 600–1,300 m (2,000–4,500 ft).

HABITAT On open, usually poorly drained sites on acidic, impoverished or very thin, often peaty soils in scrub, tussock grassland, herbfield or bog. It is also prominent on the mineral belt in Nelson–Marlborough and north-western Otago.

COLLECTED Maungatua, eastern Otago, 880 m (2,900 ft). March 1970.

Genus LEUCOPOGON

"White-beard" — referring to the hairy petals.

A large Australasian genus of some 130 species. Of the six indigenous species two reach the alpine zone.

Leucopogon fraseri A. Cunn.

After Mr C. Fraser, Superintendent of Sydney Botanic Gardens.

A distinctive, low-growing or prostrate, almost prickly shrub with ascending wiry branches up to 15 cm tall. Its creeping underground stems allow it to form quite extensive open patches. The small, hard, bronze-green leaves have a prominent sharp tip and they remain erect, almost enclosing the stem.

The small flowers have obvious bearded lobes at the top of the white tubular corolla, while the sweet, juicy, orange (to yellow) fruits with persistent styles are also distinctive.

DISTRIBUTION North, South and Stewart Islands: widespread throughout.

Coastal to low-alpine: to 1,600 m (5,500 ft).

HABITAT Usually common on open well-drained sites. In alpine areas it is most important in tussock grasslands of the drier regions east of the main divide, but in high rainfall areas it may be present on very well-drained, open sites such as the gravels of moraines or riverbeds. It also tolerates the ultrabasic soils of the mineral belt in Nelson–Marlborough and north-western Otago.

COLLECTED Both the flowering and fruiting plants from the Hooker Valley, Mt Cook National Park, 910 m (3,000 ft). November 1967 (flowering plant); March 1968 (fruiting).

Pentachondra pumila

Cyathodes empetrifolia

Leucopogon colensoi

mm

Cyathodes pumila

Leucopogon fraseri

cm

PLATE 44

Leucopogon colensoi Hook.f. *(See plate 44)*
"Fragrant".

A much stouter shrub than the other cyathodes, trailing or spreading to form large patches up to 2 m across, with upright branches reaching to 40 cm. The rigid leaves are a characteristic shape, shiny above but pale to glaucous below with 3–5 prominent veins and down-turned margins.

Flowers are in small clusters of 2–5 at the branch tips. Their white tubular corollas are only 4–5 mm long with the upper surface of their 5 lobes obviously hairy. Although male and female parts are present in all flowers there are size differences in them between plants so that they function as either male or female. Only females bear fruit which begin small and inconspicuous but when ripe are larger (4–5 mm across) and may range from white through pink and red to deep crimson.

DISTRIBUTION North and South Islands: volcanic plateau, Kaimanawa Mountains and Ruahine Range; in the South Island it is fairly widespread on the drier mountains—eastern Nelson, Marlborough, Canterbury, rather local in Otago and rare in northern Southland.

Montane to low-alpine: 600–1,600 m (2,000–5,000 ft).

HABITAT On well-drained sites, including rock outcrops in mixed tussock-scrub or snow tussock grassland. The large size of some patches can make a significant feature of the plant cover and the usually dull foliage sometimes takes on much stronger colours, especially on the volcanic plateau.

COLLECTED The Wilderness, Te Anau, *ca* 300 m (1,000 ft). January 1966.

Genus **DRACOPHYLLUM**

"Dragon leaf"—referring to a resemblance of the leaves to those of *Dracaena*, the dragon tree of Teneriffe.

Contains about 50 species from Australasia and New Caledonia. Of the 32 on the New Zealand mainland almost half reach the alpine zone. There may be some difficulty in identifying certain plants or populations due to variation caused in part by hybridism.

Dracophyllum longifolium (J. R. & G. Forst.) R.Br.   INAKA
"Long-leaved".

A highly variable shrub or small tree, reaching 12 m but usually < 1.5 m in the alpine zone. The smaller branches are slender and erect with a tuft of stiff leaves near their tips. Leaves are 10–25 cm long, gradually tapered from the base (2–5 mm wide) to a sharp-pointed tip.

From 6–15 flowers occur in one or a few prominent clusters near the base of the leafy tufts.

DISTRIBUTION North, South and Stewart Islands: rather widespread in the mountain regions from about East Cape southwards, but more common in the high rainfall areas of the South and Stewart Islands.

Coastal to low-alpine: to 1,200 m (4,000 ft).

HABITAT In open forests, especially along the coastal fringe (in Fiordland) and near the tree line. Often important in subalpine scrub, usually extending some distance above the tree line into mixed snow tussock-scrub, especially on poorly drained or peaty sites. These are extensive on the uplands in eastern Otago (Maungatua, Blue Mountains), Southland (Longwood Range) and Stewart Island.

COLLECTED Maungatua, eastern Otago, 880 m (2,900 ft). December 1970.

Dracophyllum uniflorum Hook.f.   TURPENTINE SHRUB
"Single-flowered".

A rather stout, erect, much-branched shrub up to 1 m tall with dark reddish-brown bark. The slender leafy branches are erect with tufts of overlapping leaves near their tips. Sharp-pointed leaves are thick and rigid with a broad sheath and narrow, tapering, partly rolled blade, 1.5–2 cm long.

Flowers occur singly at the tips of small branches.

DISTRIBUTION North and South Islands: Tararua Range; in the South Island it is widespread from eastern Nelson–Marlborough southwards, on both sides of the main divide.

Subalpine to low-alpine: 800–1,500 m (2,500–5,000 ft).

HABITAT One of the commonest and most widespread shrubs of the mixed snow tussock-scrub close to the tree line. It extends to higher altitudes in snow tussock-herbfield, especially on ridges and rock outcrops. Also prominent on the mineral belts in Nelson–Marlborough and north-western Otago.

COLLECTED Temple Basin track, Arthurs Pass National Park, 1,070 m (3,500 ft). January 1971.

*Dracophyllum rosmarinifolium (Forst.f.) R.Br.
"Rosemary-leaved".

Generally similar to *D. uniflorum* but altogether stouter yet somewhat shorter (to 60 cm) with the leafy branches usually more numerous. Also, the leaves may be longer (2–5 vs 1.5–3 cm), wider (1–3 vs 1–2 mm) and blunter at the tips.

Confined to south-western Otago, western Southland and Fiordland where it often occurs with *D. uniflorum*, at least up to 1,200 m (4,000 ft).

Dracophyllum acerosum Bergg.
"Sharp-leaved".

An erect shrub, 1–2 m tall, with grey bark and upright slender branches that are leafy only near their tips. The long (6–10 cm) very narrow (1–1.5 mm) leaves are also quite erect and sharp-pointed.

Flowers occur singly on very short stems usually just below the tuft of leaves.

DISTRIBUTION South Island: central Marlborough and Canterbury, as far south as the Rangitata Valley, on the drier mountains east of the main divide.

Montane to low-alpine: 600–1,200 m (2,000–4,000 ft).

HABITAT Sometimes an important member of subalpine scrub and mixed snow tussock-scrub, especially where the plant cover is depleted as in parts of the Broken River and Castle Hill basins, Canterbury.

COLLECTED Porters Pass, Torlesse Range, Canterbury, 1,070 m (3,500 ft). January 1968.

Dracophyllum longifolium

Dracophyllum acerosum

Dracophyllum uniflorum

Dracophyllum filifolium

mm

cm

PLATE 45

Dracophyllum filifolium Hook.f. *(See plate 45)*
"Very slender-leaved".

An erect, flexible, rather variable shrub, 1–2 m tall, with very slender, upright, leafy branches and dark greyish-brown rough bark. Leaves are 6–16 cm long, very narrow (up to 1 mm wide) and tapered to a very fine point.

From 4–9 flowers occur together on short slender branches near the base of the leafy tufts.

DISTRIBUTION North Island: Mt Egmont, the volcanic plateau, Kaimanawa Mountains, Ruahine and Tararua Ranges.

Montane to low-alpine: 600–1,400 m (2,000–4,500 ft).

HABITAT Usually widespread and conspicuous in subalpine scrub and mixed red tussock-scrub on the volcanic mountains; somewhat less important on the other ranges.

COLLECTED Tahurangi, Mt Egmont National Park, 1,400 m (4,600 ft). November 1967.

Dracophyllum menziesii Hook.f.   PINEAPPLE SCRUB
After Archibald Menzies, surgeon-naturalist on the *Discovery*, who first collected it.

A distinctive, low-growing to spreading, highly flexible shrub, usually <1 m tall. The broad, hard, tapered leaves (10–20 x 1.5–2 cm) are crowded near the tips of the branches, resembling the crown of a pineapple.

Rather large flowers are in 1–3 large clusters on stalks drooping below the crown of leaves which partly conceal them. In some plants the lobes of the corolla are red rather than white. Flower heads may occasionally develop above the leaves at the branch tips if stems have been damaged.

DISTRIBUTION South and Stewart Islands: south Westland, western Otago and Fiordland.

Subalpine to low-alpine: 600–1,400 m (2,000–4,500 ft).

HABITAT Isolated shrubs occur in open or short subalpine scrub, mixed snow tussock-scrub and snow tussock-herbfield. Low-growing or trailing plants may be important on steep avalanche chutes above and below the tree line, on south-facing slopes or in hollows where snow persists, and on rock bluffs.

COLLECTED Key Summit, Fiordland National Park, *ca* 1,070 m (3,500 ft). December 1964.

Dracophyllum recurvum Hook.f.
"Recurved"—referring to the leaves.

A low to prostrate but sometimes semi-erect shrub with wide-spreading branches covered with grey bark. The recurved, glaucous to dark reddish-brown leaves are distinctive. Hybridism with *D. longifolium* and *D. filifolium* produces some variable populations.

Flowers are also distinctive, 4–10 occurring in short dense spikes at the ends of the branches.

DISTRIBUTION North Island: on the central and eastern mountains— Mt Hikurangi, the central volcanoes, Kaimanawa Mountains, Ruahine Range.

Subalpine to high-alpine: 900–1,500 m (3,000–5,000 ft).

HABITAT A widespread and important plant of the central volcanic region, extending from open subalpine scrub through the red tussock grassland as a spreading or trailing shrub, and up into fellfield.

COLLECTED Whakapapanui Valley, Mt Ruapehu, Tongariro National Park, 1,220 m (4,000 ft). March 1963.

Dracophyllum kirkii Bergg.
After Mr T. Kirk, well known New Zealand botanist.

A small prostrate to sprawling shrub with stout, dark, reddish-brown branches. Broad, rather glaucous leaves are crowded on the branch tips. They vary in size on a single plant and also between populations, southern plants having distinctly narrower (*ca* 1.5 mm wide) and also shorter and less glaucous leaves than those near the northern end of its range (*ca* 4 mm wide). Populations near the centre of distribution are intermediate, as shown.

Flowers occur singly among the leaves on short branches.

DISTRIBUTION South Island: from north-west Nelson to north-west Otago, mostly in the high rainfall regions close to the main divide.

Low-alpine: 900–1,700 m (3,000–5,500 ft).

HABITAT It trails over steep exposed banks and rocky bluffs among higher altitude snow tussock-herbfield. Locally it may be an important plant.

COLLECTED Hooker Valley, Mt Cook National Park, 910 m (3,000 ft). November 1967.

Dracophyllum pubescens Cheesem.
"Covered with soft hairs".

A prostrate shrub with long, trailing or drooping, dark reddish-brown stems, and many short leafy branches. As in *D. kirkii* the leaves, although somewhat larger, taper gradually from the base to a sharp point. They are distinctive in being covered with greyish mealy pubescence, especially when young, that produces a pronounced glaucous bloom.

Most of the flowers are in small clusters of 3–5 at the branch tips, a feature distinguishing it from *D. kirkii*.

DISTRIBUTION South Island: the mountains of western Nelson, north Westland and the main divide southwards to near the Taramakau River.

Low-alpine: 1,200–1,500 m (4,000–5,000 ft).

HABITAT Drooping over steep banks, especially rocky bluffs, in rather sheltered areas.

COLLECTED Above Lake Sylvester, Cobb Valley, north-west Nelson, 1,460 m (4,800 ft). December 1967.

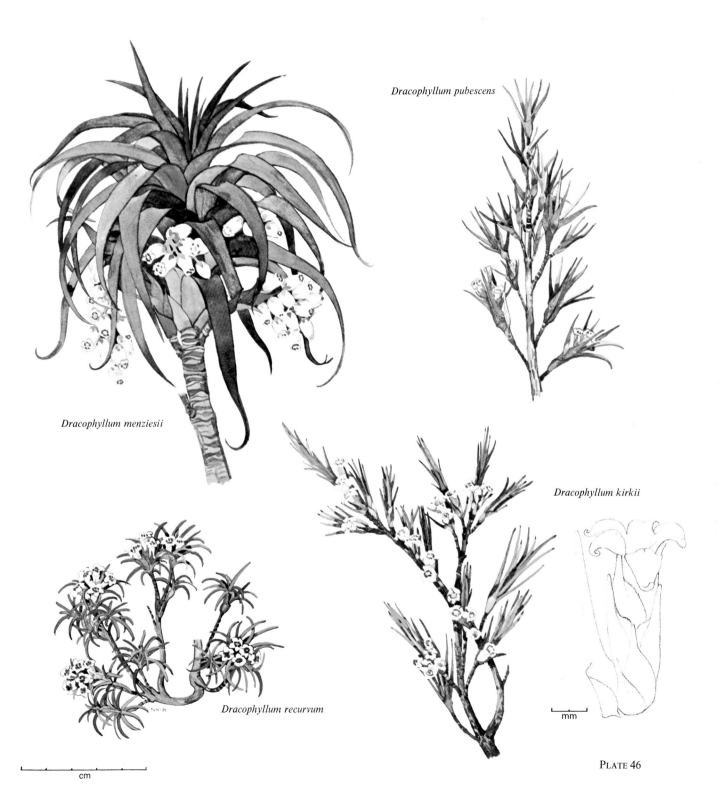

Dracophyllum pubescens

Dracophyllum menziesii

Dracophyllum kirkii

Dracophyllum recurvum

cm

mm

PLATE 46

Dracophyllum muscoides Hook.f.
"Moss-like".

The smallest species, with creeping branches, some underground, and slender, densely leafy, ascending branches up to 4 cm long that are usually tightly packed to form moss-like patches up to 60 cm across. The leaves are very small (2–3 mm long including the broad sheath) and overlapping to completely enclose the stem.

Flowers occur singly at the stem tips to be followed by an insignificant brown capsule.

DISTRIBUTION South Island: on the higher mountains of Central, northern and western Otago, extending into south Canterbury and also into south-eastern Fiordland.

Low- to high-alpine: 1,200–2,000 m (4,000–6,500 ft).

HABITAT Usually the most important member of the cushion vegetation on the extensive plateau summits in Central Otago. It also occupies well-drained sites in early snowbanks. In the other regions it colonises exposed ridge crests among snow-tussock grassland or herbfield.

COLLECTED Ohau Range, north-west Otago, 1,580 m (5,200 ft). January 1969.

Dracophyllum prostratum Kirk
"Prostrate"

A creeping or trailing shrub with stems up to 30 cm long and blackish-brown bark. The numerous, small, flexible branches, up to 4 cm long, are covered throughout by overlapping leaves since the dead ones persist near the base. A typical leaf (5–8 mm long) is shown.

Flowers occur singly at the branch tips and, although small, are quite prominent since they are not hidden by the leaves (cf. *D. politum*). Larger size, looser habit and longer, less densely overlapping leaves, together with the habitat, best distinguish it from *D. muscoides*.

DISTRIBUTION South Island: rather widespread on the mountains of south Canterbury, Otago, Southland and Fiordland.

Subalpine to low-alpine: 800–1,400 m (2,500–4,500 ft).

HABITAT Usually in sphagnum or cushion bogs (herb moor), but it may also occupy permanently wet hollows in snow tussock grassland or herbfield.

COLLECTED Key Summit, Fiordland National Park, 910 m (3,000 ft). January 1968.

Dracophyllum pronum W. R. B. Oliver
"Prostrate".

A semi-prostrate or trailing shrub, up to 50 cm tall, with stiff branches covered in rough grey bark. The smaller branches are reddish-brown with leaves only near their tips since dead ones do not persist.

Small scented flowers occur singly at the branch tips but, not being hidden by the leaves, they are quite prominent.

DISTRIBUTION South Island: almost throughout the mountain regions.

Low- to high-alpine: 800–1,800 m (2,500–6,000 ft).

HABITAT Often present in snow tussock grassland and herbfield but most common in depleted areas and on exposed ridges where it may form most of the cover. Also present on the mineral belt in Nelson.

COLLECTED Fog Peak, Torlesse Range, Canterbury, 1,520 m (5,000 ft). January 1970.

Dracophyllum politum W. R. B. Oliver
"Smooth, polished".

A prostrate shrub with short erect branches that may be so numerous as to form a dense mat or raised cushion up to 50 cm across. The closely overlapping and polished, reddish-brown leaves (8–10 mm long) completely enclose the stems and persist when dead.

Small single flowers at the branch tips are almost hidden by leaves.

DISTRIBUTION South and Stewart Islands: from Otago southwards.

Subalpine to low-alpine: 300–1,200 m (1,000–4,000 ft).

HABITAT Typically in cushion bogs (herb moor) where it may be abundant, often with *D. prostratum*. In Fiordland it also occurs locally as small cushions on exposed rocky ridges where plant cover is sparse.

COLLECTED Maungatua, eastern Otago, 880 m (2,900 ft). January 1970.

*Dracophyllum pearsonii Kirk
After Mr W. L. Pearson, who first collected it.

Generally similar to *D. politum*; branchlets in both being covered with reddish-brown leaves, but its habit is erect (up to 60 cm tall), its leaves straighter and longer (2–2.5 cm), and the flowers are in small groups of 3–6 near the branch tips.

It is confined to Fiordland and Stewart Island, there on exposed ridges both in snow tussock-herbfield and in open subalpine scrub on poorly drained sites between 300–1,000 m (1,000–3,500 ft).

The Logania Family: LOGANIACEAE

Genus MITRASACME
"Mitre Top"—referring to the resemblance of the two-lobed capsule to a bishop's mitre.

A genus of about 35 species from eastern Asia to Australasia. Both the native ones reach the alpine zone.

Mitrasacme novae-zelandiae Hook.f.
"Of New Zealand".

A glabrous herb that forms moss-like cushions up to *ca* 5 cm across. Slender upright stems are enclosed above by a tuft of small hard leaves, each with a distinct hair tip *ca* 1 mm long.

Minute but distinctive flowers occur singly at the stem tips almost hidden by the leaves and are followed by a dry 2-valved capsule.

DISTRIBUTION South and Stewart Islands: chiefly in the high rainfall areas, at least as far north as Arthurs Pass.

Montane to low-alpine: 300–1,400 m (1,000–4,500 ft).

Cont. on page 120

Dracophyllum pronum

Dracophyllum prostratum

Dracophyllum politum

mm

mm

Dracophyllum muscoides

Mitrasacme novae-zelandiae

mm

mm

cm

PLATE 47

HABITAT In cushion bogs (herb moor) but the small cushions are not often abundant. When not in flower or fruit they are easily mistaken for moss. It may occur locally in permanently wet, usually peaty depressions of snow tussock-herbfield.

COLLECTED Borland Saddle, Hunter Mountains, Fiordland National Park, 970 m (3,200 ft). January 1968.

Mitrasacme montana Hook.f.
"Growing in mountains".

Var. *helmsii* Kirk
After Mr R. Helms, who first collected it.

This variety of a Tasmanian species differs from *M. novae-zelandiae* in having blunt leaf tips. It occupies similar habitats but is confined to the Paparoa Range in north Westland.

The Myrsine Family: **MYRSINACEAE**

Genus **MYRSINE**
"Myrrh".

A large and widespread genus. All of the five mainland species are endemic but only one reaches the alpine zone.

Myrsine nummularia Hook.f.
"Coin-like"—referring to the leaves.

A small rambling shrub with slender reddish-brown stems up to 50 cm long. The thick almost round leaves have many small dark oil glands dotted over their surface and usually a dark patch near the base. Their edges are slightly down-turned and the midrib is prominent.

Minute flowers occur singly or in small clusters among the leaves. As the berries ripen they enlarge and change from green to violet-blue.

DISTRIBUTION North, South and Stewart Islands: rather widespread in the mountain regions from East Cape southwards, but absent from Mt Egmont and locally elsewhere.

Mostly montane to low-alpine: 600–1,500 m (2,000–5,000 ft).

HABITAT In sheltered sites especially on and around rock outcrops in tussock grassland, snow tussock-herbfield and open subalpine scrub.

COLLECTED Waihohonu, Mt Ruapehu, Tongariro National Park, 1,160 (3,800 ft). March 1963.

The Coffee Family: **RUBIACEAE**

Genus **COPROSMA**
"Dung-smell"—referring to the unpleasant smell of some species.

A genus of almost 100 species of the Malaysian and Pacific regions, about half of them from New Zealand. At least ten coprosmas reach the alpine zone.

Coprosma petriei Cheesem.
After Mr D. Petrie, early teacher and botanist, especially in Otago.

A creeping and taprooted sub-shrub, forming mats up to 1 m or more across. Stems are dark-brown but unlike *C. perpusilla* young branches and leaves are partly hairy except at the tip.

Flowers are similar to *C. perpusilla* except that they are at the branch tips. The shining fruits are larger, blue to whitish, almost translucent berries.

DISTRIBUTION North and South Islands: on the volcanic plateau; widespread but often local in the South Island as far south as Otago.

Montane to low-alpine: 300–1,600 m (1,000–5,500 ft).

HABITAT On open, well-drained or rocky sites in tussock grassland or on moraine or gravel river flats where it may form extensive mats.

COLLECTED Cass, mid-Canterbury, 610 m (2,000 ft). April 1963.

Coprosma atropurpurea (Ckn. & Allan) Moore
"Dark purple" — referring to the ripe fruits.

Generally similar to *C. petriei* apart from its distinctive berry colour and habitat. Leaves with a few stiff hairs on the margins and tip.

DISTRIBUTION South Island: widespread but more common in the east and north.

Lowland to low-alpine: 200–1,500 m (700–4,800 ft).

HABITAT Often local and sometimes abundant in cushion bogs, river beds, and open moist snow tussock grassland and shrubland, sometimes with *C. petriei*.

COLLECTED as for *C. petriei*, from Cass, mid-Canterbury, 610 m. April 1963.

Coprosma brunnea (Kirk) Ckn. ex Cheesem.
"Brownish"—referring to the bark.

A sprawling to prostrate shrub with brown, flexible, interlacing branches that form loose patches up to 1 m or more across. Among scrub it may reach 1 m or more in height, but on river beds and open stony sites it usually forms a wiry mat. The narrow leaves are rather sparse but paired or in opposite clusters.

Inconspicuous flowers occur singly among leaves along the branches and the berries which develop in the female plants ripen to translucent sky-blue or with pale-blue flecks.

DISTRIBUTION North, South and Stewart Islands: from the volcanic plateau southwards, although rather local or absent from some mountain areas, especially the Tararua Range and the drier regions of central and eastern South Island.

Lowland to low-alpine: to 1,500 m (5,000 ft).

HABITAT Often common on stony river beds and terraces. It may also occur in subalpine scrub and occasionally on open rocky sites in tussock-herbfield.

COLLECTED Avalanche Creek, Arthurs Pass National Park, 820 m (2,700 ft). April 1963.

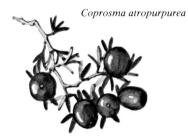

Coprosma atropurpurea

Myrsine nummularia

Coprosma petriei

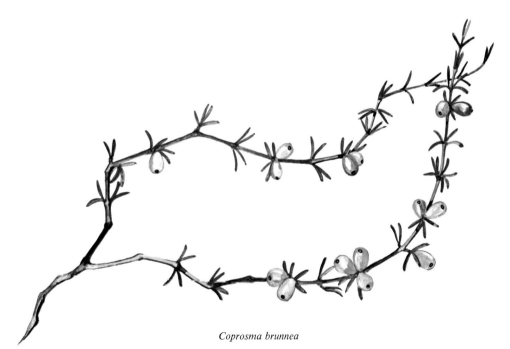

Coprosma brunnea

cm

PLATE 48

Coprosma cheesemanii W. R. B. Oliver
After Mr T. F. Cheeseman, well known New Zealand botanist.

A freely-branched sprawling shrub, up to 50 cm tall, with slender, hairy, greyish branches. The thick olive-green leaves are narrow (5–11 x 1–2 mm) except for being pointed at the tip. Only the mid-vein is obvious.

Flowers occur singly on the tips of short leafy branches and in female plants the berries ripen orange, but in a few areas plants may have white, yellow, pink, red or orange berries.

DISTRIBUTION North, South and Stewart Islands: from Mt Hikurangi southwards, but it seems to be somewhat local in occurrence.

Montane to low-alpine: 400–1,500 m (1,500–5,000 ft).

HABITAT On permanently damp, often peaty sites in tussock grassland or herbfield and open subalpine scrub.

COLLECTED Mt Ruapehu, Tongariro National Park, 1,220 m (4,000 ft). March 1963.

Coprosma depressa Col. ex Hook.f.
"Low-growing".

A low-growing or prostrate shrub with leaves (5–9 x 1–5 mm) narrowed to the petiole and to the rather blunt tip. Fruits are uniformly blood-red.

DISTRIBUTION North, South and Stewart Islands: widespread from Mt Hikurangi southwards.

Montane to low-alpine: 600–1,300 m (2,000–4,500 ft).

HABITAT On well-drained or rocky sites, often trailing over or around boulders.

COLLECTED By Dr I. Morice in the upper Otira Valley, Arthurs Pass National Park, *ca* 1,220 m (4,000 ft). April 1968.

Coprosma pseudocuneata W. R. B. Oliver
"Resembling *C. cuneata*"—from the Subantarctic Islands.

An erect to spreading or occasionally depressed shrub up to 2 m tall. Their stout grey branches have many short branchlets on which are clustered the very thick, leathery, dark-green leaves. The midrib is obvious only on the paler lower surface. Leaf size varies with the habitat but some North Island plants may have larger leaves than South Island plants.

Inconspicuous flowers occur singly on the tips of the leafy branchlets and on female plants, and the green oval berries ripen orange.

DISTRIBUTION North and South Islands: widespread in mountain regions from East Cape southwards, but not common in the driest regions of the South Island.

Subalpine to high-alpine: 700–1,800 m (2,000–6,000 ft).

HABITAT Usually abundant in subalpine forest and scrub, including open scrub of the mineral belt. Its importance decreases with altitude through the alpine zone but it can be found in most types of vegetation on stable, reasonably sheltered sites, especially on and between rock outcrops. The alpine form is considered to be a distinct species but it has not yet been formalised.

COLLECTED By Mr A. P. Druce from Mt Arthur, north-west Nelson. April 1963.

Coprosma crenulata W. R. B. Oliver
"Finely notched"—referring to the minute notching of the leaf margins.

A trailing shrub with long light-grey stems and many straw-coloured branchlets. Their leathery leaves have a characteristic shape with a distinct notch at the tip, a prominent midrib, thickened margins and a slightly foetid smell when bruised.

Flowers occur singly at the branch tips but are much less conspicuous than the round, shining, yellowish-red berries on female plants.

DISTRIBUTION South and Stewart Islands: in mountains of the high rainfall regions from central Nelson southwards.

Subalpine to low-alpine: 700–1,400 m (2,500–4,500 ft).

HABITAT Often common yet rather inconspicuous in open subalpine scrub, mixed snow tussock-scrub or herbfield on permanently damp, often peaty sites.

COLLECTED Temple Basin track, Arthurs Pass National Park, 1,160 m (3,800 ft). April 1957.

Coprosma crenulata

Coprosma cheesemanii

Coprosma depressa

Coprosma pseudocuneata

cm

PLATE 49

Coprosma serrulata Hook.f. ex Buchan.
"Minutely serrate"—referring to the leaf margins.

A handsome, erect or spreading, quite distinctive shrub, up to 1 m tall, with stout pale branches that may shed flakes of white bark. Broad, thick and leathery, the dark-green leaves are paler beneath. Their margins are slightly thickened and finely toothed with a distinct vein pattern on both surfaces.

In male plants several inconspicuous flowers occur together but in female plants they are single along the stem. Berries are relatively large, slightly oval and shining orange-red.

DISTRIBUTION South Island: widespread in the higher rainfall regions between north-west Nelson and southern Fiordland.

Subalpine to low-alpine: 800–1,500 m (2,500–5,000 ft).

HABITAT Often prominent on steep rocky bluffs in open subalpine scrub, mixed snow tussock-scrub and herbfield.

COLLECTED Twin Creeks, Arthurs Pass National Park, 910 m (3,000 ft). April 1963.

Coprosma perpusilla Col.
"Small".

A creeping and rooting glabrous herb with dark-brown to greyish branches up to *ca* 60 cm long and small, thick, almost fleshy leaves. The small funnel-shaped corolla is greenish and quite inconspicuous with 3–4 prominent stamens in male flowers or a long style with 3–4 branches in the female ones. Berries are shiny orange with 3–4 hard seeds.

DISTRIBUTION North, South and Stewart Islands: throughout the mountain regions from East Cape southwards.

Subalpine to high-alpine: 800–1,900 m (2,500–6,500 ft).

HABITAT Widespread on a range of permanently wet sites—tussock-herbfield, fellfield, cushion bog and snowbank. In the last two it may be plentiful as loose mats.

COLLECTED Tahurangi, Mt Egmont National Park, 1,460 m (4,800 ft). November 1967. A second plant (a) is from the upper Hollyford Valley, Fiordland National Park, *ca* 910 m (3,000 ft). January 1964.

*Coprosma niphophila Orchard
"Snow-loving" — referring to its habitat.

Generally similar to *C. perpusilla* apart from having two styles and fruits with only two seeds.

It is widespread but scattered in the South Island.

*Coprosma talbrockiei Moore & Mason
After H. Talbot and W. B. Brockie, who first collected it.

Generally similar to *C. atropurpurea* but with white fruits.

It is restricted to a small area in north-west Nelson, in cushion bogs.

Genus **NERTERA**
"Lowly"—referring to the habit.

Contains about 15 species from Malaysia, Central and South America, Tristan da Cunha and Australasia. Of the seven native nerteras, at least three reach the alpine zone.

Nertera balfouriana Ckn.
After Professor I. B. Balfour, keeper of the Edinburgh Botanic Garden.

A delicate, creeping and rooting, glabrous herb forming loose patches up to 25 cm or more across. Their slender almost fleshy stems have many small leaves in opposite pairs.

Fruits are often abundant and quite distinctive; bright-orange, 7–9 mm long and pear-shaped.

DISTRIBUTION North and South Islands: widespread yet apparently rather local from the Kaimanawa Mountains southwards to Foveaux Strait.

Coastal to low-alpine: to 1,400 m (4,500 ft).

HABITAT In sphagnum and cushion bogs where it may be common but quite inconspicuous unless fruiting. It often occurs among moss on permanently wet banks of streams.

COLLECTED Old Man Range, Central Otago, 1,340 m (4,400 ft). November 1969.

Nertera scapanioides Lange
"Resembling a spade"—referring to the leaf shape.

Rather more robust than *N. balfouriana*, with larger leaves that are partly hairy. Their fruits are pear-shaped and reddish-orange.

DISTRIBUTION North and South Islands: rather widespread in the wetter regions but as an alpine it is quite restricted: Ruahine Range; western Otago and Fiordland.

Lowland to low-alpine: to 1,200 m (4,000 ft).

HABITAT Usually in peat bogs or swamps often with sphagnum moss, but occasionally on damp banks in snow tussock-herbfield.

COLLECTED By Professor G. T. S. Baylis, Key Summit, Fiordland National Park, 910 m (3,000 ft). May 1965.

*Nertera depressa Banks & Sol. ex Gaertn.
"Low-growing".

Like *N. balfouriana* it is glabrous, but otherwise it more closely resembles *N. scapanioides* with its broad leaves. Their berries differ in being round, small (*ca* 4 mm across) and orange to red. Moreover, plants when bruised have a foetid smell.

DISTRIBUTION North, South and Stewart Islands: widespread in mountain regions.

Coastal to low-alpine: to 1,400 m (4,500 ft).

HABITAT More common on the forest floor than in the alpine zone but small mats occur on damp banks or permanently wet sites in snow tussock-herbfield.

Nertera scapanioides

Nertera balfouriana

Coprosma perpusilla

Coprosma serrulata

cm

PLATE 50

The Daisy Family: **ASTERACEAE**

Genus **CELMISIA**

From the Greek name Celmis, one of the attendants of Cybele, the Phrygian mother of the gods.

A large Australasian genus of more than 60 species, centred in New Zealand. More than 50 of the 60 celmisias described from the mainland reach the alpine zone. They rank with the snow tussocks as being among the most important and characteristic groups in the alpine vegetation. Their flower heads are distinctive yet rather uniform between species, but there is a remarkable assortment of vegetative forms and leaf shapes within the genus. Hybridism is widespread and several have been named, although they are not often common in the field.

Celmisia sessiliflora Hook.f.

"With sessile flowers".

A highly-branched sub-shrub forming dense, hard, greenish-grey cushions up to 1 m across. The thick rigid leaves (10–20 x 1.5–2.5 mm) are erect when young but later become reflexed.

Flower stems are very short so that the heads open among the leaves. They usually elongate (to 3–5 cm) as the fruits ripen.

DISTRIBUTION South and Stewart Islands: widespread in mountainous regions throughout.

Subalpine to high-alpine: 700–1,800 m (2,500–6,000 ft).

HABITAT Most important in short snow tussock-herbfield on permanently damp sites. It also occurs in cushion bogs, early snowbanks and on the less exposed sites in fellfield and cushion vegetation.

COLLECTED Old Man Range, Central Otago, 1,460 m (4,800 ft). January 1968.

Celmisia argentea Kirk

"Silvery".

The habit is similar to *C. sessiliflora* but the individual rosettes are smaller and more tightly packed, and the cushions more silvery. Its leaves are usually smaller (6–12 x 0.5–1.5 mm), as are the flower heads (1.5–2.5 vs 2–3 cm across) but as in *C. sessiliflora* they open among the leaves and the stalks elongate as the fruits ripen.

DISTRIBUTION South and Stewart Islands: from eastern and Central Otago southwards.

Mostly subalpine to high-alpine: 600–1,400 m (2,000–4,500 ft).

HABITAT Usually in cushion bogs (herb-moor) overlying peat, but on a few of the Central Otago ranges it occurs among other cushions on well-drained loess.

COLLECTED Maungatua, eastern Otago, 880 m (2,900 ft). January 1969.

Celmisia clavata Simpson & Thomson

"Club-shaped"—referring to the shape of the leafy branches.

It is similar to *C. argentea* except for the stems being highly divided near their tips to form terminal leafy branches that are distinctly club-shaped.

Confined to Stewart Island where it occurs in cushion bogs overlying peat.

Celmisia linearis J. B. Armst.

"Narrow and straight"—referring to the leaves.

A small tufted herb usually forming small patches. Being a hybrid, probably between *C. sessiliflora* and one of the larger species, it is variable and does not rank as a true species.

It is one of the commonest hybrids in the field, occurring usually with *C. sessiliflora* on poorly-drained often peaty areas, especially in cushion bogs, throughout much of the South Island and in Stewart Island.

COLLECTED Maungatua, eastern Otago, 880 m (2,900 ft). January 1969.

Celmisia philocremna D. R. Given

"Crag-loving".

A newly described and very distinctive sub-shrub that forms hard compact cushions up to 1 m across and 15 cm thick, quite unlike any other celmisia. Its small, very thick, leathery leaves (18 x 4 mm) are shining bright- to yellowish-green and almost glabrous above (except when young), with strongly recurved margins, while the lower surface is completely covered in soft, felt-like, pale-yellow tomentum.

Pale flower stalks reach 8–10 cm with many small, narrow, densely-woolly bracts that are tightly clustered in the bud and around the base of the flower head when it opens (to 3 cm across).

DISTRIBUTION South Island: apparently confined to a small area in the Eyre Mountains, northern Southland.

Low- to high-alpine: 900–1,600 m (3,000–5,500 ft).

HABITAT Locally common on steep exposed rock bluffs in snow tussock-herbfield and fellfield.

COLLECTED Upper Eyre Creek, Eyre Mountains, northern Southland, 1,400 m (4,600 ft). November 1969.

Celmisia sessiliflora

Celmisia argentea

Celmisia philocremna

Celmisia linearis

cm

PLATE 51

Celmisia alpina (Kirk) Cheesem.
"Alpine".

A very small tufted herb of similar habit to *C. gracilenta* but distinguished from small forms of it by the very narrow leaves (up to 5–30 x 1 mm). The leaves are thick, glabrous, grey-green and channelled above but white beneath except for the midrib. They are strongly recurved and distinctly pointed at their tips.

Flower stems are 3–5 cm long and their heads 1.5–2 cm across.
DISTRIBUTION South Island: apparently widespread.

Low-alpine: 900–1,500 m (3,000–5,000 ft).
HABITAT Confined to bogs where it may be abundant.
COLLECTED Arthurs Pass, Arthurs Pass National Park, 910 m (3,000 ft). January 1970.

Celmisia laricifolia Hook.f.
"Larch-leaved".

A slender highly-branched sub-shrub, 2–10 cm tall, that may form mats up to 50 cm or more across. Its small size and fine-pointed needle-shaped leaves (10–15 x 1–1.5 mm) with recurved margins are distinctive (except for *C. similis*). They are dark- or bronze-green above and white below.

The very slender flower stalks (5–10 cm long) are covered in soft white hairs and have a neat head (1–2 cm across).
DISTRIBUTION South Island: widespread in the mountain regions.

Subalpine to high-alpine: 700–1,900 m (2,500–6,500 ft).
HABITAT Usually present in most types of alpine vegetation except bogs. It trails or creeps when sheltered but forms low mats on exposed or high altitude sites, or where the taller cover has been depleted.
COLLECTED Rock & Pillar Range, Central Otago, 1,370 m (4,500 ft). December 1964.

*Celmisia similis D. R. Given
"Resembling"—*C. laricifolia*.

It differs from *C. laricifolia* in having stiffer slightly wider leaves with a silvery upper surface. They are more tightly clustered near the branch tips. Also, the flower stalks are darker.

Confined to north-west Nelson where both species occupy similar habitats.

Celmisia major Cheesem.
"Larger".

Var. brevis Allan
"Short, small"—compared with the lowland var. *major*.

A stout, tufted, woody-based herb with spreading leathery leaves, 10–15 cm long, gradually tapered to the tip. Their margins are recurved with the upper surface pale-green and the lower one covered with silvery-white tomentum.

Stout flower stems are shorter than the leaves with heads 2–3 cm across.
DISTRIBUTION North Island: confined to Mt Egmont.

Low- to high-alpine: 1,200–1,600 m (4,000–5,500 ft).
HABITAT Prominent in the red tussock-herbfield but extending beyond into snowbank depressions and on to the grey mossy herbfield of exposed sites where it is also conspicuous.
COLLECTED North slope, Mt Egmont National Park, 1,460 m (4,800 ft). November 1967.

Celmisia gracilenta Hook.f.
"Slender".

A rather variable, tufted, woody-based herb with 1 to few tufts together. The slender, flexible, greyish-green, usually mottled leaves (10–15 cm x 2–4 mm) have their edges recurved almost to the midrib which is prominent on the satiny-white tomentum covering the lower surface.

The 1 to few, slender, woolly to satiny flower stems (20–40 cm long) have a few small leafy bracts and a flower head 1.5–3 cm across.
DISTRIBUTION North, South and Stewart Islands: widespread from Coromandel Peninsula southwards.

Lowland to low-alpine: to 1,700 m (5,500 ft).
HABITAT A very wide range—open subalpine scrub, tussock grass-lands, herbfield, bogs, serpentine soils of the mineral belts in Marlborough-Nelson and north-western Otago. It is plentiful on the central volcanic plateau and among the valley grasslands of the South Island high rainfall regions.
COLLECTED Rock & Pillar Range, Central Otago, 1,220 m (4,000 ft). January 1969.

*Celmisia graminifolia Hook.f.
"Grassy-leaved".

The grassy habit and form are similar to *C. gracilenta*, with which it crosses, and the distinction is sometimes difficult to make. However, the leaves are usually broader (4–6 mm), sometimes longer (to 40 cm) and quite thin, with their margins flat or only slightly recurved. Both size and shape of leaves may vary on a plant. Also, the flower heads are usually larger.

Its distribution and habitats are generally similar to *C. gracilenta* but it is usually less common.

Celmisia bellidioides Hook.f.
"Resembling *Bellis*"—a genus containing the common lawn daisy.

A distinctive, creeping and rooting, much-branched, low herb. Stems end in small leafy rosettes that are usually loosely packed to form mats up to 1 m across. Small (8–12 x 3.5 mm), almost fleshy, bright-green, shining leaves are paler beneath but quite glabrous.

Only when in flower is it obviously a celmisia, with the slender purple flower stalk (*ca* 5 cm long) bearing many leafy bracts and a small head (2 cm across).
DISTRIBUTION South Island: widespread but rare in the drier regions.

Subalpine to high-alpine: 600–1,800 m (2,000–6,000 ft).
HABITAT Usually draped over permanently wet rocks, especially in cascading creeks and waterfalls, both above and below the tree line, but it may also be found creeping over shingle or moraine through which water is flowing.
COLLECTED Temple Basin, Arthurs Pass National Park, 1,340 m (4,400 ft). December 1967.

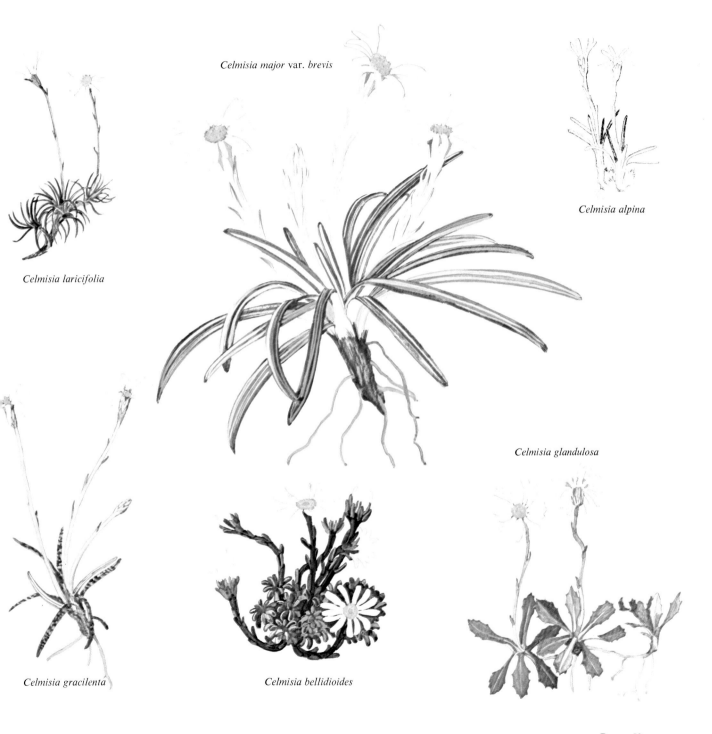

Celmisia laricifolia

Celmisia major var. brevis

Celmisia alpina

Celmisia glandulosa

Celmisia gracilenta

Celmisia bellidioides

cm

PLATE 52

*Celmisia thomsonii Cheesem.
After Mr W. A. Thomson, who first collected it.

It is similar to *C. bellidioides* except for being smaller and more compact although mats may reach 50 cm across. Leaves have a dull-green upper surface roughened with scattered fine hairs. Many plants have colourful pink flower heads.

DISTRIBUTION South Island: confined to the high-alpine zone in the central Eyre Mountains in northern Southland, where it occupies shady overhung rock ledges and crevices in fellfield.

Celmisia glandulosa Hook.f. (*See plate 52*)
"Bearing glands"—referring to the sticky glandular hairs.

A quite distinctive yet variable herb with branched creeping and rooting stems ending in small rosettes that produce loose patches up to 1 m or more across. The small (10–25 x 5–15 mm) sticky leaves are green all over but slightly paler beneath.

Slender sticky flower stalks (5–15 cm long) have a few small bracts and a small head (1.5–3 cm across).

Var. *glandulosa* is smaller (leaves 10–20 x 5–8 mm; flower stalks 5–10 cm) than the other two; var. *latifolia* Ckn., "broadleaved", is more robust (leaves 2–3 x 1–2 cm); while var. *longiscapa* Ckn., "long flower stalk", has a very slender erect stalk (12–20 cm long) and larger leaves (2–4 x 1–1.5 cm).

DISTRIBUTION North and South Islands: from the central volcanic mountains southwards, but rare or absent on the drier eastern ranges in the South Island. Var. *latifolia* is confined to the Mt Egmont region while var. *longiscapa* is in Fiordland.

Subalpine to low-alpine: 500–1,600 m (1,500–5,500 ft).

HABITAT In bogs and other permanently wet areas in snow tussock-herbfield, open subalpine scrub and valley grasslands.

COLLECTED Mt Brewster, Haast Pass, Mt Aspiring National Park, 1,430 m (4,700 ft). February 1968.

Celmisia discolor Hook.f.
"Of different colours"—referring to the two leaf surfaces.

A trailing or sprawling sub-shrub forming loose patches up to 1 m across. The leathery leaves form terminal tufts and vary in size (2–4 cm x 8–12 mm) and also somewhat in shape, but usually they have a thin covering of hairs above giving a greyish-green colour, and dense white tomentum below. Their margins are flat with a few fine teeth.

Slender pale flower stalks (10–15 cm long) are usually sticky with some white tomentum. There are several narrow bracts up to 2 cm long and a small head (2–3 cm across).

The species is somewhat variable, three varieties having been recognised: var. *intermedia* (Petrie) Allan, has smaller leaves (*ca* 15 x 6–10 mm) and flower heads (10–15 mm), while var. *ampla* Allan, has stouter stems, somewhat larger sticky leaves, and short (10 cm) flower stalks.

DISTRIBUTION South Island: widespread in mountain regions but rare or absent in the drier eastern regions and south of Westland. Var. *intermedia* occurs from Arthurs Pass south through Westland while var. *ampla* is widespread.

Subalpine to low-alpine: 1,000–1,700 m (3,500–5,500 ft).

HABITAT Its loose patches occupy openings of subalpine forest and open areas of mixed snow tussock-scrub or herbfield. In north Canterbury and Nelson it is often prominent in mixed carpet grass-snow tussock-herbfield.

COLLECTED Var. *intermedia* from the Temple Basin track, Arthurs Pass National Park, 1,070 m (3,500 ft). December 1967.

Celmisia allanii Martin
After Dr H. H. Allan, well-known New Zealand botanist.

Its habit and leaf shape are similar to *C. discolor* but the leaves are larger (3–6 x 1–1.5 cm), thinner and softer, being distinctively covered both above and below in fluffy white hairs, the upper surface being pale-grey and the lower one snow-white.

Flower stalks may be similarly hairy or almost glabrous, up to 25 cm long, but otherwise much as shown for *C. discolor*.

DISTRIBUTION South Island: Nelson and north-west Canterbury.

Low-alpine: 1,300–1,700 m (4,500–5,500 ft).

HABITAT Often common on snow hollows but it may also occur in open snow tussock-herbfield.

COLLECTED Above Lake Sylvester, Cobb Valley, north-west Nelson, 1,520 m (5,000 ft). December 1967.

Celmisia incana Hook.f.
"Hoary"—referring to the colour of the plant.

The habit is similar to *C. discolor* but the leaves (2–4 x 1–1.5 cm) are pale grey to white on both surfaces. They differ from *C. allanii* in being woolly only on the lower surface and in their leathery texture.

Flower stalks are short (*ca* 10 cm) with soft white hairs and a prominent head (2.5–3.5 cm across).

DISTRIBUTION North and South Islands: from Coromandel (Te Moehau) and East Cape (Mt Hikurangi) southwards through the central volcanic mountains, Ruahine and Tararua Ranges; on the mountains of eastern Nelson, Marlborough and Canterbury.

Subalpine to high-alpine: 900–2,000 m (3,000–6,500 ft).

HABITAT In a wide range of well-drained sites—open subalpine scrub, mixed tussock-scrub, tussock-herbfield, fellfield and rock outcrops. It is the common celmisia on the central volcanoes.

COLLECTED Whakapapanui Valley, Mt Ruapehu, Tongariro National Park, *ca* 1,460 m (4,800 ft). December 1969.

*Celmisia sinclairii Hook.f.
After Dr A. Sinclair, who first collected it.

A small low-growing sub-shrub easily distinguished from *C. discolor* and the several others with this habit by their broad, thin, bright-green leaves (5–7 x 1.5 cm) that are quite glabrous. There is a striking but superficial resemblance to *C. prorepens* from Central Otago.

DISTRIBUTION South Island: eastern Nelson and western Marlborough.

Subalpine to low-alpine: 900–1,700 m (3,000–5,500 ft).

HABITAT On damp, often peaty sites in tussock grassland, herbfield and fellfield.

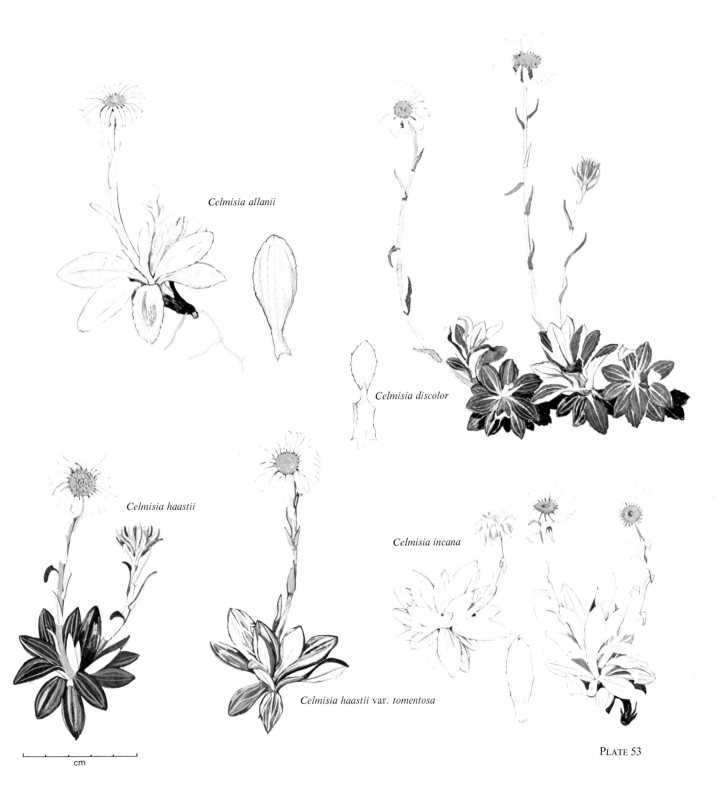

Celmisia allanii

Celmisia discolor

Celmisia haastii

Celmisia incana

Celmisia haastii var. *tomentosa*

cm

PLATE 53

Celmisia haastii Hook.f.
After Sir Julius von Haast, famous geologist and explorer.

A low-growing branching sub-shrub with very short erect stems that form diffuse patches up to 1 m or more across. The leaves (3–8 x 1–2 cm) in terminal tufts, are pale-green, glabrous and grooved above, but covered in fine greyish tomentum beneath except for the prominent midrib. The margins are down-turned and almost smooth.

Flower stems (5–15 cm long) are usually hairy with several narrow bracts and a prominent head (2.5–4 cm across).

Var. *tomentosa* Simpson & Thomson, "covered with tomentum", differs only in having a thin white tomentum on the upper surface of the leaf.

DISTRIBUTION South Island: widespread on the higher mountains. Var. *tomentosa* is confined to Rock & Pillar Range, Central Otago.
Low- to high-alpine: 1,200–2,000 m (4,000–6,500 ft).

HABITAT Usually common in permanently moist, sheltered, cold sites near the upper limit of short snow tussock-herbfield and in snowbanks where it is usually prominent.

COLLECTED Old Man Range, Central Otago, 1,520 m (5,000 ft). November 1969. Var. *tomentosa* is from Rock & Pillar Range, 1,370 m (4,500 ft). December 1964.

Celmisia ramulosa Hook.f.
"With small branches".

A highly-branched trailing to erect shrub, up to 30 cm tall, with stout stiff branches densely covered with overlapping leaves. Stiff narrow leaves (5–10 x 1–2 mm) have blunt tips, strongly recurved margins and a white tomentose lower surface.

Slender flower stalks on the ends of the branches are 1–4 cm long with a few small narrow bracts and a head 2–2.5 cm across.

Var. *tuberculata* Simpson & Thomson, "Warty", has the upper surface of the leaves studded with minute pimple-like processes (seen only with a good lens). Also, the leaves are more erect along the stem.

DISTRIBUTION South Island: widespread on the mountains of Central Otago (var. *tuberculata* only), western Otago, Southland and Fiordland.
Low-alpine: 1,000–1,400 m (3,000–4,500 ft).
Var. *tuberculata* is mostly high-alpine: 1,200–1,800 m (4,000–6,000 ft).

HABITAT Var. *ramulosa* often drapes over rock outcrops or steep bluffs but also occurs on open or rocky sites in snow tussock-herbfield. Var. *tuberculata* grows on the more sheltered sites in cushion vegetation and dwarfed herbfield.

COLLECTED Var. *tuberculata* from Rock & Pillar Range, Central Otago, 1,370 m (4,500 ft). December 1964.

Celmisia hectorii Hook.f.
After Sir James Hector, geologist and explorer.

A highly-branched silvery sub-shrub with short erect branches that form low patches or carpets up to 1 m or more across. The distinctively shaped leaves (15–20 x 5–8 mm) form a rosette at the branch tips. They are covered with tomentum on both surfaces, usually silvery above but whitish beneath, while the margins are slightly recurved.

Densely-hairy flower stalks (4–10 cm long) are rather stout, with several narrow leafy bracts and a head 2–3 cm across.

DISTRIBUTION South Island: in the high rainfall regions between the Mt Cook district and southern Fiordland, extending eastwards to the Otago Lakes district and western Southland.
Low- to high-alpine: 1,300–2,000 m (4,500–6,500 ft).

HABITAT Usually one of the most prominent plants of both fellfield and snowbanks. In the low-alpine zone it is restricted to snow hollows and exposed rocky sites.

COLLECTED Homer Saddle, Fiordland National Park, 1,220 m (4,000 ft). January 1968.

Celmisia lateralis Buchan.
"Lateral"—referring to the position of the flower stalks.

A distinctive trailing or scrambling shrub with branched stems up to 30 cm long, sometimes forming compact patches. The small narrow leaves (6–10 x 1–1.5 mm) are green on both surfaces and scattered along the stems.

Slender flower stalks (4–8 cm long) have a few small leafy bracts and a small head (1–2 cm across).

Var. *villosa* Cheesem., "hairy", differs in having the leaves and flower stalks covered in glandular hairs.

DISTRIBUTION South Island: western Nelson, as far south as the Paparoa Range in north Westland; var. *villosa* is restricted to north-west Nelson.
Low-alpine: 1,000–1,500 m (3,000–5,000 ft).

HABITAT Often locally common and prominent on rock outcrops, but inconspicuous in snow tussock-herbfield.

COLLECTED Travers Range, Nelson Lakes National Park, 1,220 m (4,000 ft). December 1967.

Celmisia brevifolia Ckn. ex Cheesem.
"Short-leaved".

A sprawling much-branched shrub with erect stems that form small clumps up to 20 cm tall. Living leaves are spread along the younger branches. The leathery blades are short and broad (10–20 x 6–9 mm), rounded at the tip, green and sticky above but with soft white tomentum beneath. Their midrib is usually obvious beneath while the margins are slightly recurved and with a few minute teeth.

Slender sticky flower stems (4–8 cm long) have a few narrow bracts and a small head (2–3 cm across).

DISTRIBUTION South Island: close to the main divide from about the Mt Cook district to western Otago, and eastwards into northern Southland, Central Otago and the Lakes district.
Low- to high alpine: 900–1,900 m (3,000–6,500 ft).

HABITAT In Central Otago and the Lakes district shrubs are scattered through herbfield and the most sheltered sites in cushion vegetation but further west they are much less common, chiefly in short snow tussock-herbfield on cold, usually rocky sites.

COLLECTED Old Man Range, Central Otago, 1,610 m (5,300 ft). January 1968.

Celmisia ramulosa

Celmisia brevifolia

Celmisia lateralis

Celmisia hectorii

cm

PLATE 54

Celmisia walkeri Kirk
After Capt. J. C. Walker, with whom Kirk first collected it.

A trailing or sprawling, sparingly-branched shrub with stems up to 1 m or more long. Slightly sticky leaves (2–5 cm x 3–5 mm) enclose the branches. Their upper surface is glabrous but white tomentum covers the lower surface except for the narrow midrib, while the margins are smooth, straight and flat or slightly recurved.

Sticky green flower stems (5–10 cm long) arise at the branch tips and have several small narrow bracts and a head 2–4 cm across.

DISTRIBUTION South Island: in the high rainfall regions close to the main divide from southern Nelson to Fiordland.

Subalpine to low-alpine: 900–1,600 m (3,000–5,500 ft).

HABITAT Often present in snow tussock-herbfield and prominent at higher altitudes, on rock outcrops, steep banks subject to snow-slides, or where it has been favoured by heavy grazing. It may establish under open subalpine scrub and beside avalanche chutes near the tree line.

COLLECTED Mt Brewster, Haast Pass, Mt Aspiring National Park, 1,280 m (4,200 ft). February 1969.

Celmisia rupestris Cheesem.
"Growing on rocks".

A trailing or straggling shrub with stems up to 1 m long. It is generally similar to *C. walkeri* but smaller in all its parts, with narrower leaves that have their margins obviously recurved and are covered both above and below in soft white tomentum.

It is confined to the low-alpine zone: 1,100–1,500 m (3,500–5,000 ft) in north-west Nelson where it occurs on rocky sites, especially ravines and outcrops, in snow tussock-herbfield.

Celmisia gibbsii Cheesem.
After Mr F. G. Gibbs, early collector in Nelson.

Its habit is also similar to *C. walkeri* but stems are shorter and less branched. Their leaves are shorter and narrower (10–20 x 2–3.5 mm), pale-green and glabrous above with the midrib sunken, and almost glabrous beneath.

DISTRIBUTION and HABITAT generally similar to *C. rupestris*.

Celmisia angustifolia Ckn.
"Narrow-leaved"—not very appropriate since many celmisias have narrower ones.

A small, occasionally-branched, sprawling shrub with the living leaves only near the branch tips. They are leathery (3–5 cm x 2–6 mm), usually with flat but wavy margins that have a few minute teeth. Their upper surface is usually green and sticky with soft white tomentum below except for the midrib, but the amount of tomentum varies—Two Thumb Range plants usually have both surfaces except for the margins covered, while Dalgety Range plants may have 3–5 veins uncovered on the lower surface.

Flower stalks (up to 15 cm long) are slender and sticky but not woolly, with a few small leafy bracts and a prominent head (3–4 cm across).

DISTRIBUTION South Island: east of the main divide from mid-Canterbury to north Otago.

Low-alpine: 1,000–1,500 m (3,000–5,000 ft).

HABITAT In the drier regions it usually occupies cold slopes in snow tussock grassland where it is encouraged by heavy grazing. Where it meets *C. walkeri* near the main divide it prefers rocky sites including large outcrops.

COLLECTED Hooker Valley, Mt Cook National Park, 910 m (3,000 ft). January 1969.

Celmisia durietzii Ckn. & Allan ex Martin
After Dr G. E. Du Rietz, eminent Swedish botanist.

A highly-variable sub-shrub occurring as single rosettes or with several forming loose patches up to 1 m across. It is best characterised by the thin, elongated, usually sticky leaves (3–6 cm x 7–10 mm) whose upper surface is both glabrous and smooth. Their lower surface except for the midrib is covered with soft white tomentum.

Flower stalks are glabrous and typically purple (5–25 cm long) with a prominent head (3–4 cm across).

DISTRIBUTION South and Stewart Islands: widespread in the mountains of the higher rainfall regions.

Montane to high-alpine: 600–1,900 m (2,000–6,500 ft).

HABITAT Typically a plant of rock outcrops: in valley grassland, open subalpine scrub and throughout the alpine zone where it is often conspicuous. Small patches may occur in open vegetation or on exposed rocky sites, while on Stewart Island a thicker-leaved form is prominent in the wet peaty grassland and herb moor.

COLLECTED Homer Tunnel, Fiordland National Park, 940 m (3,100 ft). January 1968.

Celmisia bonplandii (Buchan.) Allan
After Mt Bonpland, where it was first collected.

A low-growing shrub that forms loose patches up to 50 cm across. The broad sticky leaves (5–10 x 1.5–3 cm) are in tufts at the branch tips. Their upper surface is glabrous and shining dark-green while beneath is white tomentum, but characteristically the midrib, petiole and broad sheath enclosing the stem are all deep purple (often useful to distinguish small forms of it from *C. durietzii*).

Flower stalks are also purple (15–30 cm long) with several narrow bracts and a large head (3–5 cm across).

DISTRIBUTION South Island: western Otago—Southland and Fiordland.

Subalpine to high-alpine: 900–1,700 m (3,000–5,500 ft).

HABITAT Usually on rock outcrops in snow tussock-herbfield or subalpine scrub but smaller forms occur on rocky sites where the tussock cover is thin and sometimes in fellfield, usually with *C. durietzii*.

COLLECTED Homer Tunnel, Fiordland National Park, 1,070 m (3,500 ft). January 1968.

Celmisia walkeri

Celmisia angustifolia

Celmisia durietzii

Celmisia bonplandıı

PLATE 55

cm

Celmisia viscosa Hook.f.
"Sticky"—referring particularly to the flower stalks.

A low-growing and highly-branched sub-shrub with short erect branches that form extensive patches up to 2 m or more across. The narrow leaves (6–15 cm x 6–9 mm), confined to the branch tips, are very thick and rigid. Their upper surface is distinctly grooved and usually dull-green and glabrous but occasional plants are quite pale; there is a soft white tomentum beneath with obvious grooves but no midrib.

Stout flower stems (15–30 cm long) and their several narrow bracts are covered with sticky hairs while the relatively large head (3–4 cm across) may have pink-tinted tips to the florets before it opens.

DISTRIBUTION South Island: east of the main divide from Marlborough-Nelson to Southland and eastern Fiordland but rather local and unimportant in the high rainfall regions and in the far north and far south of its range.

Low- to high-alpine: 1,200–1,800 m (4,000–6,000 ft).

HABITAT Usually present in higher altitude snow tussock grassland and fellfield of the drier eastern mountains. In some depleted or overgrazed areas it has become a feature of the present cover, especially in Central Otago.

COLLECTED Old Man Range, Central Otago, 1,520 m (5,000 ft). December 1969.

Celmisia macmahonii Kirk
After Mr J. H. Macmahon, who first collected it.

A very distinctive small sub-shrub with branched stems that form cushions up to 40 cm across. Leaves in tufts at the branch tips are narrow (20–35 x 6–8 mm) and densely covered with silvery to buff silky hairs that turn brown when dried.

Flower stalks (8–12 cm long) and their several narrow bracts have similar silky tomentum, with a small head (2–2.5 cm across).

Var. *hadfieldii* Martin after Mr J. H. Hadfield, forms very tight cushions and has narrower (4–5 mm) rigid leaves.

DISTRIBUTION South Island: confined to Mt Stokes, east of Pelorus Sound in Marlborough while var. *hadfieldii* is further south on the Richmond Range.

Mostly low-alpine: 1,000–1,700 m (3,000–5,500 ft).

HABITAT Apparently confined to rock crevices.

Celmisia inaccessa D. R. Given
Referring to its preference for rock faces.

A low, spreading, almost glabrous sub-shrub forming loose patches up to 1 m or more across. Their crisp bright-green leaves (2–6 x 1–2 cm) have very finely toothed margins and obvious veins.

Flower stalks, *ca* 15 cm long, have several leafy bracts and a head *ca* 4 cm across.

DISTRIBUTION South Island: confined to a few sites in central Fiordland.

Low-alpine: 900–1,100 m (3,000–3,500 ft).

HABITAT This distinctive celmisia is restricted to moist shady bluffs and debris on limestone or marble.

COLLECTED Above Lake Wapiti, upper Doon Valley, Fiordland National Park, 1,070 m (3,500 ft). December 1970.

Celmisia densiflora Hook.f.
"Dense-flowered"—referring to the florets in the head.

A tufted plant with single rosettes but more often the stock is branched to form loose patches up to 1 m or more across. The thick, sometimes sticky leaves (6–15 x 1.5–3 cm) are glabrous above but have dense white tomentum beneath except for the prominent midrib. Their margins are slightly wavy and faintly toothed.

Stout flower stalks (15–30 cm long) are usually purple, glabrous and sticky with a few narrow leafy bracts and a prominent head (2.5–4 cm across).

DISTRIBUTION South Island: mostly in the medium rainfall areas of the interior from north Canterbury to Southland, but rare and local north of Otago.

Subalpine to high-alpine: 400–1,700 m (1,500–5,500 ft).

HABITAT Usually on well-drained sites, including rock outcrops, in the tussock grasslands, herbfield and occasionally in fellfield.

COLLECTED Ohau Range, north-west Otago, 1,160 m (3,800 ft). January 1969.

Celmisia prorepens Petrie
"Creeping".

This resembles *C. densiflora* except that the leaves are green and sticky on both surfaces, usually somewhat smaller and distinctly wrinkled. Also, it occurs regularly as patches.

DISTRIBUTION South Island: from eastern through Central Otago to the southern part of the Lakes district.

Subalpine to high-alpine: 600–1,800 m (2,000–6,000 ft).

HABITAT It prefers permanently moist situations in snow tussock grassland but extends into the high-alpine zone on sheltered sites around the edges of snowbanks. Plants intergrading with *C. densiflora*, especially in leaf colour, often occur in localities where both are present.

COLLECTED Old Man Range, Central Otago, 1,370 m (4,500 ft). December 1968.

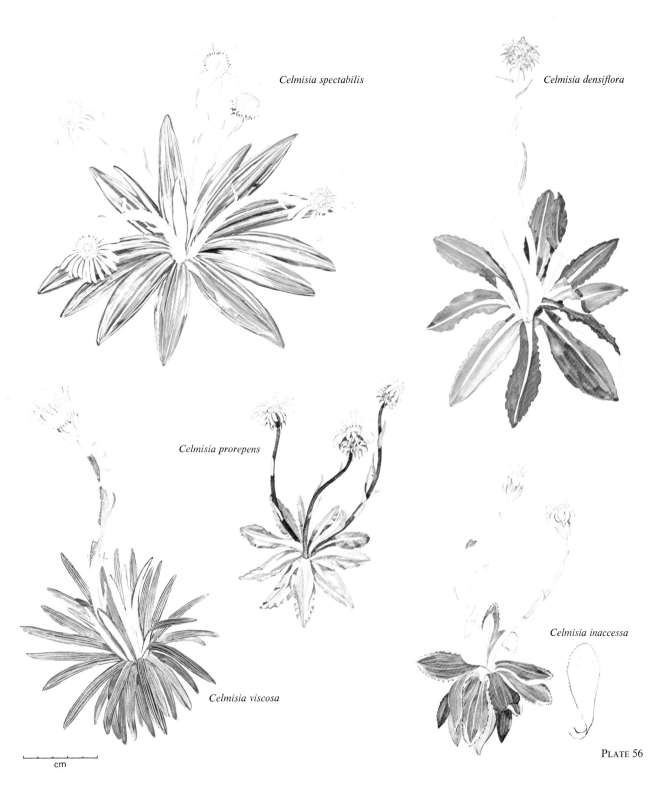

Celmisia spectabilis

Celmisia densiflora

Celmisia prorepens

Celmisia viscosa

Celmisia inaccessa

cm

PLATE 56

Celmisia holosericea (Forst.f.) Hook.f.
"Silky".

A large tufted herb, often with several tufts together in a clump. Their large leathery leaves (15–30 x 3–6 cm) are glabrous and shining above but have dense white tomentum below except for the midrib. Their margins are minutely toothed.

Flower stalks (20–50 cm) carry a large head (5–7 cm across) that is enclosed in the bud by many bracts, the outer series having white tomentum.

DISTRIBUTION South Island: restricted to southern Fiordland, south of the Homer area.

Coastal to low-alpine: to 1,200 m (4,000 ft).

HABITAT On rocky sites in open scrub below the tree line. In the alpine zone it is usually prominent in snow tussock-herbfield, but heavy grazing by deer may restrict it to inaccessible rocky bluffs.

COLLECTED Wilmot Pass, Fiordland National Park, 820 m (2,700 ft). January 1968.

Celmisia hieraciifolia Hook.f.
"Hawkweed-leaved".

A tufted herb occurring usually as single rosettes. Their leathery leaves (4–12 x 1–2 cm) are dull-green, glabrous and slightly sticky above but with pale-yellow to buff tomentum below. Their margins are wavy and slightly toothed.

Stout flower stalks (5–25 cm long) with narrow bracts are sticky and the flower heads (3–5 cm across) are enclosed in the bud by many bracts in several series.

It is a rather variable species, due in part to hybridism, and two varieties are described. Both are smaller and one, var. **gracilis**, has narrow leaves (2–4 mm wide) but their colour remains distinctive.

DISTRIBUTION North and South Islands: Ruahine and Tararua Ranges; apparently rather local in the South Island—Marlborough Sounds (Mt Stokes) and parts of Nelson.

Low-alpine: 900–1,400 m (3,000–4,500 ft).

HABITAT In snow tussock-herbfield and often prominent where the vegetation is more open, especially on exposed or rocky sites, as on the Tararua Range and the mineral belt at Dun Mountain.

COLLECTED By Mr Peter Williams from West Peak, Tararua Range, ca 1,370 m (4,500 ft). January 1969.

Celmisia dallii Buchan.
After Mr J. Dall, an early explorer and collector in Nelson.

Similar in habit and general appearance to *C. holosericea* but the leaves are shining pale-green, larger and less variable (10–15 x 2–4 cm), while their tomentum is white to pale buff. Also, the minutely toothed margins are slightly upturned and therefore white-rimmed.

Long flower stalks (20–40 cm) are also distinctive with their broad leafy bracts, the upper ones forming a false involucre beneath the large (3.5–6 cm across) flower head.

DISTRIBUTION South Island: confined to the mountains of western Nelson as far south as the Paparoa Range.

Subalpine to low-alpine: 900–1,500 m (3,000–5,000 ft).

HABITAT In open subalpine forest and scrub on stony sites but most common in snow tussock-herbfield and on the tablelands in red tussock grassland. Sometimes also prominent on rock outcrops.

COLLECTED Mt Peel, Cobb Valley, north-west Nelson, 1,490 m (4,900 ft). December 1969.

Celmisia hieraciifolia

Celmisia dallii

Celmisia holosericea

cm

PLATE 57

Celmisia semicordata Petrie

Refers to the shape of the leaf base.

The largest celmisia, a tufted herb often with several in a clump. Leaves are large and very leathery (20–50 x 2.5–8 cm), greyish- to silvery-green above but with dense white tomentum beneath. Their margins are smooth and slightly recurved.

Flower stems, up to 10 or more per tuft, are stout and long (*ca* 40 cm) with several narrow leafy bracts, all covered in white tomentum, and a large head (4–10 cm across).

Subspecies **stricta** (Ckn.) Given, "erect and very straight" and subspecies **aurigans** Given, "glittering with gold" have narrower more rigid and tapered leaves (*ca* 3 cm wide) that are silvery above in ssp. *stricta* or with a distinctly golden midrib in ssp. *aurigans*. Clumps may be larger, as much as 2 m across

DISTRIBUTION South Island: widely distributed in all except the driest regions. Ssp. *stricta* occurs in northern Southland; ssp. *aurigans* is in eastern and south-central Otago.

Mostly subalpine to low-alpine: 700–1,400 m (2,000–4,500 ft).

HABITAT Usually prominent in open subalpine scrub and snow tussock-herbfield, especially on rocky sites, in the high-rainfall regions to the south of Nelson. A combination of burning and grazing has encouraged the two subspecies so that on some mountains, the Garvies and Takitimus in particular, they now dominate extensive areas.

COLLECTED Temple Basin track, Arthurs Pass National Park, 1,040 m (3,400 ft). December 1967.

Celmisia monroi Hook.f.

After Sir D. Monro, early explorer and collector in north-eastern Nelson and Marlborough.

Generally similar to *C. semicordata* and not always easily distinguished from it, but typically the leaf blades are smaller, narrower (<15 x 2.5 cm) and they taper gradually into an obvious petiole (2–3 cm long). Their flower heads are <6 cm across.

DISTRIBUTION South Island: widespread in Marlborough and Nelson with a few records from the Canterbury alps, but its exact distribution here remains uncertain because of possible confusion with small forms of *C. semicordata*.

Mostly subalpine to low-alpine: 400–1,500 m (1,500–5,000 ft).

HABITAT Usually the most common large tufted celmisia in the tussock grasslands and snow tussock-herbfield of Marlborough-Nelson.

COLLECTED Near Lake Sylvester, Cobb Valley, north-west Nelson, 1,370 m (4,500 ft). December 1967.

Celmisia petriei Cheesem.

After Mr D. Petrie, early teacher and botanist, especially in Otago.

A stout tufted herb with thick, rigid, daggerlike leaves (20–40 x 1–3 cm). They are bright-green above with a faint midrib plus a prominent pair of parallel ribs, while the lower surface is completely covered with white tomentum.

Flower stalks (20–50 cm long) and their narrow leafy bracts are covered with soft white tomentum and the many narrow bracts surrounding the flower head (4–5 cm across) are distinctively pale brown.

DISTRIBUTION South Island: in the high rainfall regions, with an occurrence in north-west Nelson (Mt Cobb) but then a large gap southwards until it reappears in south Westland, western Otago—Southland and Fiordland.

Subalpine to low-alpine: 800–1,500 m (2,500–5,000 ft).

HABITAT This remarkable-looking celmisia is widespread and often prominent in permanently moist snow tussock-herbfield. It extends only a short distance to the east of the main divide in Otago where, under drier conditions, it is replaced by *C. lyallii*.

COLLECTED Harris Saddle, Humboldt Mountains, Mt Aspiring National Park, 1,220 m (4,000 ft). December 1969.

Celmisia spectabilis Hook.f. (*See plate 56*)   COTTON DAISY

"Beautiful".

A distinctive but variable tufted herb occurring singly but more usually in patches up to 1 m or more across. The very thick leathery leaves (5–20 x 1–2.5 cm) are shining pale- or yellowish-green, glabrous and grooved above, with the lower surface entirely covered in soft, feltlike, buff to almost white tomentum.

Flower heads (3–5 cm across) sit on stout stalks (20–25 cm tall) that are covered in loose hairs and have a few narrow bracts mostly on the upper half.

Var. **angustifolia** Martin, "narrow-leaved", is altogether smaller: leaves 8–15 cm x 3–5 mm; flower stalk 10 cm long; flower head 3 cm across; while var. **magnifica** Allan, is larger with leaves up to 35 cm long, and forms large patches.

DISTRIBUTION North and South Islands: on the interior mountains from Hikurangi and the central volcanoes southwards. In the South Island it is widespread in the mountains, mostly along and east of the main divide, as far south as Canterbury. Var. *angustifolia* is in Nelson and Marlborough, usually with var. *spectabilis*, while var. *magnifica* occurs mostly alone in south-eastern Canterbury.

Montane to low-alpine: 300–1,700 m (1,000–5,500 ft).

HABITAT The most widespread and versatile of the celmisias, it spans the widest altitudinal, geographical, climatic and vegetational ranges. It is associated with red tussock grassland and fellfield—the central volcanoes; snow tussock-herbfield in the high rainfall regions—the Tararua Range, in north-west Nelson and at Arthurs Pass; and very much drier tussock grasslands—the South Island interior including the mineral belt in Marlborough. On the foothill ranges of Canterbury in particular, the cotton daisy has become abundant as a fire weed following depletion of the tussock cover.

COLLECTED Mt Ruapehu, Tongariro National Park, *ca* 1,220 m (4,000 ft). January 1968.

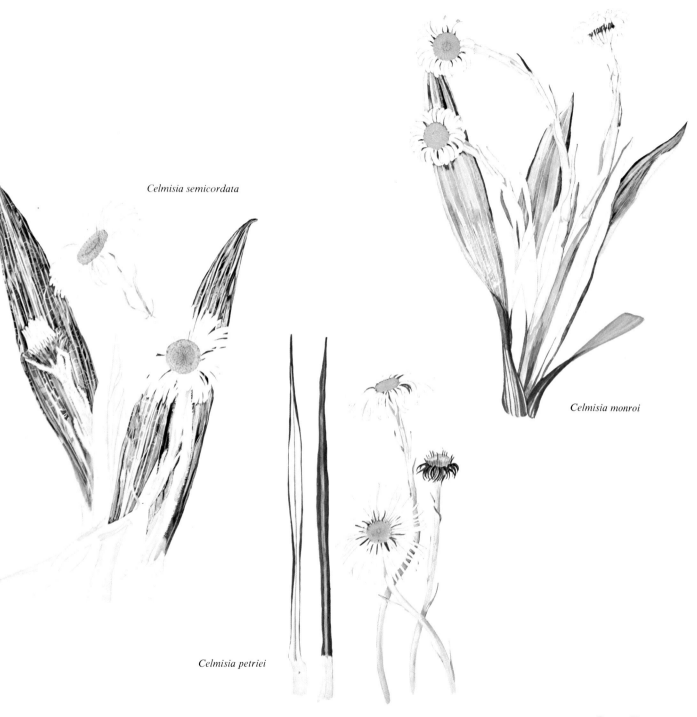

Celmisia semicordata

Celmisia monroi

Celmisia petriei

cm

PLATE 58

Celmisia lyallii Hook.f. FALSE SPANIARD

After Dr Lyall, surgeon-naturalist on HMS *Terror* in the 1840s.

A distinctive tufted herb with narrow (20–40 x 1–2.5 cm), rigid, very leathery, sharp-pointed leaves. The upper surface is glabrous and often finely striated while the lower one is obviously striped due to white tomentum occupying 6–12 distinct grooves.

The one to several flower stalks (15–30 cm long) and their several narrow leafy bracts are covered in soft white hairs and the flower head (3–4 cm across) is surrounded by brown papery bracts.

DISTRIBUTION South Island: widespread in mountain regions east of the main divide from Marlborough to northern Southland, but most plentiful in the interior.

Subalpine to low-alpine: 800–1,700 m (2,500–5,500 ft).

HABITAT Often a prominent member of tussock grasslands and snow tussock-herbfield, especially where tussock cover has been depleted by burning and/or grazing. When not in flower it may be mistaken for a speargrass.

COLLECTED Mt Richmond, Two Thumb Range, south Canterbury, 1,400 m (4,600 ft). January 1969.

Celmisia vespertina D. R. Given

"Western"—referring to its distribution.

A smaller tufted herb, occurring singly or in small clumps. The narrow rigid leaves (5–15 cm x 3–6 mm) have a grooved dark-green upper surface with strongly recurved margins. Their lower surface is covered in white tomentum except for the midrib.

Flower stalks (10–15 cm long) and their few narrow bracts are covered with soft white hairs, while the flower head is 3–4 cm across.

DISTRIBUTION South Island: chiefly in Westland between the Taramakau and Waiatoto Valleys.

Low- to high-alpine: 1,100–1,600 m (3,500–5,500 ft).

HABITAT Usually on rock outcrops and open snow tussock-herbfield on steep well-drained sites in South Westland. Further north it is most abundant in fellfield towards the upper limit of vegetation.

COLLECTED Marks Range, Mt Aspiring National Park, 1,160 m (3,800 ft). January 1969.

Celmisia markii Lee & Given NEEDLE-LEAVED CELMISIA

After A.F.M. who collected it.

This plant is similar to *C. vespertina* but is easily distinguished by its needle-like leaves (7 cm x 1.5 mm) and habit: it forms dense patches or mats up to 1 m across.

DISTRIBUTION South Island: so far it is recorded from only two small areas: above the Turnbull and Waiatoto Valleys in south Westland near the southern limit of *C. vespertina*, and further south in central Fiordland. The similar *C. spedenii* is locally common on ultrabasic rocks at West Dome, northern Southland.

Low-alpine: 1,100–1,500 m (3,500–5,000 ft).

HABITAT The mats are locally common and quite conspicuous on exposed bluffs or ridges in snow tussock-herbfield.

COLLECTED Drake Range, Mt Aspiring National Park, 1,370 m (4,500 ft). January 1969.

Celmisia armstrongii Petrie

After Mr J. B. Armstrong, who first collected it.

A large tufted herb, either single or in clumps. The tapered leathery leaves (20–35 x 1–2 cm) are quite rigid and swordlike with their smooth margins slightly recurved. Their upper surface is grooved and distinctively coloured while thick white tomentum covers the lower surface except for the prominent thickened midrib.

One to several flower stems (*ca* 25 cm long) and their many narrow bracts are covered in soft white tomentum, while the heads are usually *ca* 5 cm across.

DISTRIBUTION South Island: in the high rainfall regions along and west of the main divide from Nelson to about Harris Saddle in the Humboldt Mountains, western Otago.

Subalpine to low-alpine: 800–1,500 m (2,500–5,000 ft).

HABITAT The most prominent celmisia in snow tussock-herbfield throughout most of Westland. As can be seen near Arthurs Pass, it also extends down into open subalpine scrub.

COLLECTED Temple Basin track, Arthurs Pass National Park, 1,070 m (3,500 ft). December 1967.

Celmisia vespertina

Celmisia lyallii

Celmisia armstrongii

Celmisia markii

cm

PLATE 59

Celmisia coriacea (Forst.f.) Hook.f.

"Leathery" — referring to the leaves.

The habit and general appearance are much as for *C. armstrongii* but its leaves are wider (2.5–4 cm) with a stout yellowish to orange midrib rather than the pair of lateral yellow bands that characterise *C. armstrongii*. Also, the flower head may be larger (5–7 cm across).

DISTRIBUTION South Island: southern Fiordland and western Southland (Longwood Range).

Mostly low-alpine: 800–1,200 m (2,500–4,000 ft).

HABITAT An occasional or locally common plant in very poorly drained, usually peaty areas of snow tussock-herbfield.

COLLECTED Borland Saddle, Hunter Mountains, Fiordland National Park, 970 m (3,200 ft). January 1969.

Celmisia verbascifolia Hook.f. ssp. *verbascifolia*

"Verbascum- (Mullein-) leaved".

A large tufted herb with broad, elliptical, soft to slightly leathery leaves (15–24 x 2.5–5 cm). Their upper surface is shining bright-green and usually glabrous when mature, with prominent veins and sometimes a distinct white hairy edge due to the upturned margins. Beneath is dense white to pale-buff tomentum and a prominent sometimes purple midrib which expands into a distinct, often pale purple petiole.

One-to-few flower stalks (20–40 cm long) have several narrow leafy bracts and a large head (5–8 cm across).

DISTRIBUTION South Island: a wide distribution in the higher rainfall regions from southern Nelson to Fiordland. Subalpine to low-alpine: 700–1,700 m (2,500–5,500 ft).

HABITAT Usually common in mixed snow tussock-scrub on rocky sites and in snow tussock-herbfield on all but highly exposed and permanently wet areas. It often extends to the upper limit of the alpine grasslands.

COLLECTED Percy Saddle, Turret Range, Fiordland National Park, 1,200 m (4,000 ft). January 1968. The form with a purple midrib and petiole previously referred to *C. petiolata* (see plate 60) but now is included in *C. verbascifolia*. It was collected on Mt Burns, Hunter Mountains, Fiordland National Park, 1,370 m (4,500 ft). January 1968. *Celmisia verbascifolia* ssp. *membranacea* (Kirk) Given, is somewhat smaller with fewer sometimes single rosettes. It replaces ssp. *verbascifolia* north of about Amuri and Lewis Passes. Subspecies *rigida* (Kirk) Given, occurs under scrub on coastal cliffs and ledges of southern Stewart Island.

Celmisia traversii Hook.f.

After Mr W. T. L. Travers, who first collected it.

A most distinctive and handsome tufted herb. Their thick leaves (15–30 x 4–6 cm) are glabrous above except for the midrib and margins, but beneath they are covered in soft, velvety, rusty-brown tomentum, except for the prominent purple midrib. Petioles are also deep purple.

One to few flower stalks (20–40 cm long) with their few narrow bracts are also distinctively brown with tomentum, and at the top is a large head (4–6 cm across).

DISTRIBUTION South Island: a discontinuous pattern, occurring in high rainfall regions both in the north-west (Nelson—north-western Canterbury) and the south-west (southern Fiordland—western Southland). Even in these two regions its distribution seems somewhat erratic.

Low-alpine: 900–1,600 m (3,000–5,500 ft).

HABITAT In permanently moist snow tussock-herbfield where it may be sufficiently common and spectacular, even when not in flower, to impart a distinct character to the vegetation.

COLLECTED Near Lake Sylvester, Cobb Valley, north-west Nelson, 1,430 m (4,700 ft). December 1967.

A few minor alpine celmisias are not described here. All are of rather limited distribution and we have not yet seen them in the field:

C. cockayneana Petrie, from the Kaikoura Ranges, Marlborough.
C. cordatifolia Buchan., from the Richmond Range, Marlborough.
C. dubia Cheesem. and *C. parva* Kirk, both from north-west Nelson.
C. rutlandii Kirk, from northern Marlborough.

Genus **VITTADINIA**

After Carlo Vittadini, an Italian botanist.

A small genus of about 15 species from New Guinea, New Caledonia, Australasia and southern South America. The single native vittadinia reaches the alpine zone.

Vittadinia australis A. Rich.

"Southern".

A spreading rather weedy-looking sub-shrub, up to 30 cm tall, with a stout root. The green younger branches and the deeply 3–5-toothed pale-green leaves (up to 1.5 cm long) are thinly covered in white and glandular hairs. Small flower heads (1–1.5 cm across) with white rays and a yellow centre occur singly at the branch tips.

It occurs from Great Barrier Island and Whangarei southwards, but is rather local north of East Cape. In the South Island it is widespread east of the main divide where it reaches the low-alpine zone (to 1,500 m; 5,000 ft). Here it is found chiefly in depleted stony and eroding tussock grassland, especially on the drier grey-wacke mountains of Canterbury and Marlborough.

Celmisia coriacea

Celmisia traversii

Celmisia "petiolata"

Celmisia verbascifolia

cm

PLATE 60

Genus BRACHYSCOME

"Short hair"—the long hairs characteristic of most daisy fruits are here much reduced.

A rather widespread genus but concentrated in Australia. Most of the New Zealand brachycomes are variable and not yet properly resolved, although several varieties have been described.

Brachyscome sinclairii Hook.f.

After Dr Andrew Sinclair, surgeon and early New Zealand botanist.

A usually glabrous rosette herb, the rosettes occurring singly or several together. The single leaf shows the typical shape and with the blade only shallowly lobed. In some populations the lobing may be deeper, in others it is absent. It may even vary within a plant.

The single flower stalks are usually slender, 4–20 cm long, without any leafy bracts, but covered in fine short and swollen glandular hairs, discernible only with a good lens. Flower heads are 1–2.5 cm across with yellow centres surrounded by white petal-like rays. Surrounding the florets is a series of green scales usually with purple jagged tips or borders.

DISTRIBUTION North, South and Stewart Islands: widespread from East Cape southwards but rather local in the North Island.
    Lowland to high-alpine: to 2,000 m (6,500 ft).

HABITAT Usually present but rarely abundant in most types of open vegetation on stable sites from lowland tussock grassland to fellfield and early snowbanks. Its size usually decreases with altitude; the one shown is typical of many alpine habitats.

COLLECTED Old Man Range, Central Otago, 1,580 m (5,200 ft). January 1968.

*Brachyscome radicata Hook.f.

"Long-rooted".

Another highly variable species but generally similar to B. sinclairii. They are distinguished by their dry fruits (but a microscope or good lens may be needed for the features concerned): in B. sinclairii they are quite flattened with no or very few glandular hairs; in B. radicata they are not very compressed and are densely covered with short glandular hairs. In addition, plants of B. radicata may be covered with glandular hairs and there may be some leafy bracts on the flower stalk.

Distribution and habitats are similar to B. sinclairii except that it may also occur in open forest and has not been recorded from the high-alpine zone. It is altogether less common than B. sinclairii.

Brachyscome humilis Simpson & Thomson

"Low-growing".

A very small tufted herb that occurs singly or as loose mats up to 5 cm across. The narrow rather fleshy leaves sometimes have 1–2 fine notches near the tip.

Flower stalks are very slender, 3–5 cm long, and capped with a head ca 6 mm across. The series of 9–10 bracts surrounding the head have purplish margins.

DISTRIBUTION South Island: apparently restricted to Rock & Pillar Range in Central Otago.
    High-alpine: 1,200–1,400 m (4,000–4,500 ft).

HABITAT Confined virtually to the slopes of early snowbanks.

COLLECTED Rock & Pillar Range, Central Otago, 1,370 m (4,500 ft). December 1969.

Genus LAGENIFERA

"Flagon-bearing" — referring to the shape of the whorl of bracts (involucre) surrounding the flower head.

Contains about 25 species from South America, southern Asia and Australasia. Of the 11 native species one reaches the alpine zone.

Lagenifera cuneata Petrie

"Wedge-shaped" — referring to the leaves.

A small rosette herb, usually spreading by wiry underground stems to form small open patches. Leaves are usually slightly hairy with 1–3 pairs of small notches.

The flower head is very small (5–7 mm across) on a long (5–15 cm) slender stalk.

DISTRIBUTION North and South Islands: the base of the central volcanic mountains; in the South Island it is widespread east of the main divide.
    Montane to low-alpine: 200–1,600 m (500–5,500 ft).

HABITAT Often common yet inconspicuous in tussock grasslands, but usually becoming more prominent where the plant cover is depleted.

COLLECTED Mt Richmond, Two Thumb Range, south Canterbury, 1,460 m (4,800 ft). January 1969.

Genus ABROTANELLA

"Small Abrotanus"—the ancient herbal name for Artemisia.

This genus contains about 20 South American—Australasian species. All abrotanellas from mainland New Zealand reach the alpine zone (two from Stewart Island do not) and most have a similar small, almost mosslike habit.

Abrotanella caespitosa Petrie ex Kirk

"Turf-forming".

Branching and rooting stems, mostly pale and below ground, produce very small leafy rosettes that together form mats up to 1 m or more across. Narrow strap-shaped leaves (6–15 x 1–1.5 mm) are thick, blunt-tipped and usually mottled dark-green.

Minute flower heads (2–4 mm across) are sunk among the leaves at the stem tips but as the fruits ripen their stalks elongate (to 1 cm) exposing the heads.

DISTRIBUTION North and South Islands: Ruahine and Tararua Ranges; widespread in Nelson and southwards, east of the main divide, to Southland and south-eastern Fiordland.

Cont. on page 148

Brachyscome sinclairii

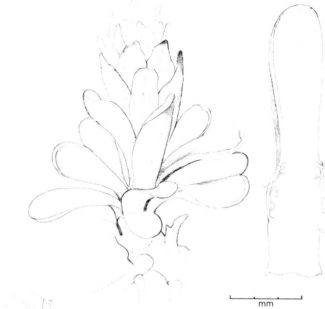

Rock & Pillar *Abrotanella*

mm

Brachyscome humilis

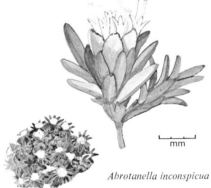

mm

Abrotanella inconspicua

Lagenifera cuneata

Abrotanella linearis

Abrotanella caespitosa

cm

PLATE 61

Low- to high-alpine: 900–1,800 m (3,000–6,000 ft).
HABITAT In bogs and permanently wet hollows, especially snowbanks, but being so small and inconspicuous it may be overlooked.
COLLECTED Rock & Pillar Range, Central Otago, 1,370 m (4,500 ft). December 1970. The ripe fruit is from Mt Richmond, Two Thumb Range, south Canterbury, 1,340 m (4,400 ft). January 1969.

Abrotanella linearis Bergg. (*See plate 61*)
"Linear"—referring to the leaves.

A small tufted herb, often with a few or several tufts produced from branches of the wiry underground stem. The narrow leaves (3–7 cm x 1–2 mm) are blunt or sharp-pointed.

Flower heads (*ca* 5 mm across) may be single or 2–3 together on a slender leafy stalk that elongates (to 1–10 cm) as the fruits mature.

Var. **apiculata** Simpson & Thomson, "sharp-pointed"—referring to the leaves, looks more like *A. caespitosa* but the leaves are distinctly sharp-pointed.

DISTRIBUTION South and Stewart Islands: in the high rainfall regions, chiefly close to the main divide, from Nelson southwards. Var. *apiculata* is rather rare in south Westland and Fiordland.

Mostly subalpine to low-alpine: 800–1,300 m (2,500–4,500 ft).
HABITAT In permanently wet, sometimes peaty areas or steep shady banks in snow tussock-herbfield, open subalpine forest or scrub. Var. *apiculata* is more strictly alpine, on wet banks or rocks.
COLLECTED Temple Basin, Arthurs Pass National Park, 1,280 m (4,200 ft). January 1970.

*Abrotanella pusilla Hook.f.
"Very small".

A small mat-forming herb with branched, creeping and rooting stems that are covered in very narrow, pointed, sickle-shaped leaves (5–15 x 1 mm). Small flower heads (5 mm across) develop among the tuft of leaves at the branch tips and emerge on stalks up to 2 cm long as the fruits ripen.

The mats are usually common but inconspicuous in turf on wet, often peaty sites, especially snow hollows, on the Ruahine and Tararua Ranges at 1,000–1,500 m (3,000–5,000 ft).

*Abrotanella spathulata Hook.f.
"Spathulate"—referring to the spatula-shaped leaves.

It forms small dark-green rosettes, up to 3 cm across, often with a few together from a branched stock. Leaves are rather broad (1–2.5 cm x 2–5 mm) with flattened purple petioles. Up to 5 small, almost sessile heads are crowded at the centre of the rosette but become more prominent when the stalks elongate (to 2–5 cm) as the fruits ripen.

A common species on the Subantarctic Islands, it also occurs sporadically in Fiordland, chiefly in crevices and on rocky ledges in fellfield at 1,300–1,500 m (4,500–5,000 ft).

Abrotanella inconspicua Hook.f. (*See plate 61*)
"Insignificant".

Its habit is similar to *A. muscosa*; plants form bright-green moss-like mats 10 cm or more across. Thick awl-shaped leaves are narrow (3–10 x 1 mm), pointed at the tip and usually curved. They persist along the stems. Very small heads (3 mm across) occur singly among the leaves at the stem tips and barely extend beyond them as the fruits ripen.

DISTRIBUTION South Island: widespread on the higher mountains of Central Otago and the Lakes district but extending west, in places almost to the main divide.

Low- to high-alpine: 1,200–2,000 m (4,000–6,500 ft).
HABITAT Usually common in cushion vegetation on the high plateaux of Central Otago, but avoiding the most exposed sites and late snowbanks. Further west it is much more local, in fellfield and on wind-swept ridges near the upper limit of snow tussock-herbfield.

A generally similar plant but with broader (1.5–2 mm) blunt leaves and flower stalks that elongate beyond the leaves as the fruits ripen, substitutes for the typical *A. inconspicua* on the Rock & Pillar Range, Central Otago.

COLLECTED Old Man Range, Central Otago, 1,580 m (5,200 ft). January 1968. A plant from Rock & Pillar is also shown, 1,370 m (4,500 ft). November 1967.

Genus HAASTIA

After Sir Julius von Haast, famous geologist and explorer.

An endemic genus. All three haastias are strictly alpine.

Haastia pulvinaris Hook.f.　　　　　　　VEGETABLE SHEEP
"Cushion-shaped".

A remarkable plant that forms woolly buff-coloured cushions up to 2 m across and 30 cm or more thick. Their branches are very tightly packed, 1–2 cm across, including the closely-overlapping leaves which persist around the stem long after they have died and become incorporated in the cushion.

The small yellow flower heads lack the prominent rays of many daisies and remain inconspicuous, sunken within the leafy branch tips.

Var. **minor** Laing, "smaller", is altogether smaller with hairs whiter and much shorter so that the individual leaves are more obvious.

DISTRIBUTION South Island: Marlborough and the drier mountains of south-eastern Nelson. Var. *minor* also occurs in this region.

Low- to high-alpine: 1,300–1,900 m (4,500–6,500 ft).
HABITAT These remarkably sheep-like cushions occupy partly-stable fellfield on greywacke where the rock outcrops are being shattered. They are also found on stable rock debris but are absent from mobile scree.

COLLECTED Both var. *minor* and the more usual form from Julius Rocks, Travers Range, Nelson Lakes National Park, 1,710 m (5,600 ft). December 1967.

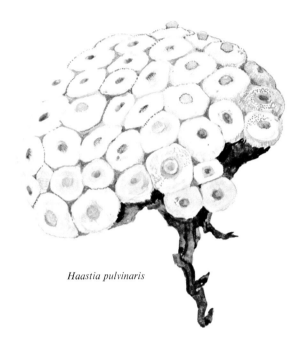

Haastia pulvinaris

Haastia pulvinaris var. *minor*

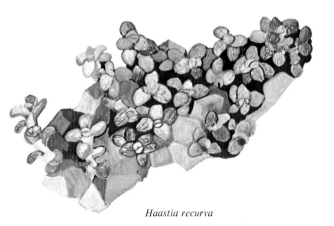

Haastia recurva

Haastia sinclairii

cm

PLATE 62

Haastia recurva Hook.f. (*See plate 62*)
"Recurved"—referring to the leaves.

A trailing, usually much-branched sub-shrub with stems up to 25 cm long that form loose patches up to 50 cm or more across. Densely overlapping and persistent leaves (*ca* 2 x 1 cm) are strongly recurved and smothered in long yellowish- to reddish-brown hairs. Small white flower heads (5–8 mm across) remain inconspicuous almost within the leaves at the branch tips, but as the fruits ripen their long white hairs become prominent.

DISTRIBUTION South Island: on the drier greywacke mountains of Marlborough, eastern Nelson and Canterbury, southwards to the Waimakariri catchment, but somewhat local in occurrence.

Low- to high-alpine: 1,300–1,900 m (4,500–6,500 ft).

HABITAT Usually on scree slopes but it may also occur on loose but stable rock debris and in the crevices of outcrops.

COLLECTED Craigieburn Range, Canterbury, 1,770 m (5,800 ft). January 1968.

Haastia sinclairii Hook.f. (*See plate 62*)
After Dr Andrew Sinclair, surgeon and early New Zealand botanist.

A trailing sub-shrub, sparingly to much branched, up to 30 cm long, with the tips usually erect. Leaves vary from broad, as shown, to narrower and more pointed, and also in size (up to 3.5 x 1.5 cm). They are covered in whitish to buff tomentum which is thicker and more persistent in the low rainfall regions, as shown. As the hairs thin in older leaves the wrinkled upper surface is seen.

A white flower head up to 3 cm across protrudes from the leaves at the branch tips and becomes more prominent as the fruits ripen.

Var. *fulvida* Allan, "dull yellow", has distinctly buff tomentum (also present along the leaf margins in many eastern populations of var. *sinclairii*), smaller leaves and flower heads (except for high-altitude populations of var. *sinclairii*). More distinctively, the black-tipped bracts surrounding the flower head in var. *fulvida* have broad, thin, papery margins (seen only with a good lens).

DISTRIBUTION South Island: widespread in mountain regions throughout. Var. *fulvida* occurs alone in parts of Central Otago but mixes with var. *sinclairii* in western Otago—Southland and Fiordland.

Low- to high-alpine: 1,300–2,000 m (4,500–6,500 ft).

HABITAT Typically a plant of stable or partly mobile debris in fellfield; occasionally on scree.

COLLECTED St Arnaud Range, Nelson Lakes National Park, 1,680 m (5,500 ft). December 1967.

Genus LEPTINELLA

"Slender" – referring to the habit of several species.

A genus of some 33 species from New Zealand, New Guinea, Australia, and sub-antarctic South America, formerly included in *Cotula*. Of the 17 native species eight reach the alpine zone.

Leptinella atrata (Hook.f.) D. Lloyd & C. Webb
"Black" – referring to the florets.
(= *Cotula atrata* Hook.f.)

A creeping herb with branched underground stems and ascending leafy branches up to 10 cm long. Thick, greyish-green, fleshy leaves (1.5–3 x 0.5–2 cm) are quite feather-like and partly hairy.

A striking button-like flower head (1–2 cm across) with black florets that open to reveal bright-yellow stamens, sits on a leafy stalk 3–6 cm tall.

DISTRIBUTION South Island: widespread on the drier mountains from Marlborough to north Otago. North of Canterbury the typical form is replaced by subspecies *luteola* which has yellow florets with dark red tips, not unlike *C. dendyi* except that the bracts surrounding the flower head are shorter than the florets.

Low- to high-alpine: 1,000–2,000 m (3,500–6,500 ft).

HABITAT Confined to screes. It is often one of the more common plants in this highly demanding habitat but the foliage blends so well with the rocky background that it is easily overlooked.

COLLECTED Fog Peak, Torlesse Range, Canterbury; 1,520 m (5,000 ft). January 1968.

Leptinella dendyi (Ckn.) D. Lloyd & C. Webb
After Professor A. Dendy, early Canterbury zoologist.
(= *Cotula dendyi* Ckn.)

Very similar to *C. atrata* and their yellow florets with dark-red tips resemble those of *C. atrata* ssp. *luteola* but they are easily distinguished when flowering by the bracts surrounding the head being shorter than the florets. The heads may also be larger, up to 2 cm across.

DISTRIBUTION South Island: on the greywacke mountains of eastern Nelson-Marlborough southwards to Mt Hutt in Canterbury.

HABITAT As for *C. atrata* and often more plentiful.

COLLECTED Island Pass, upper Wairau Valley, Nelson; 1,400 m (4,600 ft). December, 1969.

Leptinella goyenii (Petrie) D. Lloyd & C. Webb
After Mr P. Goyen, early collector.
(= *Cotula goyenii* Petrie)

A very small creeping and rooting herb with highly-branched wiry stems and many short, erect leafy branches that may form loose mats up to 20 cm across. Their minute glabrous leaves (3–5 mm long) are distinctively cut into 5–7 teeth.

Purplish flower heads are likewise small (3–4 mm wide) and hardly raised above the leaves at the branch tips. The enlarged flower head shows the outer ring of female florets and the inner bisexual ones.

DISTRIBUTION South Island: widespread on the higher mountains of Central Otago with one record in south-eastern Fiordland (Hunter Mts).

High-alpine: 1,200–1,900 m (4,000–6,500 ft).

HABITAT A common but insignificant plant on the most exposed and frost-heaved sites among dwarfed cushion vegetation of the Central Otago plateau summits. Here it tolerates one of the most severe environments of any alpine plant.

COLLECTED Rock & Pillar Range, Central Otago, 1,370 m (4,500 ft). October 1967.

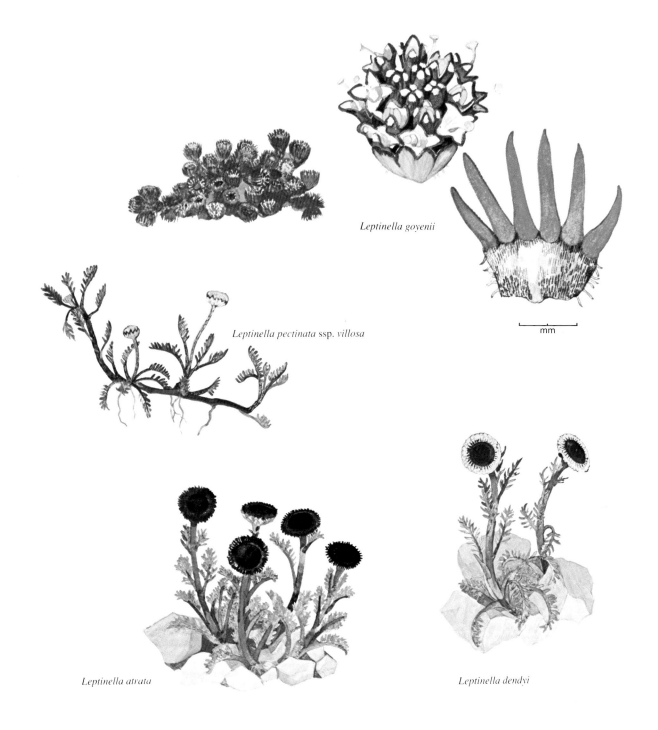

Leptinella goyenii

Leptinella pectinata ssp. *villosa*

mm

Leptinella atrata

Leptinella dendyi

cm

PLATE 63

Leptinella pectinata (Hook.f.) D. Lloyd & C. Webb
"Comb-like" – referring to the leaves.
(= *Cotula pectinata* Hook.f.)

The subspecies **pectinata** has a habit similar to ssp. **villosa** but plants are less hairy, usually almost glabrous, and the leaves are divided into 1–10 pairs of narrow, pointed, awl-shaped leaflets.

White flower heads (5–7 mm across) are on slender leafless stalks up to 10 cm long but usually only 2–4 cm in alpine areas.
DISTRIBUTION South Island: widespread yet usually not abundant on the drier mountains east of the main divide between southern Marlborough and north Otago.
Subalpine to high-alpine: 500–2,400 m (1,500–8,000 ft).
HABITAT A wide ranging plant but usually in open vegetation-depleted tussock grassland, stony herbfield and loose fine debris on rather inactive screes.
COLLECTED Pisa Range, Central Otago, 1,800 m (5,900 ft). February 1970.

Leptinella pectinata subspecies **willcoxii** (Cheesem.) D. Lloyd & C. Webb
After Mr W. Willcox, who first collected it.
(= *Cotula pectinata* ssp. *wilcoxii* Cheesem.)

Its habit is similar to ssp. *pectinata* but the glabrous leaves (5–10 x 5–10 mm) are almost fleshy and deeply divided with one terminal leaflet plus 1–2 pairs (but up to 4) of lateral ones, much as in small forms of *C. pyrethrifolia*.
Flower heads are similar to ssp. *pectinata*, containing both male and female florets, but the slender stalk never exceeds 4 cm and florets are yellow to yellow-red.
DISTRIBUTION South Island: in high rainfall areas on the higher mountains of western Otago - Southland and northern Fiordland.
Low- to high-alpine: 900–2,400 m (3,000–8,000 ft).
HABITAT Common in fellfield as small open patches on loose stony areas or trailing out from the crevices of rock outcrops. Rare in the low-alpine zone on exposed rocky sites and stony creekbeds.
COLLECTED Upper Eyre Creek, Eyre Mountains, northern Southland, 1,520 m (5,000 ft). December 1970.

Leptinella pectinata subspecies **villosa** (D. Lloyd) D. Lloyd & C. Webb
"Shaggy-hairy".
(= *Cotula pectinata* ssp. *villosa* (Simp.) Lloyd)

Its habit is similar to ssp. *pectinata* but plants are usually densely covered in greyish hairs, including the stout, short (1–2 cm) flower stalk, and florets are yellow to yellow-red.
DISTRIBUTION South Island: confined to the drier mountains of south Canterbury and Otago, Southland and southeastern Fiordland.
Low- to high-alpine: 1,000–2,000 (3,000–6,500 ft).
HABITAT Often common in cushion vegetation, snowbanks and exposed sites in herbfield and depleted snow tussock grassland.
COLLECTED Pisa Range, Central Otago, 1,800 m (5,900 ft). February 1970.

Leptinella albida (D. Lloyd) D. Lloyd & C. Webb
"Whitish" – plants are silvery-white.
(= *Cotula albida* Lloyd)

A compact densely-hairy herb, similar in habit to *C. pectinata*, that forms silver-white patches up to 20 cm or more across.
It is known only from high-alpine cushion vegetation on three ranges in Central Otago: Pisa, Old Man, Mt Cardrona.

Leptinella pyrethrifolia (Hook.f.) D. Lloyd & C. Webb
"With leaves like *Pyrethrum*".
(= *Cotula pyrethrifolia* Hook.f.)

The common var. **pyrethrifolia** is a highly variable creeping and rooting aromatic herb, much more robust than the other cotulàs. Copiously branched stems with leafy ascending tips form loose patches up to 1 m or more across. Rather fleshy glabrous leaves (10–20 x 4–15 mm) are deeply cut into 1–5 pairs of lobes.
Prominent white flower heads (8–16 mm across) on slender stalks (5–10 cm long) have florets that are either all male or female or a mixture of both.
DISTRIBUTION North and South Islands: Tararua Range; widespread in most South Island mountain regions as far south as Canterbury and central Westland.
Subalpine to high-alpine: 600–2,000 m (2,000–6,500 ft).
HABITAT Common on moist open sites, especially shady rock ledges, stream beds and damp areas of snow tussock-herbfield and fellfield.
COLLECTED Temple Basin, Arthurs Pass National Park, 1,340 m (4,400 ft). December 1967.

Leptinella pyrethrifolia var. **linearifolia** (Cheesem.) D. Lloyd & C. Webb
"Narrow-leaved".
(= *Cotula pyrethrifolia* var. *linearifolia* (Cheesem.) Lloyd)

Smaller and darker green than ssp. *pyrethrifolia* with narrow undivided leaves, forming loose patches up to 30 cm across.
Flower heads are smaller (7–10 mm across), surrounded by thin purple-edged bracts and on slender stalks up to 8 cm long.
DISTRIBUTION South Island: confined to the mountains along the lower Wairau Valley, Marlborough, including the mineral belt.
Low- to high-alpine: 900–1,500 m (3,000–5,000 ft).
HABITAT Usually in fellfield and open rocky areas of tussock grassland.
COLLECTED Red Hill, Wairau Valley, Marlborough, 1,340 m (4,400 ft). January 1971.

Leptinella squalida (Hook.f.) D. Lloyd & C. Webb
"Gloomy, unattractive".
(= *Cotula squalida* Hook.f.)

A highly-variable creeping and rooting herb with branched, mostly underground, wiry stems and short, erect, leafy branches that may form an open turf. The partly-hairy to glabrous, usually bright-green leaves (3–5 cm x 5–10 mm) are divided into 8–15 pairs of leaflets, the middle ones being of quite distinctive shape.
Flower stalks (usually 1–2 cm long in the alpine zone) are slender and hairy without any bracts. The white heads are unisexual with male heads (4–5 mm across) smaller than female ones (6–9 mm).
DISTRIBUTION North, South and Stewart Islands: widespread from the Bay of Plenty southwards chiefly west of the main divide.
Lowland to low-alpine: to 1,400 m (4,500 ft).
HABITAT Often common in permanently damp open areas—gravel

Cont. on page 154

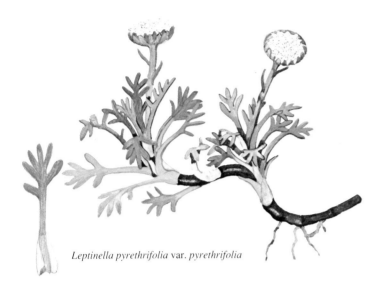

Leptinella pectinata ssp. *willcoxii*

Leptinella pyrethrifolia var. *pyrethrifolia*

Leptinella pectinata

Leptinella pyrethrifolia var. *linearifolia*

Leptinella squalida

cm

PLATE 64

river beds, avalanche chutes, closely-grazed grassland or herbfield not far above the tree line, and occasionally in bogs.

COLLECTED Rock & Pillar Range, Central Otago, 1,370 m (4,500 ft). December 1969.

Leptinella pusilla (Hook.f.) D. Lloyd & C. Webb
"Small".

(= *Cotula perpusilla* Hook.f.)

It is smaller but generally similar to *L. squalida* including the deeply cut leaves (1–3 cm x 3–7 mm). Flower stalks are stouter and shorter (5–10 mm).

It is more local than *L. squalida* in the North Island but wide-spread in the South Island, mainly to the east of the divide and in similar habitats.

Genus GNAPHALIUM
"Downy" – referring to the soft woolly tomentum on the leaves.

A large and widespread genus with about ,150 species. Of the 17 described gnaphaliums from New Zealand about 3 reach the alpine zone.

Gnaphalium mackayi (Buchan.) Ckn.
After Mr A. McKay, who first collected it.

A small tufted herb with much-branched creeping and rooting stems that form small loose mats up to 20 cm or more across. Their soft leaves (10–20 x 3–4 mm) are pale-grey to almost white and closely overlapping.

Very small, single, yellow flower heads (4–5 mm across) are buried among leaves at the stem tips but they emerge on stalks (1–4 cm long) as the fruits ripen.

DISTRIBUTION North and South Islands: widespread from the Ruahine Range southwards.

Subalpine to high-alpine: 900–1,900 m (3,000–6,500 ft).

HABITAT Often common in permanently-wet, sometimes peaty areas in open or depleted grassland and herbfield, as well as in snow hollows.

COLLECTED Old Man Range, Central Otago, 1,370 m (4,500 ft). Flowering mat, December 1969; fruiting plant, March 1970.

Gnaphalium traversii Hook.f.
After Mr W. T. L. Travers, an early collector of native plants.

Generally similar to *G. mackayi* and tends to intergrade with it, but differs in being somewhat taller (to 10 cm), having larger leaves (2–5 cm x 3–6 mm) that are more erect, and a larger head (*ca* 1 cm across). Also, the tufts usually occur singly or in small groups rather than as mats. Distribution appears to be similar to *G. mackayi* except that it does not extend far beyond the tree line.

Gnaphalium nitidulum Hook.f.
"Rather bright".

Its habit is similar to *G. mackayi* but the mats are more rigid, the leaves denser and the younger ones are covered in pale brownish-grey tomentum. As in *G. mackayi* the small single heads are buried among the leaves but unlike it, they do not emerge at all as the fruits ripen.

DISTRIBUTION South Island: on the drier mountains of south-eastern Nelson, north-western Canterbury and Marlborough.

Low-alpine: 1,000–1,700 m (3,000–5,500 ft).

HABITAT Their loose mats are conspicuous in open depleted snow tussock grassland.

COLLECTED Island Pass, upper Wairau Valley, south-eastern Nelson, 1,370 m (4,500 ft). December 1967.

Genus PSEUDOGNAPHALIUM
"False *Gnaphalium*" — it differs in some floral features.

A widespread genus of some 40 species, distinguished from *Gnaphalium* on the floral bracts. The only native species may reach the alpine zone.

Pseudognaphalium luteoalbum (L.) Hilliard & B. L. Burt
"Yellowish-white" — flower heads are yellowish-brown; the plant is almost white.

(= *Gnaphalium luteo-album* L.)

Colour and texture are similar to *G. mackayi* but plants are erect, up to 20 cm tall in alpine areas, with one to several stems from a branched base. Leaves may be similar to *G. traversii* but flowering plants are easily distinguished by their several heads that are clustered into a compound one at the branch tips. It is common in open areas throughout, mostly below the alpine zone, but occasionally in open depleted grassland or herbfield up to about 1,400 m (4,500 ft).

COLLECTED Upper Dart Valley, Mt Aspiring National Park, 1,100 m (3,800 ft). January 1968.

Genus RAOULIA
After M. E. Raoul, surgeon-botanist to the French vessels *L' Aube* and *L'Allier* in the early 1840s.

A rather large, predominantly New Zealand genus of mat and cushion plants; there are a few species in New Guinea. Of the 20 New Zealand raoulias, one is confined to Stewart Island. This one and at least 15 others reach the alpine zone.

Raoulia subsericea Hook.f.
"Rather silky".

Forms rather loose mats, 20 cm or more across, from the much-branched creeping and rooting stems that have densely leafy tips. The rather loosely-packed, overlapping, pale-green leaves (3–6 x 1 mm) have a thin covering of silvery to golden tomentum on their lower surface only except for a small tuft at the rather blunt tip.

Prominent flower heads (7–10 mm across) are each surrounded by papery, straw-coloured, petal-like scales with obvious blunt white tips.

DISTRIBUTION South Island: widespread in all but the wettest mountain regions.

Subalpine to low-alpine: 400–1,500 m (1,500–5,000 ft).

HABITAT Usually the commonest mat plant in the tussock grasslands of the South Island and often abundant where the cover is partly depleted and soil is eroding.

COLLECTED Old Man Range, Central Otago, 1,370 m (4,500 ft). January 1968.

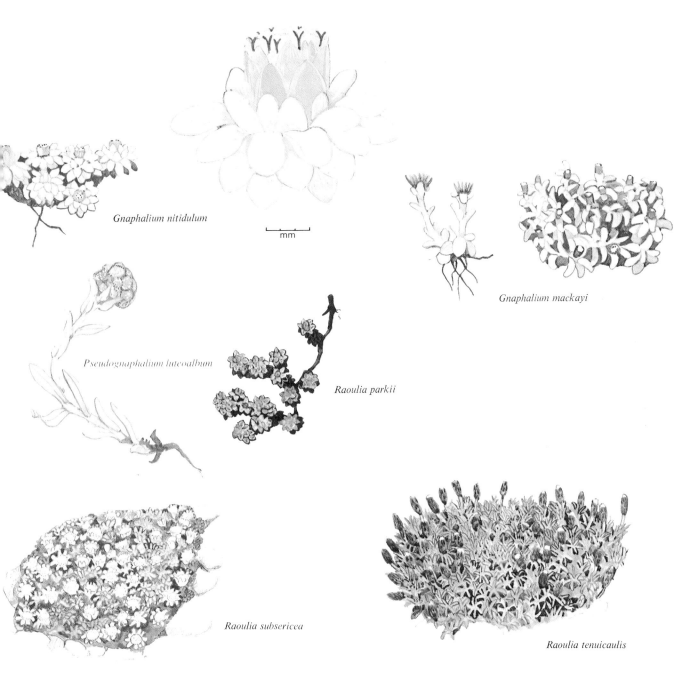

Gnaphalium nitidulum

mm

Gnaphalium mackayi

Pseudognaphalium luteoalbum

Raoulia parkii

Raoulia subsericea

Raoulia tenuicaulis

cm

PLATE 65

Raoulia parkii Buchan.
After Professor J. Park, early geologist.

Its habit is similar to *R. subsericea* but mats are usually smaller and more open and their leaves more closely overlapping, almost recurved at their tips and broader (3–5 x 2 mm). They are covered with pale-yellow to yellowish-green tomentum except near the base.

Flower heads are generally similar but smaller (4–7 mm across).
DISTRIBUTION South Island: east of the main divide from mid-Canterbury to Central Otago.

Subalpine to high-alpine: 900–1,600 m (3,000–5,500 ft).
HABITAT Usually a minor plant in cushion vegetation, fellfield, and exposed or depleted areas of snow tussock grassland.
COLLECTED Old Man Range, Central Otago, 1,460 m (4,800 ft).

*Raoulia glabra Hook.f.
"Without hairs".

Plants are similar to *R. subsericea* but distinguished by their looser mats, bright-green glabrous leaves and usually smaller heads in which the surrounding papery scales have less-prominent, pointed, white tips.
DISTRIBUTION North, South and Stewart Islands: Mount Egmont, and from the Ruahine Range southwards; in all but the driest regions of the South Island.

Lowland to low-alpine: to 1,300 m (4,500 ft).
HABITAT A plant of open, often stony or rocky sites, especially rock outcrops and gravel of moraine or valley floors in wet regions.

Raoulia hookerii Allan
After Sir J. D. Hooker, famous early botanist.

Forms rather soft silvery mats up to 50 cm or more across. Leaves are thickened and turned up near their rounded tip (2–3 x 1 mm). Both surfaces are covered in white or sometimes pale-yellow tomentum except near the base.

Flower heads (5–7 mm across) have only *ca* 15 florets surrounded by yellowish papery scales.

Two varieties occur in the alpine zone:
Var. **apicinigra** (Kirk) Allan, "black-pointed" — referring to the distinctive papery scales surrounding the flower heads, is further distinguished by having leaves entirely covered with tomentum.

Var. **albosericea** (Col.) Allan, "white-silky", has shining snow-white tomentum and rather dark tips to the scales of the flower heads.
DISTRIBUTION Var. *apicinigra* is confined to the South Island, chiefly in Marlborough, while var. *albosericea* is in the North Island: the volcanic plateau, Kaweka, Kaimanawa and Ruahine Ranges.

Both are mostly low- to high-alpine: 1,000-1,800 m (3,500-6,000 ft).
HABITAT Both varieties occupy fellfield and exposed or open depleted sites in tussock grassland.
COLLECTED Var. *apicinigra* from above Island Pass, upper Wairau Valley, Nelson. 1,680 m (5,500 ft). January 1971.

Raoulia tenuicaulis Hook.f. (*See plate 65*)
"Thin-stemmed".

Forms rather loose, circular or extensive silvery-green mats up to 1 m or more across. Leaves are narrow and pointed (to 5 x 2 mm) with thin whitish tomentum only near their tips.

Usually abundant flower heads (to 6 mm across) are surrounded by narrow papery scales with pointed brownish tips. Plants may be almost smothered by the hairy fruits as they are being shed.
DISTRIBUTION North and South Islands: widespread from about Auckland southwards.

Lowland to low-alpine: to 1,500 m (5,000 ft).
HABITAT Often the commonest mat plant on gravel river beds but in the low-alpine zone it also colonises loose fine debris on moist sites.
COLLECTED Upper Eyre Creek, Eyre Mountains, northern Southland, 1,160 m (3,800 ft). December 1970.

Raoulia petriensis Kirk
After Mr D. Petrie, early teacher and botanist, especially in Otago.

A distinctive, almost shrubby plant with branched stems, often trailing downhill, and short, upright, leafy branches that form loose mats up to 30 cm or more across. Minute golden-green leaves are tightly packed, with thickened and recurved tips that give a corrugated texture and appearance to the stems.

Prominent white heads (6–7 mm across) conceal the leaves at the tips of the flowering branches.
DISTRIBUTION South Island: on the higher greywacke mountains of south Canterbury and north Otago but rather isolated in occurrence.

High-alpine: 1,400–1,700 m (4,500–5,500 ft).
HABITAT Often rare yet in places locally abundant, among frost-shattered rocks in fellfield and on semi-stable scree.
COLLECTED Mt Ida, Hawkdun Range, north Otago, 1,610 m (5,300 ft). December 1969.

Raoulia subulata Hook.f.
"Awl-shaped"—referring to the leaves.

Forms remarkably moss-like mats or loose patches up to 20 cm or more across. Dark-green, pointed, awl-shaped leaves (3–8 x 0.5–1 mm) are quite glabrous and among them at the stem tips the small (4 mm across) white flower heads develop.
DISTRIBUTION South Island: widespread on the higher mountains.

High-alpine: 1,400–2,000 m (4,500–6,500 ft).
HABITAT Usually present in late snowbanks and sheltered permanently wet sites in fellfield, but when not in flower it is easily mistaken for moss.
COLLECTED Old Man Range, Central Otago, 1,650 m (5,400 ft). January 1968.

Raoulia youngii (Hook.f.) Beauverd
After Mr W. Young, Haast's assistant.

Its habit is similar to *R. grandiflora* but the mats are snow-white and soft because the densely-overlapping and spreading leaves (3–6 x 2–2.5 mm) are smothered in soft white or sometimes pale-buff tomentum. Persistent dead leaves are grey.

Inner•scales enclosing the large flower heads (8–15 mm across) are glistening white and petal-like but the outer ones are light-brown and smaller.
DISTRIBUTION South Island: widespread on the higher mountains from about central Canterbury southwards.

High-alpine: 1,200–2,000 m (4,000–6,500 ft).

Cont. on page 158

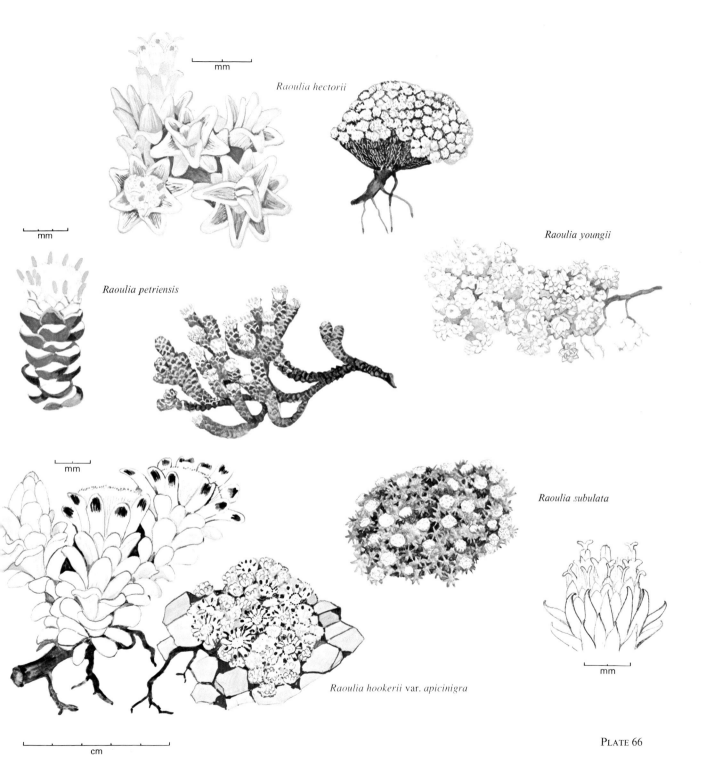

Raoulia hectorii

Raoulia youngii

Raoulia petriensis

Raoulia subulata

Raoulia hookerii var. *apicinigra*

PLATE 66

HABITAT A plant of virtually snow-free windswept sites in fellfield and cushion vegetation.

COLLECTED Mt Anstead, upper Dart Valley, Mt Aspiring National Park, 1,980 m (6,500 ft). January 1968.

Raoulia hectorii Hook.f. *(See plate 66)*
After Sir James Hector, geologist and explorer.

Forms hard silvery-green mats up to 1 m or more across. Their tightly-packed, short, erect, leafy branches are enclosed by small, tightly-overlapping, tapered leaves (2–4 mm long) that are obviously thickened at the tip and covered in silvery tomentum (sometimes slightly golden at the tips of younger leaves).

The small flower heads (*ca* 4 mm across) at the stem tips are enclosed by pale straw-coloured scales with tapered tips.

DISTRIBUTION South Island: on the higher and drier mountains from south Canterbury southwards through Central Otago.

High-alpine: 1,200–2,000 m (4,000–6,500 ft).

HABITAT One of the most important plants of cushion vegetation on the broad plateaux summits, in all but the most exposed sites. Its silvery colour contrasts with the other cushions.

COLLECTED Hawkdun Range, north Otago, 1,610 m (5,300 ft). December 1969.

Raoulia eximia Hook.f.   VEGETABLE SHEEP
"Exceptional".

Forms very dense light-grey cushions up to 2 m across and 30 cm or more thick. Both leaves and stems are very tightly packed but the dense covering of soft woolly hairs on the rounded leaf tips gives a velvety texture to the cushions. The pattern of hairs on the leaves is a key feature.

Small flower heads (*ca* 3 mm across), sunken among the leaves at the stem tips, have 10–15 minute crimson florets.

DISTRIBUTION South Island: on the drier greywacke mountains from mid-Canterbury to north Otago.

High-alpine: 1,100–1,800 m (3,500–6,000 ft).

HABITAT This remarkable plant usually colonises frost-shattered but relatively stable rocks in fellfield. Although often surrounded by scree and appearing from a distance to be on it, the vegetable sheep is not a scree plant.

COLLECTED Fog Peak, Torlesse Range, Canterbury, 1,740 m (5,700 ft). January 1968.

Raoulia mammillaris Hook.f.   VEGETABLE SHEEP
"Breast-like" referring to the shape of the short, thick, leafy branches.

Its habit is similar to *R. eximia* but the cushions rarely reach 1 m across. Also, shorter hairs at the leaf tips give the cushions a harsh texture, not soft as in *R. eximia*. The patterns of hairs on the leaf surfaces also distinguish the two species but a good lens is needed to see this.

Flower heads are usually larger (up to 6.5 mm across), but more distinctive are the inner bract scales that surround the heads—they have prominent, blunt, white tips only in *R. mammillaris*.

DISTRIBUTION South Island: confined to the drier greywacke moun-tains of mid and north Canterbury between about the Waiau and Rangitata Rivers.

High-alpine: 1,200–1,800 m (4,000–6,000 ft).

HABITAT As for *R. eximia*, with which it often occurs in mid-Canterbury.

COLLECTED Fog Peak, Torlesse Range, Canterbury, 1,710 m (5,600 ft). January 1968.

Raoulia bryoides Hook.f.   VEGETABLE SHEEP
"Moss-like".

Its cushion habit is similar to *R. mammillaris* and its texture is equally harsh. They are best distinguished by the hairs on the leaves. Shorter more appressed hairs at the tips of the leaves mean that the leaf shape is not at all obscured from above: it is partly concealed by the tuft of long hairs in *R. mammillaris*; com-pletely so in *R. eximia*.

Flower heads are generally similar to *R. mammillaris*.

DISTRIBUTION South Island: on the drier mountains of eastern Nelson-Marlborough and north Canterbury.

Low- to high-alpine: 1,200–1,800 m (4,000–6,000 ft).

HABITAT As for *R. eximia* but often occurring in association with the more massive brownish cushions of *Haastia pulvinaris*.

COLLECTED Mt Robert, Travers Range, Nelson Lakes National Park, 1,400 m (4,600 ft). December 1967.

Raoulia rubra Buchan.
"Red"—referring to the florets.

Forms hard, dense, whitish-green cushions up to 50 cm or more across and 20 cm thick. The tightly overlapping leaves have a fringe of hairs projecting beyond their broad tips which gives the cushions a velvety texture.

Small flower heads (3 mm across) with 10–15 deep-crimson florets are sunken among the leaves at the stem tips.

DISTRIBUTION North and South Islands: Tararua Range; the moun-tains of north-west and western Nelson, at least as far east and south as the Travers and Paparoa Ranges, respectively. Near its eastern limits it appears to cross with *R. bryoides*.

Low- to high-alpine: 1,200–1,800 m (4,000–6,000 ft).

HABITAT Usually on rock outcrops where the cushions may be quite prominent. They also colonise loose stony debris on windswept sites in fellfield.

COLLECTED Above Lake Sylvester, Cobb Valley, north-west Nelson, 1,490 m (4,900 ft). December 1967.

Raoulia buchananii Kirk
After Mr J. Buchanan, early New Zealand botanist.

Closely related and very similar to *R. rubra*. Hair patterns on the two leaf surfaces are distinctive: in *R. rubra* the lower portion of both surfaces is glabrous but long straight hairs project beyond the tip from both surfaces.

DISTRIBUTION South Island: south of about the Haast Valley in south Westland and west of the lakes in Otago-Southland-Fiordland, but apparently absent south of about Doubtful Sound.

Cont. on page 160

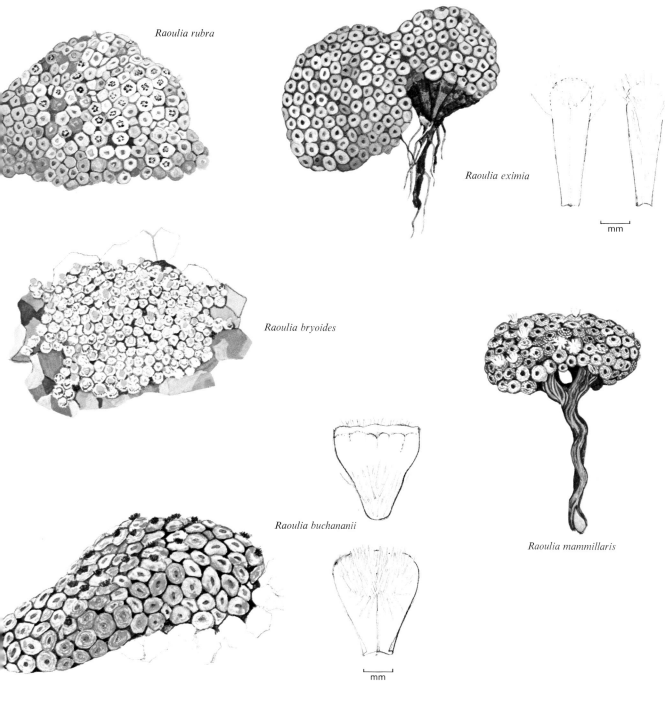

Raoulia rubra

Raoulia eximia

mm

Raoulia bryoides

Raoulia mammillaris

Raoulia buchananii

mm

cm

PLATE 67

Low- to high-alpine: 1,200–1,800 m (4,000–6,000 ft).
HABITAT On rock outcrops and steep exposed bluffs in snow tussock-herbfield and fellfield.
COLLECTED Gertrude Saddle, upper Hollyford Valley, Fiordland National Park, 1,430 m (4,700 ft). January 1968.

Raoulia goyenii Kirk
After Mr P. Goyen, who first collected it.

Its habit and colour are similar to *R. buchananii* but the cushions are somewhat larger, up to 1 m or more across. Leaves are narrower (0.5–1 vs 2–3 mm) but their pattern of hairs is almost identical.
DISTRIBUTION Stewart Island: confined to its higher peaks.
    Subalpine to low-alpine: 300–970 m (1,000–3,200 ft).
HABITAT Usually prominent both on exposed rock outcrops and in the wet peaty meadows and herb-moor.

Raoulia grandiflora Hook.f.
"Large-flowered".

Small, erect, leafy stems, 1–2 cm tall, form loose silvery mats up to 10 cm or more across. Their closely-overlapping tapered leaves (5–10 x 1–2 mm) are covered in silvery tomentum.

Relatively large flower heads (1–1.5 cm across) with prominent, white, petal-like scales surrounding the group of yellow florets, develop at the stem tips.
DISTRIBUTION North and South Islands: widespread on the higher mountains from East Cape (Mt Hikurangi) and the central North Island, southwards.
    Low- to high-alpine: 1,000–1,900 m (3,500–6,500 ft).
HABITAT Present in most types of alpine vegetation except for very dry, unstable or late snowmelt sites. In snow tussock grassland and herbfield it prefers openings but it is more widespread in the short high-alpine vegetation.
COLLECTED Old Man Range, Central Otago, 1,430 m (4,700 ft). December, 1969.

Genus LEUCOGENES
"White race (or genus)".
    Contains four species, all alpines and endemic to New Zealand.

Leucogenes leontopodium (Hook.f.) Beauverd
NORTH ISLAND EDELWEISS
Generic name of the european Edelweiss which it resembles in habit.

A trailing or creeping and rooting, much-branched sub-shrub with ascending leafy branches 5–15 cm tall. Closely-packed, pointed sessile leaves (8–20 x 4–5 mm) are covered in shining silvery to, pale-yellow tomentum.

Terminal flower stalks (to 10 cm tall) have many leafy bracts and a large compound head of 8–15 smaller ones clumped together and all surrounded by 10–20 woolly petal-like bracts.

DISTRIBUTION North and South Islands: from Mt Hikurangi southwards through the central and southern mountains; more scattered in the northern South Island: north-west Nelson (Tasman Mountains) and above the Wairau Valley in eastern Nelson-western Marlborough.
    Low- to high-alpine: 1,200–1,800 m (4,000–6,000 ft).
HABITAT This distinctive and beautiful alpine plant is quite reminiscent of the Swiss edelweiss in both its habit and habitat. It is often prominent on windswept rocky sites in the low-alpine zone and continues up into fellfield but on more sheltered sites, especially rock outcrops.
COLLECTED By Mr P. Williams from the Tararua Range, *ca* 1,400 m (4,600 ft). January 1969.

Leucogenes grandiceps (Hook.f.) Beauverd
"Large-headed".
SOUTH ISLAND EDELWEISS

Its branching semi-woody habit is similar to *L. leontopodium* but the leafy erect stems are shorter, while the leaves are smaller (5–10 x 2–4 mm) and less pointed, with softer tomentum. Basal leaves never form rosettes as they often do in North Island edelweiss.
DISTRIBUTION South and Stewart Islands: widespread in mountain regions almost throughout.
    Low- to high-alpine: 800–1,900 m (2,500–6,500 ft).
HABITAT With a wide distribution and distinct preference for rock outcrops, where it is often conspicuous, South Island edelweiss is probably the best known alpine throughout the South Island.
COLLECTED Upper Bealey Valley, Arthurs Pass National Park, 910 m (3,000 ft). December 1967.

Two recently described species are:

* Leucogenes neglecta Molloy
"Overlooked" — as a separate species.

Generally similar to *L. leontopodium* but differs in their longer, thinner stems, narrower more appressed leaves and shorter flower stems with smaller heads and silvery-blue floral bracts. The habitat is also similar but it is confined to and locally common on the Marlborough mountains between the Wairau and Awatere Rivers.

* Leucogenes tarahaoa Molloy
Tarahaoa is the legendary Maori name for Mt Peel.

Forms dense silvery white cushions of small closely packed rosettes 1.5 cm across with crowded narrow pointed leaves and short (2–4 cm) flower stems with a distinctive small edelweiss type head 1–2.5 cm across. Within the general geographic range of *L. grandiceps* it is restricted to fellfield and rock ledges on Mt Peel in mid Canterbury.

Leucogenes leontopodium

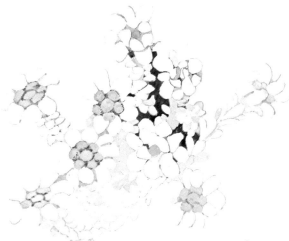

Leucogenes grandiceps

Raoulia grandiflora

PLATE 68

cm

Genus **HELICHRYSUM**
"Sun Gold".

A large and widespread genus of about 500 species. Of the nine native helichrysums, seven reach the alpine zone.

Helichrysum bellidioides (Forst.f.) Wild.   EVERLASTING DAISY
"Resembling *Bellis*" — a genus containing the common lawn daisy.

A somewhat variable low-growing sub-shrub with trailing or creeping and rooting stems up to 50 cm long that may form loose patches. Leaves vary in size (4–10 x 2–8 mm) and are grey to green and glabrous above when mature, but covered beneath in soft white tomentum.

Slender woolly flower stems (up to 10 cm long) have many erect leafy bracts and a single prominent head (1.5–3 cm across) in which the persistent inner bracts (30–50) are papery but large and petal-like.

Somewhat stouter plants with broader leaves that are often hairy on the supper surface may occur at higher elevations.

DISTRIBUTION   North, South and Stewart Islands: widespread in mountain regions from East Cape and Mt Egmont southwards.

Lowland to low-alpine: to 1,600 m (5,500 ft).

HABITAT   One of the most common and widespread plants in open or depleted vegetation — scrub, tussock grasslands, herbfield, riverbed and morainic gravels, roadsides, burned-over forests, rock outcrops and ultrabasic soils of the mineral belts.

COLLECTED   A robust form from the north slope, Mt Egmont National Park, 1,460 m (4,800 ft). November 1967.

Helichrysum filicaule Hook.f.
"Slender-stemmed".

A very slender sub-shrub with creeping buried stems and a few delicate erect branches 8–20 cm long. Leaves are not unlike *H. bellidioides* but are in two rows and flowering stems are quite different: a small head (7–10 mm across), without the surrounding petal-like bracts, sits atop a very slender stalk.

DISTRIBUTION   North, South and Stewart Islands: widespread in mountain regions south of about Rotorua.

Lowland to low-alpine: to 1,400 m (4,500 ft).

HABITAT   Usually common yet inconspicuous in tussock grasslands and herbfield. In high rainfall regions it is restricted to well-drained sites and is often abundant in valley grassland on gravel.

Helichrysum depressum (Hook.f.) Benth. & Hook.f.
"Low-growing".

A distinctive, dead-looking, dwarfed shrub, usually < 20 cm tall in alpine areas. Small, greyish-green, leafy branches are enclosed by the persistent, narrow, almost scale-like silky leaves.

Small sessile flower heads (5 mm across) are at the branch tips.

DISTRIBUTION   North and South Islands: recorded only from Hawke's Bay (Tukituki River); more widespread in the South Island, at least as far south as Canterbury.

Montane to low-alpine 300–1,300 m (1,000–4,500 ft).

HABITAT   Almost confined to loose gravel, especially shingle river beds, terraces and moraine. It so easily passes for a dead shrub that it is usually overlooked.

Helichrysum intermedium Simpson
"Intermediate — between other species".

A highly-branched variable shrub, up to 40 cm tall, with crowded branches (2–4 mm across) enclosed by minute but thick triangular scale-leaves (3–4 mm long but up to 8 mm in young plants) that are shining green and glabrous on the back when mature. Dense white hairs on the base and inside of the leaves and on the stems, usually outline each leaf on the stem.

Single yellow to almost white sessile flower heads are usually wider (3–7 mm) than the leafy stems they terminate.

DISTRIBUTION   South Island: widespread on the drier mountains from Nelson to Southland.

Mostly subalpine to high-alpine: 800–1,600 m (2,500–5,500 ft).

HABITAT   Virtually confined to crevices on rock outcrops, occasionally coastal.

COLLECTED   The smaller form from Hawkdun Range, north Otago, 1,370 m (4,500 ft). December 1969. The more robust form came from the upper Wairau Valley, Nelson, 1,160 m (3,800 ft). December 1967. It has some features of *H. coralloides* and is possibly a hybrid.

Helichrysum parvifolium Yeo
"Few-leaved".

Its habit is similar to *H. intermedium* but the leafy branchlets are finer (1–2 mm across) and the flower head somewhat larger (*ca* 1 cm across) yet with fewer florets (20–25 vs 25–45).

It grows on the dry mountains of the upper Wairau, Awatere and Clarence catchments in southern Nelson-Marlborough and north Canterbury, with a habitat and altitudinal range similar to *H. intermedium*.

Helichrysum coralloides (Hook.f.) Benth. & Hook.f.
"Resembling coral".

Its habit is similar to *H. intermedium* but the plants look much more remarkable—shrubs may reach 60 cm, their leafy branches are much stouter (7.5–10 mm across) than in *H. intermedium* and the individual leaves are larger (*ca* 5 x 2.5 mm). Also, overlap of the leaves is such that only the upper green and thickened half is exposed.

DISTRIBUTION   South Island: on the dry mountains of Marlborough to the south of Blenheim.

Montane to high-alpine: 400–1,900 m (1,500–6,500 ft).

HABITAT   Almost confined to rock outcrops.

COLLECTED   Mt Gladstone, Inland Kaikoura Range, Marlborough, 1,830 m (6,000 ft). January 1970.

Helichrysum bellidioides

Helichrysum coralloides

Helichrysum intermedium

Helichrysum plumeum

cm

PLATE 69

Helichrysum plumeum Allan
"Downy" — referring to the leafy branches.

Most features are similar to *H. intermedium* except for the distinctive loose, dull-yellow (rarely white) hairs that persist on the leaves to give shrubs a downy appearance.

DISTRIBUTION South Island: on the drier mountains of south Canterbury from the Two Thumb Range southwards.

Low- to high-alpine: 900–1,700 m (3,000–5,000 ft).

HABITAT Confined to rock outcrops.

COLLECTED Mt Dalgety, Dalgety Range, south Canterbury, 1,220 m (4,000 ft). January 1969.

Genus CRASPEDIA
"Fringed"—referring to the white margin on the leaves (of *C. uniflora*).

A small Australasian genus. At least three of the six craspedias described for New Zealand reach the alpine zone.

Craspedia incana Allan
"Hoary".

A summer-green rosette herb in which the basal leaves (5–10 x 2–3 cm) and rather stout flower stem (10–25 cm long) with its several narrow leafy bracts are all covered in thick, soft, snow-white tomentum. The tight head (2–3 cm across) of florets is distinctly yellow.

DISTRIBUTION South Island: on the drier eastern and interior mountains from central Marlborough to Otago, but somewhat local.

Low- to high-alpine: 1,000–1,800 m (3,500–6,000 ft).

HABITAT Most common on screes of the greywacke mountains where the hoary colour makes it one of the more conspicuous even if less important plants. It sometimes colonises loose stony debris in fellfield but on these sites plants often share some features of *C. lanata*.

COLLECTED Fog Peak, Torlesse Range, Canterbury, 1,160 m (3,800 ft). February 1969.

Craspedia uniflora Forst.f.
"Single-flowered"—inappropriate, since the head consists of many minute flowers.

A green rosette herb in which the degree of hairiness is much less than in the other two alpine species but highly variable. Only the leaf margins and sometimes the flower stalks are distinctly white with hairs. Flower stalks (15–45 cm long) have leafy bracts and a small to large head (1.5–3 cm across) that is white to yellow.

Var. *uniflora* has relatively small leaves (7 x 1.5 cm), short slender flower stalks and small heads, while var. *grandis* Allan, has larger (10–15 x 2 cm) sparsely hairy leaves, variable flower stalks and medium heads (*ca* 2 cm across).

DISTRIBUTION North and South Islands: widespread from about Rotorua southwards to Fiordland and Southland, but often replaced in the drier regions of the South Island by one or both of the other alpine species. Var. *grandis* is in the southern North Island.

Coastal to low-alpine: to 1,600 m (5,500 ft).

HABITAT Usually present but seldom abundant in moist grassland and snow tussock-herbfield. Being small leafy rosettes they are usually inconspicuous when not in flower.

COLLECTED Homer Tunnel, upper Hollyford Valley, Fiordland National Park, 970 m (3,200 ft). January 1968.

Craspedia lanata (Hook.f.) Allan
"Woolly".

Typical plants are generally intermediate between *C. uniflora* and *C. incana*. Their tomentum is greyish-white and more tightly pressed against the surface than in *C. incana*; flower heads are somewhat smaller (1.5–2 cm across) than in the other two, but like *C. uniflora* they are either white or yellow.

Var. *elongata* Allan, has more narrow pointed leaves (8–10 x 1–2.5 cm) on longer petioles and longer flower stalks (to 50 cm).

DISTRIBUTION South Island: much as for *C. incana* but apparently less erratic.

Montane to high-alpine: 500–1,900 m (1,500–6,500 ft).

HABITAT A plant of the tussock grasslands, herbfield, fellfield and cushion communities on the drier mountains east of the main divide.

COLLECTED Old Man Range, Central Otago, 1,220 m (4,000 ft). January 1968.

Genus TARAXACUM
From medieval Latin but ultimately from the Persian "bitter potherb"—after its medicinal use.

A widespread genus of about 150 species. The sole native dandelion, also in South America, reaches the alpine zone.

Taraxacum magellanicum Comm. ex Sch. Bip.   NATIVE DANDELION
"South American".

Similar to, and often confused with introduced dandelion. Native dandelion differs in being smaller and less succulent, but particularly in the bracts surrounding the flower head—they have distinct margins that are thin, white and almost translucent.

DISTRIBUTION North, South and Stewart Islands: widespread in mountain regions from the Coromandel Range southwards.

Mostly montane to high-alpine: 500–1,900 m (1,500–6,500 ft).

HABITAT Often common in open grassland and herbfield on moist sites, especially valley grasslands in the wet forested regions and where alpine vegetation has been depleted by heavy grazing. In the high-alpine zone it is confined to sheltered sites, especially shallow snowbanks.

COLLECTED Old Man Range, Central Otago, 1,610 m (5,300 ft). December 1969.

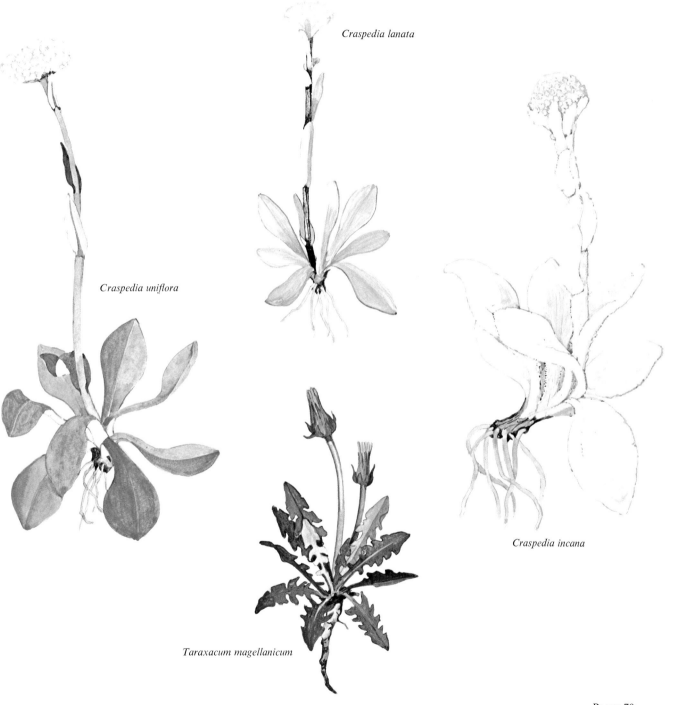

Craspedia lanata

Craspedia uniflora

Craspedia incana

Taraxacum magellanicum

cm

PLATE 70

Genus CASSINIA

After Cassini, French botanist.

A small Australasian—South African genus of about 20 species. Of the five native cassinias, one reaches the alpine zone.

Cassinia leptophylla (Forst.f.) R.Br. TAUHINU; COTTONWOOD
"Narrow-leaved".

A variable shrub up to 3 m tall but usually < 1 m in alpine areas. Small leathery leaves (3–12 x 2–3 mm) have slightly recurved margins and on their lower surface a prominent midrib and dull yellowish-brown to white tomentum.

Many (10–20) small flower heads (3–4 mm across), each with several white-tipped petal-like bracts, occur together on very short stalks in tight clusters at the branch tips.

The considerable local variation including leaf colour (white to yellowish-brown) is partly related to habitat, including elevation but variable plants may occur together. Upland plants have previously been called *C. vauvilliersii* but this name has now been abandoned and all native cassinias are referred to *C. leptophylla*. No subspecies or varieties have yet been recognised.

DISTRIBUTION North, South and Stewart Islands: rather widespread from East Cape and Taupo southwards.

Lowland to low-alpine: to 1,500 m (5,000 ft).

HABITAT Most important in open forest and scrub, and sometimes conspicuous in subalpine scrub. In the alpine zone it is widespread in mixed snow tussock-scrub but is common usually only where burning and grazing have favoured it, because of an ability to resprout quickly from the basal crown.

COLLECTED Temple Basin track, Arthurs Pass National Park, 1,160 m (3,800 ft). January 1971.

Genus SENECIO

From "senex, old man" — referring probably to the conspicuous white hairs (pappus) on the fruits.

A very large cosmopolitan genus. Of the 18 native species one reaches the alpine zone.

* Senecio glaucophyllus Cheesem.
"With glaucous leaves".

A highly variable prostrate to erect almost glabrous perennial herb with a somewhat woody base. The deeply toothed rather fleshy leaves are dark green above and often purplish beneath.

The bright yellow flower heads occur singly or in small clusters; the ripe seed heads are spherical and fluffy.

DISTRIBUTION North and South Islands: from the volcanic plateau southward to north Otago, mostly on the drier eastern mountains.

Montane to low-alpine: 300–1,650 m (1,000–5,500 ft).

HABITAT Often present on screes and rocky ground, including limestone crevices.

Genus BRACHYGLOTTIS

"Short tongue" — referring to the strap of the ray florets.

An endemic genus of some 30 species, six of which reach the alpine zone.

Brachyglottis bellidioides (Hook.f.) Nordenstam
"Resembling *Bellis*" — a genus containing the common lawn daisy.

A highly variable woody-based rosette herb with slightly leathery to almost fleshy, broad, rounded leaves (1–5 cm long) that usually have hairy margins, but the two surfaces may be glabrous or with sparse hairs. Leaves usually lie flat on the ground.

Simple or branched flower stalks (3–30 cm long) may be hairy or glabrous. They have a few, small, narrow bracts and a head (2–3 cm across) with yellow rays.

Several varieties have been distinguished, based largely on differences in degree and type of hairs and size, shape and texture of leaves, but the complex is still poorly understood.

DISTRIBUTION South and Stewart Islands: widespread in mountain regions almost throughout.

Mostly montane to high-alpine: 300–1,800 m (1,000–6,000 ft).

HABITAT Often present in a wide range of communities but being low growing it may be overlooked when not in flower. In the drier tussock grasslands it prefers moist sites but in wet regions it has a wide range from scrub through snow tussock-herbfield, both on the ground and on rocks. In the high-alpine zone it is confined to sheltered sites.

COLLECTED A common alpine form with a single head from Key Summit, Fiordland National Park, 910 m (3,000 ft). January 1969.

Brachyglottis lagopus (Raoul) Nordenstam
"Hare's foot" — referring to the abundant hairs.

A highly variable rosette herb with a stout rootstock smothered above in long brownish hairs. The characteristic colour of the leathery leaves is shown but their shape may vary from elliptic to almost round and their size from 2.5–15 x 3–10 cm. Hairs become sparse on the upper leaf surface but persist as a dense woolly cover beneath.

Simple or branched flower stems may reach 35 cm with a few narrow leafy bracts and yellow heads 2–4 cm across.

DISTRIBUTION North and South Islands: rather widespread from the Taupo region and Ruahine Range southwards through Canterbury. In the South Island smaller mountain forms may resemble hairy forms of *B. bellidioides* but their leaves are more erect and are distinctly woolly beneath.

Lowland to low-alpine: to 1,500 m (5,000 ft).

HABITAT Often common in open scrub, tussock grassland and snow tussock-herbfield, especially on rocky sites.

COLLECTED By Mr A. P. Druce from Tararua Range, 1,460 m (4,800 ft).

Brachyglottis haastii (Hook.f.) Nordenstam
After Sir Julius von Haast, famous geologist and explorer.

Its habit is similar to *B. bellidioides* except that the leaves are more erect, but dense, soft, white tomentum covers most of the plant. Shallow rounded teeth on the leaf margins are usually more pronounced than in *B. bellidioides*.

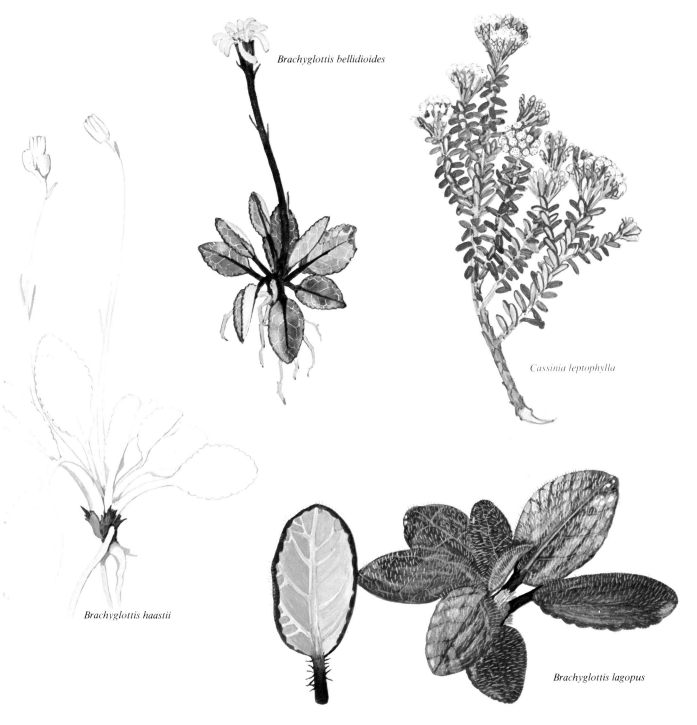

Brachyglottis bellidioides

Cassinia leptophylla

Brachyglottis haastii

Brachyglottis lagopus

cm

PLATE 71

DISTRIBUTION South Island: on the drier mountains of the interior from eastern Nelson – western Marlborough southwards to the Otago Lakes district.

Montane to low-alpine: 400–1,500 m (1,500–5,000 ft).

HABITAT In relatively dry grasslands and scrub but often most abundant and conspicuous on rock outcrops.

COLLECTED Mt Dalgety, Dalgety Range, south Canterbury, 1,220 m (4,000 ft). January 1969.

Brachyglottis revolutus (Kirk) Nordenstam
"Rolled towards the lower side" — referring to the leaves.

A low-growing usually spreading shrub, 10–20 cm tall, with ascending leafy branches like the one shown. Sticky leathery leaves (3–6 x 1–3 cm) are wrinkled and almost glabrous above but are covered beneath, except for the midrib, in dense whitish tomentum. Their slightly wavy margins are turned down.

Bright yellow flower heads (2 cm across) are produced in a broad cluster on a leafy flower stalk at the branch tips.

DISTRIBUTION South Island: on the mountains of western Southland-Fiordland and southern Central Otago as far north as about Harris Saddle and Lake Wakatipu.

Subalpine to high-alpine: 900–1,600 m (3,000–5,500 ft).

HABITAT Sometimes locally common in moist often rocky hollows or shady faces among low scrub in snow tussock grassland or herbfield.

COLLECTED Homer Tunnel, Fiordland National Park, 1,040 m (3,400 ft). January 1968.

Brachyglottis adamsii (Cheesem.) Nordenstam
After Mr J. Adams, with whom Cheeseman first collected it.

Its habit and many other features are similar to B. revolutus but plants are often larger (to 1 m tall) and stickier. Leaves are thicker and somewhat smaller and the flower stems more openly branched.

DISTRIBUTION North and South Islands: Tararua Range only; confined to the mountains of northern Marlborough–Nelson.

Subalpine to low-alpine: 1,100–1,600 m (3,500–5,500 ft).

HABITAT In mixed snow tussock-scrub and snow tussock-herbfield where it may be both common and conspicuous.

COLLECTED By Dr L. B. Moore from the Mt Arthur Plateau, north-west Nelson.

Brachyglottis bidwillii (Hook.f.) Nordenstam
After Mr J. C. Bidwill, early explorer and collector, especially in the central volcanic and Nelson regions.

A low branching shrub up to 1 m tall with stout rough branches. Very thick, broad, rounded leaves (2–3 x 1–2 cm) are glabrous and shining above but completely covered below in dense, soft, pale-grey to-buff tomentum.

Small dull flower heads (7–15 mm across) without any petal-like rays are in tight clusters on branched hairy, but almost leafless flower stems.

Var. **viridis** (Kirk) Cheesem., "green", is taller (to 1.5 m) and more slender with larger less leathery leaves.

DISTRIBUTION North and South Islands: widespread on the mountains from East Cape and Taupo southwards to Cook Strait. The larger South Island form is var. *viridis* which occurs as far south as the Rakaia Valley.

Subalpine to high-alpine: 800–1,700 m (2,500–5,500 ft).

HABITAT Scattered through subalpine low scrub and snow tussock-herbfield, becoming quite dwarfed with altitude to be only 20–30 cm tall on rock outcrops near its upper limit. It is plentiful on the central North Island volcanoes where it even extends into fellfield.

COLLECTED Mt Ruapehu, Tongariro National Park, ca 1,220 m (4,000 ft). The flowering twig is of var. *viridis* from the Temple Basin track, Arthurs Pass National Park, 1,160 m (3,800 ft). January 1971.

Genus DOLICHOGLOTTIS
"Long-tongue" — referring to the strap of the ray florets.

A small endemic genus of two species, both alpines. Hybrids between the species are not uncommon in the many areas they occupy together. Flower colour in the hybrids is cream to pale pink as shown here in the plant collected in the Craigieburn Range.

Dolichoglottis lyallii (Hook.f.) Nordenstam
After Dr Lyall, surgeon-naturalist on the H.M.S. *Terror* in the early 1840s.

A leafy herb with a buried woody stock covered in old leaf bases that produces many almost grass-like, rather fleshy, glabrous leaves (10–25 cm x 2–10 mm)

Leafy flower stems exceed the basal leaves and branch near the top into a broad cluster of large yellow heads (4–5 cm across). The upper part of the flower stem is usually purplish with dense glandular hairs.

DISTRIBUTION South and Stewart Islands: widespread almost throughout but rather local in the driest sites.

Montane to high-alpine: 600–1,800 m (2,000–6,000 ft).

HABITAT In permanently wet, usually flushed but well-lit sites, especially open creek beds, avalanche chutes or waterfalls in forest or scrub. In the alpine zone it occupies seepage areas, bogs, wet depressions, stream-sides and damp shaded sides of rock outcrops.

COLLECTED Craigieburn Range, Canterbury, ca 1,370 m (4,500 ft). January 1966.

Dolichoglottis scorzoneroides (Hook.f.) Nordenstam
"Resembling *Scorzonera*", Black Salsify or Viper's Grass from Europe.

Its habit is similar to D. lyallii but the leaves are broader (up to 2 cm) and usually slightly hairy. Much more distinctive are the flower heads which are white rather than yellow and often larger (4–6 cm across).

DISTRIBUTION South and Stewart Islands: widespread in the higher rainfall regions near the main divide.

Low- to high-alpine: 900–1,700 m (3,000–5,500 ft).

HABITAT Generally similar to D. lyallii; the two species often grow together, but being more tolerant of snow and a shorter growing season it is also successful in snowbanks and permanently moist sites in fellfield.

COLLECTED Craigieburn Range, Canterbury, 1,370 m (4,500 ft). January 1966.

Brachyglottis adamsii

Brachyglottis revolutus

Brachyglottis bidwillii

hybrid

Dolichoglottis lyallii

Dolichoglottis scorzoneroides

cm

PLATE 72

The Gentian Family: **GENTIANACEAE**

Genus **GENTIANA**
After Gentius, an Illyrian king.

A very large and widespread but typically alpine genus. New Zealand members belong to a group in which the corolla is deeply lobed. This and some other features indicate that they should be separated into another genus. *Gentianella* has been used but formalised for only some species, so *Gentiana* will be retained as the only valid name for all 19 indigenous species from the three main islands. Most of these reach the alpine zone but several are quite local in occurrence. They are usually among the last of the alpines to flower, in late January–April, or even later.

Gentiana lineata Kirk
"Linear"—referring to the leaves.

A curious little dark-green herb, 5–10 cm tall, easily recognised by its much-branched wiry stems that produce dense patches up to 10 cm or more across. Its many basal leaves are small and narrow (8–16 x 1–2 mm) and the 1–3 sometimes paired stem leaves are even smaller.

Single, small, terminal flowers (6–15 mm long) have the calyx deeply cut into narrow pointed lobes that are obviously shorter than the pointed lobes of the white corolla.

DISTRIBUTION South and Stewart Islands: a curious pattern—south Otago (Blue Mts), western Southland (Longwood Range), southern Fiordland and Stewart Island.

Lowland to low-alpine: to 1,100 m (3,500 ft).

HABITAT Apparently confined to cushion herb-moor, usually overlying peat.

COLLECTED Blue Mountains, south Otago, 910 m (3,000 ft). December 1964.

Gentiana gibbsii Petrie
After Mr F. G. Gibbs, who first collected it.

A rather erect herb, 6–15 cm tall, often forming small clumps with several stems from the base. The basal leaves may be shed, leaving the few pairs of smaller pointed stem leaves.

Flowers have pointed calyx and corolla lobes as in *G. lineata*, yet are distinct in that here the calyx lobes are about as long (15–20 mm) as the corolla. Also, the flowers are larger.

DISTRIBUTION Stewart Island: apparently confined to Mt Anglem.

Subalpine to low-alpine: 400–900 m (1,500–3,000 ft).

HABITAT Common under open subalpine scrub and especially in the saturated grassy meadow and herb moor on the upper slopes.

COLLECTED A late flowering plant from Mt Anglem, Stewart Island, 790 m (2,600 ft). May 1964.

Gentiana bellidifolia Hook.f.
"Daisy-leaved".

A stout-rooted herb that varies considerably with locality and habitat. Its stock may be single or branched with many thick, almost fleshy overlapping leaves (blades 10–15 × 5–7mm) in a basal rosette. These produce several to many stems (4–12 cm tall) that may be branched. Stem leaves are smaller than the basal ones, almost sessile and in 3–4 pairs.

Flowers are single or with 2–6 together in a tight flat-topped head. The calyx (8–9 mm long) is about half the corolla length and deeply cut into narrow pointed lobes, while the bell-shaped corolla (15–18 mm long), also deeply divided, has broad blunt lobes and sometimes fine purple veins.

Var. **australis** Petrie, is stouter and often forms low dense patches (6–12 cm across) with abundant large flowers (to 2.5 cm across).

DISTRIBUTION North and South Islands: widespread but sometimes local on the mountains from Mt Hikurangi southwards.

Subalpine to high-alpine: 600–1,800 m (2,000–6,000 ft).

Var. *australis* is in the South Island and mostly high-alpine.

HABITAT Usually a plant of the higher altitude tussock grasslands and herbfield. In fellfield along the Southern Alps it is usually represented by the smaller but more spectacular var. *australis*.

COLLECTED A richly-coloured plant from fellfield on Mt Ruapehu, Tongariro National Park, *ca* 1,500 m (5,000 ft). February 1971.

Gentiana amabilis Petrie, "pleasing",
is now considered to be a uniform dwarfed form of *G. bellidifolia*, modified by its bog habitat. It usually has only a single dark stem (4–5 cm tall) and a large terminal flower. On the mountains of Central Otago it grows in association with the larger form of *G. bellidifolia* from better drained sites.

COLLECTED Old Man Range, Central Otago, 1,370 m (4,500 ft). February 1967.

Gentiana matthewsii Petrie
After Mr H. J. Matthews, a forester and native plant enthusiast.

Rather similar to *G. grisebachii* but with stouter, more erect, squarish stems up to 25 cm tall. The few basal leaves and smaller but very broad stem leaves are sessile, with their bases clasping the stem. Single (or paired) flowers are on less slender stalks while their calyx and corolla lobes are less pointed than in *G. grisebachii*.

DISTRIBUTION South Island: western Otago and south Westland.

Subalpine to low-alpine: 800–1,300 m (2,500–4,500 ft).

HABITAT In wet areas of snow tussock-herbfield. On open sites it may be plentiful, especially on grassy valley floors below the tree line.

COLLECTED Park Pass, Humboldt Mountains, Mt Aspiring National Park, 1,220 m (4,000 ft). February 1968.

Gentiana gibbsii

Gentiana matthewsii

Gentiana lineata

Gentiana amabilis

Gentiana bellidifolia

cm

PLATE 73

Gentiana patula (Kirk) Cheesem.
"Spreading".

Another variable herb with several features of *G. bellidifolia* but the stems are usually at least 20 cm long and the blades of the basal leaves usually exceed 2 cm (vs 1–1.5 cm in *G. bellidifolia*). There are 1–several rather stout stems that radiate away from the basal rosette before becoming erect.

Flower heads vary as in *G. bellidifolia* and the flowers are also similar.

DISTRIBUTION North and South Islands: from the Tararua Range southwards, but it appears to be rare or absent along and west of the main divide south of Nelson.

Montane to low-alpine: 400–1,200 m (1,500–4,000 ft).

HABITAT Usually on wet sites in grassland.

COLLECTED Cobb Valley, north-west Nelson, 850 m (2,800 ft). December 1967.

Gentiana vernicosa Cheesem.
"Very glossy".

A dark-green glossy herb, *ca* 10 cm tall, with a long slender root and 1–5 creeping stems that end in upright leafy shoots. They produce small patches 5–10 cm across. Leaves (20 x 4 mm) are thick, narrow and pointed.

Flower stems have a few pairs of smaller leaves and a small terminal head of 1–7 flowers.

DISTRIBUTION South Island: rather widespread on the mountains of Nelson, but more common towards the west.

Low-alpine: 1,200–1,500 m (4,000–5,000 ft).

HABITAT This very distinctive alpine is often prominent in red tussock and snow tussock-herbfields.

COLLECTED Above Lake Sylvester, Cobb Valley, north-west Nelson, 1,430 m (4,700 ft). February 1969.

Gentiana cerina Hook.f.
"Waxy"—referring probably to the shining leaves.

Both the species and its more trailing var. *suberecta* are confined to the Auckland Islands. They are included to highlight the contrast in flower colour that we see in this and several other genera between mainland New Zealand and the Subantarctic Islands (see p. 16).

COLLECTED By Dr R. A. Falla. January 1963.

Gentiana grisebachii Hook.f.
After A. H. R. Grisebach, German botanist.

A variable openly-branched herb with few to many slender weak stems (7–20 cm long). The thin basal leaves (15–20 x 8–10 mm) are on petioles of similar length but the smaller stem leaves are almost sessile.

Single or paired flowers (8–15 mm long) are on very thin stalks up to 3 cm long. Both the calyx and corolla are deeply cut into narrow pointed lobes.

DISTRIBUTION North, South and Stewart Islands: from the central volcanoes and Mt Egmont southwards, but often quite local.

Lowland to low-alpine: to 1,400 m (4,500 ft).

HABITAT Usually in very wet grassland and herbfield or along forest margins.

COLLECTED Hen and Chickens, Mt Egmont National Park, 1,310 m (4,300 ft). February 1966.

172

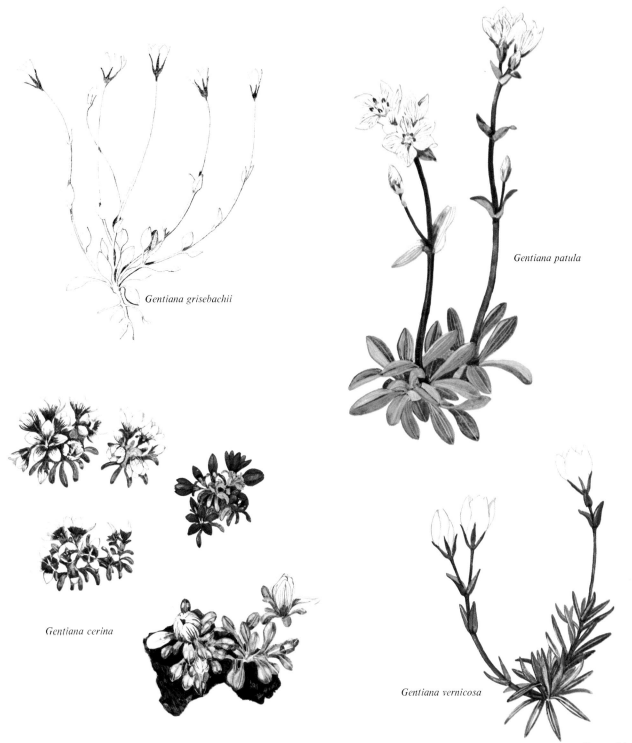

Gentiana grisebachii

Gentiana patula

Gentiana cerina

Gentiana vernicosa

cm

PLATE 74

Gentiana montana Forst.f.
"Growing in mountains".

Rather stout with a basal rosette (or sometimes a few together from a branched stock) of leathery dark-green leaves (15–25 x 8–16 mm) that are typically reddish beneath and have 3–5 prominent veins.

Usually a single stem (10–40 cm tall) from each rosette, with 2–6 pairs of smaller sessile leaves, branches above and ends in a cluster of up to 10 flowers that may form a flattened head.

Var. **stolonifera** Cheesem., "stolon-forming", is more slender with creeping stolons (10–15 cm long) radiating from its base. Leaves on the stolons are smaller and paired, as in the erect stems, and there are fewer flowers.

DISTRIBUTION South and Stewart Islands: widespread in the high rainfall regions along and near the main divide from north-west Nelson southwards. Var. *stolonifera* is restricted to Westland.

Subalpine to low-alpine: 500–1,500 m (1,500–5,000 ft).

HABITAT In snow tussock-herbfield from most high rainfall South Island regions. South of Nelson it is usually the most common low-alpine gentian near the main divide. It descends into subalpine scrub, wet avalanche chutes and sphagnum bog or wet grassland on the higher valley floors. Var. *stolonifera* is much less common.

COLLECTED Var. *montana* from Harris Saddle, Humboldt Mountains, Mt Aspiring National Park, 1,160 m (3,800 ft). January 1970. The few branches of a var. *stolonifera* are from Mt Brewster, Haast Pass, Mt Aspiring National Park, 1,520 m (5,000 ft). March 1968.

Gentiana spenceri Kirk
After Rev. F. H. Spencer, who first collected it.

The habit and colour are similar to *G. montana* but it is easily distinguished by the distinctive whorl of 5–7 large leafy bracts that surround the 1–3 tight clusters of flowers on each of the 1–few slender stems.

DISTRIBUTION South Island: from north-west Nelson southwards to central Westland.

Subalpine to low-alpine: 900–1,600 m (3,000–5,500 ft).

HABITAT Usually common in snow tussock-herbfield but extending into scrub and open forest.

COLLECTED Near Lake Sylvester, Cobb Valley, north-west Nelson, 1,370 m (4,500 ft). January 1971.

Gentiana lilliputiana C. Webb
"Minute".

A minute annual herb with an unbranched stem up to 2 cm tall and a single 4-petalled flower at its tip.

DISTRIBUTION South Island: Known only from the Kirkliston Range in south Canterbury and the northern Dunstan Mountains of Central Otago.

Low- to high-alpine: 1,200–1,800 m (1,380–6,000 ft).

HABITAT Often abundant, though quite inconspicuous when not in flower, among low turf in bogs and flushes.

COLLECTED Northern Dunstan Mountains, Central Otago, 1,580 m (5,420 ft). February 1985.

Gentiana lilliputiana

Gentiana montana var. *stolonifera*

Gentiana montana

Gentiana spenceri

cm

PLATE 75

Gentiana divisa (Kirk) Cheesem.
"Divided"—referring to the stems.

A stout-rooted herb with a distinctive habit. The basal rosette of overlapping, broad, rounded often reddish leaves is concealed in flowering plants by a compact mass of many usually short (5–20 cm), but highly-branched stems.

The globose mass of large terminal flowers is often so dense as to entirely mask the leaves. Plants usually die after flowering.

Var. **magnifica** (Kirk) Allan, is a short form that has few or no stem leaves.

DISTRIBUTION South Island: on the high mountains from southern Nelson southwards, chiefly close to the main divide but with a few eastern outliers. Var. *magnifica* is from the Amuri district.

Low- to high-alpine: 900–1,900 m (3,000–6,500 ft).

HABITAT In fellfield or occasionally cushion vegetation where it is often common and highly conspicuous when in flower, the heads looking quite like snowballs. It may also occur on windswept, stony or cold sites in snow tussock-herbfield.

COLLECTED Pisa Range, Central Otago, 1,520 m (5,000 ft). January 1968.

Gentiana corymbifera Kirk
"Bearing corymbs"—referring to the type of flower head.

A stout herb, 10–50 cm tall, with a large deep taproot and a basal rosette of thick, almost fleshy, long but narrow leaves (5–15 x 1–2 cm).

The 1–few stiff erect stems are usually unbranched below but much-branched above to form a compact, almost flat-topped head or corymb (5–15 cm across) of many large flowers. Most plants die after flowering.

DISTRIBUTION South Island: on the mountains of the interior from Marlborough—Nelson to Otago, but somewhat erratic.

Montane to high-alpine: 400–1,500 m (1,500–5,000 ft).

HABITAT A plant of the drier tussock grasslands where the prominent flower heads can make it most conspicuous. The deep taproot allows it to persist in depleted eroding grassland. In high rainfall regions it is confined to well-drained sites, especially moraine.

COLLECTED Hooker Valley, Mt Cook National Park, 1,280 m (4,200 ft). March 1968.

Cobb Valley *Gentiana*

A handsome much-branched herb that produces rather compact patches, up to 25 cm across, out of many basal rosettes that have stems 6–15 cm tall. Basal leaves have blades 8–12 x 5–6 mm with an equally long petiole. Flower stems have 2–4 pairs of leaves and may be single-flowered or branched above into small compact heads of up to 10 12 flowers (12–20 cm long).

These plants show certain resemblances to *G. bellidifolia*, to *G. spenceri*, as well as to *G. cerina* of the Auckland Islands, but their real status has not yet been clarified.

It is common where collected, from poorly-drained sites in snow tussock-herbfield above Lake Sylvester in the Cobb Valley, north-west Nelson, 1,430 m (4,700 ft). February 1969.

Other minor alpine gentians include:

*G. *filipes* Cheesem., a pale-green annual (< 8 cm tall) with solitary terminal flowers that forms little ball-like clumps; from Mt Arthur, north-west Nelson.

***G. gracilifolia** Cheesem., forms small patches up to 15 cm across, with narrow, dark-green, glossy leaves that are smaller (8–15 x 2–3 mm) than in *G. vernicosa* but otherwise similar. Flowering stems reach 15 cm with only 1–3 small flowers. They grow on the wet peaty margins of tarns on the Mt Arthur Plateau, north-west Nelson.

Gentiana corymbifera

Cobb Valley *Gentiana*

Gentiana divisa

cm

PLATE 76

The Plantain Family: PLANTAGINACEAE

Genus PLANTAGO
"Sole of the foot" — referring to the broad leaves flattened against the ground.

A large genus of some 260 mostly temperate species. Of the six mainland plantains only three commonly reach the alpine zone.

Plantago lanigera Hook.f.
"Woolly".

A small rosette herb, readily distinguished by the many long hairs covering the upper surface of at least the young leaves. These give a pale colour to the plants.

Several short, usually densely-hairy flower stems have small heads with only a few (up to 6) flowers.

DISTRIBUTION North and South Islands: on the mountains from the Ruahine Range southwards, but south of Nelson it occurs only east of the main divide.

Low- to high-alpine: 1,100–1,900 m (3,500–6,500 ft).

HABITAT Often prominent in damp hollows of snowbank depressions, but as a minor species it has a wider range, from exposed ridges to wet cold depressions in snow tussock grassland and herbfield.

COLLECTED Old Man Range, Central Otago, 1,520 m (5,000 ft). December 1968.

Plantago uniflora Hook.f.
"Single-flowered".

A variable rosette herb with narrow (1–3 cm x 1–7 mm), distinctively-shaped, glabrous leaves (sometimes with a few hairs on the basal half of the upper surface). Their edges may be smooth to strongly toothed.

Flower stems have very small heads of just one (or 2) flowers.

DISTRIBUTION North, South and Stewart Islands: on the volcanic mountains, Ruahine and Tararua Ranges; in the wetter western mountains of the South Island and locally further east.

Mostly subalpine to low-alpine: 1,000–1,500 m (3,500–5,000 ft).

HABITAT Usually in alpine bogs and permanently wet depressions in snow tussock grassland and herbfield.

COLLECTED Old Man Range, Central Otago, 1,520 m (5,000 ft). January 1970.

Plantago novae-zelandiae L. B. Moore
"Of New Zealand".

The habit is similar to *P. uniflora* but the leaves are more oval to elliptic (1–4 cm x 6–10 mm) with sparse long hairs and smooth or at most indistinctly-toothed edges.

Flower heads are up to 1 cm long with a tight cluster of 2–12 flowers. It has now been merged with *P. lanigera* which has therefore become more variable in both form and habitat.

DISTRIBUTION North and South Islands: widespread in mountain regions from East Cape (Mt Hikurangi) southwards.

Montane to low-alpine: 500–1,700 m (1,500–5,500 ft).

HABITAT Common, if rather inconspicuous, in grasslands and herbfields, including rock outcrops, except on dry sites.

COLLECTED Above Lake Wapiti, upper Doon Valley, Fiordland National Park, 1,070 m (3,500 ft). December 1970.

The Bellflower Family: CAMPANULACEAE

Genus WAHLENBERGIA
After Professor G. Wahlenberg, Swedish botanist.

A genus of some 120 widely distributed species, particularly in the southern hemisphere. Of the ten native wahlenbergias, three are alpines.

Wahlenbergia albomarginata Hook.
"White-margined"—referring to the leaves.

A small herb with branched, wiry, underground stems that produce usually scattered rosettes (1–2 cm across). Leaves vary (5–15 x 1–10 mm) but usually they are leathery, almost smooth-edged and have a white margin. They are wider and rather glacous towards the north and very small in semi-arid areas.

One very slender flower stalk (3–20 cm tall, depending on the habitat) per rosette has a white or pale-blue, usually drooping flower (1–3 cm long), often with deeper coloured veins.

DISTRIBUTION South and Stewart Islands: widely distributed but more common in the drier mountain regions east of the main divide.

Lowland to low-alpine: to 1,400 m (4,500 ft).

HABITAT A wide-ranging plant in open, even depleted tussock grassland, herbfield and occasionally scree. In high rainfall regions it may be restricted to well-drained sites, especially gravel of river beds and moraine.

COLLECTED Wairau Gorge, south-eastern Nelson, 1,160 m (3,800 ft). December 1967.

Wahlenbergia pygmaea Col.
"Very small".

Generally similar to *W. albomarginata* and sometimes difficult to distinguish from it, but it is more uniformly small with unthickened, shallowly-toothed leaf margins and almost fleshy glossy-green blades.

Flowers appear large for the plant. They droop, as in *W. albomarginata*, with pale-blue lobes and prominent veins, but the usually white throat of the corolla is much broader.

DISTRIBUTION North and South Islands: from the volcanic mountains southwards in the higher rainfall regions but rather local in central and southern South Island.

Subalpine to low-alpine: 700–1,700 m (2,500–5,500 ft).

HABITAT On open, often depleted but well-drained sites in scrub, valley grasslands and tussock-herbfields.

COLLECTED Mt Ruapehu, Tongariro National Park, *ca* 1,500 m (5,000 ft). March 1963.

Plantago lanigera

Plantago novae-zelandiae

Plantago uniflora

Wahlenbergia pygmaea

Wahlenbergia cartilaginea

Wahlenbergia albomarginata

cm

PLATE 77

Wahlenbergia cartilaginea Hook.f. (*See plate 77*)
"Cartilaginous"—referring to the leaf margins.

A distinctive rhizomatous plant, easily recognised by its small star-like rosette of thick, leathery, glaucous to purplish leaves (6–20 x 5–15 mm) with even thicker, white, minutely-toothed margins.

Flowers are white to light blue, quite erect and distinctly sweet-scented.

DISTRIBUTION South Island: on the drier mountains of Marlborough and eastern Nelson.

Low- to high-alpine: 1,100–1,700 m (3,500–5,500 ft).

HABITAT Almost confined to scree but sometimes on partly-stabilised debris and among crevices.

COLLECTED Shingle Peak, upper Awatere Valley, Marlborough, 1,310 m (4,300 ft). January 1970.

The Donatia Family: **DONATIACEAE**

Genus **DONATIA**
After Vitalianus Donati, of Padua near Venice.

Contains but two species, one in southern South America and the other in New Zealand where it reaches the alpine zone.

Donatia novae-zelandiae Hook.f.
"Of New Zealand".

Forms dense, hard, dark-green cushions up to 1 m or more across from its highly-branched and densely-leafy stems. Small, thick, glossy, pointed leaves (5–10 x 1 mm) completely enclose the erect stems, while fleshy white roots emerge from among the persistent dead leaves below the surface of the cushion.

Single white flowers (8–10 mm across) occur sunken among the leaves. They characteristically have 5 rather fleshy white petals but only 2 short stamens that a good lens will show are joined to the base of the split styles.

DISTRIBUTION North, South and Stewart Islands: from the Tararua Range southwards.

Mostly subalpine to low-alpine: 800–1,500 m (2,500–5,000 ft).

HABITAT Usually common in cushion bogs overlying peat. Small cushions sometimes occur in permanently-wet depressions in snow tussock or red tussock grassland or herbfield.

COLLECTED Key Summit, Fiordland National Park, 910 m (3,000 ft). January 1968.

The Stylidium Family: **STYLIDIACEAE**

Genus **PHYLLACHNE**
"Glume-like leaves"—referring to the somewhat chaffy leaves.

A small genus from southern South America, Tasmania and New Zealand. All of the native phyllachnes are alpine.

Phyllachne colensoi (Hook.f.) Bergg.
After Rev. W. Colenso, early New Zealand botanist.

Forms bright- to dark-green cushions or mats up to 50 cm across. Leaves are shorter (4 mm) than in *Donatia* and tapered from the papery base to blunt tips where there is a microscopic pore.

Small white flowers among the terminal leaves have 5 spreading lobes and a prominent central column (stylidium) of the 2 stamens with purple anthers surrounding the style.

DISTRIBUTION North, South and Stewart Islands: widespread in mountain regions from Mt Hikurangi and the volcanic mountains southwards.

Low- to high-alpine: 900–1,900 m (3,000–6,500 ft).

HABITAT A versatile cushion plant—herb-moor overlying peat, short open snow tussock-herbfield both in snow hollows and on exposed ridges at higher elevations, fellfield, cushion vegetation and shallow snowbanks.

COLLECTED Mt Brewster, Haast Pass, Mt Aspiring National Park, 1,680 m (5,500 ft). March 1968.

*Phyllachne clavigera (Hook.f.) F. Muell.
"Club-bearing"—referring to the slightly thickened knob at the leaf tip.

Similar to *P. colensoi* except for having the column in the flowers hardly protruding beyond the lobes of the corolla. It is recorded only from the South Island, but we have not yet seen fully developed flowers that were not referable to *P. colensoi*.

Phyllachne rubra (Hook.f.) Cheesem.
"Red"—referring to the usual colour of spent flowers.

Distinguishing features are its paler yellowish-green colour and a distinct apical knob on the leaves. Cushions are usually < 30 cm across.

DISTRIBUTION South Island: on the higher mountains of Central Otago and the Lakes district.

High-alpine: 1,200–1,900 m (4,000–6,500 ft).

HABITAT Usually common on the more exposed areas of cushion vegetation and in shallow snowbanks.

COLLECTED Old Man Range, Central Otago, 1,650 m (5,400 ft). December 1968.

Genus **OREOSTYLIDIUM**
"Mountain *Stylidium*".

Contains but a single endemic species that reaches the alpine zone.

Oreostylidium subulatum (Hook.f.) Bergg.
"Awl-shaped"—referring to the leaves.

A small, glabrous, rosette herb, sometimes with offset plants produced from slender creeping stems. Densely-tufted spreading leaves are needle-like (10–40 x 1–2 mm), sharp-pointed and light-green, often mottled with red.

Small white flowers (4–5 mm across) occur singly on 1–2 short (0.5–2 cm) but stout stalks. Details of the flower show distribution of glandular hairs, lobing on the 2-lipped calyx and the short central

Cont. on page 182

Oreostylidium subulatum

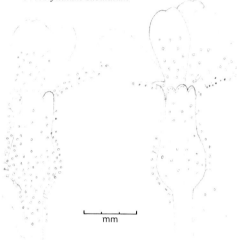

Donatia novae-zelandiae

Phyllachne rubra

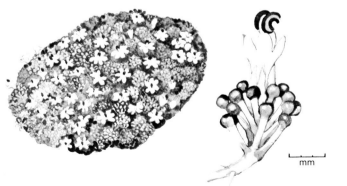

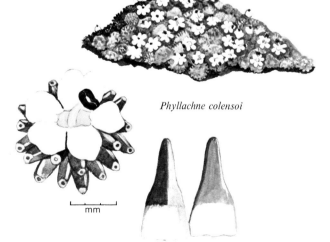

Phyllachne colensoi

PLATE 78

column with a split anther on either side of the stigma. Fruits are dry roundish capsules (4–5 mm across).

DISTRIBUTION North, South and Stewart Islands: widespread but highly erratic from the central volcanoes southwards.

Lowland to low-alpine: to 1,200 m (4,000 ft).

HABITAT An inconspicuous plant of well-lit, permanently wet, usually peaty or acidic sites in bogs, tussock grassland, herbfield, dwarfed woodland or scrub.

COLLECTED By Mr A. P. Druce from the slopes of Mt Tongariro, Tongariro National Park. November 1967.

Genus FORSTERA

After one or other of the Forsters, father and son who accompanied Cook as botanists on his second voyage to New Zealand.

A small genus from southern South America, Tasmania and New Zealand. All four native forsteras reach the alpine zone.

Forstera sedifolia Forst.f.

"*Sedum*-leaved".

A small glabrous sub-shrub with trailing or creeping and rooting slightly-branched stems that become erect and 3–15 cm tall. Glossy leathery leaves (4–8 x 2–4 mm) are sessile and overlapping on the stem. Their smooth edges are thickened and translucent while the usually reddish lower surface has a prominent, broad, tapering midrib.

Slender flower stalks (5–10 cm long) arise among the terminal leaves and bear 1–2 flowers (6–12 mm long) each with 6 petal lobes. Fruits are dry capsules (6–7 mm long).

DISTRIBUTION South and Stewart Islands: widespread on the wetter mountains along and near the main divide.

Mostly subalpine to low-alpine: 800–1,500 m (2,500–5,000 ft).

HABITAT Usually common in wet snow tussock-herbfield, but more prominent wherever the tall cover is thinner and shorter, especially on bluffs or rocky sites. Also in open scrub and below the tree line especially on wet rocks alongside waterfalls or avalanche chutes.

COLLECTED Mt Brewster, Haast Pass, Mt Aspiring National Park, 1,520 m (5,000 ft). March 1968.

Forstera bidwillii Hook.f.

After Mr J. C. Bidwill, early explorer and collector, especially in the central volcanic and Nelson regions.

Generally similar to *F. sedifolia* except that the leaves are usually less densely overlapping, but more distinctive, the midrib is narrow and quite indistinct, while the margins are less pronounced.

Flower stalks bear up to 3 flowers that sometimes have a dark-red eye, a feature seen only rarely in *F. sedifolia*.

Var. **densifolia** Mild., is more highly branched, with the leaves larger and more closely set. Its flowers are longer (up to 15 mm).

DISTRIBUTION North and South Islands: from Mt Hikurangi and the volcanic mountains southwards; in Nelson, but seems to be rare or absent elsewhere. Var. *densifolia* is on the volcanic mountains.

Subalpine to high-alpine: 800–1,800 m (2,500–6,000 ft).

HABITAT Generally similar to *F. sedifolia* except that it also extends into the high-alpine zone, at least on stable moist sites on Mt Egmont.

COLLECTED Mangatepopo Valley, Tongariro National Park, *ca* 1,070 m (3,500 ft). March 1964. Var. *densifolia* is from the north slope of Mt Egmont, 1,460 m (4,800 ft). November 1967.

Forstera tenella Hook.f.

"Rather delicate".

Its habit is similar to the others but the leaves are often purplish, thinner, narrower and much less crowded. Moreover, they have short (1 mm) but distinct petioles. Their flower stalks are very slender and delicate.

DISTRIBUTION North and South Islands: widespread yet rather local from the Ruahine Range southwards.

Montane to low-alpine: 500–1,400 m (1,500–4,500 ft).

HABITAT Most common in sphagnum and cushion bogs where it is often abundant, but it may be locally plentiful in permanently wet depressions among grassland and herbfield or below the tree line on wet avalanche chutes or waterfalls.

COLLECTED Maungatua, eastern Otago, 880 m (2,900 ft). January 1969.

*Forstera mackayi Allan

After Mr W. Mackay, who first collected it.

Generally similar to *F. sedifolia*, except that the leaves are longer and narrower (8–10 x 2–2.5 mm). Distribution is quite restricted— along and west of the main divide from central Nelson to north Westland (Paparoa Range), where it occupies similar habitats to *F. sedifolia*.

Forstera bidwilli var. *densifolia*

Forstera bidwillii

Forstera sedifolia

Forstera tenella

cm

Plate 79

The Lobelia Family: **LOBELIACEAE**

Genus **LOBELIA**
After M. de l'Obel or Lobelius, 17th century Flemish botanist and physician to James I.

A widespread genus containing about 350 species. Of the three native lobelias, two are alpines.

Lobelia linnaeoides (Hook.f.) Petrie
"Resembling *Linnaea*"—a small boreal and northern hemisphere alpine herb.

A small, sparingly-branched, creeping and rooting herb with milky sap, slender stems and thick leaves (4–8 x 4–8 mm) that are distinctively shaped and coloured.

Small white to pink or pale-blue flowers occur singly on delicate erect stalks (2–8 cm long).

DISTRIBUTION South Island: on the mountains of the interior between about the Ashburton catchment in Canterbury, and Otago.

Montane to high-alpine: 500–1,800 m (1,500–6,000 ft).

HABITAT On permanently moist but thinly-vegetated sites from short tussock grassland upwards, through snow tussock grassland and herbfield. In the high-alpine zone it is restricted to damp hollows in shallow snowbanks.

COLLECTED Rock & Pillar Range, Central Otago, 1,220 m (4,000 ft). January 1968.

Lobelia roughii Hook.f.
After Captain Rough, early collector, especially in the Nelson mountains.

A glabrous summer-green herb with bitter milky sap. Slender, underground, branched stems and roots weave among loose rock debris while short leafy branches (to 10 cm) emerge through it. The dark to bronze-coloured, almost fleshy leaves (10–20 x 10–15 mm) have a characteristic shape.

Small white to partly-red flowers (10 mm long) occur among the foliage on short stalks. These elongate (to *ca* 5 cm) as the large, dry, bladder-like capsules, tipped with persistent sepals, ripen.

DISTRIBUTION South Island: on the drier, especially greywacke mountains from Marlborough–Nelson (including the mineral belt) to north Otago, but rather uncommon.

Low- to high-alpine: 1,000–1,800 m (3,500–6,000 ft).

HABITAT Essentially confined to scree where the dark foliage makes it one of the most conspicuous if less common members.

COLLECTED Vegetative plants from Island Pass, upper Wairau Valley, Nelson, 1,400 m (4,600 ft): the flowering one from Shingle Peak, upper Awatere Valley, Marlborough, 1,310 m (4,300 ft). January 1970. Those in fruit from Fog Peak, Torlesse Range, Canterbury, 1,520 m (5,000 ft). March 1968.

Genus **PRATIA**
After Prat, French botanist and naval officer.

Contains about 25 species from Asia, South America and Australasia. Two of the five native pratias reach the alpine zone.

Pratia angulata (Forst.f.) Hook.f.
"Angled".

A highly variable creeping and rooting herb that may form small diffuse patches. The usually thick leaves are rounded but highly variable in size (4–10 x 4–10 mm) and coarsely yet shallowly-toothed.

Flowers are white with purple veins and have a short corolla tube, but their size is highly variable (7–20 mm long). The slender flower stalks elongate (to 2–6 cm) as the shining purplish-red berries ripen.

Groups have been recognised to reconcile some of the range of variation in this highly plastic species but no varieties have yet been described.

DISTRIBUTION North, South and Stewart Islands: almost throughout.

Lowland to low-alpine: to 1,300 m (4,500 ft).

HABITAT Often common on well-lit permanently moist sites. In the alpine zone it may be common along streamsides and on closely grazed or depleted sites, especially near the tree line.

COLLECTED By Professor G. T. S. Baylis from Fiordland National Park. May 1965.

Pratia macrodon Hook.f.
"Large-toothed"—referring to the coarsely-toothed leaves.

This species also varies in size, especially with the habitat. Distinction from *P. angulata* is based both on the leaves, which are somewhat fleshy, and the fragrant flowers—here the corolla tube is relatively long and cylindrical but more or less swollen at the base. The berry is globose and purplish on a short (3–10 mm) stalk.

DISTRIBUTION South Island: widespread in mountain regions.

Subalpine to high-alpine: 700–1,900 m (2,000–6,500 ft).

HABITAT In the drier regions it is confined to permanently moist sites, but elsewhere it is much less restricted—valley grassland, open subalpine forest and scrub, snow tussock-herbfield, fellfield and snowbanks.

COLLECTED Mt Brewster, Haast Pass, Mt Aspiring National Park, 1,680 m (5,500 ft). March 1968.

Lobelia roughii

Lobelia linnaeoides

mm

Pratia macrodon

Pratia angulata

cm

PLATE 80

The Borage Family: **BORAGINACEAE**

Genus **MYOSOTIS**

"Mouse-ear"—referring to the leaves.

Contains about 50 mostly temperate species, 34 of which are native to New Zealand. Of these about 18 reach the alpine zone, but several are local in occurrence and even the more widespread forget-me-nots are seldom prominent in the vegetation.

Myosotis pulvinaris Hook.f.

"Cushion-shaped".

Forms soft grey cushions up to 10 cm across. Individual stems are erect (1–3 cm long), unbranched above and crowded with small silky-hairy leaves (5–7 x 3–5 mm). Towards the west and south of its range the cushions are looser and the leaves greener due to fewer and shorter hairs.

Small white flowers occur singly among the leaves at the stem tips and may cover most of the cushion.

DISTRIBUTION South Island: on the higher mountains of central-western Otago and northern Southland with one record from south-eastern Fiordland (Hunter Mts).

High-alpine: 1,300–1,900 m (4,500–6,500 ft).

HABITAT A characteristic plant of exposed sites in cushion vegetation of the Central Otago high plateaux. In the wetter regions further west it colonises ridge crests and rock outcrops in fellfield.

COLLECTED: Old Man Range, Central Otago, 1,520 m (5,000 ft). November 1967.

Myosotis glabrescens L. B. Moore

"Almost glabrous".

The cushion habit and single flowers resemble *M. pulvinaris* but only the young leaves are hairy.

It is reported from fellfield in the Lakes district of Otago, within the range of *M. pulvinaris*, but has not been collected recently.

Myosotis cheesemanii Petrie

After Mr T. F. Cheeseman, well-known New Zealand botanist.

The loose cushion habit is similar to *M. glabrescens* but the colour and hairiness match *M. pulvinaris*. Two distinct features are branching near the tips of the short erect stems, and flowers occurring 2–4 together in a small head rather than singly. It is apparently confined to cushion vegetation on the Pisa Range and Dunstan Mts, Central Otago.

Myosotis albosericea Hook.f. with silvery loose cushions, and *M. oreophilo* Petrie, a dark grey rosette species, are confined to the Dunstan Mountains of Central Otago.

Myosotis elderi L. B. Moore

After Mr N. L. Elder, who noted it on the Tararua Range.

A small rosette herb, usually with a few short trailing branches that form patches up to 8 cm across. The rosette leaf shows numerous long, soft, spreading hairs but only on the upper surface.

Short flower heads carry up to 12 congested white (or blue or pinkish) flowers (4–8 mm across) in which the anthers barely protrude beyond the corolla tube and the styles are much longer than the calyx lobes.

DISTRIBUTION North and South Islands: Tararua Range; much more widespread on South Island mountains—Canterbury, Central and western Otago, south Westland and Fiordland.

Low- to high-alpine: 1,000–1,700 m (3,000–5,500 ft).

HABITAT Usually on loose fine debris in fellfield or in open depleted snow tussock grassland or herbfield.

COLLECTED Rock & Pillar Range, Central Otago, 1,160 m (3,800 ft). November 1967.

Myosotis tenericaulis Petrie

"Delicate-stemmed".

A very slender herb with a few delicate branches arising from the mostly-buried main stem. Branches are usually only 2–5 cm long in alpine areas and their sparsely-hairy small leaves (6–12 x 3–6 mm) are on long slender petioles.

In alpine areas the very small flowers may be single but at lower elevations there are usually several, widely spaced along an elongated head.

DISTRIBUTION North and South Islands: Ruahine Range; more widespread in the South Island, but as an alpine apparently restricted to Central Otago.

Lowland to low-alpine: to 1,500 m (5,000 ft).

HABITAT In the alpine zone it appears to be confined to bogs, where it will probably be overlooked unless flowering.

COLLECTED Rock & Pillar Range, Central Otago, 1,220 m (4,000 ft). December 1970. Seen among moss.

Myosotis pygmaea Col.

"Very small".

A variable little rosette herb with a few to several simple or divided trailing branches up to 8 cm long, that may form loose or dense patches. Only the upper leaf surface has a sparse covering of hairs.

Minute white flowers (0.5–3 mm across) are in few- to many-flowered heads. As the single flower shows, the calyx is split less than halfway and the anthers do not protrude beyond the end of the corolla. The style is shorter than the calyx.

Four varieties are recognised but a good lens will be needed to identify these (see Allan's *Flora of New Zealand* 1961, p. 815).

DISTRIBUTION North, South and Stewart Islands: widespread from the Auckland Isthmus southwards.

Coastal to high-alpine: to 1,700 m (5,500 ft).

HABITAT Usually on well-drained open sites, especially on otherwise bare soil among depleted vegetation. In high-alpine areas it may occupy shallow snowbanks, fellfield and rock outcrops.

COLLECTED Old Man Range, Central Otago, 1,220 m (4,000 ft). November 1967.

Myosotis lyallii Hook.f.

After Dr Lyall, surgeon-naturalist on the HMS *Terror* in the early 1840s.

A variable rosette herb, with a few short (to 8 cm), hairy, trailing branches. Basal leaves (15–35 x 4–7 mm) and their long petioles

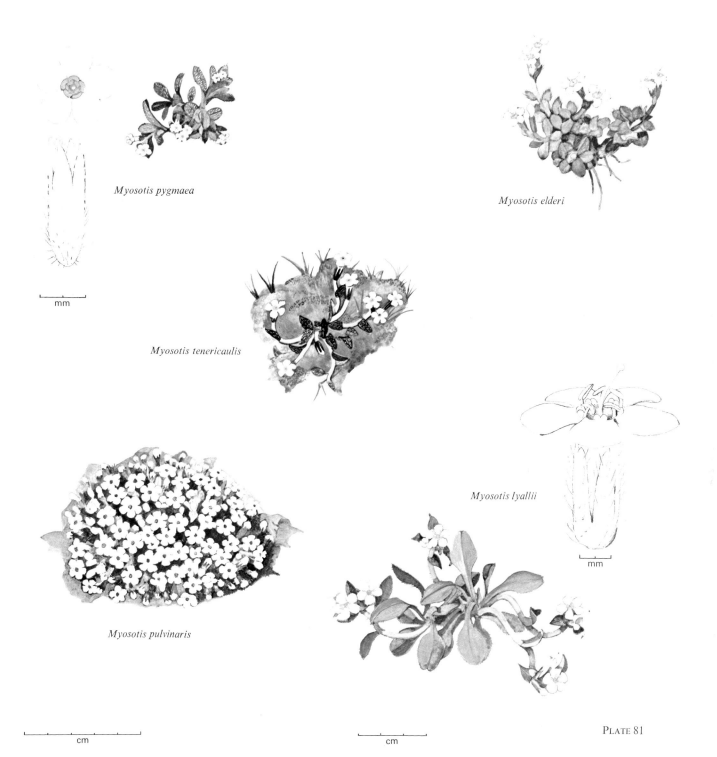

Myosotis pygmaea

Myosotis elderi

mm

Myosotis tenericaulis

Myosotis lyallii

Myosotis pulvinaris

mm

cm

cm

PLATE 81

have fine hairs on their upper surface and margins but they are sparse or absent beneath.

Small, few-flowered (< 8) heads are on the tips of the stems; the lower 2–3 flowers are associated with small leafy bracts. Anthers project beyond the white corolla tube.

Var. *lyallii* is a compact plant with dense hairs on the leaves and calyx, while var. *townsonii* (Cheesem.) L. B. Moore, "after Mr W. Townson", is more lax, with fewer hairs.

DISTRIBUTION South Island: in the high rainfall regions along and west of the main divide from the Buller district southwards. Var. *lyallii* is in western Otago and Fiordland while var. *townsonii* is further north.

Low- to high-alpine: 1,200–1,800 m (4,000–6,000 ft).

HABITAT On loose debris slopes and rock outcrops in fellfield, sometimes descending into the low-alpine zone on exposed sites where the plant cover is sparse.

COLLECTED Gertrude Saddle, upper Hollyford Valley, Fiordland National Park, 1,220 m (4,000 ft). January 1968.

Myosotis traversii Hook.f.
After Mr W. T. L. Travers, early collector, especially in Nelson.

A pale-green herb forming rosettes, often with several clumped together, and with pinkish branches up to 15 cm tall. Rather thick leaves (2–7 cm x 4–9 mm) are covered with fine but stiff white hairs on both surfaces and have broad petioles.

Rounded heads contain many crowded, white to pale-yellow flowers, sometimes with a yellow eye.

Three varieties are recognised, based on the type of hairs and shape of the heads (see Allan's *Flora of New Zealand* 1961, p. 817).

DISTRIBUTION South Island: on the greywacke mountains from eastern Nelson–Marlborough southwards through Canterbury to north-western Otago.

Subalpine to high-alpine: 800–1,900 m (2,500–6,500 ft).

HABITAT Present on screes and fellfield where it may be conspicuous when in flower.

COLLECTED Island Pass, upper Wairau Valley, Nelson, 1,400 m (4,600 ft). December 1967.

Myosotis australis R.Br.
"Southern".

A highly-variable greenish-brown herb, occurring usually as single rosettes with a few to many, hairy, erect branches, 5–25 cm long. Thin leaves (2–6 cm x 4–12 mm) have a distinctly hairy upper surface but are much less hairy beneath.

Small yellow (or white) flowers are on short stalks in a tight head which unrolls, elongates and becomes erect as the fruits ripen. The tube of the corolla and the style are hardly longer than the calyx.

A number of varieties have been described but the complex has not yet been satisfactorily resolved.

DISTRIBUTION North and South Islands: the most widespread form, shown here, is apparently local in the North Island (Kaimanawa Range), but less so in the South Island where it occurs in Canterbury and north Otago. A form with slightly larger white flowers is in Marlborough.

Mostly subalpine to low-alpine: 500–1,500 m (1,500–5,000 ft).

HABITAT In the alpine zone it is most common in depleted, often eroding snow tussock grassland or occasionally on loose debris that is almost scree.

COLLECTED Porters Pass, Torlesse Range, Canterbury, 1,220 m (4,000 ft). January 1968.

Fiordland *Myosotis*

A handsome herb, resembling perhaps large forms of *M. suavis*, with several rosettes arising from a branched stock and a few lateral branches *ca* 12 cm long. Large but thin basal leaves (3.5–4.5 x 1.5–2 cm) and their broad petioles have a thin covering of hairs, none of which are bent sharply backwards (in *M. suavis*, hairs on the lower surface are so bent, except near the tip).

Compact flower heads at the branch tips have no leafy bracts and in the faintly scented flowers (*ca* 6 mm across) the trumpet is short (*ca* 5 mm) and the anthers hardly protrude beyond the rather large scales.

The plant is known so far only from above Lake Wapiti in the upper Doon Valley, Fiordland National Park, where it grows on moist shady sites on small rock outcrops in fellfield at 1,460 m (4,800 ft). This plant was collected by Mr J. Anderson in January 1971.

Myosotis suavis Petrie
"Pleasing".

A compact distinctly-hairy plant with small dense heads of white flowers. It occupies scree and loose rocky debris in fellfield, mostly along and near the main divide from the Mt Cook district to central Fiordland but is not common.

Myosotis macrantha (Hook.f.) Benth. & Hook.f.
"Large-flowered".

A variable pale-green herb, occurring as single rosettes or several together, with one to few erect hairy branches (10–30 cm long) per rosette. Large leaves (3–12 x 0.6–2 cm) and their long broad petioles have a fine covering of stiff hairs that gives them a harsh texture.

Rather compact rounded heads of many flowers are most striking, with a range in colour between plants or localities: brownish-yellow, brownish-orange, reddish-brown or occasionally bluish-green, usually with an iridescent sheen.

DISTRIBUTION South Island: rather widespread in the wetter regions from Nelson to western Otago.

Subalpine to low-alpine: 600–1,500 m (2,000–5,000 ft).

HABITAT This handsome plant is confined to moist rocky or stony sites, especially shady ledges, damp shady ravines or rock gutters, wet scree or moraine.

COLLECTED Craigieburn Range, Canterbury, 1,430 m (4,700 ft). January 1968.

Myosotis explanata Cheesem.
"Spread out"—referring to the stems that spread from the base.

Plants resemble *M. macrantha* in vegetative features but flowers

Cont. on page 190

Fiordland *Myosotis*

Myosotis australis

Myosotis macrantha

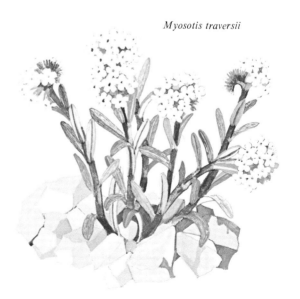

Myosotis traversii

cm

PLATE 82

are white (rarely blue) with shorter trumpets (6–10 vs 10–15 mm) and their anthers only partly project beyond the corolla tube—in *M. macrantha* they are fully exposed.

It has been recorded only in the Arthurs Pass region, in similar habitats to *M. macrantha*.

Myosotis concinna Cheesem.
"Elegant".

This also has the habit of *M. macrantha* but is distinguished by its more silky hairs and pale-yellow flowers with short trumpets (*ca* 6 mm). It is confined to limestone debris and outcrops at 1,000–1,400 m (3,500–4,500 ft) in Nelson (Mt Owen).

At least two other forget-me-nots reach the alpine zone (for details see Webb et al. *Flora of New Zealand* Vol. IV, 1988).

Myosotis monroi Cheesem.
After Sir D. Munro.

Is confined to the mountains of Nelson and north-western Marlborough, chiefly in fellfield on the mineral belt.

Myosotis amabilis Cheesem.
"Pleasing".

Apparently is confined to broken shingle on the summit of Mt Hikurangi on the Raukumara Range.

The Bladderwort Family: **LENTIBULARIACEAE**

Genus **UTRICULARIA**
"A small bladder"—referring to the small bladders on the submerged leaves.

A large and widespread genus of insectivorous plants. Only one of the four native bladderworts appears to reach the alpine zone.

Utricularia monanthos Hook.f.   MOUNTAIN BLADDERWORT
"Single-flowered".

A distinctive minute herb, with very slender creeping stems bearing several, small, white bladders (1.5–2.5 mm across). Plants often grow tangled in loose mats. Their narrow leaves (5–20 mm long) are all basal and summer-green.

Relatively large and colourful (rarely whitish) flowers occur usually singly on very slender stalks (2–10 cm long).
DISTRIBUTION North, South and Stewart Islands: apparently restricted to the central mountainous region; more widespread in the South Island.
    Lowland (in the south) to low-alpine: to 1,400 m (4,500 ft).
HABITAT Almost confined to peat bogs where it may cover small patches, but only when flowering is it obvious.
COLLECTED Key Summit, Fiordland National Park, 910 m (3,000 ft). January 1968. Flower details are from a Broken River plant, Craigieburn Range, Canterbury, *ca* 760 m (2,500 ft). January 1966.

The Figwort Family: **SCROPHULARIACEAE**

Genus **EUPHRASIA**
"Eye-medicine"—a herbal name: application of the plant was supposed to brighten the eyes, whence the common name, eyebright.

Semi-parasitic plants containing about 200 species from the temperate regions. Most of the 15 native eyebrights reach the alpine zone.

Euphrasia dyeri Wettst.
After Sir W. T. Thistleton-Dyer, English botanist.

A delicate fleshy annual, 1–5 cm tall, with a few weak spreading branches from the base. Plants are often massed together into loose mats. Small sessile leaves (4–8 x 2–6 mm) are distinctively toothed.

One to few flowers near the stem tips have stalks up to 2 cm long and a slender tube to the corolla that may be white or brightly coloured, as shown.
DISTRIBUTION South and Stewart Islands: rather local on the mountains from mid-Canterbury southwards.
    Montane to low-alpine: 200–1,500 m (500–5,000 ft).
HABITAT Confined to bogs where it is easily overlooked unless in flower.
COLLECTED Rock & Pillar Range, Central Otago, 1,280 m (4,200 ft). January 1970.

Euphrasia zelandica Wettst.
"Of New Zealand".

An almost fleshy, variable, annual herb, 1–10 cm tall, usually with a few branches from the base. Its sessile leaves (4–9 x 2–6 mm) are widely spaced below but crowded near the branch tips. They have a characteristic shape with 2–5 pairs of pointed teeth, and sparse hairs on the upper surface.

Flowers on short stalks occur singly or, in larger plants, in small clusters at the stem tips. They usually have purple anthers and a yellow eye.
DISTRIBUTION North and South Islands: widespread on the mountains from Mt Hikurangi southwards.
    Subalpine to high-alpine: 700–1,800 m (2,000–6,000 ft).
HABITAT A very wide range—open subalpine scrub or wet mossy avalanche chutes below the tree line, moist sites in tussock grassland or herbfield, highly exposed well-drained sites in high-alpine cushion vegetation. Here flowering plants are only 1–2 cm tall and, even though abundant, are easily overlooked.
COLLECTED Maungatua, eastern Otago, 880 m (2,900 ft). January 1970.

Euphrasia cheesemanii Wettst.
After Mr T. F. Cheeseman, well-known New Zealand botanist.

It resembles larger forms of *E. zelandica* but is best distinguished by the longer flower stalks (to 3 cm) which carry the flowers well

Cont. on page 192

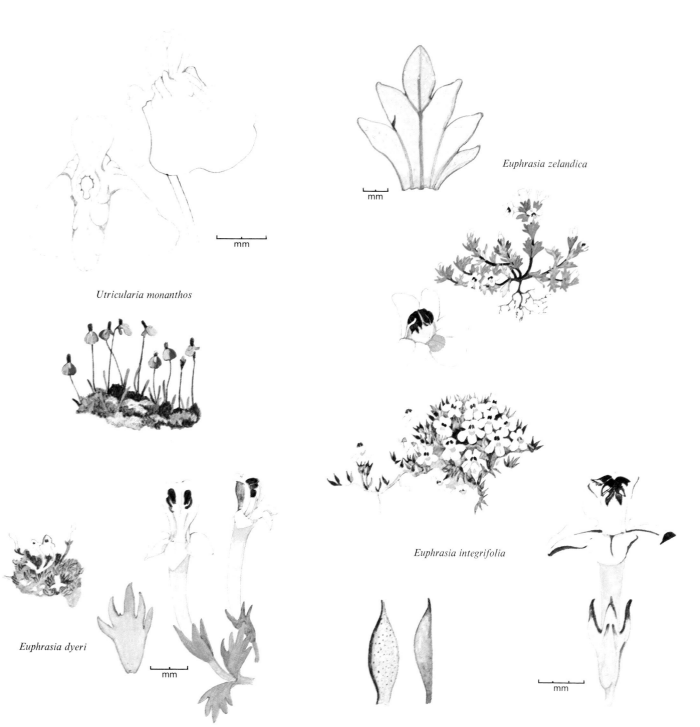

Euphrasia zelandica

Utricularia monanthos

Euphrasia integrifolia

Euphrasia dyeri

PLATE 83

beyond the leaves, and blunt lobes to the leaves.

It occupies wet open sites, especially bog edges, in the subalpine and low-alpine zones of western Nelson.

Euphrasia australis Petrie
"Southern".

It also resembles *E. zelandica* but, as in *E. cheesemanii*, flowers are on stalks which elongate to *ca* 2.5 cm in the fruit. Leaves are larger (10–12 x 7–8 mm) and their lobes sharply-toothed.

It is confined to south Westland and Fiordland in wet meadows, especially in snow tussock-herbfield.

Euphrasia integrifolia Petrie (*See plate 83*)
"With undivided leaves".

An insignificant creeping and rooting herb that weaves among other plants or forms loose mats. Minute narrow leaves (3–4 x 1 mm) are fleshy and sharp-pointed. They stand erect in opposite pairs along the stem.

A few prominent flowers (8–13 mm long) develop singly towards the branch tips.

DISTRIBUTION South Island: confined to the mountains of southern Fiordland.

Low-alpine: 1,200–1,500 m (4,000–5,000 ft).

HABITAT In permanently wet hollows, flushes and streamsides in snow tussock-herbfield. Only when flowering is it noticed and obviously an eyebright.

COLLECTED Mt Burns, Hunter Mountains, Fiordland National Park, 1,280 m (4,200 ft). January 1968.

Euphrasia cockayneana Petrie   YELLOW EYEBRIGHT
After Dr L. Cockayne, famous New Zealand botanist and pioneer ecologist.

An almost fleshy, partly-hairy, annual herb, 5–10 cm tall, that is quite distinct from the rest in having bright-yellow flowers.

DISTRIBUTION South Island: in the high rainfall region from north-west Nelson to Arthurs Pass.

Low-alpine: 1,000–1,500 m (3,000–5,000 ft).

HABITAT Often abundant and if in flower quite conspicuous, in damp open areas of mixed snow tussock-scrub and herbfield.

COLLECTED Temple Basin track, Arthurs Pass National Park, 1,130 m (3,700 ft). March 1958.

Euphrasia petriei M. B. Ashwin
After Mr D. Petrie, early teacher and botanist, especially in Otago.

Another variable plant with a habit similar to *E. revoluta*, but usually distinguishable by the leaf shape (at high altitudes they may be reduced to 3 lobes) and the fine but swollen glandular hairs on the calyx (a good lens will be needed to see these). Northern populations are stouter (up to 12 cm tall) and have larger flowers (10–20 mm long and across), as shown, than southern (west Otago-Southland-Fiordland) populations (*ca* 5 cm tall; flowers 8–12 mm).

DISTRIBUTION South Island: widespread in the higher rainfall regions of north-west Nelson and from about Arthurs Pass southwards.

Subalpine to high-alpine: 800–1,800 m (2,500–6,000 ft).

HABITAT Often common in damp, rather open or exposed areas of snow tussock-herbfield and sometimes under open subalpine scrub, on moraine or in fellfield or shallow snowbanks.

COLLECTED Temple Basin, Arthurs Pass National Park, 1,370 m (4,500 ft). December 1967.

Euphrasia townsonii Petrie
After Mr W. Townson, who first collected it.

A variable plant, 5–15 cm tall, the small forms closely resembling *E. revoluta*. Larger plants are distinct with sessile almost glabrous leaves (4–15 x 2–6 mm) that have 1–2 pairs of fine teeth. Thickened down-turned margins are similar to *E. revoluta*.

The few flowers near the stem tips are on slender stalks (5–20 mm long), so that even in dwarfed forms the flowers and later the capsules are conspicuous beyond the leaves. A good lens will show that the calyx has swollen glandular hairs as well as tapered white ones. Both the margins and midribs of the calyx lobes are usually reddish and thickened.

DISTRIBUTION South Island: the mountains of north-west Nelson, southwards to the Paparoa Range. It tends to replace *E. revoluta* in this region.

Subalpine to low-alpine: 500–1,500 m (1,500–5,000 ft).

HABITAT Small forms, as shown, are often common in cushion bogs while larger plants may be prominent among red tussock or in snow tussock-herbfield.

COLLECTED Near Lake Sylvester, Cobb Valley, north-west Nelson, 1,430 m (4,700 ft). December 1967.

Euphrasia revoluta Hook.f.
"Rolled towards the lower side"—referring to the leaf margins.

A small tufted herb, up to 5 cm tall, with a slightly woody stock and several, very slender, very slender, partly-trailing stems that turn upright and leafy. Their narrow, glabrous, sessile leaves (2–10 x 1–5 mm) have a characteristic shape with one pair of small teeth and very thick down-turned margins.

One to few large flowers at the stem tips may have short (to 5 mm) hairy stalks and a calyx that is uniformly covered in fine white hairs.

DISTRIBUTION North and South Islands: Ruahine and Tararua Ranges; in the South Island it is much more widespread though rather local, close to the main divide.

Low- to high-alpine: 900–1,700 m (3,000–5,500 ft).

HABITAT A rather wide range but usually in damp sites in snow tussock-herbfield. A dwarfed form may occupy snowbank depressions.

COLLECTED Temple Basin, Arthurs Pass National Park, 1,370 m (4,500 ft). December 1967. The dwarfed form is from Mt Brewster, Mt Aspiring National Park, 1,680 m (5,500 ft). March 1968.

Euphrasia monroi Hook.f.
After Sir D. Munro, early explorer and collector in north-eastern Nelson and Marlborough.

Rather similar to *E. cuneata* but smaller (5–20 cm tall), less branched and with the leaves grouped and overlapping near the

Cont. on page 194

Euphrasia monroi

Euphrasia cuneata

Euphrasia cockayniana

Euphrasia revoluta

Euphrasia townsonii

Euphrasia petriei

cm

PLATE 84

tips of the erect stems. Thick leaves (5–10 x 3–6 mm) are sessile with thickened margins and 1–2 pairs of shallow nicks near their broad blunt apex.

A few large flowers on short hidden stalks occur in a tight cluster at the stem tips. As in *E. cuneata*, flowering branches do not persist over winter.

DISTRIBUTION South Island: on the mountains of Nelson, Marlborough and north-west Canterbury, including the mineral belt.

Low-alpine: 1,000–1,500 m (3,500–5,000 ft).

HABITAT Often common and when in flower a colourful plant on rocky sites in snow tussock-herbfield.

COLLECTED St Arnaud Range, Nelson Lakes National Park, 1,580 m (5,200 ft). December 1967.

Euphrasia laingii Petrie
After Mr R. M. Laing, Canterbury botanist.

Generally similar to *E. monroi* and in the north may be difficult to distinguish from it, but the leaves are usually longer (6–15 x 3–6 mm) and more widely spaced. Also, flowers are on distinct stalks up to 10 mm long.

It occurs on the mountains of eastern Nelson-Marlborough and Canterbury, southwards at least to the Mt Cook district where it is prominent. Its altitudinal range is similar to *E. monroi* but it may occupy drier, partly depleted snow tussock grassland in addition to snow tussock-herbfield of wet regions.

Euphrasia drucei M. B. Ashwin
After Mr A. P. Druce, North Island botanist.

Also similar in habit to *E. monroi* but plants are somewhat smaller (3–8 cm tall) and with a distinctive leaf shape: about as broad as they are long, widest near the centre rather than the tip, with 3 or 5 lobes.

It is confined to open, permanently wet, often boggy sites in snow tussock-herbfield on the Tararua Range.

Euphrasia cuneata Forst.f. *(See plate 84)*
"Wedge-shaped"—referring to the leaves.

A variable erect sub-shrub, 10–60 cm tall (but usually < 20 cm in the alpine zone) and highly-branched from a woody base. Widely-spaced, often brownish leaves are distinctively shaped (5–20 x 3–10 mm) with 1–3 pairs of teeth and a short petiole.

The flower head may be much-branched but in the alpine zone it is usually simple. In the flowers the 3-lobed lower lip of the corolla is distinctly longer than the upper lip. When mature, the long narrow capsules exceed the glabrous calyx.

DISTRIBUTION North and South Islands: widespread on the mountains from East Cape, Lake Taupo and Mt Egmont southwards; in the South Island it is almost strictly coastal, in the north-east.

Coastal to low-alpine: to 1,200 m (4,000 ft).

HABITAT At higher altitudes it may be common in open subalpine scrub or among red tussock, especially on the volcanic plateau where it is both abundant and colourful.

COLLECTED Mangatepopo Valley, Tongariro National Park, *ca* 1,070 m (3,500 ft). March 1964.

Genus OURISIA
After Ouris, Governor of the Falkland Islands, who procured the first species.

A small genus of about 27 species divided between South America and New Zealand, apart from one in Tasmania. A revision in 1984 recognised 14 native species, 10 of which may reach the alpine zone.

Ourisia macrophylla Hook.f.
"Large-leaved"

A large leaved, rather variable herb with erect tufts produced at the end of stout (1–2 cm thick) creeping and rooting stems. Leaves have blades 4–15 cm long with a glabrous surface and petioles that may be densely hairy.

The erect flower stem (up to 60 cm tall in fruit) reaches well above the leaves and has 1–8 series of stalked flowers in whorls, each accompanied by a whorl of 2–4 sessile leaf-like bracts. Distinctively the slender individual flower stalks (3–5 cm long) and often other parts as well, are hairy. Also, the lobes of the calyx are narrow and tapering.

Subspecies *macrophylla* Hook. has leaf blades about as broad as long and widest near the base, while subspecies *robusta* (Col.) Arroyo has leaves wider than broad that are widest near the middle.

DISTRIBUTION North Island: subspecies *macrophylla* is confined to Mt Egmont including the Pouakai Range where it is often common in subalpine scrub and low-alpine herbfield; 800–1,400 m (2,600–4,000 ft). Subspecies *robusta* extends from the Raukumara Range southwards through the central mountains to Manawatu and eastern Taranaki, from the montane to low-alpine zones; 100–1,000 m (300–3,300 ft).

HABITAT In alpine regions plants may be prominent in tussock-herbfield but in heavily grazed areas they are often restricted to inaccessible sites, especially bluffs.

COLLECTED An alpine form of var. *macrophylla* from Manganui Skifield, Mt Egmont National Park, 1,370 m (4,500 ft). November 1967.

Ourisia lactea (Moore) Arroyo
"Milky" — referring to the flower colour.
(= *O. macrophylla* Hook. var. *lactea* Moore)

Generally similar to *O. macrophylla* and occurring with it on the Volcanic Plateau but distinguished by the presence of hairs on the upper surface of the leaves, generally smaller flower heads and fewer bracts per whorl on the flower stems.

Subspecies *lactea* has the calyx and uppermost bracts covered in hairs with swollen glandular tips while in subspecies *drucei* (Moore) Arroyo these hairs are tapered and non-glandular.

DISTRIBUTION North, South and Stewart Islands: subspecies *lactea* is confined to the South and Stewart Islands where it is widespread on the wetter mountains from the subalpine to low-alpine zones: 900–1,400 m: (3,000–4,600 ft) where it is often common in shrubland and snow tussock herbfield, but in heavily grazed areas plants are often restricted to inaccessible sites, especially bluffs. Subspecies

Ourisia vulcanica

Ourisia spathulata

Ourisia macrophylla var. *macrophylla*

cm

PLATE 85

drucei is widespread on the North Island mountains from Mt Hikurangi to the Tararua Range, including Mt Egmont where it may be common in similar habitats to those of ssp. *lactea*.

Ourisia macrocarpa Hook.f.
"Large-fruited".

Its habit is similar to *O. macrophylla* but plants are stouter and their leaf blades always glabrous, more leathery and often larger (4–15 x 2–10 cm). The lower surface and petioles of leaves, as well as the flowering stems, are often dark-purple.

Flower stems may reach 70 cm when the fruits ripen. As distinct from *O. macrophylla*, the calyx has broad rather blunt lobes that are often notched at the tips. Flowers are somewhat larger (2–3 vs 1.5–2 cm across), as are the dry capsules.

There are two varieties: var. **macrocarpa** has very broad, almost round leaves and a glabrous flowering stalk; var. **calycina** (Col.) Ckn., has longer leaves and a sparsely-hairy flower stalk.

DISTRIBUTION South Island: widespread in the high rainfall regions — var. *calycina* occurs from Nelson to south Westland and is replaced further south by var. *macrocarpa*. Hybrids with *O. caespitosa* were previously referred to as *O. cockayneana*.

Mostly subalpine to low-alpine: 800–1,300 m (2,500–4,500 ft).

HABITAT Only where animal pressure has been light do these magnificent alpine plants continue to be prominent in open subalpine scrub, mixed snow tussock-scrub and snow tussock-herbfield. This can still be seen along the track to Temple Basin above Arthurs Pass but large plants are often restricted to inaccessible bluffs.

COLLECTED ssp. *calycina* from Temple Basin track, Arthurs Pass National Park, 1,160 m (3,800 ft). December 1967.

The eight smaller alpine species with more or less horizontal leaves distributed along creeping stems or forming rosettes, and with bracts on the flowering stems usually in pairs, can be distinguished as follows (for use of key see Glossary):

A	Upper surface of leaves essentially glabrous (perhaps a few hairs on the margins):	B
AA	Upper surface of leaves densely hairy:	C
B	Flower stems and stalks glabrous; petioles broad; widespread:	*O. caespitosa*
BB	Flower stems and stalks hairy; petioles slender; confined to central North Island mountains:	*O. vulcanica*
C	Older basal leaves glabrous apart from a few very long hairs on upper surface:	*O. glandulosa*
CC	Older basal leaves permanently hairy on upper surface:	D
D	All calyx lobes divided to the base:	*O. sessilifolia*
DD	Two calyx lobes (posterior pair) united for at least half their length:	E
E	Corolla throat with 3 rows of hairs:	*O. remotifolia*
EE	Corolla throat entirely glabrous:	F
F	Corolla throat yellow at base, purple on the sides:	*O. simpsonii*
FF	Corolla throat entirely yellow to greenish yellow:	G
G	Plants forming distinct rosettes, densely hairy upper leaf surface a mixture of long pointed and short gland-tipped hairs; lower leaf surface glabrous:	*O. confertifolia*
GG	Plants with distinct rhizomes; scattered hairs on upper leaf surface a mixture of pointed and gland-tipped hairs; lower surface with distinct but sparse glandular hairs:	*O. spathulata*

Ourisia vulcanica L. B. Moore (*See plate 85*)
"Volcanic"—referring to its location.

Its habit is similar to *O. caespitosa* but the stems are less branched, mostly buried, and the mats are smaller (5–15 cm across). Leaves (25 x 6–15 mm) are crowded and often flattened against the ground. They have equally long petioles, and only a few hairs on the margins and the midrib beneath.

Hairy flower stems (*ca* 12 cm tall) have bracts in pairs and a few flowers on long hairy stalks.

DISTRIBUTION North Island: confined to the central volcanic mountains and the nearby Kaimanawa Range.

Subalpine to low-alpine: 1,100–1,500 m (3,500–5,000 ft).

HABITAT Widespread and often abundant on damp sites in red tussock grassland on the central volcanoes.

COLLECTED Whakapapanui Stream, Mt Ruapehu, Tongariro National Park, 1,160 m (3,800 ft). November 1968.

Ourisia caespitosa Hook.f.
"Turf-forming".

A highly branched creeping and rooting low-growing herb that may form loose mats. Thick glabrous leaves (6–10 x 3–5 mm) have a distinctive shape with up to 3 notches on either side. They are usually crowded and roughly in two rows on either side of the stem.

Erect glabrous flower stems (4–10 cm tall) have bracts in pairs and the individual flowers are on glabrous stalks at least as long as the flowers.

DISTRIBUTION North, South and Stewart Islands: widespread in mountain regions from Mt Hikurangi southwards but absent from Mt Egmont.

Smaller forms with single flowers, previously recognised as var. "*gracilis*", may occur intermixed in Canterbury and western Otago but essentially alone on the Central Otago mountains.

Montane to high-alpine: 700–1,800 m (2,000–6,000 ft).

HABITAT A wide range but most common on damp or shady rocky sites in the low-alpine zone. It may also be found in open subalpine scrub, valley grassland and on avalanche chutes below the tree line, as well as in fellfield and shallow snowbanks of the high-alpine zone.

Ourisia caespitosa var. "*gracilis*"

Ourisia caespitosa

Ourisia "*cockayneana*"

Ourisia macrocarpa ssp. *calycina*

cm

PLATE 86

COLLECTED Hooker Valley, Mt Cook National Park, 910 m (3,000 ft). November 1967. Var. *"gracilis"* is from Rock & Pillar Range, Central Otago, 1,220 m (4,000 ft). December 1964.

Ourisia glandulosa Hook.f. *(See plate 87)*
"Bearing glands" — referring to the numerous glandular hairs.

Its habit is similar to *O. caespitosa* but plants are easily distinguished by the many, long, jointed hairs near the margins of the horizontally-arranged leaves. Older leaves become almost glabrous.

Flowering stems (3–10 cm tall) are erect and covered mostly in swollen glandular hairs, with 1–2 pairs of hairy bracts below the few-flowered (2–6) head. The flowers are entirely glabrous.

DISTRIBUTION South Island: from south Canterbury southwards through Otago to northern Southland.

Low- to high-alpine: 1,200–1,800 m (4,000–6,000 ft).

HABITAT On rather severe but moist well-lit sites — exposed ridge crests, rock outcrops in snow tussock-herbfield, early snowbanks and sheltered sites in fellfield and cushion vegetation.

COLLECTED Rock & Pillar Range, Central Otago, 1,220 m (4,000 ft). December 1964.

Ourisia sessilifolia Hook. f.
"With sessile leaves".

A creeping and rooting somewhat variable herb with the closely overlapping, rounded to spathulate leaves 1–5 cm long and dying but persistent behind the stem tips.

Flowering stems are hairy, 6–12 cm tall and with up to 4 pairs of leafy bracts. Flowers are 1.5–2.5 cm across.

Subspecies **splendida** (Moore) Arroyo differs from ssp. **sessilifolia** Hook. f. in having 1 rather than 3 rows of hairs on the throat of the corolla and in its almost round leaves (up to 2.5 x 2.5 cm) rather than somewhat narrower and usually smaller (<2 cm long) leaves.

DISTRIBUTION South and Stewart Islands: subspecies *sessilifolia* is widespread on the South Island mountains apart from mid and south Canterbury, while ssp. *splendida* is largely confined to the Canterbury and southern Nelson mountains.

Low- to high-alpine: 1,000–1,830 m (3,300–6,000 ft).

HABITAT Subspecies *sessilifolia* occurs in rather open, often rocky sites including outcrops in snow tussock herbfield and sheltered fellfield, while ssp. *splendida* is more common near the upper limits of snow tussock herbfield and is often common in fellfield and early snowbanks.

COLLECTED Subspecies *sessilifolia* is from Temple Basin, Arthurs Pass National Park, 1,460 m (4,800 ft). January 1970; ssp. *splendida* is from Mt Brewster, Mt Aspiring National Park, 1,970 m (6,000 ft). February 1970.

Ourisia simpsonii (Moore) Arroyo
After Mr G. Simpson, Dunedin botanist.
(= *Ourisia sessilifolia* Hook. f. var. *simpsonii* Moore)

Generally similar to *O. sessilifolia* but differing in having the posterior lobes of the calyx joined for at least half their length and in the throat of the corolla being quite glabrous.

DISTRIBUTION South Island: throughout much of the range of *O. sessilifolia* but more common north of Arthurs Pass.

Low-alpine: 1,200–1,500 m (4,000–5,000 ft).

HABITAT Similar to *O. sessilifolia* with which it often occurs.

COLLECTED St Arnaud Range, Nelson Lakes National Park 1,460 m (4,800 ft). December 1967.

* *Ourisia confertifolia* Arroyo
"With leaves pressed close together".

A compact rhizomatous herb with soft and shaggy more or less separate rosettes 2–3.5 cm across. The pale green leaves are thick, rounded, closely packed and covered with dense long hairs (long pointed ones mixed with shorter gland-tipped hairs) on their upper surfaces, but are glabrous and often reddish beneath. They do not persist after dying.

Flower stems are also hairy, up to 7 cm long, often curved, with several pairs of leafy bracts and 1–3 flowers. The hairy calyx has purple-blue streaks while the corolla is glabrous, *ca* 2 cm wide and white except for a yellow-green throat. Anthers are purple. Capsules are glabrous, up to 8 mm long, and protected by the persistent, hairy (both long glandular and non-glandular hairs) calyx.

DISTRIBUTION South Island: along the main divide from south Westland to Fiordland.

Low- to high-alpine: 1,200–2,100 m (4,000–6,900 ft).

HABITAT The main divide counterpart to *O. glandulosa* (with which it shares glabrous flowers), it was previously identified as *O. sessilifolia*. It is often common on exposed sites in snow tussock herbfield and fellfield.

Ourisia remotifolia Arroyo
"Remote leaves" — the leaves are widely separated on the stems.

Plants are generally similar to *O. sessilifolia* but easily distinguished by their straggly lax, semi-erect habit and soft rather delicate, long-petioled leaves (2–7 cm long) that are widely spaced on the stems.

Sparse long hairs also occur on the flower stem and calyx. Flowers are distinguished by their united calyx lobes and the 3 lines of hairs on the corolla throat.

DISTRIBUTION South Island: locally common along the main divide from mid Canterbury to Fiordland.

Low- to high-alpine: 1,000–1,700 m (3,500–5,600 ft).

HABITAT Locally common on shaded rocky sites in snow tussock grassland, herbfield and fellfield, sometimes in association with *O. confertifolia*.

COLLECTED Mt Burns, Fiordland National Park, 1,400 m (4,500 ft). January 1968.

Ourisia spathulata Arroyo
"Spathulate" — referring to the leaf shape.

A tufted, creeping rhizomatous herb with glabrous reddish stems and broad petioles. Their soft, hairy (mixed long glandular and non-glandular hairs), pale green leaves are distinctly spathulate, wavy edged and up to 6 cm long. The lower leaf surface has only sparse glandular hairs.

Ourisia sessilifolia ssp. *sessilifolia*

Ourisia remotifolia

Ourisia simpsonii

Ourisia sessilifolia ssp. *splendida*

Ourisia glandulosa

cm

PLATE 87

The very slender hairy flower stems are 8–11 cm long and usually curved with several pairs of spathulate bracts *ca* 1 cm long. The hairy calyx has purple-blue streaks while the glabrous white corolla has a yellow throat.

DISTRIBUTION South Island: confined to the mountains of central northern Southland (Eyre, Thomson and southern Garvie Mountains).

Low-alpine: 900–1,600 m (3,000–5,000 ft).

HABITAT The ecological equivalent of *O. simpsonii* from northern South Island, it has been most frequently confused with *O. splendida*. It is largely restricted to open rocky areas of snow tussock grassland and induced fellfield.

COLLECTED Jane Peak, Eyre Mountains, 1,220 m (4,000 ft). November 1969.

Genus **CHIONOHEBE**

"Snow-loving *Hebe*".

A small genus of five species, all alpines, previously referred to as *Pygmea*.

Chionohebe pulvinaris (Hook.f.) Briggs & Ehrendorfer

"Cushion-shaped".

Forms dull, greyish-green moss-like cushions 5–15 cm across and 2–4 cm thick. Usually they are dense and tight but some are more loosely packed. The stems are highly branched near the tips and their leaves rather loosely arranged, giving a soft texture to the cushion. Distribution of hairs on the leaves is diagnostic but in this species it is rather variable.

In the 4 cushion species the flowers are similar.

DISTRIBUTION South Island: widespread on the mountains of Nelson, Marlborough and Canterbury.

Low- to high-alpine: 1,400–1,900 m (4,500–6,500 ft).

HABITAT On highly-exposed rocky sites, especially eroding ridge crests, in snow tussock grassland and herbfield, and on loose debris or outcrops in fellfield.

COLLECTED Temple Basin, Arthurs Pass National Park, 1,610 m (5,300 ft). December 1967.

Chionohebe thomsonii (Buchan.) Briggs & Ehrendorfer

Probably after Mr J. T. Thomson, early Otago surveyor.

Its habit and colour are similar to *C. pulvinaris* but the cushions are more dense and rigid and the leaves broader (1–3 vs 1 mm) and more tightly packed so that usually only the tips show. Leaves are much more hairy but with a distinctive pattern, as shown.

The single flower shows the pair of purplish anthers and the protruding style.

DISTRIBUTION South Island: on the higher mountains of Otago and northern Southland.

High-alpine: 1,400–2,400 m (4,500–8,000 ft).

HABITAT On windswept rock outcrops and loose debris in fellfield, and with other cushion plants on the high plateaux of Central Otago where they may be confused, especially if not flowering, with *Myosotis pulvinaris*.

COLLECTED Intact cushion from the Richardson Mountains, western Otago, 1,680 m (5,500 ft). December 1967. Details are from a Central Otago (Old Man Range) plant, 1,610 m (5,300 ft). December 1968.

Chionohebe myosotoides (Ashwin) Briggs & Ehrendorfer

"Resembling *Myosotis* (*pulvinaris*)".

Cushions are similar to *C. thomsonii* and easily confused with it but the leaves are more loosely packed and their pattern of hairs is distinct, as shown.

So far it has been found only on the summit plateaux of the Pisa and Rock & Pillar Ranges in Central Otago, among cushion vegetation.

COLLECTED Pisa Range, Central Otago, 1,830 m (6,000 ft). March 1968.

Chionohebe ciliolata (Hook.f.) Briggs & Ehrendorfer

"With minute hairs" — referring to the leaf margins.

Pale green cushions vary in size and tightness but the leaves are quite distinct with hairs confined to their margins. Three varieties cover differences in cushion size and rigidity, leaf shape, size and hairiness, and geographic distribution (see Allan's *Flora of New Zealand*, 1961, p. 873).

DISTRIBUTION South Island: in the high-rainfall regions, usually not far east of the main divide, between Nelson and Fiordland—western Southland.

Low- to high-alpine: 1,100–2,100 m (3,500–7,000 ft).

HABITAT Usually on fine debris and rock outcrops in both exposed and sheltered fellfield. In the low-alpine zone it is restricted to highly-exposed ridges and rock outcrops.

COLLECTED Mt Brewster, Haast Pass, Mt Aspiring National Park, 1,650 m (5,400 ft). December 1967.

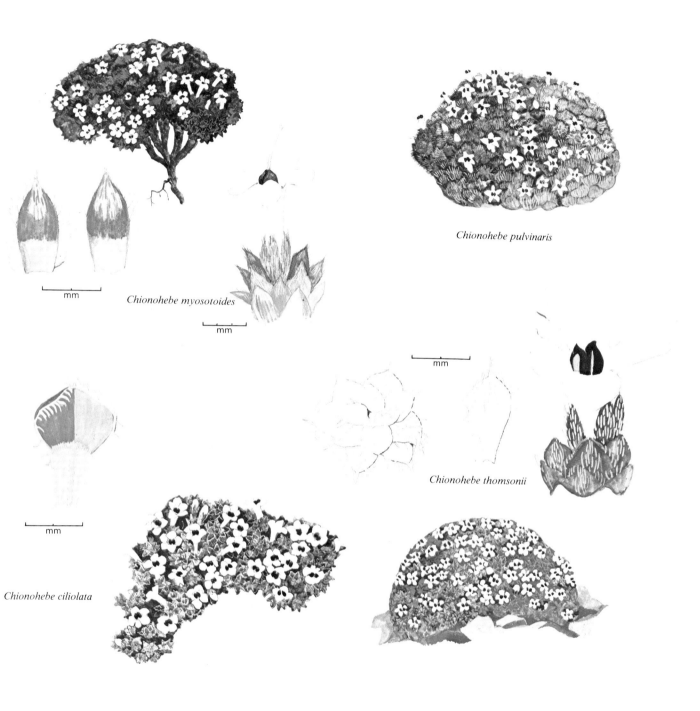

Chionohebe myosotoides

Chionohebe pulvinaris

Chionohebe thomsonii

Chionohebe ciliolata

mm

mm

mm

mm

mm

cm

PLATE 88

Chionohebe densifolia (F. Muell.) Briggs & Ehrendorfer
"With densely leafy (stems)".

A low, trailing or creeping and rooting, laxly-branched shrub forming small loose patches 5–15 cm across. Short branches (2–5 cm high) are squarish with four rows of leathery brownish-green leaves (3–6 x 1.5–3.5 mm) that have a few hairs along their margins.

Large white to pale lilac flowers (1–1.5 cm across) occur singly at the branch tips. Both the calyx and corolla are very deeply cut and 5-lobed.

DISTRIBUTION South Island: on the higher mountains of the Lakes district, Central and north Otago.

Low- to high-alpine: 1,100–1,800 m (3,500–6,000 ft).

HABITAT Chiefly on exposed open sites in snow tussock grassland or sheltered moist sites in fellfield and cushion vegetation.

COLLECTED Rock & Pillar Range, Central Otago, ca 1,220 m (4,000 ft). December 1964.

"Pygmea armstrongii" (Buchan.) Ashwin

After Mr J. B. Armstrong, early Canterbury botanist.

Its habit is similar to *C. densifolia* but plants are smaller and more compact, leaves are very tightly packed into 4 distinct rows and flowers are only half as large.

Perhaps it represents hybrids between *C. densifolia* and one of the cushion species which it resembles in its small overlapping and tightly-packed leaves and a few other features. It is a rare high-alpine plant from the Lakes District where both *C. densifolia* and *C. thomsonii* are present, but it also extends in places to the main divide,

beyond the range of *C. densifolia*.

COLLECTED Richardson Mountains, western Otago, 1,770 m (5,800 ft). December 1967.

Genus **PARAHEBE**

"Beside *Hebe*"—referring to its close relationship to this genus.

An endemic genus containing 11 species, all but one of them reaching the alpine zone.

Parahebe planopetiolata (Simpson & Thomson) W. R. B. Oliver
"With flattened petioles".

Its habit may be similar to *P. linifolia* but plants are usually smaller and more compact. Leaves are shining dark-green, sometimes purplish, but best distinguished from *P. linifolia* by being broader, sometimes almost rounded (1.5–6 mm wide), but narrowing into a distinct yet broad flattened petiole.

Single or a pair of small white, lavender or pink flowers (4–6 mm across) occur among the leaves on very short stalks near the branch tips.

DISTRIBUTION South Island: on the mountains of Fiordland and western Otago where it may occur with *P. linifolia*, except that it rarely if ever descends below the tree line.

Low- to high-alpine: 900–1,800 m (3,000–6,000 ft).

HABITAT Similar to *P. linifolia*.

COLLECTED Forbes Range, Mt Aspiring National Park, 1,460 m (4,800 ft). January 1968.

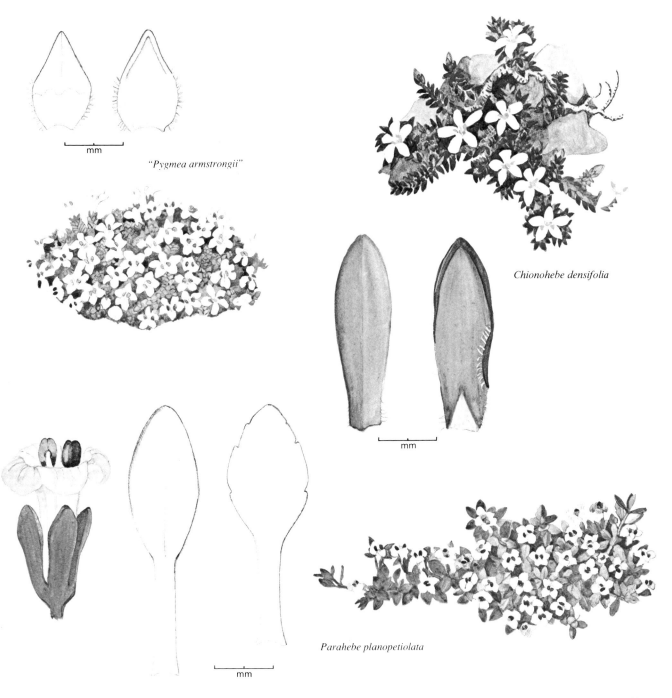

"Pygmea armstrongii"

Chionohebe densifolia

Parahebe planopetiolata

PLATE 89

Parahebe decora M. B. Ashwin
"Ornamental".

A slender, highly-branched, creeping and rooting sub-shrub that forms loose mats up to 50 cm or more across. Usually reddish leaves are minute (1.5–4 x 1–4 mm), almost-fleshy, glabrous and rounded, with usually one notch on either side.

Most distinctive are the long (5–15 cm) erect flower stalks with several (10–15) white to pink flowers, the lowest ones usually being in a rather separate cluster of three.

DISTRIBUTION South Island: mostly to the east of the main divide as far south as northern Southland.

Montane to low-alpine: 300–1,500 m (1,000–5,000 ft).

HABITAT On well-drained usually stony sites, especially gravel river beds, moraine and fairly stable scree.

COLLECTED Eyre Mountains, northern Southland, 910 m (3,000 ft). January 1970.

Parahebe lyallii (Hook.f.) W. R. B. Oliver
After Dr Lyall, surgeon-naturalist on HMS *Terror* in the early 1840s.

A variable, trailing or creeping and rooting, highly-branched shrub, distinguished by its small but broad, often reddish leaves (5–10 x 2–8 mm) that have 2–3 teeth on each side.

Flower stalks (3–8 cm long) are much less erect than in *P. decora* but the flowers are similar except that the lowest ones are not in a separate cluster of three.

DISTRIBUTION South Island: widespread in the mountain regions.

Lowland to low-alpine: to 1,300 m (4,500 ft).

HABITAT Usually on moist, rocky, open sites, especially streamsides, but also in snow tussock-scrub, herbfield, river gravels and moraine. East of the divide it may occur with *P. decora* and small forms may be difficult to distinguish from it.

COLLECTED Mt Brewster, Haast Pass, Mt Aspiring National Park, 1,280 m (4,200 ft). December 1970.

Parahebe linifolia (Hook.f.) W. R. B. Oliver
"*Linum*- (linen flax) leaved".

A sprawling, much-branched, glabrous sub-shrub, the stems, up to 20 cm long, crowded with narrow, pointed, smooth-edged, sessile leaves (8–25 x 1.5–4 mm).

Short flower stalks (1–2 cm long) near the branch tips carry a few (1–7) distinctively coloured bowl-shaped flowers (10–15 mm across).

DISTRIBUTION South Island: widespread on the wet mountains from southern Nelson to western Otago.

Subspecies **brevistylis** Garnock-Jones, "short style", has recently been recognised as distinct on the basis of several flower characters associated with pollination. It occurs from central Westland-Canterbury (Whataroa-Rangitata Rivers), southwards.

Subalpine to low-alpine: 500–1,600 m (1,500–5,500 ft).

HABITAT On damp rocky sites—creek beds, waterfalls, rock ledges and loose debris, especially moraine.

COLLECTED Twin Creeks, Arthurs Pass National Park, 880 m (2,900 ft). December 1967.

Parahebe hookeriana (Walp.) W. R. B. Oliver
After Sir J. D. Hooker, famous early botanist.

A stout, trailing to creeping and rooting, highly-branched sub-shrub. Thick leathery leaves (4–12 x 3–8 mm) are crowded along the stems.

Short stout flower stalks (2–6 cm long) carry only a few (4–8) rather large flowers.

Two varieties differ in the shape and hairiness of the leaves, but some forms are difficult to place. Var. **hookeriana** has leaves with a sparse covering of jointed hairs on both surfaces. Flower stems have dense, swollen, glandular hairs and their flowers are mostly lavender. Var. **olsenii** (Col.) M. B. Ashwin, after Mr A. Olsen, who first collected it, has glabrous leaves with more pointed tips, shallower teeth and a flattened petiole. Flower stems are more slender, usually with only pointed non-glandular hairs and white flowers.

DISTRIBUTION North Island: Mt Hikurangi and those of the central volcanoes; Kaimanawa, Kaweka and Ruahine Ranges. Var. *hookeriana* is on the volcanic mountains while var. *olsenii* is on the Ruahine Range.

Subalpine to high-alpine: 900–1,800 m (3,000–6,000 ft).

HABITAT On rocky sites, especially exposed ridges in tussock-herbfield or loose stony debris in fellfield.

COLLECTED Var. *hookeriana* from Mt Ruapehu, Tongariro National Park, *ca* 1,830 m (6,000 ft). March 1963.

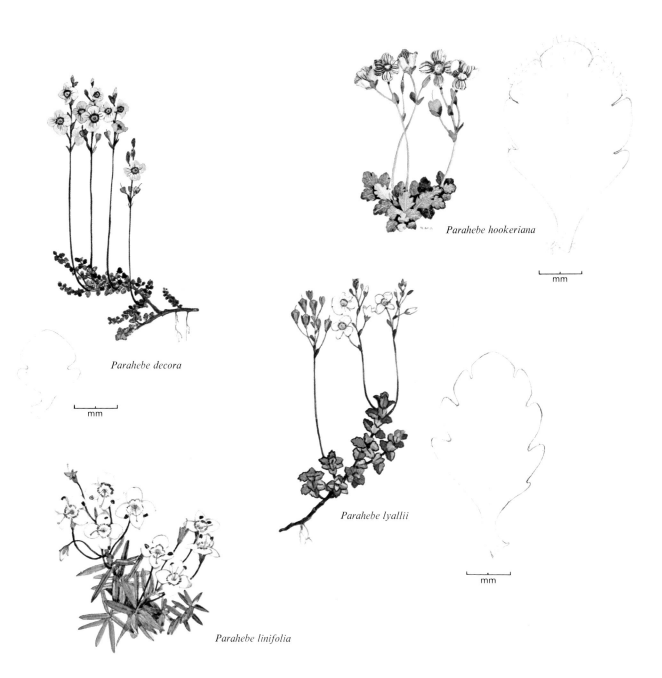

Parahebe hookeriana

Parahebe decora

mm

Parahebe lyallii

mm

Parahebe linifolia

cm

PLATE 90

Parahebe spathulata (Benth.) W. R. B. Oliver

"Spathulate"—referring particularly to the shape of the leafy bracts on the flower stems.

A prostrate highly-branched sub-shrub that forms distinctive, low, pale patches up to 25 cm across. Branchlets, leaves and flower stems are all pale with a dense covering of white hairs.

Very short flower stems (5–20 mm) carry small heads of 2–7 pure-white or rarely pale-lavender flowers.

DISTRIBUTION North Island: the central volcanic mountains; Kaweka, Kaimanawa and Ruahine Ranges.

Low- to high-alpine: 1,300–2,000 m (4,500–6,500 ft).

HABITAT Confined to loose stony debris of both shingle and scoria.

COLLECTED Mt Ruapehu, Tongariro National Park, *ca* 1,680 m (5,500 ft). March 1963.

Parahebe cheesemanii (Benth.) W. R. B. Oliver

After Mr T. F. Cheeseman, well-known New Zealand botanist.

A much-branched sub-shrub with a deep taproot and creeping and rooting partly-buried stems that form dull greyish-green cushions or loose patches 5–10 cm across. The small hairy leaves (3–5 x 2–3 mm) are deeply toothed.

Small white flowers (6–7 mm long) occur usually singly (but up to 3) almost hidden among the leaves on very short stalks.

DISTRIBUTION South Island: rather erratic between the mountains of Nelson–western Marlborough and the Arthurs Pass region.

Low- to high-alpine: 1,000–1,700 m (3,000–5,500 ft).

HABITAT On screes and loose stony debris in fellfield where it may be common yet easily overlooked.

COLLECTED Mt Peel, Cobb Valley, north-west Nelson, 1,580 m (5,200 ft). December 1967.

Parahebe trifida W. R. B. Oliver

"Three-cleft"—referring to the leaf tips.

A trailing or creeping and rooting, sparingly-branched sub-shrub that forms loose patches up to 30 cm or more across. Glossy but wrinkled, brownish-green, almost fleshy leaves (4–9 x 2–5 mm) are usually crowded near the tips of the long stems. They have a characteristic shape.

From 1–3 large white flowers (15–20 mm across) are on short hairy stalks (2–10 mm long) near the stem tips.

DISTRIBUTION South Island: on a few of the Central Otago mountains and those above the southern end of Lake Wakatipu.

Mostly high-alpine: 1,200–1,700 m (4,000–5,500 ft).

HABITAT Virtually confined to snowbanks.

COLLECTED Old Man Range, Central Otago, 1,630 m (5,350 ft). January 1970.

Parahebe birleyi (N. E. Brown) W. R. B. Oliver

After Mr H. Birley, who collected it.

A distinctive, dark, straggling sub-shrub, with both trailing and short erect branches up to 10 cm tall, that form loose patches up to 20 cm across. Almost-fleshy leaves (6–10 x 4–9 mm) are usually dark reddish-purple and have a characteristic shape.

Flowers and fruits are similar to *P. trifida*.

DISTRIBUTION South Island: on the higher mountains, mostly along and close to the main divide between the Mt Cook district and Otago.

High-alpine to nival: 2,000–2,900 m (6,500–9,600 ft).

HABITAT Confined to loose debris and rock clefts in fellfield.

COLLECTED Mt Brewster, Haast Pass, Mt Aspiring National Park, 2,160 m (7,100 ft). March 1968.

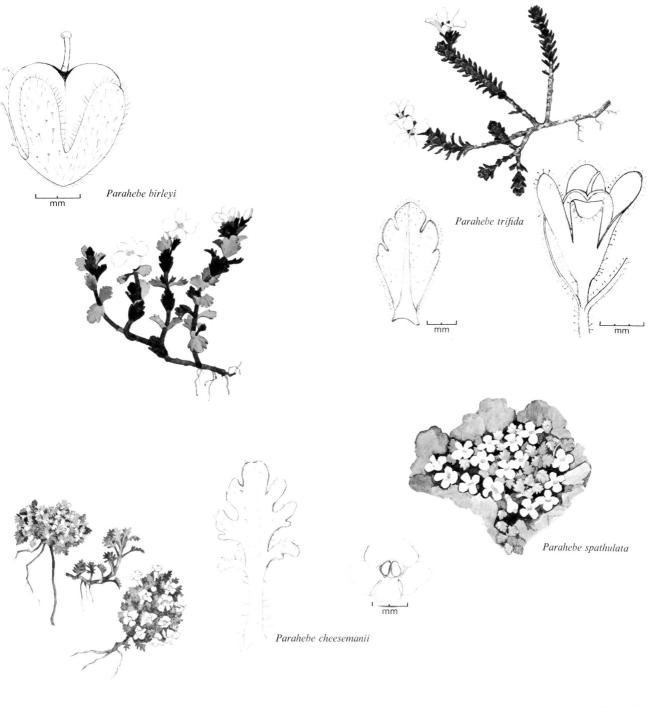

Parahebe birleyi

mm

Parahebe trifida

mm

mm

Parahebe cheesemanii

mm

Parahebe spathulata

cm

PLATE 91

Genus HEBE

From the classics: "the Greek goddess of youth".

A largely New Zealand genus of almost 100 species but also represented in South America, Tasmania, south-east Australia and New Guinea. About half of the native hebes reach the alpine zone.

Important among the several criteria used in recognising species are: the position (lateral or terminal) and degree of branching of the flower head; leaf size—in the whipcord group they are reduced to small scales; in the leafy species the presence or absence of a sinus (see Glossary), and if present, its shape. But despite these and the more usual criteria of size, leaf margins, colour of leaves and flowers, and geographical distribution, the genus is not an easy one to master.

Recent revisions by Heads which erected a new genus *Leonohebe* for 28 *Hebe* species (and two *Chionohebe* species) have not received general acceptance and are not included here but one new species (*H. crawii*) and two resurrected ones (*H. biggarii and H. dilatata*) from southern South Island are included.

Hebe odora (Hook.f.) Ckn.
"Fragrant".

A bright-green shrub up to 1.5 m or more tall but with a wide range of forms. Glabrous leaves (usually 8–15 x 4–5 mm) are shining above but dull below with a distinctly bevelled edge that may also be finely milled like a coin. Usually the midrib is pronounced on the lower surface. The rounded leaf base joins a narrow but distinct petiole so that in the bud there is a sinus which is broad and heart-shaped.

Tight conical flower heads at the branch tips consist usually of a terminal and 1–2 pairs of lateral spikes.

DISTRIBUTION North, South and Stewart Islands: widespread on the mountains from Mt Hikurangi southwards.

Subalpine to low-alpine: 600–1,400 m (2,000–4,500 ft).

HABITAT Usually present in short subalpine scrub and mixed snow tussock-scrub but it may extend for some distance into snow tussock grassland or herbfield on permanently moist sites.

A range of forms can be recognised: a very robust one from Fiordland (leaves 15–25 x 5–8 mm); an almost prostrate form from boggy meadows; a dense, compact, ball-like habit is often seen in grassland or herbfield.

COLLECTED Rock & Pillar Range, Central Otago, 1,160 m (3,800 ft). December 1970.

Hebe pauciramosa (Ckn. & Allan) L. B. Moore
"With few branches".

A sparingly-branched shrub reaching to 50 cm with a distinctly erect habit produced by the upright stems. Very thick leaves, confined to upper parts, are shining all over, concave and almost square (6–8 x 4–6 mm) with a blunt tip, rounded margins and a prominent midrib below. A short petiole makes for a broad heart-shaped sinus in the bud.

Var. *masoniae* L. B. Moore, after Miss R. Mason, botanist, has terminal flower heads and the midrib beneath the leaf is equally keeled or sharp throughout; var. *pauciramosa* "sparsely branched" usually has lateral heads so that the tip of the stem continues to grow, while the keel is distinctly flattened just below the leaf tip.

DISTRIBUTION South Island: rather widespread but chiefly in the wetter regions. Var. *masonae* is in Nelson, being replaced further south by var. *pauciramosa*.

Subalpine to low-alpine: 600–1,700 m (2,000–5,500 ft).

HABITAT Usually in seepage areas or flushes among grassland or herbfield but sometimes on moraine and gravel river beds.

COLLECTED Var. *masonae* from above Lake Sylvester, Cobb Valley, north-west Nelson, 1,370 m (4,500 ft). December 1967. Var. *pauciramosa* is from the Hooker Valley, Mt Cook National Park, 910 m (3,000 ft). January 1969.

Hebe cockayneana (Cheesem.) Ckn. & Allan
After Dr L. Cockayne, famous early botanist and pioneer ecologist.

An erect shrub, up to 1 m tall, with many stout branches that are very rough due to the old leaf scars. Thick leaves (10–17 x 5–8 mm) are shining above but glaucous beneath, except for their prominent midrib and the rounded slightly-thickened margin. A narrow sinus separates the leaves in the bud.

At the branch tips are 2–4 rather loose flower heads, each consisting of a single lateral stem up to 2.5 cm long. Details of a flower are shown.

DISTRIBUTION South Island: in the high rainfall regions of western Otago—Southland and Fiordland.

Subalpine to low-alpine: 800–1,500 m (2,500–5,000 ft).

HABITAT Similar to *H. odora* with which it may occur.

COLLECTED Homer Tunnel, Fiordland National Park, *ca* 1,070 m (3,500 ft). December 1964.

Hebe canterburiensis (J. B. Armst.) L. B. Moore
"Canterbury"—referring to its location.

A spreading shrub with erect branches up to 1 m tall and leaves twisted so as to be arranged in one plane along the stem. They are short, broad (7–17 x 6–8 mm) and rather blunt-tipped with a glossy upper surface. There is a long narrow sinus in the bud.

Flower heads are simple, lateral and up to 2.5 cm long, but they do not project far beyond the leaves.

DISTRIBUTION North and South Islands: Tararua Range; more widespread in the wetter mountains of the South Island from Nelson–western Marlborough to Arthurs Pass.

Subalpine to low-alpine: 900–1,400 m (3,000–4,500 ft).

HABITAT Often prominent in snow tussock-herbfield and mixed tussock-scrub but less important in subalpine scrub.

COLLECTED Temple Basin, Arthurs Pass National Park, 1,340 m (4,400 ft). January 1971.

Hebe pauciramosa

Hebe pauciramosa var. *masoniae*

Hebe canterburiensis

Hebe odora

Hebe cockayneana

cm

PLATE 92

Hebe buchananii (Hook.f.) Ckn. & Allan
After Mr J. Buchanan, early New Zealand botanist.

A low-growing shrub, 10–20 cm tall, with dark, stout, rough branches and dull, sometimes glaucous, thick leaves that vary (3–7 x 3–5 mm) with the habitat. They are usually concave with a distinct midrib but without an obvious petiole so that the bud lacks a sinus.

Flower heads near the branch tips are short and simple (1–2 cm long) with crowded flowers.

DISTRIBUTION South Island: on the drier mountains of the interior from Canterbury (Godley Valley) southwards to Central Otago and the Lakes district.

Low- to high-alpine: 900–2,100 m (3,000–7,000 ft).

HABITAT On rock outcrops and other highly-exposed sites, especially in cushion vegetation and fellfield.

COLLECTED Rock & Pillar Range, Central Otago, 1,220 m (4,000 ft). December 1970.

Hebe macrantha (Hook.f.) Ckn. & Allan
"Large-flowered".

A rather straggling shrub, 20–60 cm tall, with thick leaves of a distinctive size and shape.

Very large pure-white flowers occur 2–6 together, on one or more lateral branches near the stem tips.

Minor differences in leaf size and shape separate two varieties: var. **brachyphylla** (Cheesem.) Ckn. & Allan, "short-leaved", has shorter leaves (13–15 x 9–10 mm) than var. **macrantha** (12–25 x 5–10 mm).

DISTRIBUTION South Island: chiefly in the wetter regions—var. *brachyphylla* is in Nelson and north-west Canterbury while var. *macrantha* replaces it southwards to Fiordland.

Subalpine to low-alpine: 1,000–1,500 m (3,500–5,000 ft).

HABITAT On damp often rocky sites in mixed snow tussock-scrub and herbfield.

COLLECTED Var. *macrantha* is from the Humboldt Mountains, Mt Aspiring National Park, 1,370 m (4,500 ft). February 1968.

Hebe pinguifolia (Hook.f.) Ckn. & Allan
"Thick-leaved".

A highly-variable stout shrub ranging from depressed to erect, 15 cm to 1 m tall. Thick leaves (8–15 x 5–10 mm) are usually concave and glaucous, often with reddish margins. Their midrib is faint and there is no petiole and hence no sinus in the bud.

Several lateral flower heads near the branch tips extend well beyond the leaves and often conceal the tip.

DISTRIBUTION South Island: widespread on the drier mountains of the interior from Nelson–Marlborough southwards as far as south Canterbury.

Subalpine to high-alpine: 800–1,800 m (2,500–6,000 ft).

HABITAT Most common on rock outcrops but also in open or depleted snow tussock grassland, herbfield and occasionally on loose rocky debris.

COLLECTED Island Pass, upper Wairau Valley, south-eastern Nelson, 1,430 m (4,600 ft). December 1967.

Hebe decumbens (J. B. Armst.) Ckn. & Allan
"Decumbent"—the stems lie along the ground before turning up.

Shrubs reach 30–80 cm and may resemble *H. pinguifolia* but their branches are shining purplish-black and the almost flat fleshy leaves (12–30 x 5–10 mm) are not glaucous but usually have a red margin. Buds lack a sinus.

Flowers have very short stalks rather than being sessile as in *H. pinguifolia*.

DISTRIBUTION South Island: confined to the drier areas in the north-east—Marlborough, eastern Nelson and north Canterbury.

Subalpine to low-alpine: 900–1,500 m (3,000–5,000 ft).

HABITAT It favours rocky sites in grassland.

COLLECTED Mt Blowhard, Raglan Range, Wairau Valley, Marlborough, 1,340 m (4,400 ft). January 1971.

*Hebe amplexicaulis (J. B. Armst.) Ckn. & Allan
"Stem-clasping"—referring to the leaf bases.

Rather similar to *H. pinguifolia*, but with larger leaves (12–15 x 8–12 mm) which have broad rounded bases that clasp the stem.

It is on the mountains of central Canterbury (Mt Peel, upper Rangitata Valley) where it colonises rocks in snow tussock grassland from 1,100–1,400 m (3,500–4,500 ft).

Hebe allanii Ckn., is similar to *H. amplexicaulis* and with a similar distribution but differs in that both twigs and leaves are covered in dense hairs. It has been reduced to a form of *H. amplexicaulis*.

Hebe gibbsii (Kirk) Ckn. & Allan, resembles *H. amplexicaulis* and *H. allanii* but differs in the distribution of hairs and shape of calyx lobes. It is confined to a small area near the southern end of the Richmond Range in northern Marlborough–Nelson.

* *Hebe dilatata* Simpson and Thomson, is similar to *H. cockayneana* with a narrow sinus but the plant is more prostrate. The leaves are pointed, with thickened and bevelled edges and a conspicuous midrib. It occurs on loose rocky debris on the Garvie Mountains, southern Central Otago in the low-alpine zone at 1,300–1,400 m (4,300–4,600 ft).

Hebe biggarii Ckn., resembles *H. pinguifolia*, particularly in leaf shape and colour, including the reddish margins, and habitat (mainly rock outcrops). It is restricted to south-central South Island, on the Eyre, Garvie and Thomson Mountains in the low-alpine zone at 1,200–1,450 m (4,000–4,800 ft).

COLLECTED Upper Eyre Creek, Eyre Mountains, 1,370 m (4,500 ft) December 1970.

Hebe crawii Heads, is a spreading shrub up to 40 cm tall with distinctly glaucous leaves that are thick, broad and rounded at the tip. There is a narrow sinus and the branched flower heads are lateral rather than terminal. It occurs in low- to high-alpine shrubland, and among rocky debris at 800–1,650 m (2,500–5,400 ft) on the Eyre, Takitimu and southern Garvie Mountains of northern Southland.

Hebe macrantha

Hebe decumbens

Hebe pinguifolia

Hebe biggarii

mm

Hebe buchananii

cm

PLATE 93

Hebe haastii (Hook.f.) Ckn. & Allan
After Sir Julius von Haast, famous geologist and explorer.

A trailing or sprawling variable shrub with twisted branches that are ascending and densely leafy towards the tips. Almost fleshy leaves (6–13 x 4–9 mm) are in four distinct rows with the broad bases of each pair of opposite leaves joined together.

Large compact heads at the branch tips consist of several small flower stems.

Three varieties are recognised on differences in leaves and flowers (see Allan's *Flora of New Zealand*, 1961, p. 939).

DISTRIBUTION South Island: from Nelson southwards along the main divide at least to the Mt Cook district and through much of Canterbury to the Two Thumb Range.

High-alpine to nival: 1,200–2,900 m (4,000–9,600 ft).

HABITAT On scree and loose rocky debris or crevices in fellfield. It extends into the nival zone in clefts on snow-free sites, sharing with *Parahebe birleyi* the highest recorded elevation for a vascular plant.

COLLECTED Var. *humilis* is from above Lake Sylvester, Cobb Valley, north-west Nelson, 1,580 m (5,200 ft). December 1967. The non-flowering plant is var. *haastii* from above Cass, mid-Canterbury.

Hebe epacridea (Hook.f.) Ckn. & Allan
"Resembling *Epacris*".

Generally similar to *H. haastii* but distinguished by its smaller size, more rigid habit and especially by its leaves which are curved sharply backwards and usually glaucous.

The terminal head, although of several small flower stems as in *H. haastii*, is usually shorter (1.5 vs 1.5–3 cm).

DISTRIBUTION South Island: on the higher mountains from Nelson Marlborough southwards along and east of the main divide to north Otago and the Lakes district.

High-alpine: 1,200–2,100 m (4,000–7,000 ft).

HABITAT On screes and debris slopes or rock crevices in fellfield, sometimes with *H. haastii*.

Hebe vernicosa* (Hook.f.) Ckn. & Allan
"Smooth and shining"—referring to the leaves.

Similar to *H. canterburiensis* and best distinguished by its more horizontal branches, spreading leaves, and longer flower heads (3–5 cm) which project well beyond the leaves.

It is plentiful in eastern Nelson–Marlborough and north Canterbury, especially under beech forest, but it may extend a short distance beyond the tree line into mixed tussock-scrub, including that of the mineral belt.

COLLECTED St Arnaud Range, Nelson Lakes National Park, 1,680 m (5,500 ft). December 1967.

Hebe ramosissima* Simpson & Thomson, "Highly-branched", forms low mats, 20–30 cm across, with fleshy leaves (5 x 2 mm) that are recurved. It has been recorded only from moist debris at 2,150 m (7,050 ft) on the eastern slope of Mt Tapuaenuku on the Inland Kaikoura Range, Marlborough.

Hebe petriei (Buchan.) Ckn. & Allan
After Mr D. Petrie, early teacher and botanist, especially in Otago.

A distinctive, small, trailing or straggling, much-branched shrub, with stems up to 50 cm long and short (5–15 cm), erect, leafy branches, as shown. Bright-green to slightly glaucous leaves (6–10 x 2–5 mm) have their bases joined.

Flower heads are relatively large and compact at the branch tips.

DISTRIBUTION South Island: on the higher mountains above Lake Wakatipu, extending to south-western Otago, western Southland and Fiordland.

Low- to high-alpine: 1,300–2,100 m (4,500–7,000 ft).

HABITAT Usually on shady rock ledges and loose stony debris in fellfield.

COLLECTED Eyre Mountains, northern Southland, 1,740 m (5,700 ft). December 1969. The non-flowering branch is from Mt Burns, Hunter Mountains, Fiordland National Park, 1,370 m (4,500 ft)

Hebe pauciflora Simpson & Thomson, "With few flowers", is a low straggling shrub, up to 20 cm tall, not unlike *H. petriei*, but with pale-green, crowded, shining leaves (5–7 x 3.5–5 mm) in four distinct rows. Leaves have a prominent midrib and a broad petiole so that a sinus is present in the bud. Flower heads are quite inconspicuous, with only a short (1 cm) spike on either side of the tip, each with only 2 small white flowers. It is confined to the Fiordland mountains south of about Lake Te Anau, chiefly on open rocky sites or in crevices.

COLLECTED Murchison Mountains, Fiordland National Park, 1,220 m (4,000 ft). February 1973.

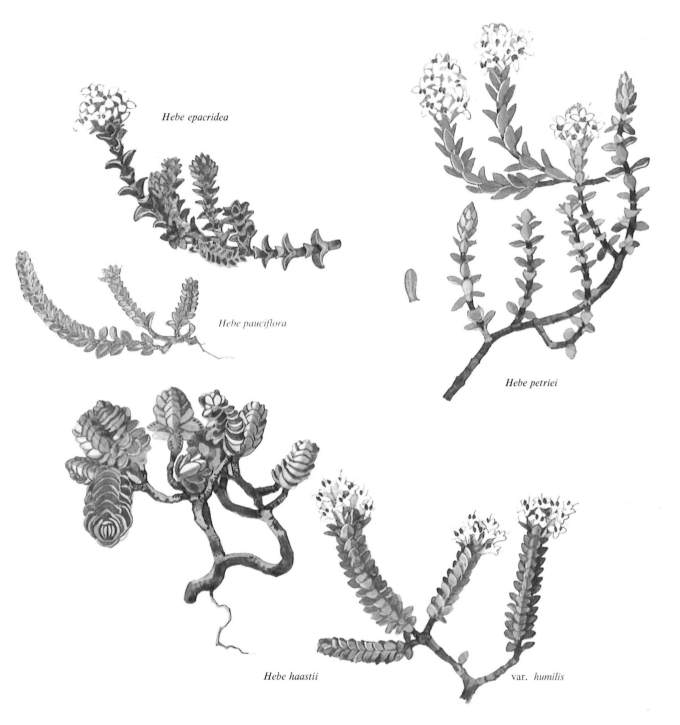

Hebe epacridea

Hebe pauciflora

Hebe petriei

Hebe haastii

var. *humilis*

cm

PLATE 94

Hebe ciliolata (Hook.f.) Ckn. & Allan
"With minute hairs"—referring to the leaf margins.

A low straggling shrub, often forming loose patches up to 20 cm or more across and 10–20 cm tall. Stems have almost a whipcord form with small, closely-overlapping, narrow leaves (4 x 1 mm) in four distinct rows. Individual leaves are trough-shaped with a row of fine hairs along their upturned edges.

Small white flowers occur on several short stems that almost conceal the branch tips. A single flower is shown.

DISTRIBUTION South Island: on the wetter mountains from Nelson southwards, along or close to the main divide, at least to Otago.

Low- to high-alpine: 1,000–2,000 m (3,500–6,500 ft).

HABITAT Most common on rock ledges and clefts, especially in fell-field, but it may colonise moraine and exposed rocky sites in snow tussock-herbfield.

COLLECTED B'limit Col, Temple Basin, Arthurs Pass National Park, 1,800 m (5,900 ft). December 1967.

Hebe tumida (Kirk) Ckn. & Allan
"Swollen"—referring to the leaves.

A trailing or straggling highly-branched shrub that forms rather compact low patches 10–50 cm across. Their short leafy branches are squarish (1.5–2 mm across) but rough and serrated in outline because of the projecting blunt tips of the four rows of swollen scale leaves.

Flowers are in rather loose heads (*ca* 12 mm long) at the branch tips.

DISTRIBUTION South Island: on the drier mountains of eastern Nelson–western Marlborough.

Low- to high-alpine: 1,100–1,700 m (3,500–5,500 ft).

HABITAT Usually on rock ledges and crevices in snow tussock-herbfield and fellfield.

COLLECTED St Arnaud Range, Nelson Lakes National Park, 1,460 m (4,800 ft). December 1967.

Hebe tetrasticha (Hook.f.) Ckn. & Allan
"Arranged in four rows"—referring to the leaves.

Its 'habit is similar to *H. tumida* but the twigs are stouter (2.5 mm across) and leaves thin and flattened on their outer surface rather than swollen. Also, their tips are sharp, not blunt as in *H. tumida*, and the flower heads at the branch tips are much more compact (*ca* 5 mm long).

DISTRIBUTION South Island: confined to the Canterbury mountains.

Subalpine to high-alpine: 800–1,800 m (2,500–6,000 ft).

HABITAT On ledges or clefts of rock outcrops and occasionally also among loose stony debris.

COLLECTED Above Lake Lyndon, Torlesse Range, Canterbury, 790 m (2,600 ft). December 1967.

Hebe cheesemanii (Buchan.) Ckn. & Allan
After Mr T. F. Cheeseman, well-known botanist.

Similar to *H. tumida* but the leafy twigs are distinctly greyish-green and almost square in section (1.5–2 mm across). Short, stiff, white hairs along the leaf margins are quite obvious on younger twigs.

Flower heads are small (*ca* 5 mm long) but the stalk elongates later to be much beyond the leaves when the fruits mature, as shown.

DISTRIBUTION South Island: on the drier mountains to the east of the main divide, but rare south of Canterbury.

Low- to high-alpine: 1,100–1,700 m (3,500–5,500 ft).

HABITAT On rock outcrops, exposed rocky ridge crests and occasionally among loose rocky debris.

COLLECTED Upper Cass River, Godley Valley, Canterbury, 1,160 m (3,800 ft). May 1969.

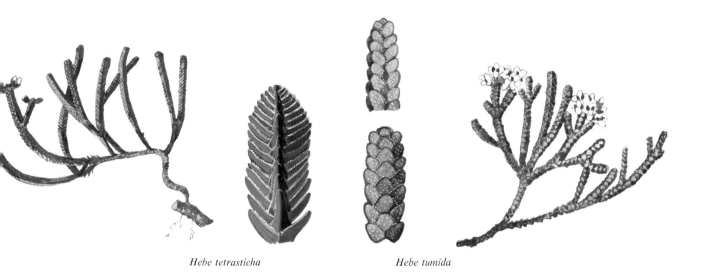

Hebe tetrasticha

Hebe tumida

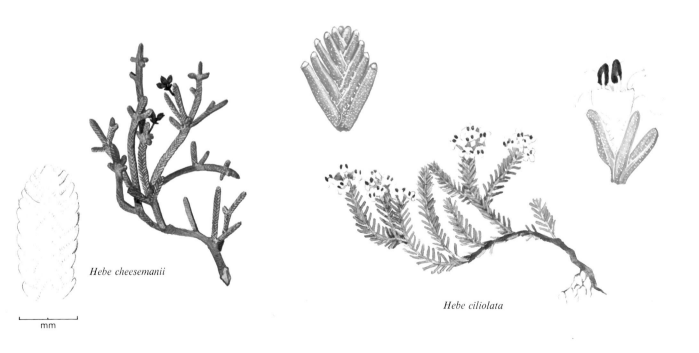

Hebe cheesemanii

Hebe ciliolata

mm

cm

PLATE 95

Hebe hectorii (Hook.f.) Ckn. & Allan
After Sir James Hector, geologist and explorer.

A robust whipcord shrub, 10–70 cm tall, usually highly-branched with many short (3–10 cm) but stout (2.5–3.5 mm across) erect branches that are rounded except for their squarish tips. Scale leaves are broad and thick (2–2.5 mm long), rounded on the back and typically with broad blunt tips.

Short flower spikes at the branch tips are crowded to form small terminal heads.

DISTRIBUTION South Island: widespread on the mountains from about the Mt Cook district and south Canterbury southwards to Foveaux Strait.

Subalpine to high-alpine: 900–1,800 m (3,000–6,000 ft).

HABITAT Often prominent in snow tussock-herbfield and mixed snow tussock-scrub. Small forms may extend into shallow snowbanks and moist depressions in fellfield and cushion vegetation.

COLLECTED Borland Saddle, Hunter Mountains, Fiordland National Park, 1,010 m (3,300 ft). January 1968.

Hebe tetragona (Hook.) Ckn. & Allan
"Four-angled"—referring to the branches.

A rigid yellowish-green shrub, similar in habit to *H. hectori*, but distinguished by its 4-angled stems and narrower, more pointed scale leaves. Plants vary in the degree of overlapping and appression of the leaves and pronouncement of their tips.

Compact flower heads at the branch tips are similar to *H. hectori*.

DISTRIBUTION North Island: from Mt Hikurangi southwards through the central North Island mountains to the northern end of the Ruahine Range. Here it is replaced by *H. subsimilis*.

Subalpine to low-alpine: 700–1,700 m (2,000–5,500 ft).

HABITAT In mixed tussock-scrub, tussock-herbfield and also in the low scrub covering vast areas of pumice on the central volcanoes.

COLLECTED Mt Ruapehu, Tongariro National Park, ca 1,070 m (3,500 ft). November 1964.

Hebe laingii (Ckn.) Ckn. & Allan
After Mr R. M. Laing, Canterbury botanist.

A low shrub up to 25 cm tall that resembles small forms of *H. hectori*, but the twigs are squarish and finer (2–2.5 mm across).

It occurs in damp grassy meadows of Fiordland and Stewart Island (Mt Anglem).

COLLECTED Above Lake Wapiti, upper Doon Valley, Fiordland National Park, 1,370 m (4,500 ft).

***Hebe subsimilis** (Col.) M. B. Ashwin
"Rather similar"—to *H. tetragona*.

It differs from *H. tetragona* in its lower habit and smaller size (to ca 30 cm), in the branches being rounded or only slightly squared, and in the leaves being distinctly swollen and only faintly keeled, not unlike those of *H. coarctata*. Flower heads have fewer and smaller flowers than in *H. tetragona*.

It is confined to the Pouakai Range of Mt Egmont and the Ruahine and Tararua Ranges, in subalpine scrub, mixed snow tussock-scrub and snow tussock-herbfield up to ca 1,500 m (5,000 ft).

Hebe coarctata (Cheesem.) Ckn. & Allan
"Compressed"—referring to the leaves.

A spreading very highly-branched shrub, 30–80 cm tall, usually with a distinctive habit: horizontal or arching stems bearing short (to 5 cm) erect branches. These final branches are rounded and shining (1.5–2 mm across), with thick, strongly-curved, scale leaves that have a slightly thickened keel below the tips.

Flowers are in small heads at the branch tips, as in *H. hectori*.

DISTRIBUTION South Island: in the north-west, extending east to the Nelson Lakes and south to north Westland.

Low-alpine: 1,200–1,700 m (4,000–5,500 ft).

HABITAT Its place in the damp snow tussock-herbfields is similar to that of *H. hectori* in the south.

COLLECTED Near Lake Sylvester, Cobb Valley, north-west Nelson, 1,370 m (4,500 ft). January 1971.

Hebe ochracea M. B. Ashwin
"Ochre-coloured"—referring to the branch tips.

Stout arching stems and short erect branches are similar to *H. coarctata* but the shrubs are shorter and usually flat-topped. Their ochre colour is distinctive.

DISTRIBUTION South Island: within the range of *H. coarctata* but more restricted to the north-west. Its habitat and altitudinal range is also similar to *H. coarctata*, the two species often occurring together.

COLLECTED Mt Peel, Cobb Valley, north-west Nelson, 1,520 m (5,000 ft). December 1967.

Hebe subulata Simpson
"Awl-shaped" — referring to the leaves.

A low-growing yellow-green whipcord shrub up to 20 cm tall, often rooting with erect branches ca 2 mm diameter. It is rather like *H. poppelwellii* and *H. lycopodioides* but with less obviously pointed leaf tips than the latter.

DISTRIBUTION South Island: confined to the eastern mountains of Central Otago.

Low- to high-alpine: 900–1,300 m (3,000–4,300 ft).

HABITAT Often common in open low-alpine snow tussock grassland and early snowbanks.

COLLECTED Umbrella Mountains, Central Otago, 1,300 m (4,300 ft). December 1985.

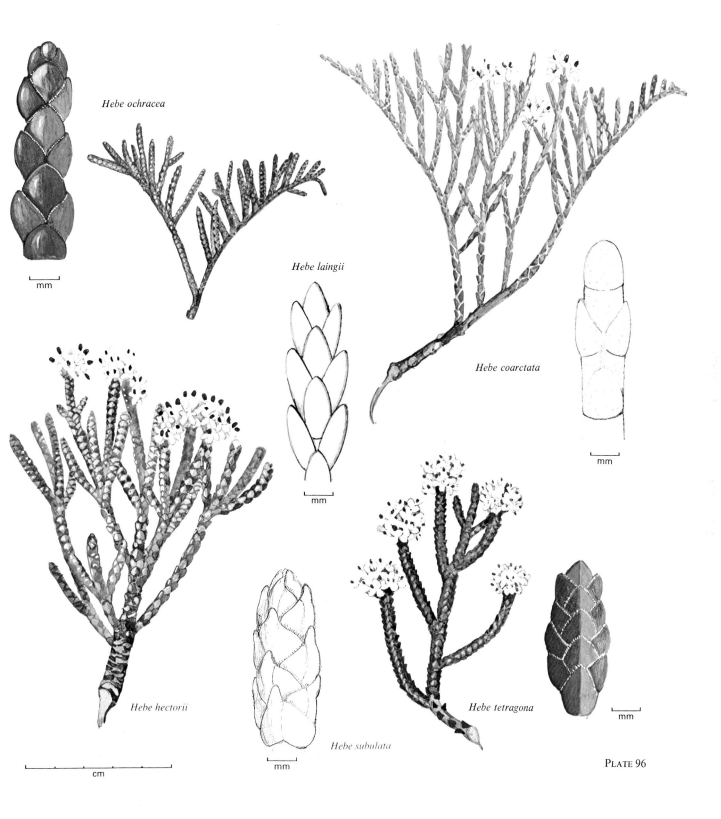

Hebe ochracea

Hebe laingii

Hebe coarctata

Hebe hectorii

Hebe subulata

Hebe tetragona

PLATE 96

Hebe lycopodioides (Hook.f.) Ckn. & Allan
"Resembling *Lycopodium*".

A rigid yellowish-green shrub, rather similar in habit to *H. hectori* but distinguished by the obviously squared branches and their scale leaves. These have yellow margins, faint stripes and pronounced but blunt tips. Towards the north of its range branches tend to be stouter (to 3 mm across) and the pointed leaf tips less pronounced.

Flower heads at the branch tips are similar to *H. hectori*.

Var. **patula** Simpson & Thomson "Slightly spreading", is altogether smaller and forms low patches rather similar to *H. poppelwellii*.

DISTRIBUTION South Island: mostly on the drier mountains from eastern Nelson–Marlborough southwards through Canterbury to north Otago, but extending in several places, e.g. Arthurs Pass, to the main divide. Var. *patula* occurs along the main divide between Amuri and Harper Passes in north Canterbury.

Subalpine to low-alpine: 900–1,700 m (3,000–5,500 ft).

HABITAT Usually the most common whipcord hebe of the drier eastern tussock grasslands and herbfields.

COLLECTED St Arnaud Range, Nelson Lakes National Park, 1,580 m (5,200 ft). December 1967.

Hebe poppelwellii (Ckn.) Ckn. & Allan
After Mr D. L. Poppelwell, who collected it.

A low, slender, much-branched shrub, forming small yellowish-green clumps 5–20 cm tall. Branches are glossy and squarish (1.5–2 mm across) and their tightly packed leaves are finely striped.

Small flower heads develop at the stem tips.

DISTRIBUTION South Island: a very limited range in Central Otago—Rock & Pillar and Old Man Ranges; Garvie Mountains.

Low- to high-alpine: 1,200–1,700 m (4,000–5,500 ft).

HABITAT In somewhat sheltered moist sites, especially depressions in cushion vegetation. It may descend some way into herbfield or snow tussock grassland on exposed sites.

COLLECTED Rock & Pillar Range, Central Otago, ca 1,220 m (4,000 ft). December 1964.

***H. imbricata** Ckn. & Allan, "Referring to the small overlapping leaves", is a much-branched, whipcord, round-headed shrub, 40–60 cm tall, with the final branches shining and rounded (2–2.5 mm across). Leaves are striped as in *H. poppelwellii* but with some features of *H. hectori* and could be a hybrid. Apparently confined to the Hunter Mountains, Fiordland.

Hebe propinqua (Cheesem.) Ckn. & Allan
"Resembling"—*H. armstrongii*.

A highly-branched, spreading, rather flat-topped shrub, 20–60 cm tall and up to 1 m or more across. The many final branches are slender (1–2 mm across) and rounded, with distinctive, thick, rounded, scale leaves.

Small flower heads develop at the branch tips.

DISTRIBUTION South Island: from eastern Otago to the Lakes district with one record from Canterbury (Rangitata Valley).

Low-alpine: 800 1,400 m (2,500–4,500 ft).

HABITAT Usually on poorly drained, often peaty areas, of mixed snow tussock-scrub.

COLLECTED Maungatua, eastern Otago, 880 m (2,900 ft). December 1970.

Hebe cupressoides (Hook.f.) Ckn. & Allan
"Resembling *Cupressus*"—referring to the twigs.

A highly-branched rounded and glaucous shrub, usually 1–1.5 m tall, with numerous, fine, flexible branches (1 mm across) that are further distinguished by the very widely-spaced, rather fleshy, scale leaves. These have a distinct turpentine smell when crushed.

Small, pale, bluish-purple (rarely white) flowers occur 3–8 together at the branch tips.

DISTRIBUTION South Island: widespread to the east of the main divide from Marlborough to the Otago Lakes district but now rather rare.

Subalpine to low-alpine: 600–1,400 m (2,000–4,500 ft).

HABITAT On stony well-drained sites, especially gravel river beds and terraces among the tussock grasslands. Grazing by stock has greatly reduced its numbers.

COLLECTED From a cultivated plant from the upper Wairau Valley, Nelson.

Several other alpine hebes have limited distribution or occurrence:

***Hebe venustula** (Col.) L. B. Moore, "Charming", is erect, up to 1.5 m tall. Leaves are bright-green above but dull below (10–20 x 3–6 mm) with a pointed tip, slightly bevelled margins and a tapered base. The leaf bud has a long narrow sinus. Flower heads are lateral, sometimes branched, and up to 3.5 cm long. It occurs between 800–1,500 m (2,500–5,000 ft) from Mt Hikurangi to the central volcanic mountains.

***Hebe armstrongii** (J. B. Armst.) Ckn. & Allan, is a yellowish-green whipcord shrub, ca 1 m tall, with rounded branches, occurring from mid-Canterbury (Rangitata Valley) to north Otago. It is rare in the field but common in cultivation.

***Hebe salicornioides** (Hook.f.) Ckn. & Allan, "Like *Salicornia*", is an erect shrub, ca 1 m tall, with dull, soft, fleshy, rounded twigs (2–2.5 mm across) and widely-spaced leaves that have broad rounded tips. It occurs sporadically from Nelson to western Otago, but only in very wet sites.

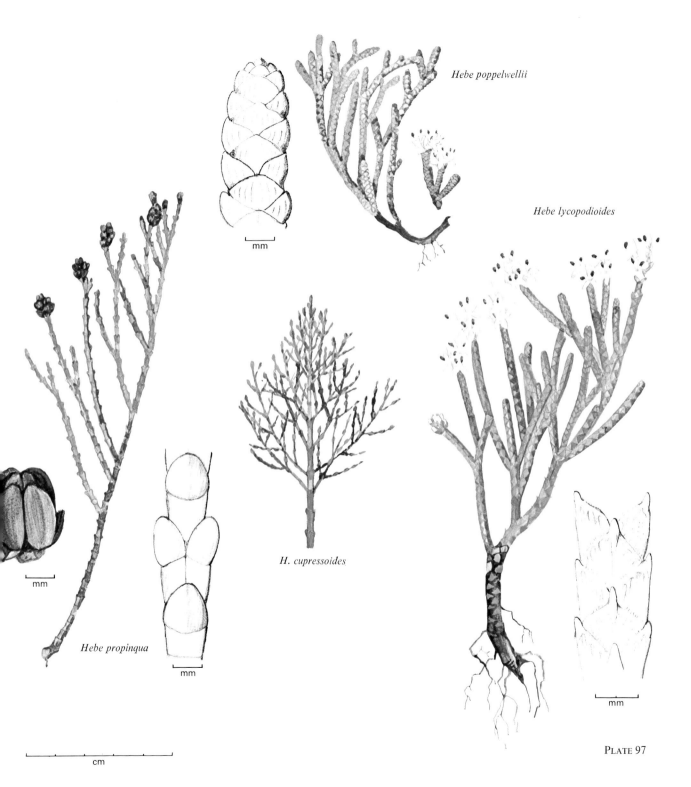

Hebe poppelwellii

Hebe lycopodioides

mm

mm

H. cupressoides

Hebe propinqua

mm

mm

cm

PLATE 97

FLOWERING PLANTS

THE MONOCOTYLEDONS

The Lily Family: **LILIACEAE**

Genus **ASTELIA**
"Without a stem"

Contains about 25 species distributed around the Pacific Ocean but centred in New Zealand. Here there are 13 and seven reach the alpine zone. All plants are unisexual.

Astelia petriei Ckn.
After Mr D. Petrie, early teacher and botanist, especially in Otago.

Leafy tufts form patches that are quite distinctive because of the shining, glabrous, pale-green upper leaf surface, silvery-white lower surface and conspicuous veins on both.

Flower heads are prominent among the upper leaves, with greenish flowers and orange fruits.

DISTRIBUTION South Island: in the higher rainfall regions, chiefly along and near the main divide, from Nelson to Fiordland.

Mostly low-alpine: 900–1,500 m (3,000–5,000 ft).

HABITAT Usually rather rare in snow tussock-scrub and herbfield. In heavily grazed areas it is now almost restricted to inaccessible bluffs.

COLLECTED A female plant from Mt Burns, Hunter Mountains, Fiordland National Park, 1,220 m (4,000 ft). January 1969.

Astelia petriei

cm

PLATE 98

Astelia nervosa Banks & Sol. ex Hook.f.
"Nerved"—referring to the leaves.

The leafy tufts may form small or large clumps that vary with altitude and location, but alpine forms have leaves up to 80 cm long. They have a pair of stout lateral veins and may be pale-green with only a thin, silvery, skin-like covering on the upper leaf surface, or greyish-white with a thick almost hairy covering, especially near the margins. The lower leaf surface is more silky than the upper.

Flower heads are usually small and hidden among the leaves but in female plants fruiting heads become prominent in autumn.

DISTRIBUTION North, South and Stewart Islands: widespread in mountain regions from Mt Hikurangi, Mt Egmont and Taupo southwards.

Lowland to low-alpine: to 1,500 m (5,000 ft).

HABITAT In the alpine zone it is usually in damp, often peaty areas of mixed tussock-scrub, tussock grassland and herbfield.

COLLECTED A female plant from Swampy Summit, Dunedin district, 670 m (2,200 ft). April 1969.

Astelia graminea L. B. Moore
"Grass-like".

Its habit is similar to *A. nivicola* but the tufts are more grasslike, with the leaves narrower (5–10 vs > 10 mm wide), strongly folded and with fewer (< 6) nerves on either side of the midrib.

Flower heads are both more common and more prominent than in *A. nivicola*, with male flowers maroon and female ones greenish, as shown, with pinkish petals. Fruits are bright orange.

DISTRIBUTION South Island: western Marlborough and Nelson, including the mineral belt at Dun Mountain.

Low-alpine: 1,200–1,600 m (4,000–5,500 ft).

HABITAT Its small clumps occupy open grassland, especially among carpet grass.

COLLECTED Travers Range, Nelson Lakes National Park, 1,250 m (4,100 ft). December 1967.

Astelia skottsbergii L. B. Moore
After Professor C. Skottsberg, Swedish botanist who studied astelias.

It resembles small plants of *A. petriei* except that young leaves are light bluish-green and older ones are glabrous on both surfaces with their margins recurved.

As in *A. petriei* flowers are greenish and the fruits orange.

It is confined to western Nelson between Mt Arthur and the Paparoa Range, growing chiefly on rocky sites at *ca* 1,200 m (4,000 ft).

Astelia nervosa

Astelia graminea

cm

PLATE 99

Astelia linearis Hook.f.
"Narrow and straight"—referring to the leaves.

Small tufts develop on rhizomes that branch to produce almost a turf up to 50 cm or more across. The thick leathery leaves (usually 3–10 cm x 2–7 mm) have recurved margins and a pair of prominent lateral nerves.

Flower heads are small and inconspicuous but the bright red fruits on female plants are more prominent.

Var. **novae-zelandiae** Skottsb. differs from var. **linearis** in having the lower surface of the leaves glabrous except for brownish hair-like scales on the margins and midrib.

DISTRIBUTION North, South and Stewart Islands: var. *novae-zelandiae* is found on the Raukumara, Ruahine and Tararua Ranges; throughout much of the South Island mountain region and on Stewart Island. Var. *linearis* is also on Stewart Island, in western Southland and Nelson.

Mostly subalpine to low-alpine: 800–1,500 m (2,500–5,000 ft).

HABITAT Usually plentiful in bogs and damp, open, often peaty areas of snow tussock-herbfield.

COLLECTED Var. *novae-zelandiae* from the Little Red Hill Range, north-west Otago, 1,070 m (3,500 ft). December 1969.

Astelia subulata Cheesem.
"Awl-shaped"—referring to the leaves.

Its habit is similar to *A. linearis* but the plants are much smaller and form a dense matted turf. Leaves are shining bright-green (1–2.5 cm long) with pointed tips.

Flower heads are very small with a single flower, but the elongated fruits are more conspicuous.

DISTRIBUTION South and Stewart Islands: on Frazer Peaks, Stewart Island, Ajax Bog in south-east Otago and the Paparoa Range in north Westland.

HABITAT A most insignificant plant among cushions in subalpine and low-alpine peat bogs.

COLLECTED By Dr I. Morice from Mt Watson, Paparoa Range, north Westland. April 1968.

Astelia nivicola Ckn.
"Growing at high altitudes".

Tufts are usually 10–30 cm high with stout prostrate stems that branch to form patches up to 50 cm or more across.

Flowering is rare in the field but heads are very short and compact, as are the orange fruits.

DISTRIBUTION South Island: widespread in the higher rainfall regions.

Mostly low-alpine: 1,100–1,700 m (3,500–5,500 ft).

HABITAT Usually common in damp snow hollows among snow tussock-herbfield, especially near its upper limit.

COLLECTED Mt Brewster, Haast Pass, Mt Aspiring National Park, 1,460 m (4,800 ft). March 1968.

Genus **HERPOLIRION**
"Creeping lily".

An Australasian genus with but one species. It may reach the alpine zone.

Herpolirion novae-zelandiae Hook.f.　　　　　　　GRASS LILY
"Of New Zealand".

A grass-like glaucous herb with pale-brown wiry rhizomes that branch to form diffuse patches. Leaves are flattened (2–5 cm long), the older ones spreading and the younger ones shorter and erect.

Relatively large lilac or white flowers are almost sessile, and the fruit is a swollen triangular capsule.

DISTRIBUTION North, South and Stewart Islands: Kaimanawa and Ruahine Ranges and a few non-alpine localities in the North Island; widespread in the South Island.

Mostly montane to low-alpine: 500–1,200 m (1,500–4,000 ft).

HABITAT Often common in bogs and open, usually damp sites in tussock grassland or herbfield.

COLLECTED Rock & Pillar Range, Central Otago, 910 m (3,000 ft). December 1969.

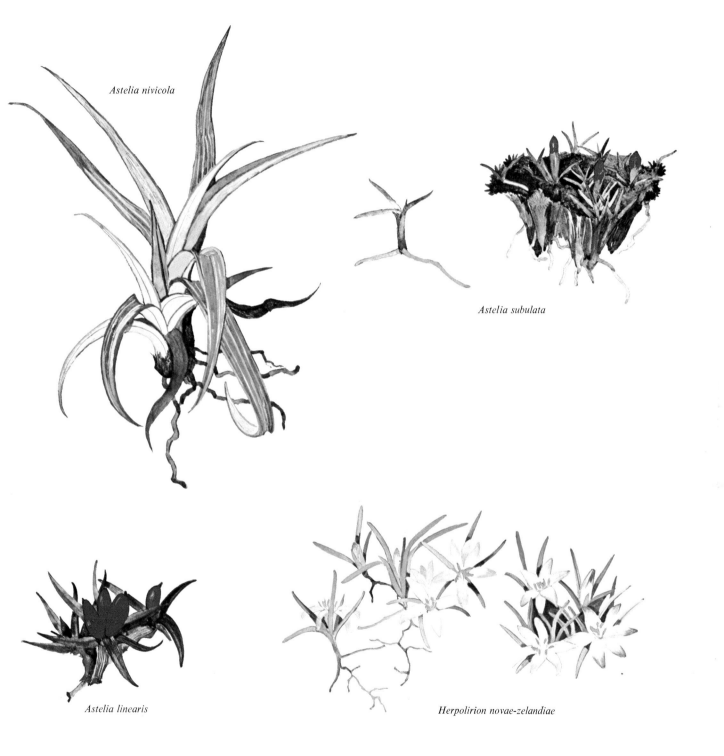

Astelia nivicola

Astelia subulata

Astelia linearis

Herpolirion novae-zelandiae

cm

PLATE 100

Genus BULBINELLA

"Small bulb"—inappropriate since the roots only are swollen.

Contains about 20 species from South Africa and New Zealand. Of the five mainland bulbinellas at least three reach the alpine zone.

Bulbinella hookerii (Hook.) Cheesem.
After Sir J. D. Hooker, famous early botanist.

Usually robust and from 20–50 cm tall, with mostly erect leaves that are blunt-tipped and longitudinally ribbed beneath. Some western Nelson and Marlborough populations have glaucous leaves.

Flower stems exceed the leaves and the heads have large bracts that conceal the flower buds. Flowers have large petals that later shrivel and hang from the base of the ripening capsule, as in *B. angustifolia*. But it differs from this species in that both the ovary and ripe capsule are on a short but distinct stalk.

DISTRIBUTION North and South Islands: Mt Egmont, parts of the volcanic plateau, north-west Ruahine Range; widespread in mountain regions of Nelson, Marlborough and north Canterbury.

Montane to low-alpine: 200–1,500 m (500–5,000 ft).

HABITAT Often prominent on moist sites in tussock grassland and herbfield, specially on shady slopes and seepage areas.

COLLECTED A glaucous form from above Lake Sylvester, Cobb Valley, north-west Nelson, 1,460 m (4,800 ft). December 1967.

Bulbinella angustifolia (Ckn. & Laing) L. B. Moore   MAORI ONION
"Narrow-leaved".

Its habit is similar to *B. hookerii* but the leaves are uniformly narrow (< 1.5 cm wide) and often channelled above. Flower heads have smaller bracts that never conceal the buds while the ovary and later the capsule are quite sessile.

DISTRIBUTION South Island: on the drier mountains of the eastern and interior regions from north Canterbury (Hurunui catchment) southwards.

Montane to low-alpine: 500–1,700 m (1,500–5,000 ft).

HABITAT Similar to *B. hookerii*. Often common in depleted tussock grassland.

COLLECTED Coronet Peak, Otago Lakes district, 1,070 m (3,500 ft). December 1968.

Bulbinella gibbsii Ckn.
Presumably after Mr F. G. Gibbs who collected on Stewart Island.

It differs from the other two in that the petals remain firm, smooth and erect against the maturing fruit. Also, older leaves are usually strongly arched.

Var. *balanifera* L. B. Moore, "resembling an acorn"—referring to the developing fruit with its barrel-shaped capsule and persistent petals around the base, is distinguished from var. *gibbsii* on ovary and fruit shape (in var. *gibbsii* they are globose, sessile and broad-based), on the lower bracts in the flower head (shorter than the flower stalks in var. *balanifera* but at least equal to them in var. *gibbsii*), and on distribution.

DISTRIBUTION Var. *gibbsii* is confined to Stewart Island while var. *balanifera* is on the southern Ruahine and Tararua Ranges and in the high rainfall regions of western South Island south of about Arthurs Pass.

Mostly montane to low-alpine: 500–1,400 m (1,500–4,500 ft).

HABITAT Var. *gibbsii* occupies wet often peaty grassland, open scrub and bog, while var. *balanifera* may be common in moist yet well-drained often rocky sites in tussock-herbfield, open scrub or below the tree line on avalanche chutes.

COLLECTED Var. *balanifera* from Borland Saddle, Hunter Mountains, Fiordland National Park, 850 m (2,800 ft). January 1968.

The Flax Family: PHORMIACEAE

Genus PHORMIUM

"Basket, wickerwork"—a plant from which mats and other items are woven.

Contains only two species, both in New Zealand, but one also in Norfolk Island. Only one reaches the alpine zone.

Phormium cookianum Le Jolis   MOUNTAIN FLAX
After Captain James Cook.

Distinguished from the lowland flax (*P. tenax*) by its less rigid leaves, smaller size (leaves 0.6–1.5 m long), flower colour (yellow or yellowish-red vs reddish-purple) and long (10–17 vs 5–10 cm) twisted and drooping capsules (in *P. tenax* they are erect).

DISTRIBUTION North, South and Stewart Islands: widespread but mostly in mountain regions.

Lowland to low-alpine: to 1,400 m (4,500 ft).

HABITAT In the alpine zone it may be common on poorly-drained, often peaty areas of mixed tussock-scrub, tussock grassland or herbfield, usually not far above the tree line. Plants reshoot quickly after fire and may increase if burning is regular.

COLLECTED Both flowers and fruit from Temple Basin track, Arthurs Pass National Park, 1,160 m (3,800 ft). January 1971.

Bulbinella gibbsii var. *balanifera*

Bulbinella angustifolia

Bulbinella hookerii

Phormium cookianum

cm

PLATE 101

The Orchid Family: **ORCHIDACEAE**

Genus **APOROSTYLIS**
"Perplexing column"—referring to the flower.

Contains but a single endemic species which reaches the alpine zone.

Aporostylis bifolia (Hook.f.) Rupp & Hatch
"With two leaves".

A variable herb, up to 25 cm tall, with small, white, rounded tubers and a pair of mottled basal leaves that vary in shape but are usually of unequal size.

Flower stems have a single sheathing bract and 1 (or 2) white or pink flowers.

DISTRIBUTION North, South and Stewart Islands: widespread in moist mountains regions from Mt Egmont and Lake Taupo southwards.

Mostly montane to low-alpine: 500–1,400 m (1,500–4,500 ft).

HABITAT Often common in moist tussock grassland, herbfield, bog, open forest and scrub.

COLLECTED Key Summit, Fiordland National Park, 910 m (3,000 ft). January 1968.

Genus **PTEROSTYLIS**
"Winged style".

Contains about 60 species, mostly Australasian. Of the 19 native ones, several reach the upper forest margin but only one of these and the truly grassland species are included here.

Pterostylis mutica R.Br.
"Blunt"—referring to the lack of long pointed lobes that occur on the flowers of most species.

A small but distinctive rather stout herb, up to 10 cm tall, with a basal rosette of up to 8 small pointed leaves that often wither as the fruits ripen. Stems have 1–6 sheathing brownish-grey bracts and 2–8 small greenish-brown flowers *ca* 6 mm long.

DISTRIBUTION North, South and Stewart Islands: on the volcanic plateau; more widespread in the drier eastern and interior regions of the South Island.

Lowland to low-alpine: to 1,300 m (4,500 ft).

HABITAT Apparently uncommon in drier tussock grasslands, but being quite insignificant it is easily overlooked.

COLLECTED Cass, mid-Canterbury, *ca* 900 m (3,000 ft). November 1956.

Pterostylis irsoniana Hatch
After Messrs J. B. Irwin and O. E. Gibson, for their work on Mt Egmont orchids.

A usually colourful erect herb, up to 35 cm tall, with green or red stems and 3–5 narrow linear leaves, the lower ones larger (4–15 cm x 5–12 mm), with obvious sheathing bases. Leaves often have a red

midrib or may be striped with green, red and white. They usually overtop the single large flower.

DISTRIBUTION North and South Islands: Mt Egmont and near Kaitoke, Wellington; Nelson and north Westland with a few records from central Westland and Marlborough.

Mostly subalpine to low-alpine: 700–1,300 m (2,500–4,500 ft).

HABITAT Usually in subalpine scrub, forest margins or mixed snow tussock-scrub; sometimes abundant on moist banks.

COLLECTED North slope, Mt Egmont National Park, 1,220 m (4,000 ft). January 1966.

Genus **CALADENIA**
"Beautiful gland"—referring to the lip of the flower.

Contains about 75 species, mostly Australian. Two reach New Zealand, and one of these extends to the alpine zone.

Caladenia lyallii Hook.f.
After Dr Lyall, surgeon-naturalist on HMS *Terror* in the early 1840s.

A slender herb, 10–25 cm tall, with tubers as in *Aporostylis* and a single narrow (3–5 mm) leaf from near the base of the stem.

Its hairy flower stem has a sheathing bract near the middle and 1–2 prominent white to pink flowers that have a colourful 3-lobed lip.

DISTRIBUTION South and Stewart Islands: widespread in moist regions.

Mostly subalpine to low-alpine: 600–1,500 m (2,000–5,000 ft).

HABITAT In bogs and damp often peaty areas of tussock grassland, herbfield or open scrub.

COLLECTED Key Summit, Fiordland National Park, 910 m (3,000 ft). December 1964.

Genus **PRASOPHYLLUM**
"Leek-leaf".

Contains about 90 species, mostly Australian. Of the four in New Zealand only one reaches the alpine zone.

Prasophyllum colensoi Hook.f.
After Rev. W. Colenso, early New Zealand botanist.

A stout or slender glabrous herb, 10–25 cm tall, with tuberous roots. Its stem is ensheathed for much of its length by the single, rounded, fleshy leaf and ends in a many-flowered (5–20) spike of small, reddish- or yellowish-green, slightly fragrant flowers.

DISTRIBUTION North, South and Stewart Islands: widespread in hilly and mountainous regions but more abundant in the South Island.

Lowland to low-alpine: to 1,500 m (5,000 ft).

HABITAT A wide range—swamps and bogs, moist tussock grassland or herbfield, moraine, and occasionally open depleted well-drained sites in grassland and herbfield.

COLLECTED Mt Richmond, Two Thumb Range, south Canterbury, 1,370 m (4,500 ft). January 1969.

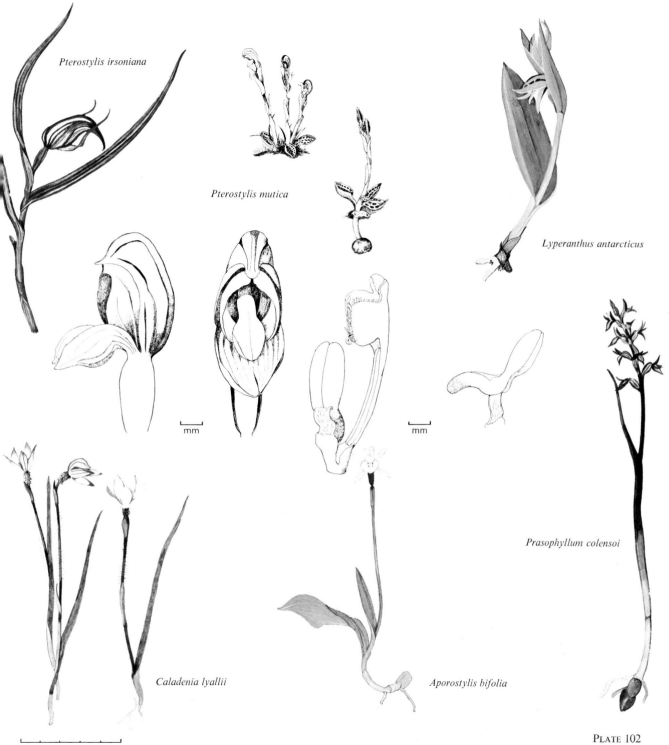

Pterostylis irsoniana

Pterostylis mutica

Lyperanthus antarcticus

mm

mm

Caladenia lyallii

Aporostylis bifolia

Prasophyllum colensoi

cm

PLATE 102

Genus LYPERANTHUS
"Dull flower".

Contains about 10 species from Australia and New Caledonia. The only native one reaches the alpine zone.

Lyperanthus antarcticus Hook.f. (See plate 102)
"Antarctic".

A glabrous herb, 7–30 cm tall, with small rounded tubers. From 1–3 leaves, the upper smaller and narrower, ensheath the base of the stem which has a head of 1–4 greenish flowers, each associated with a sheathing bract.

DISTRIBUTION North, South and Stewart Islands: Tararua Range; more widespread in the wetter regions of the South Island.

Mostly subalpine to low-alpine: 800–1,200 m (2,500–4,000 ft).

HABITAT Rather uncommon in bogs and wet often peaty areas of tussock grassland, herbfield, open scrub and forest margins.

COLLECTED Maungatua, eastern Otago, 880 m (2,900 ft). January 1970.

The Rush Family: JUNCACEAE

Genus ROSTKOVIA
After Rostkov, a Russian.

Contains two species, one from Tristan da Cunha, the other Subantarctic and reaching New Zealand where it is rare.

Rostkovia magellanica (Lam.) Hook.f.
"South American".

Forms a very open turf of small tufts, 5–20 cm tall, interconnected by rhizomes. Both the stems and bright-green leaves are stiff and bristle-like (< 1 mm wide). Brown sheaths persist at the base.

Flowers are small (5–10 mm long) and single at the stem tips with a stiff leafy bract extending up to 3 cm beyond.

On the mainland it is recorded only from wet sites in Takahe Valley, Fiordland and on a few ranges in Central Otago from 900–1,600 m (3,000–5,500 ft).

COLLECTED Carrick Range, Central Otago, 1,580 m (5,200 ft). December 1970.

Genus JUNCUS
"Rush".

A large and widely distributed genus. Of the 16 native species only three reach the alpine zone.

Juncus antarcticus Hook.f.
"Antarctic".

Quite distinctive and easily recognised by the small tufts of many rounded leaves and the leafless flower stems, 3–10 cm long, that usually exceed the leaves and end in brown 2–8-flowered heads.

DISTRIBUTION North, South and Stewart Islands: as an alpine only from Nelson southwards where it is widespread.

Mostly montane to low-alpine: 500–1,600 m (1,500–5,500 ft).

HABITAT In swamps, bogs, permanently wet depressions or avalanche chutes, usually associated with mosses.

COLLECTED Hunter Mountains, Fiordland National Park, 910 m (3,000 ft). April 1967.

Juncus novae-zelandiae Hook.f.
"Of New Zealand".

Forms tufts or dense patches, up to 15 cm high, of very slender much-branched stems. Round leaves are equally slender and striated with prominent, long, papery sheaths. Flowers are in a cluster of 2–5 at the stem tips or with 1–2 additional lateral clusters. Ripe capsules are rounded, shining, black and conspicuous.

DISTRIBUTION North, South and Stewart Islands: widespread in mountain regions.

Lowland to low-alpine: to 1,500 m (5,000 ft).

HABITAT Confined to swamps, bogs, edges of tarns, wet depressions or seepage areas.

COLLECTED A fruiting plant from Maungatua, eastern Otago, 460 m (1,500 ft). April 1957.

*Juncus pusillus Buch.
"Very small".

Similar to J. novae-zelandiae but plants are smaller and even more slender. Flowers are pale while the capsules are narrower and not much longer than the scales surrounding them. It is almost as widespread as J. novae-zelandiae and in similar habitats but is less common.

Genus MARSIPPOSPERMUM
"Seed in a pouch"—probably referring to the capsule.

Contains only four species from southern South America and New Zealand. The only native is an alpine.

Marsippospermum gracile (Hook.f.) Buch.
"Slender"—referring to the habit.

Its smooth, round, rigid stems, 10–30 cm tall, are in tufts or scattered along the stout rhizome, together with longer but equally smooth round and rigid leaves. Several pale- to dark-brown sheaths are conspicuous around the leaf bases.

Single flowers develop at the stem tips surrounded by 6 narrow pointed scales and the fruit is a hard, dry, chestnut-brown capsule enclosed by the persistent scales.

DISTRIBUTION South Island: widespread on the higher mountains, more especially in the higher rainfall regions.

Low- to high-alpine: 1,100–2,100 m (3,500–7,000 ft).

HABITAT Often prominent in snowbanks or late snow-melt or seepage areas in fellfield and locally in damp hollows or on exposed ridges near the upper limits of snow tussock grassland or herbfield.

COLLECTED Temple Basin, Arthurs Pass National Park, 1,370 m (4,500 ft). December 1967.

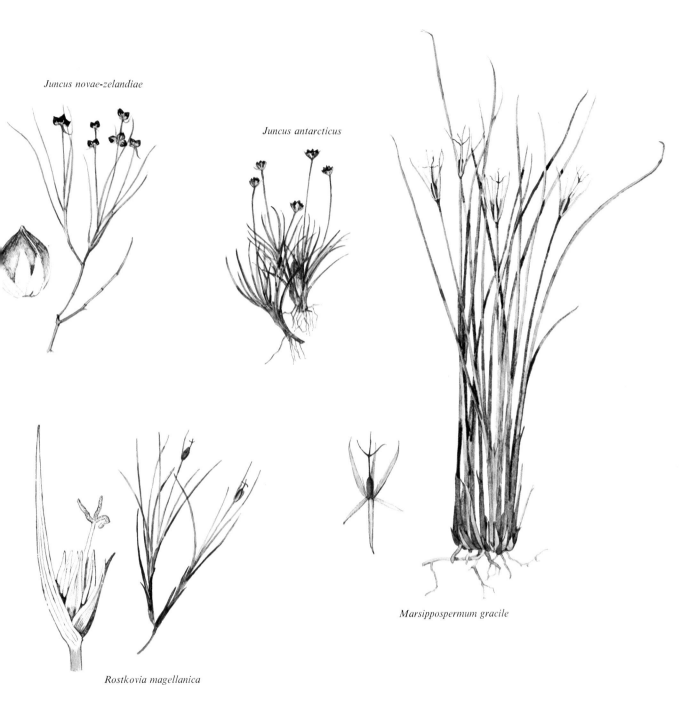

Juncus novae-zelandiae

Juncus antarcticus

Marsippospermum gracile

Rostkovia magellanica

cm

PLATE 103

Genus LUZULA

Said to be from "luzziola, firefly"—referring to the shining seed head.

Contains about 80 species, mostly from the northern temperate zone. A characteristic feature is the long white hairs scattered over their grass-like leaves, especially along the edges of the younger ones. Nine of the 11 native woodrushes reach the alpine zone, and the following key should allow most alpine plants to be identified (for use of key see Glossary):

A	Leaves with sharp tips	B
AA	Leaves with blunt tips	C
B	Margins and back of leaves with tangled white hairs	L. ulophylla
BB	Only leaf margins with hairs; flower heads usually drooping	L. traversii
C	Plants forming low cushion-like clumps < 6 cm tall	D
CC	Plants grass-like	E
D	Flower stems shorter than leaves even in fruit	L. colensoi
DD	Flower stems exceeding the leaves, especially in fruit	L. pumila
E	Leaves few and very narrow, < 0.5 mm wide	L. leptophylla
EE	Leaves numerous and wider, > 1.0 mm wide	F
F	Flower head usually compact and globose; floral scales reddish-brown	L. rufa
FF	Flower head of 3 or more equal-sized clusters on distinct stalks; floral scales not reddish-brown	G
G	Floral scales very dark, sometimes with very narrow red-brown margins	L. crinita
GG	Floral scales light- or dark-brown, often with wide white or cream margins	L. banksiana

DISTRIBUTIONS AND HABITATS

Luzula ulophylla (Buch.) Ckn. & Laing
"Woolly-leaved".

South Island: east of the main divide from southern Nelson—Marlborough to the Otago Lakes district.

Montane to low-alpine: 300–1,700 m (1,000–5,500 ft).

Its distinctive, small, woolly-leaved patches are on open stony ground, especially wind-eroded moraine and river flats, or on bare patches in depleted tussock grassland.

COLLECTED Upper Rees Valley, western Otago, 1,070 m (3,500 ft). December 1970.

*Luzula traversii (Buch.) Cheesem. var. **traversii**
After Mr W. T. L. Travers, early botanist, especially in the northern South Island.

South Island: east of the main divide as far south as Otago.

Montane to low-alpine: 600–1,700 m (2,000–5,500 ft).

Usually on rocks or moraine but plants vary in size (2–40 cm tall) according to altitude and exposure.

Luzula colensoi Hook.f.
After Rev. W. Colenso, early botanist.

North and South Islands: on most of the higher North Island mountains; rather sporadic in the South Island—Nelson, Southern Alps between Arthurs and Whitcombe Passes, the mountains of Fiordland and Southland.

Low- to high-alpine: 1,200–2,000 m (4,000–6,500 ft).

In fellfield and exposed ridges in snow tussock-herbfield.

COLLECTED North slope, Mt Egmont National Park, 1,520 m (5,000 ft). November 1967.

Luzula pumila Hook.f.
"Very small".

South Island: widespread on the higher mountains but more common east of the main divide.

Low- to high-alpine: 1,200–2,000 m (4,000–6,500 ft).

Its small tufts or loose cushions are usually common on exposed sites in cushion and fellfield, bogs and on rock outcrops, and sometimes also in snowbanks,

COLLECTED Two forms from Rock & Pillar Range, Central Otago, 1,370 m (4,500 ft). December 1969.

*Luzula crenulata Buch., forms similar cushions to L. pumila but their leaves are narrower (< 0.7 vs > 0.7 mm wide) and closely overlapping. Also, their flower heads contain < 5 florets whereas in L. pumila there are 4–12 florets per head.

It is recorded only from the summit of the Old Man Range in Central Otago but is rare.

*Luzula leptophylla Buch. & Petrie
"Slender-leaved".

North and South Islands: Ruahine and Kaimanawa Ranges; near Ashburton (Mt Somers), Otago and Southland.

Subalpine to low-alpine: 700–1,500 m (2,500–5,000 ft).

In bogs, damp hollows, flushes and water courses.

Luzula rufa Edgar var. **rufa**
"Reddish-brown"—referring to the floral scales.

South and Stewart Islands: widespread but chiefly to the east of the main divide.

Lowland to high-alpine: to 1,700 m (5,500 ft).

Its reddish-green tufts are common in the drier tussock grasslands of the interior and eastern regions. It may extend into cushion or fellfield or occasionally into wet herbfield west of the main divide.

COLLECTED Old Man Range, Central Otago, 1,220 m (4,000 ft). January 1970.

Luzula crinita Hook.f.
"Long-haired"—referring to the leaf hairs.

Var. **petrieana** (Buch.) Edgar
After Mr D. Petrie, early teacher and botanist, especially in Otago.

Cont. on page 234

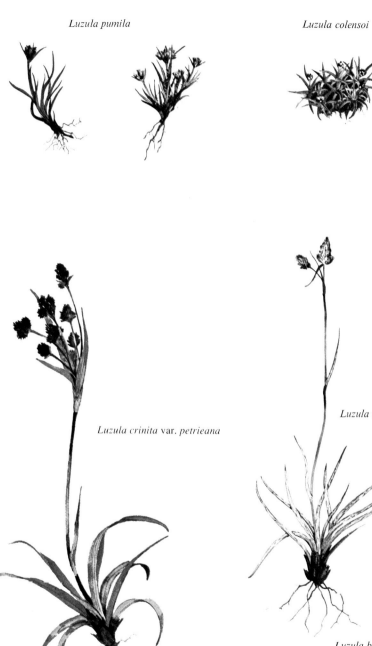

Luzula pumila

Luzula colensoi

Luzula rufa

Luzula crinita var. *petrieana*

Luzula ulophylla

Luzula banksiana var. *migrata*

cm

PLATE 104

Flower heads vary from single to numerous clusters on erect stalks.

South and Stewart Islands: widespread in the high rainfall regions. Subalpine to high-alpine: 700–2,000 m (2,500–6,500 ft).

Usually common in fellfield, on moraine, avalanche chutes, rock outcrops and in snow tussock-herbfield.

COLLECTED Temple Basin track, Arthurs Pass National Park, 1,160 m (3,800 ft). December 1967.

Luzula banksiana E. Mey. (*See plate 104*)
After Sir Joseph Banks, naturalist on Cook's first New Zealand voyage.

One of its 5 varieties reaches the alpine zone.

Var. *migrata* (Buch.) Edgar
"Migrated"—from the Old World.

North and South Islands: widespread in North Island mountain regions; the Marlborough Sounds and western South Island, southwards to about the Haast Valley.

Lowland to low-alpine: to 1,700 m (5,500 ft).

Occurs both on rock outcrops and in tussock-herbfield.

COLLECTED North slope, Mt Egmont National Park, 1,460 m (4,800 ft). November 1967.

The Centrolepis Family: **CENTROLEPIDACEAE**

Genus **CENTROLEPIS**
"Pointed scale"—referring to the floral bracts.

Contains about 25 species, chiefly Australian. Two of the three native ones reach the alpine zone.

Centrolepis ciliata (Hook.f.) Druce
"With hairs"—referring to the leaf sheaths.

Forms soft moss-like cushions up to 50 cm or more across and up to 8 cm thick. Leaves are bristle-like with broad papery sheaths covered in fine white hairs. Short erect flower stalks usually exceed the leaves and produce 2 almost opposite floral bracts, each enclosing a minute flower.

DISTRIBUTION North, South and Stewart Islands: widespread in mountain regions.

Mostly subalpine to low-alpine: 700–1,500 m (2,500–5,000 ft).

HABITAT Almost confined to bogs.

COLLECTED Arthurs Pass, Arthurs Pass National Park, 910 m (3,000 ft). December 1967.

**Centrolepis pallida* (Hook.f.) Cheesem.
"Pale".

Differs in forming smaller pale-green cushions. Leaves have white transparent sheaths that are quite glabrous, and less pronounced tips. Flower stems are usually shorter than the leaves. It also occupies bogs, both in the North (Ruahine Range, bases of the central volcanoes) and southern South Island, but is not common.

Genus **GAIMARDIA**
From Gaimard, French zoologist on the *Astrolabe* in 1827.

Contains three species, only one of which is in New Zealand where it reaches the alpine zone.

Gaimardia setacea Hook.f.
"With bristle-like leaves".

Its habit is similar to *Centrolepis ciliata* but leaves are glabrous, and with prominent hair tips. Flower stalks are also generally similar but the 2–3 floral bracts at the tip are obviously alternate.

Its distribution and habitat are as for *C. ciliata*.

COLLECTED Arthurs Pass, Arthurs Pass National Park, 910 m (3,000 ft). January 1971.

The Restio Family: **RESTIONACEAE**

Genus **EMPODISMA**
"Tangle-foot".

A small Australasian genus of two species. The single native one also occurs in southeastern Australia and Tasmania.

Empodisma minus (Hook.f.) Johnson & Cutter   WIRE RUSH
"Small".

Very distinctive, with wiry, interlacing, much-branched, green to brown stems *ca* 1 mm thick, and leaves reduced to persistent sheathing scales. Male and female flowers are on separate plants and in both, the spikelets are small and occur usually singly towards the stem tips, partly hidden by the leaf sheath.

DISTRIBUTION North, South and Stewart Islands: widespread throughout except for the southern North Island but rare in the driest parts of the South Island.

Lowland to low-alpine: to 1,500 m (5,000 ft).

HABITAT Often common in swamps and permanently wet often peaty areas of tussock grassland, herbfield and mixed scrub.

COLLECTED Whakapapanui Valley, Mt Ruapehu, Tongariro National Park, 1,160 m (3,800 ft). November 1968.

The Sedge Family: **CYPERACEAE**

Genus **ISOLEPIS**
"With equal scales".

A widespread genus of annuals or slender aquatic perennials. Two of the 13 native species reach the alpine zone.

Isolepis aucklandica (Hook.f.) Soják
From Auckland Islands.

Forms dense grass-like patches up to 20 cm or more across, but plants are rather variable and 2–15 cm tall. Stems are highly branched

Cont. on page 236

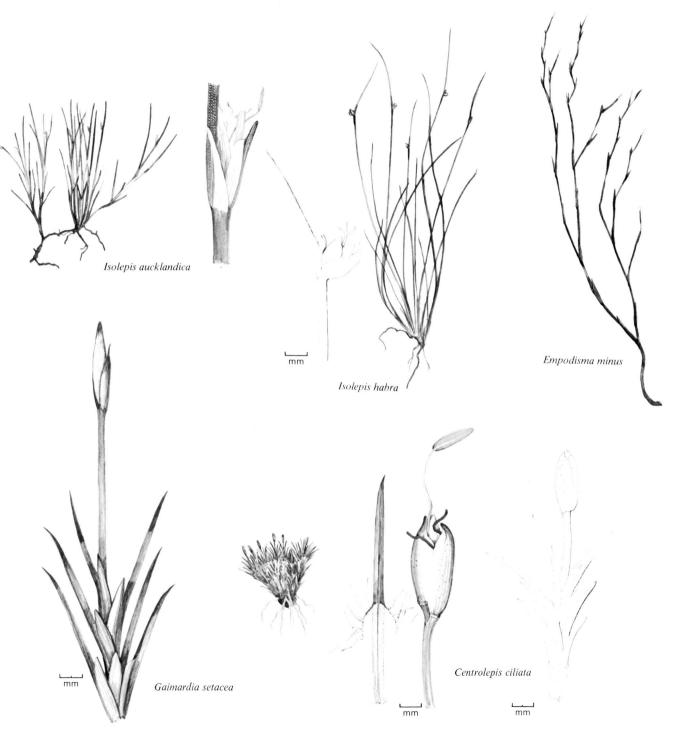

Isolepis aucklandica

Isolepis habra

Empodisma minus

Gaimardia setacea

Centrolepis ciliata

mm

mm

mm

mm

cm

PLATE 105

at the base with many rigid blunt-tipped leaves that may overtop the stems.

Spikelets are small (2–3 mm long), usually single on the stem and dark chestnut-brown or rarely very pale-green.

DISTRIBUTION North, South and Stewart Islands: the central volcanic mountains, Ruahine and Tararua Ranges; widespread in the South Island.

Mostly subalpine to high-alpine: 800–1,800 m (2,500–6,000 ft).

HABITAT Confined to bogs, edges of tarns and permanently wet often peaty areas of snow tussock grassland and herbfield.

COLLECTED Maungatua, eastern Otago, 880 m (2,900 ft). December 1970.

Isolepis habra (Edgar) Sojäk (See plate 105)
"Soft, delicate".

Its bright green tufts have soft, slender, hair-like stems, 5–30 cm long, and shorter leaves. Sheaths may be tinted red-purple. It is best distinguished from *I. aucklandica* by its many soft leaves and 1–3 oval, pale-green or reddish-black spikelets (2.5–4 x 2–3 mm).

DISTRIBUTION North, South and Stewart Islands: the central and southern mountains; widespread in the South Island except the drier eastern regions.

Mostly montane to low-alpine: 600–1,500 m (2,000–5,000 ft).

HABITAT In bogs, along stream banks or on wet sites in tussock grassland, herbfield, scrub or open forest.

COLLECTED Secretary Island, Fiordland National Park, sea level. February 1967.

Genus **SCHOENUS**
"Rush".

Contains about 100 species from temperate regions. Of the eight native species, one is a common alpine.

Schoenus pauciflorus (Hook.f.) Hook.f.
"Few-flowered".

Forms dense tufts with slender, rounded, deeply-grooved stems, up to 80 cm long that are erect or trailing and green or purplish-red. Most leaves are distinctively reduced to very dark reddish-purple shining sheaths at the base of the stem.

Small flower heads contain up to 9 narrow, compressed, usually dark-brown spikelets, 6–7 mm long, each with up to 4 florets. The fruit is a shining pale-brown nut.

DISTRIBUTION North, South and Stewart Islands: widespread in mountain regions throughout.

Mostly montane to low-alpine: 600–1,700 m (2,000–5,500 ft).

HABITAT One of the commonest plants of flushes and wet banks in tussock grasslands, herbfield, open scrub, moraine and avalanche chutes.

COLLECTED Eyre Mountains, northern Southland, 1,070 m (3,500 ft). November 1970.

Genus **CARPHA**
"Hay or straw"—probably referring to the persistent dried flower stalks.

A small southern Hemisphere genus. The only native carpha is an alpine.

Carpha alpina R.Br.
"Alpine".

Tufted and grass-like, 10–30 cm tall. Leaves are flat and blunt-tipped with broad papery sheaths.

The flower head at the stem tip is a cluster of spikelets with a pair of leafy bracts. In each spikelet the two small outer and two large inner glumes are pale but shining and as the dry fruit ripens, 6 feathery bristles enlarge to equal or exceed the glumes.

DISTRIBUTION North, South and Stewart Islands: widespread in mountain regions almost throughout.

Mostly subalpine to low-alpine: 700–1,700 m (2,500–5,500 ft).

HABITAT Often common in bogs, flushes and wet often peaty areas of tussock grassland, herbfield or open scrub.

COLLECTED Temple Basin, Arthurs Pass National Park, 1,160 m (3,800 ft). January 1970.

Genus **OREOBOLUS**
"Mountain mass or clod"—referring to the cushions.

Contains about 12 species, mostly from the Southern Hemisphere. All three native ones reach the alpine zone.

Oreobolus pectinatus Hook.f.   COMB SEDGE
"Comb-like"—referring to the leaf arrangement.

Forms dense circular cushions up to 50 cm or more across. Leaves are distinctively arranged in one plane with broad sheathing bases.

Flowers are in single spikelets that are quite inconspicuous among the leaves at the tips of short stems. These elongate and usually exceed the leaves as the fruits ripen.

DISTRIBUTION North, South and Stewart Islands: widespread in mountain regions throughout.

Mostly subalpine to low-alpine: 600–1,700 m (2,000–5,500 ft).

HABITAT Usually common in alpine bogs, especially herb-moor, and sometimes in wet depressions among tussock grassland and herbfield.

COLLECTED Mt Brewster, Haast Pass, Mt Aspiring National Park, 1,430 m (4,700 ft). December 1967.

Oreobolus strictus Bergg.
"Erect and straight"—referring to the leaves.

Forms a loose turf, 4–8 cm thick and up to 30 cm or more across. The very narrow leaves are channelled above with blunt tips and broad papery sheaths.

Cont. on page 238

236

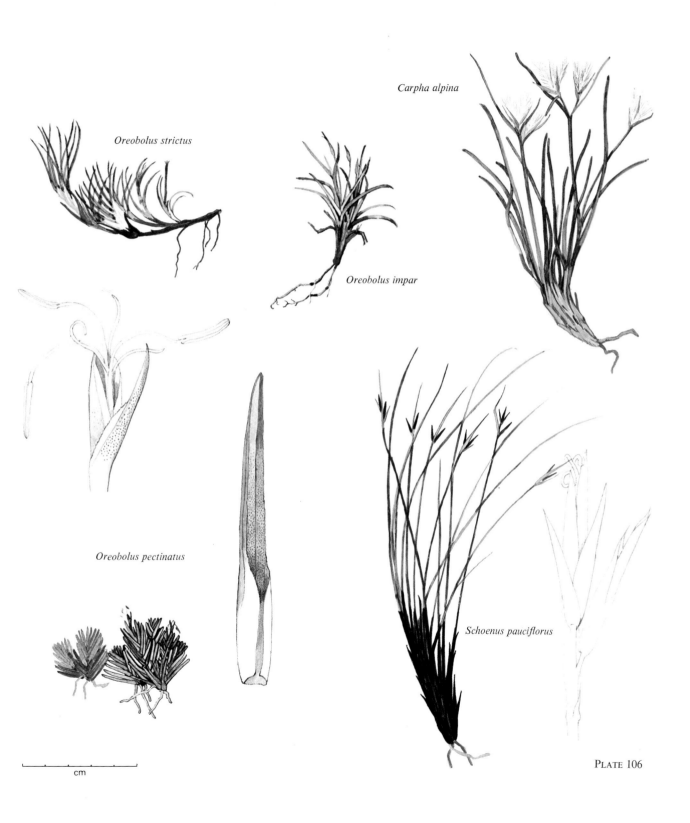

Oreobolus strictus

Carpha alpina

Oreobolus impar

Oreobolus pectinatus

Schoenus pauciflorus

cm

PLATE 106

Usually single spikelets, often with pinkish glumes, are on stalks that emerge above the leaves. After the small dry fruit is shed, the 6 narrow, pointed scales that surround it, persist. Distinction from *O. impar* may be difficult (see under *O. impar*).

DISTRIBUTION North, South and Stewart Islands: widespread in mountain regions from the southern Tararua Range, southwards.

Mostly montane to low-alpine: 500–1,400 m (1,500–4,500 ft).

HABITAT Usually common in peat bogs, often with *O. pectinatus*, and in wet areas of grassland, open forest or scrub.

COLLECTED Maungatua, eastern Otago, 880·m (2,900 ft). December 1970.

Oreobolus impar Edgar (*See plate 106*)

"Dissimilar"—referring to the differences between the two leaf surfaces.

Plants form a close mat up to 10 cm or more across rather than a cushion or loose turf. Leaves are spreading, not obviously arranged in one plane, and are flattened except for being channelled near the base.

Flowers and fruit are generally similar to *O. strictus* except that there are usually 2 spikelets and the 6 scales are slightly longer than the small dry fruit they surround (in *O. strictus* they are shorter).

DISTRIBUTION North, South and Stewart Islands: very local in the North Island; widespread in the high rainfall regions of the South Island along and near the main divide.

Subalpine to low-alpine: 800–1,500 m (2,500–5,000 ft).

HABITAT Usually on areas of otherwise bare soil or among open depleted vegetation on damp but usually freely-drained sites. Only rarely in bogs.

COLLECTED Mt Brewster, Haast Pass, Mt Aspiring National Park, 1,280 m (4,200 ft). December 1967.

Genus UNCINIA

"Hooked sedge".

Contains about 50 species concentrated in Australasia but extending to New Guinea, South and Central America.

They are easily characterised by hooked fruits but separation of species may be difficult. Of some 32 native uncinias at least seven reach the alpine zone. The following key should allow most alpine uncinias to be identified (for use of key see Glossary):

A	Plants dark red to reddish-green	*U. rubra*
AA	Plants not reddish	B
B	Persistent chaffy scales (glumes) enclosing each floret	*U. fuscovaginata*
BB	Glumes shed as the fruits ripen	C
C	Glumes pale brown or translucent with a green midrib; fruits green	D
CC	Glumes opaque, brownish, sometimes with a green midrib; fruits yellow or brown and shining	E

D	Leaves narrow (1.5–2 mm); few (5–15) female flowers per head	*U. viridis*
DD	Leaves wider (2–4 mm); many (20–35) female flowers per head	*U. caespitosa*
E	Leaves uniformly very narrow, < 1 mm wide	*U. nervosa*
EE	Leaves wider, gradually tapered, flat	F
F	Leaves 2–4 mm wide; fruits yellowish with a red-brown tip	*U. divaricata*
FF	Leaves 1–1.5 mm wide; fruits dark brown	*U. drucei*

Uncinia rubra Boott

"Red".

Their loose reddish tufts, 15–35 cm tall, develop from short rhizomes.

DISTRIBUTION North and South Islands: on the volcanic plateau; Nelson and the mountains east of the main divide in the South Island.

Montane to low-alpine: 500–1,400 m (1,500–4,500 ft).

HABITAT Usually in damp, often peaty areas of tussock grassland or open scrub. Occasionally in bogs.

Uncinia fuscovaginata Kük.

"Dark-sheathed"—referring to the brown sheaths around the base of the tuft.

Their small tufts, 10–30 cm tall, arise from branching of the dark underground stems. Leaves are rough on the margins and upper surface. On the flower head deciduous glumes are pale-brown with a green midrib. Var. **caespitans** Hamlin, has a denser, more tussock-like habit and narrower leaves (1–2 mm wide) than var. **fuscovaginata** (3–4 mm wide).

DISTRIBUTION North, South and Stewart Islands: the volcanic plateau, Ruahine and Tararua Ranges; more widespread in the South Island but rare in Westland. Var. *caespitans* is confined to the South Island.

Subalpine to high-alpine: 800–1,700 m (2,500–5,500 ft).

HABITAT Usually the commonest uncinia in the drier tussock grasslands and herbfields of the South Island. Dwarf forms may extend into early snowbanks.

COLLECTED Var. *caespitans* from Rock & Pillar Range, Central Otago, 1,370 m (4,500 ft). February 1969.

Uncinia caespitosa Boott

"Tufted, forming tussocks".

Forms loose tussocks, up to 35 cm tall, with flat rather stiff leaves that are rough on the edges and upper surface.

DISTRIBUTION North, South and Stewart Islands: widespread in mountain regions almost throughout but absent from Mt Egmont.

Mostly subalpine to low-alpine: 800–1,800 m (2,500–6,000 ft).

HABITAT Often common in damp snow tussock grassland, herbfield, scrub or forest margins.

238

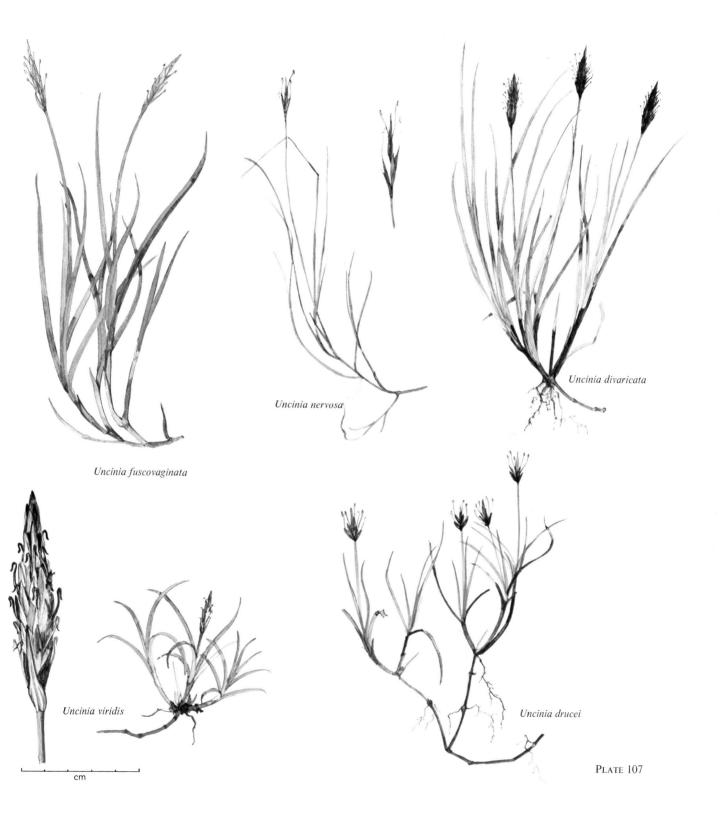

Uncinia fuscovaginata

Uncinia nervosa

Uncinia divaricata

Uncinia viridis

Uncinia drucei

cm

PLATE 107

Uncinia viridis (C. B. Clarke) Edgar *(See plate 107)*

"Green".

Also forms loose tussocks but usually shorter (to 20 cm) than in *U. caespitosa*.

DISTRIBUTION North and South Islands: widespread but rather rare on the higher North Island mountains; absent only from Marlborough and Canterbury.

Mostly low-alpine: 1,000–1,600 m (3,500–5,500 ft).

HABITAT Usually in tussock grassland and herbfield.

COLLECTED Pisa Range, Central Otago, 1,740 m (5,700 ft). January 1970.

Uncinia nervosa Boott *(See plate 107)*

"Nerved"—referring to the sac surrounding the fruits.

Very slender and wiry, forming loose to dense tufts, 10–25 cm tall.

DISTRIBUTION North, South and Stewart Islands: a patchy distribution—Ruahine and Tararua Ranges; Nelson and a few records from Canterbury, Westland, Otago and Fiordland.

Mostly montane to low-alpine: 500–1,700 m (1,500–5,500 ft).

HABITAT Most common on wet, sometimes peaty sites under *Dracophyllum* scrub mixed with snow or red tussock.

COLLECTED Maungatua, eastern Otago, 880 m (2,900 ft). March 1970.

Uncinia divaricata Boott *(See plate 107)*

"Much-branched"—probably referring to the short rhizome.

Loose tufts, up to 35 cm tall, with flat, pointed, dark yellowish-green leaves that are rough on their edges.

DISTRIBUTION North and South Islands: Mt Hikurangi, the central mountains and Ruahine Range; widespread in mountain regions of the South Island.

Montane to high-alpine: 500–1,800 m (1,500–6,000 ft).

HABITAT Usually present in damp tussock grassland and herbfield, especially on open or rocky sites, moraine, river beds, under open forest or scrub and occasionally in fellfield or bogs.

COLLECTED Upper West Matukituki Valley, Mt Aspiring National Park, 1,130 m (3,700 ft). January 1970.

Uncinia drucei Hamlin *(See plate 107)*

After Mr A. P. Druce, New Zealand botanist.

Readily distinguished by its creeping wiry stolons, many soft, narrow (1–1.5 mm), bright-green leaves up to 10 cm long and short (1–2 cm) flower heads.

DISTRIBUTION North, South and Stewart Islands: present records suggest a rather curious pattern—Mt Egmont and Ruahine Range; Nelson, Central and western Otago and Fiordland.

Low- to high-alpine: 1,000–1,800 m (3,500–6,000 ft).

HABITAT Usually on rocky sites in snow tussock-herbfield or occasionally fellfield, except in Central Otago and the Lakes district where it prefers moist snowbank depressions.

COLLECTED Rock & Pillar Range, Central Otago, 1,220 m (4,000 ft). January 1970.

Genus CAREX

"To cut"—referring to the cutting leaf edge.

A very large and widespread genus, especially in tropical mountain and temperate regions.

Of some 73 native species about 12 reach the alpine zone. They should be separable with the following key (for use of key see Glossary):

A	Flower head of a single undivided spikelet	B
AA	Flower head of more than one spikelet	D
B	Leaves flat and grassy; flower head without a leafy bract	C. pyrenaica
BB	Leaves rounded, erect and wiry; flower head accompanied by a leafy bract	C
C	Plants forming a dense close turf; female flowers 2–3 per head	C. enysii
CC	Plants tufted; female flowers 5–7	C. acicularis
D	Spikelets sessile, arranged in a compact cluster; no separate male spikelets	E
DD	Spikelets usually stalked, rather loosely arranged with a smaller male spikelet at the top	H
E	Plants stout but dwarfed and rigid, forming low patches; flower stem short, almost hidden among leaves	C. pterocarpa
EE	Plants grassy in habit; flower stem not hidden	F
F	Plants stout and tall (15–35 cm); spikelets 4–10 in a dense head 1–2.5 cm long; W. Nelson	C. trachycarpa
FF	Plants more slender, smaller; fewer spikelets (2–5)	G
G	Leaves narrow, rolled; spikelets pale-green	C. kirkii
GG	Leaves almost flat, grassy; spikelets red-brown	C. lachenalii
H	Plants small, flower stems < 8 cm tall, overtopped by leaves	I
HH	Plants taller	J
I	Plants dull-red (rarely glaucous) with broad, flat, linear leaves rounded at the tips	C. berggrenii
II	Leaves green, tapered and pointed	C. hectorii
J	Plants reddish-brown with curled leaf tips and broad sheaths	C. petriei
JJ	Plants not as above	K
K	Spikelets very dark-brown to black; often all slender	C. gaudichaudiana
KK	Spikelets pale- to dark-brown; only the upper male spikelets slender	C. wakatipu

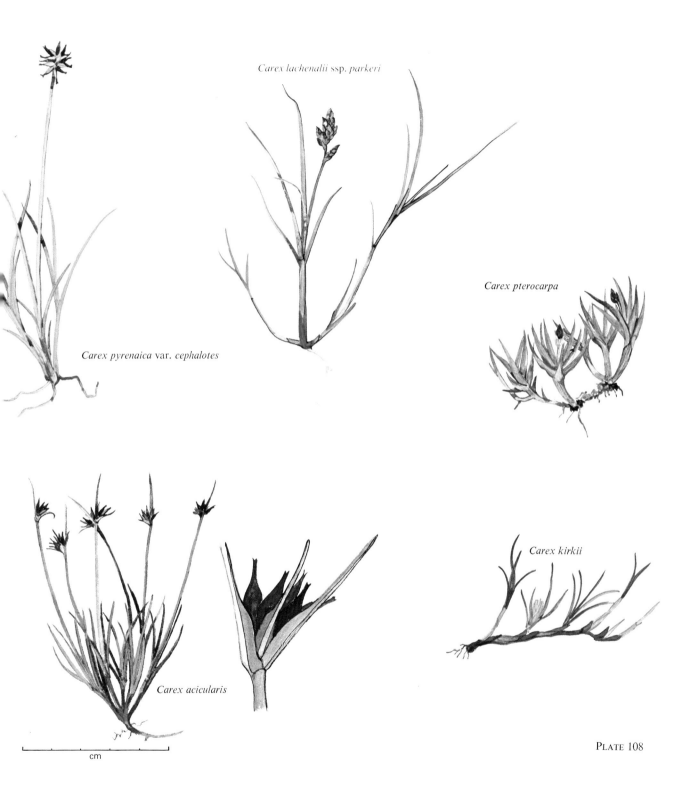

Carex lachenalii ssp. *parkeri*

Carex pyrenaica var. *cephalotes*

Carex pterocarpa

Carex kirkii

Carex acicularis

cm

PLATE 108

Carex pyrenaica Wahl. (*See plate 108*)
"Pyrenean"—from the Pyrenees.

Var. ***cephalotes*** (F. Muell.) Kük., "headed"—referring to the spikelet, which is much smaller (0.7–1 vs 1–2 cm) than in var. *pyrenaica*, and almost rounded. Only var. *cephalotes* occurs in New Zealand.

North and South Islands: Mt Egmont, Ruahine and Tararua Ranges; widespread on the higher mountains in the South Island.

Low- to high alpine: 1,100–2,000 m (3,500–6,500 ft).

In bogs, snowbanks and late melt areas in fellfield, cushion, high-altitude snow tussock grassland and herbfield.

COLLECTED Old Man Range, Central Otago, 1,610 m (5,300 ft). January 1970.

*Carex enysii Petrie
After Mr J. D. Enys, early Canterbury botanist.

A bog plant, so far collected only from the alpine zone of central Canterbury.

Carex acicularis Boott (*See plate 108*)
"Needle-shaped"—referring to the leaves.

North, South, and Stewart Islands: rather widespread in mountain regions except for Mt Egmont and the driest areas of the South Island.

Mostly low-alpine: 900–1,800 m (3,000–6,000 ft).

On damp, open, often rocky sites in snow tussock-herbfield.

COLLECTED Temple Basin, Arthurs Pass National Park, 1,160 m (3,800 ft). January 1970.

Carex pterocarpa Petrie (*See plate 108*)
"Wing-seeded"—referring to the winged fruit sac.

South Island: confined to the higher mountains of south Canterbury and Central Otago.

High-alpine: 1,500–2,000 m (5,000–6,500 ft).

In dwarfed cushion vegetation from exposed sites and in early snowbanks.

COLLECTED Old Man Range, Central Otago, 1,650 m (5,400 ft). December 1970.

*Carex trachycarpa Cheesem.
"Rough-seeded"—referring to the rough fruit sac.

It occurs in bogs on the mountains of western Nelson.

Subalpine to low-alpine: 1,000–1,700 m (3,500–5,500 ft).

Carex kirkii Petrie (*See plate 108*)
After Mr T. Kirk, early New Zealand botanist.

South Island: a few isolated occurrences in western Nelson, mid-Canterbury and Central Otago.

Low- to high-alpine: 900–1,900 m (3,000–6,500 ft).

It may occur in snow tussock grassland, cushion vegetation or in snowbanks, but is not common.

COLLECTED Old Man Range, Central Otago, 1,610 m (5,300 ft). February 1964.

Carex lachenalii Schkukr (*See plate 108*)
After W. de la Chenal, Swiss botanist.

Ssp. *parkeri* (Petrie) Toinoven, only ssp. *parkeri* occurs in New Zealand.

South Island: there are isolated occurrences in Nelson, Canterbury, Otago and Fiordland.

Low- to high-alpine: 1,100–1,800 m (3,500–6,000 ft).

Confined to bogs, seepage areas and damp hollows in snowbanks.

COLLECTED Rock & Pillar Range, Central Otago, 1,220 m (4,000 ft). December 1969.

Carex berggrenii Petrie
After Dr S. Berggren, Swedish botanist who collected in New Zealand.

South Island: widespread except for Marlborough, but rare in Westland.

Montane to high-alpine: 300–1,600 m (1,000–5,500 ft).

Almost confined to bogs and damp river flats.

COLLECTED Old Man Range, Central Otago, 1,580 m (5,200 ft). November 1969.

Carex hectorii Petrie
After Sir James Hector, geologist and explorer.

North and South Islands: Mt Egmont; Nelson and Central Otago.

High-alpine: 1,200–1,800 m (4,000–6,000 ft).

Almost restricted to snowbanks.

COLLECTED Rock & Pillar Range, Central Otago, 1,370 m (4,500 ft). December 1970.

Carex petriei Cheesem.
After Mr D. Petrie, early teacher and botanist, especially in Otago.

North and South Islands: Kaimanawa Range; widespread in the South Island south to about Otago, but absent from Westland.

Montane to low-alpine: 700–1,500 m (2,000–5,000 ft).

A rather uncommon plant of moist, even swampy, open sites in tussock grassland and herbfield.

COLLECTED Upper Dart Valley, Mt Aspiring National Park, 1,010 m (3,300 ft). January 1968.

Carex gaudichaudiana Kunth
After the French botanist and traveller C. Gaudichaud-Beaupré.

North and South Islands: widespread in mountain regions throughout.

Lowland to low-alpine: to 1,700 m (5,500 ft).

Often common in bogs, swamps and seepage areas.

COLLECTED Rock & Pillar Range, Central Otago, 1,220 m (4,000 ft). December 1969.

Carex wakatipu Petrie
It was first collected above Lake Wakatipu.

Highly variable in size according to habitat conditions, with flower stems 5–40 cm long.

South Island: widespread in mountain regions almost throughout but rare in Westland and Fiordland.

Montane to high-alpine: 500–1,800 m (1,500–6,000 ft).

Many well-drained habitats are tolerated, including tussock grassland, herbfield, moraine and snowbanks.

COLLECTED Pisa Range, Central Otago, 1,520 m (5,000 ft). February 1970.

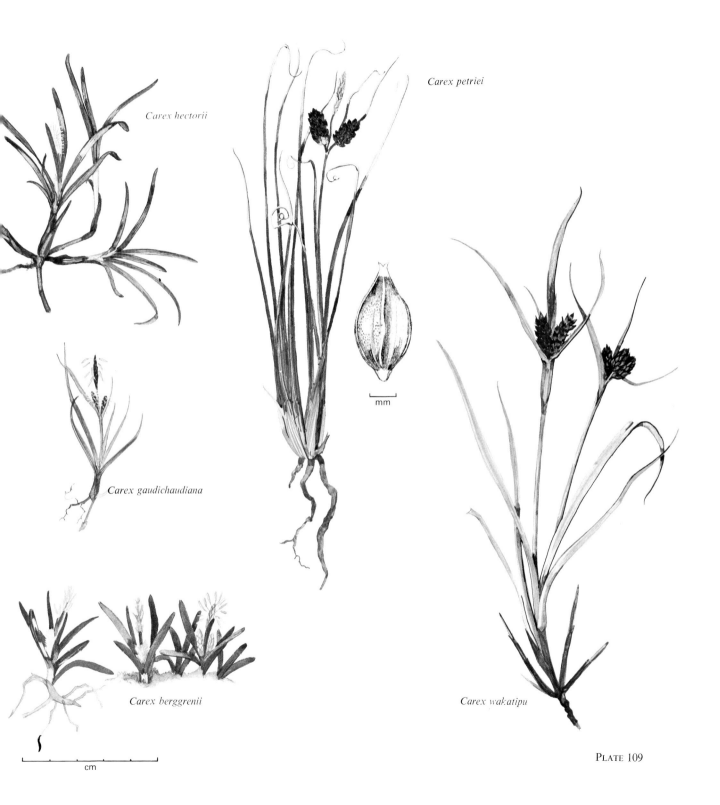

Carex hectorii

Carex petriei

Carex gaudichaudiana

mm

Carex berggrenii

Carex wakatipu

cm

PLATE 109

The Grass Family: POACEAE

The grasses make an important contribution to the alpine vegetation and its flora. Several genera and even species are recognisable without close examination but for many, a careful study of the flower head is needed. Grass heads consist of a cluster of separate spikelets. A spikelet usually contains an outer pair of empty chaffy scales, called glumes, which partly or completely enclose one or more small flowers (florets), each within its own one or two glumes (flowering glumes). The number of florets within the spikelet and the size of their glumes in relation to the empty outer pair, together with their shape and a few other features, are important criteria in recognition of the grass genera.

A vegetative feature that is often useful for identification is the ligule, an appendage at the junction of the leaf blade with its sheath on the leaf's inner surface. In a few grasses, notable *Chionochloa*, the ligule is hairy but in most it is thin and chaffy. Even here, however, and in other genera it may vary from one species to another and so be useful in identification.

Most of the genera have been revised recently but a few, notably *Festuca* are still in need of attention.

Genus AGROSTIS
"Field grass".

A large genus of about 125 species, mostly from the temperate and subpolar zones. Most of the native species reach the alpine zone.

Agrostis muelleriana Vick.
After F. Mueller, early Australian botanist.
(= *A. subulata* Hook.f.)

Distinguished by its small tufts of erect, crowded, very narrow, rolled leaves that are smooth and glabrous, and the taller (3–20 cm) slender flower stems with 1 (or 2) nodes near the base and a narrow pale green to purplish head. As is typical of the genus, the individual spikelets contain only 1 floret and the chaffy glume that encloses it is translucent and much smaller than the empty pair of green to purplish glumes outside it.

DISTRIBUTION North and South Islands: on the central volcanoes and the Ruahine and Tararua Ranges; widespread on the higher central and western mountains of the South Island.

Low- to high-alpine: 900–1,900 m (3,000–6,500 ft).

HABITAT Usually present in most alpine vegetation — snow tussock grassland and herbfield especially on exposed or depleted rather open sites, cushion vegetation, early snowbanks, fellfield, rock outcrops and moraine.

COLLECTED Hawkdun Range, Central Otago, 1,520 m (5,000 ft). December 1969.

Agrostis magellanica Lam.
"South American".

Very similar to *A. muelleriana*, but distinguished by the short bristle-like awn that projects from each spikelet in the flower head.

DISTRIBUTION South Island: from western Otago-south Westland southwards to Fiordland and western Southland.

Low- to high-alpine: 1,000–1,900 m (3,500–6,500 ft).

HABITAT Similar to *A. subulata* and often associated with it, but less common.

COLLECTED Mt Brewster, Haast Pass, Mt Aspiring National Park, 1,830 m (6,000 ft). March 1968.

Agrostis muscosa Kirk
"Moss-like".

Minute dense tufts form soft cushions up to 10 cm across and 2 cm thick. Very fine rolled leaves are pale glaucous-green and only 5–20 mm long, and the minute flowering stems do not usually emerge beyond them.

DISTRIBUTION North and South Islands: rather widespread from Taupo and Mt Egmont southwards, but in the South Island it is almost confined to the drier interior and eastern regions.

Mostly montane to low-alpine: 500–1,500 m (1,500–5,000 ft).

HABITAT Typically it colonises patches of bare soil in tussock grassland, but only the careful observer will recognise the moss-like cushions as a grass.

COLLECTED Old Man Range, Central Otago, 1,220 m (4,000 ft). December 1968.

Agrostis dyeri Petrie
After Sir W.T. Thistleton-Dyer, English botanist.

The tufts are kept small by new shoots emerging from within the old leaf sheaths rather than breaking through them at the base. Leaves are flat and slightly rough and those along the flowering stem have striated green sheaths.

Flowering stems have 2–3 nodes and extend (to 10–45 cm) beyond the leaves into a green or brownish-green, rarely purplish-green head (5–12 cm long) that is usually more open than in the other alpine species of *Agrostis*.

DISTRIBUTION North, South and Stewart Islands: widespread in mountain regions from East Cape, Taupo and Mt Egmont southwards.

Montane to low-alpine: 300–1,500 m (1,000–5,000 ft).

HABITAT Usually present but rarely plentiful in tussock grasslands and herbfield.

Genus HIEROCHLOE
"Holy Grass" — refers to its use in religious ceremonies.

A small genus, widespread in the temperate and sub-polar zones. All but two of the six native species are alpines. A common one is shown.

Hierochloe novae-zelandiae Zotov
"Of New Zealand".

Somewhat rhizomatous with erect tufts of flat glabrous leaves with striated glossy, purple sheaths and flower stems with distinctive open heads of compressed, glossy yellowish-brown spikelets containing obvious short bristle-like awns. These features are shared by most of

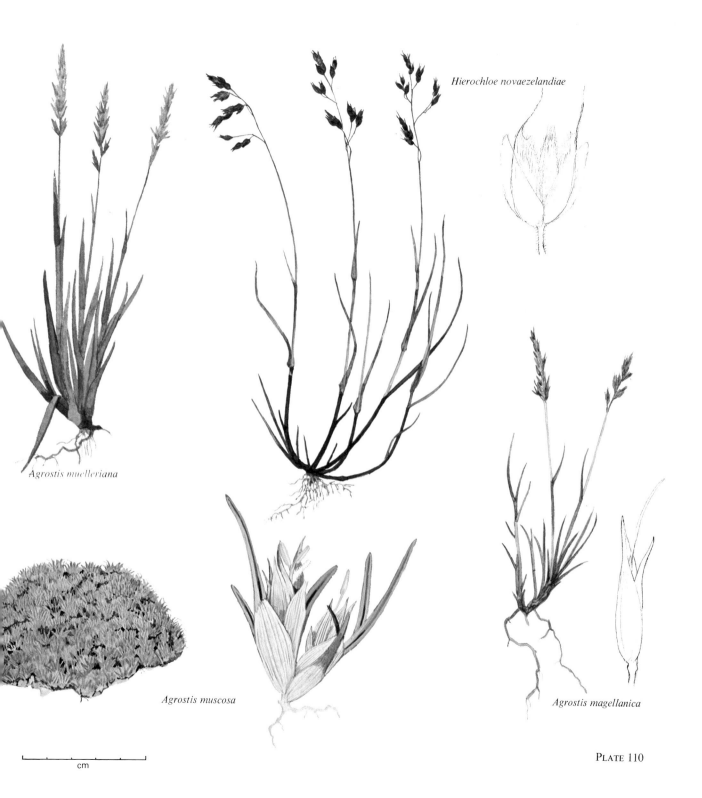

Hierochloe novaezelandiae

Agrostis muelleriana

Agrostis muscosa

Agrostis magellanica

cm

PLATE 110

the four alpine species. *H. novae-zelandiae* is distinguished by the short (*ca* 4 mm) outer pair of glumes in each spikelet; in the other four they are *ca* 7 mm long.

DISTRIBUTION South and Stewart Islands; widespread; mostly low- to high-alpine: 900–1,750 m (3,000–5,700 ft).

HABITAT Often common but inconspicuous in snow tussock grasslands, herbfield and open scrub.

COLLECTED A small high-altitude form from the Pisa Range, Central Otago, 1,740 m (5,700 ft). January 1970.

The other three alpine species occupy similar habitats and are best distinguished by their floral features — length and shape of the pair of outer sterile glumes and of the three inner fertile florets plus the hairs and long bristle-like awn near the tip of the florets. *H. recurvata* (Cheesem.) Zotov is widespread in the North and South Islands, *H. equiseta* Zotov (referring to the awn length) occurs east of the main divide in the South Island, and *H. cuprea* Zotov (referring to the copper colour of mature florets) occurs from Mt Taranaki (Egmont) and the Ruahine Mountains southward along the wet western ranges to southern Fiordland.

Genus LACHNAGROSTIS
"Soft hairy *Agrostis*" — perhaps referring to the silky flowering glume.

A small mostly Australasian genus that was recently revised. The few native alpines were previously included in *Deyeuxia*.

They are characterised by very lax fragile flower heads and usually single-flowered spikelets in which the two outer empty glumes are much longer than the flowering glume within, a bristle-like, bent or sometimes straight awn attached to the back of the flowering glume, and by having the inner glume of the pair enclosing the floret at least half as long as the outer member of the pair. The flower heads detach when mature and may blow in the wind.

Limited to Australasia, New Guinea and Easter Island. Of the 12 native species five reach the alpine zone.

Lachnagrostis lyallii (Hook.f.) Zotov
After Dr Lyall, surgeon-naturalist on the HMS *Terror* and *Acheron* in 1840-60.

Rather lax tufts up to 50 cm tall with wide flat or narrow folded (0.3-5 cm) bright or dull green leaves. Flower heads are relatively large and very lax, up to 25 x 16 cm, with filiform branches, each with 1-2 or sometimes several spikelets at the tips and florets with a prominent bent awn 2-6 mm long.

DISTRIBUTION North and South Islands: southwards from East Cape, generally widespread in the mountain regions.

Lowland to low-alpine: to 1,400 m (4,600 ft).

HABITAT Often present in tussock grassland, herbfield and rocky morainic or ultramafic areas.

COLLECTED Temple Basin, Arthurs Pass National Park, 1,220 m (4,000 ft). January 1970.

Lachnagrostis striata
"Striated" — referring to the leaves.

A smaller more slender grass (than *L. lyallii*) up to 15 cm tall, with obviously striated leaves. The open flower head usually has 5 branches in the lowermost whorl. Branchlets typically have two partly-purple spikelets on stalks of unequal length. Florets have small anthers (0.2–0.5 mm) and short straight awns.

It is widespread but mostly in high rainfall regions of the North and South Islands from the lowlands to low-alpine zone, mostly in damp tussock grassland but also on rocks and raw moraine.

Lachnagrostis elata Edgar
"Tall" — referring to the plant's height.

A slender tufted grass, 30–80 cm tall with narrow (0.4–2 mm) leaves, flat or folded. Flower heads are very lax, often wider than long and sparsely branched with single light green to purplish spikelets at the tips and straight or curved usually prominent awns 1-5 mm long. It occurs on the North, South and Stewart Islands from the volcanic mountains and Ureweras southwards, mainly along and west of the main divide, from lowland to low-alpine zones; to 1,200 m (4,000 ft), mostly in damp tussock grassland.

Lachnagrostis uda Edgar
"Moist" — referring to its habitat.

Forms rather lax tufts 10–35 cm tall with light green to dull brown, flat or rolled narrow (1–2 mm) leaves. Flower heads are lax when mature, up to 14 x 8 cm with filiform branches and a few pale green or faint purple spikelets at the tips. The florets have prominent hairs and anthers 0.7–1.3 mm long) and a short straight awn up to 2.5 mm long.

Confined to the South Island, in western south Canterbury-Central Otago and northern Southland, in the low-alpine zone: 900–1,200 m 3,000–4,000 ft), typically in seepage areas and bogs.

Lachnagrostis pilosa (Buchan.) Edgar
"Hairy" — referring to the inner glume (lemma) of a floret.

Plants are more robust than the other species, up to 90 cm tall with dull green rather broad (2–7 mm) flat leaves and long stiff multiflowered heads. The mainland variety *pilosa* has a very prominent bent awn (4–8.5 mm) on the florets. It occurs in the North and South Island from coastal to low-alpine: to 1,200 m (4,000 ft), but in the mountains it is common only locally in Nelson-Marlborough and western Otago, south Westland and Fiordland, mainly on river flats and rock outcrops.

Genus MICROLAENA
"Small cover" — referring to the very small outer glumes in the flower head.

A small Australasian genus. Two of the four native species reach the alpine zone.

Microlaena colensoi (Hook.f.) J.C. Smith
After Rev. W. Colenso, early botanist.

Easily distinguished by its habit: plants usually trail or droop and

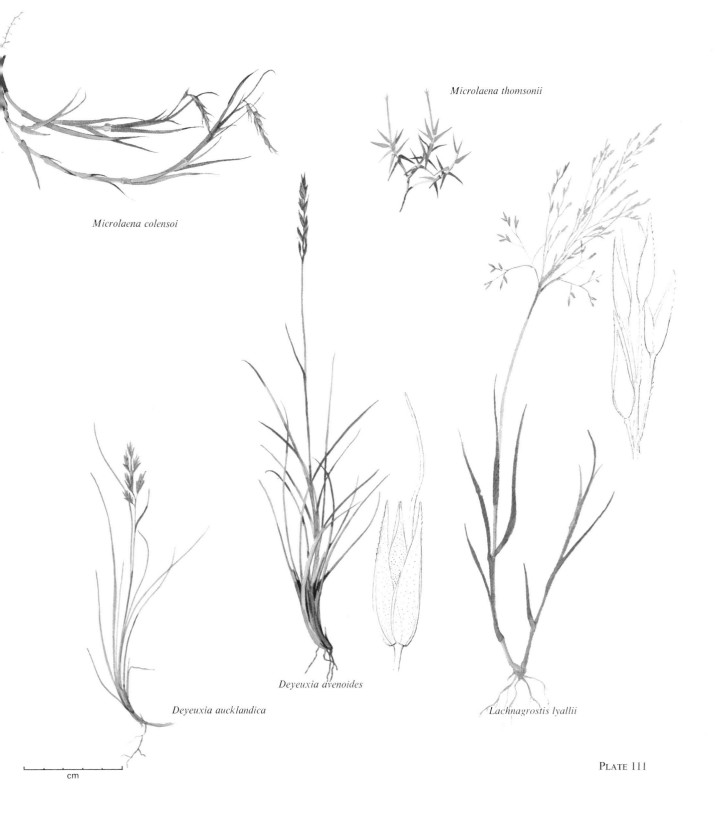

Microlaena thomsonii

Microlaena colensoi

Deyeuxia avenoides

Deyeuxia aucklandica

Lachnagrostis lyallii

cm

PLATE 111

their leaves are arranged in a vertical plane, while the single flowering spike (3–10 cm long) tends to nod.

DISTRIBUTION North and South Islands: Mt Egmont, Ruahine and Tararua Ranges; widespread on the wetter mountains of the South Island.

  Low- to high-alpine: 1,000–1,700 m (3,500–5,500 ft).

HABITAT Usually present in snow tussock-herbfield and often conspicuous drooping over steep banks or on sunny but wet rocks in herbfield and occasionally also in fellfield.

COLLECTED Temple Basin track, Arthurs Pass National Park, 1,160 m (3,800 ft). January 1970.

Microlaena thomsonii (Petrie) Petrie
After Mr G.M. Thomson, who first collected it with Petrie.

A very small but distinctive grass with much branched stems that may weave or form loose mats up to 10 cm or more across. Leaves are flat and arranged in one plane while the small heads have only 2–5 spikelets on a short stalk which barely extends beyond the leaves.

DISTRIBUTION South and Stewart Islands: apart from one record in Nelson (Mt Rochfort) it is confined to southern Fiordland, western Southland and Stewart Island.

  Mostly subalpine to low-alpine: 600–1,300 m (2,000–4,500 ft).

HABITAT Confined to bogs or very wet, open, usually peaty areas of tussock-herbfield.

COLLECTED Mt Anglem, Stewart Island, 670 m (2,200 ft). May 1964.

Genus DEYEUXIA
After N. Deyeux, 19th century French chemist.

A widespread genus in southern temperate regions, with more than 100 perennial species. Flower heads are usually narrow and dense and their spikelets are single flowered with awns. The individual spikelets are continued beyond the floret as a silky bristle (rhachilla), but a good lens will be needed to see it.

Of the seven native species at least two reach the alpine zone.

Deyeuxia aucklandica (Hook.f.) Zotov
From the Auckland Islands.

Forms small tufts of very fine, almost bristle-like rolled leaves and longer, erect, wiry flower stems (4–30 cm tall) with narrow contracted heads.

Spikelets have 2 subequal, often purplish pale brown outer glumes and a slightly shorter flowering glume which has very long silky hairs from its base and an awn 2–4.5 mm long attached to the middle of its back and reflexed. The silky bristly rhachilla is clearly visible.

DISTRIBUTION North, South and Stewart Island: widespread on the mountains from East Cape and Mt Egmont southwards.

  Subalpine to low-alpine: 800–1,500 m (2,500–5,000 ft), mostly along and west of the main divide.

HABITAT On damp, even boggy, yet open grassland and herbfield, moist sites on rock outcrops and on avalanche chutes below the tree line.

COLLECTED Park Pass, Humboldt Mountains, Mt Aspiring National Park, 1,250 m (4,100 ft). February 1968.

Deyeuxia avenoides Buchan.   MOUNTAIN OAT GRASS
"Oat-like" — referring to the large spikelets.

Its small tufts and slender rolled leaves are similar to *D. aucklandica* but the flower stems are longer (15–75 cm), far exceeding the leaves. Even more distinctive are the narrower, very congested and longer flower heads (3–20 cm) in which the prominent awn is attached below the middle of the flowering glume and the hairs at the base of this glume are quite short.

DISTRIBUTION North, South and Stewart Islands: widespread on the mountains throughout.

  Lowland to low-alpine: to 1,400 m (4,500 ft).

HABITAT One of the most common small grasses of the drier eastern tussock grasslands and herbfields, and usually abundant on partly depleted sites.

COLLECTED Porters Pass, Torlesse Range, Canterbury, 1070 m (3,500 ft). February 1969.

Deyeuxia youngii (Hook.f.) Buchan.
After Mr W. Young, Haast's assistant.

Forms rather narrow tufts up to 50 cm tall with stiff usually flat (1–4 mm) obviously ridged and roughened leaves. Flower heads to 130 cm with narrow branched heads 7–20 cm long with densely crowded light green to purplish spikelets and obviously hairy florets with a brush of hairs on the anthers and a short (1–3 mm) straight awn. South Island: northwest Nelson and Marlborough, more scattered in mid south Canterbury and Otago, from the lowland to low-alpine zones, in tussock grassland, shrubland and open rocky sites.

Genus DESCHAMPSIA
After M.H. Deschamps, French naturalist.

A rather small genus but widespread through most of the cold and temperate regions. It is characterised by 2-flowered spikelets in which the thin translucent flowering glumes are shorter than the empty, thin, shining outer pair. The flowering glumes are finely toothed at their tips and have only a short awn if any.

Of the five mainland species at least four reach the alpine zone.

Deschampsia caespitosa Beauv.
"Tufted; forming tussocks".

Forms rather distinctive tussocks, 30 cm to 1 m tall, with stiff narrow leaves and shining sheaths. Flower heads (10–30 cm long) are usually nodding above, with shining pale yellowish-green or purplish spikelets. The pair of outer glumes are pointed but the flowering glumes have broad tips with 4 teeth, and are silky at the base. A short awn attached near the middle of the glume hardly projects beyond it.

DISTRIBUTION North, South and Stewart Islands: widespread from the lower Waikato southwards.

  Lowland to low-alpine: to 1,400 m (4,500 ft).

HABITAT Mostly confined to waterlogged sites; among alpine vegetation it may be common locally in bogs and other very wet depressions.

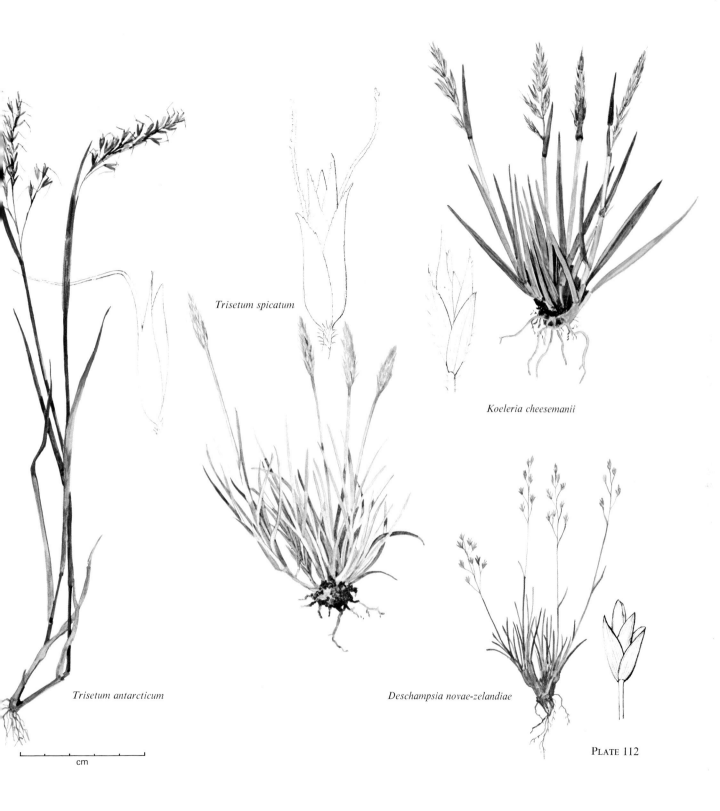

Trisetum spicatum

Koeleria cheesemanii

Trisetum antarcticum

Deschampsia novae-zelandiae

cm

PLATE 112

Deschampsia novae-zelandiae Petrie
"Of New Zealand".

Its short tufts have very narrow bristle-like leaves up to half the length of the flower stems (4–20 cm tall). Slender erect flower heads are quite distinctive with their small, shining, 2-flowered spikelets. The 2 empty outer glumes are unequal while the translucent flowering glumes are glabrous at the base. They are awnless with broad tips that have several minute teeth.

DISTRIBUTION South Island: rather widespread in the mountains from about central Canterbury-Westland southwards.
Montane to high-alpine: 300–1,900 m (1,000–6,500 ft).

HABITAT Similar to *D. caespitosa* but more important than it in the alpine zone. Dwarfed forms extend into moist snowbanks.

COLLECTED A small form from Old Man Range, Central Otago, 1,650 m (5,400 ft). January 1959.

*Deschampsia pusilla Petrie
"Very small".

Forms small compact patches with leaves shorter than the flower stems (2.5–5 cm tall). Flower heads (1–2 cm long) have only a few shining straw-yellow spikelets in which the outer glumes are of almost equal length and the flowering glume may have a few hairs at the base. Recorded only from Otago Lakes district (Hector and Humboldt Mts) in the high-alpine zone but small forms of *D. novae-zelandiae* in this area may share some of its features.

* Deschampsia tenella Petrie
"Tender, delicate".

Flowering heads are similar to *D. novae-zelandiae* but plants are taller (to 15–35 cm) and their leaves very narrow and bright-green.

As an alpine it occurs chiefly in the southern North Island (Ruahine and Tararua Ranges) and north-western South Island (Mt Arthur), up to 1,400 m (4,500 ft).

Genus **TRISETUM**

"Three awns" — referring to the 3-awned (2 terminal and 1 dorsal) flowering glumes.

Characterised by flat leaves and small, usually 2-flowered spikelets in which the flowering glumes equal or exceed the length of the 2 empty outer glumes and have 3 awns — a prominent one from the back just below the tip and a much smaller pair at the tip.

A widespread genus of about 60 species from alpine regions and the temperate zone, especially of the Northern Hemisphere. The few native species all reach the alpine zone.

Trisetum spicatum (L.) Richt.
"Spiked" — referring to the short dense flower head.

Forms small tufts with flat usually hairy leaves, striped sheaths and much taller hairy flower stalks (to 5–30 cm). Flower heads are dense and cylindrical (2–5 cm long) with pale-green (rarely purplish) shining spikelets. Prominent awns that are attached part way down the back of each flowering glume and emerge well beyond the spikelet, best distinguish *T. spicatum* from species of *Koeleria*.

DISTRIBUTION South Island: rather widespread in mountain regions.
Low- to high-alpine: 1,000–1,900 m (3,500–6,500 ft).

HABITAT Usually a minor plant in snow tussock grassland and herbfield, especially on moist sites. A small form may be more abundant and conspicuous in cushion vegetation, fellfield or early snowbanks.

COLLECTED Rock & Pillar Range, Central Otago, 1,250 m (4,100 ft). January 1970.

Trisetum antarcticum Trin.
"Antarctic".

Plants are almost glabrous, 15 to 60 cm tall, and easily recognised by their distinctive flower heads. They are erect or slightly nodding with pale-green or brownish-green shining spikelets in which the 2–3 florets each have recurved awns that are much longer than the spikelet.

Var. *tenellum* Petrie, "tender, delicate", is smaller, not unlike *T. spicatum*, but more slender and glabrous.

DISTRIBUTION North, South and Stewart Islands: widespread in mountain regions.
Lowland to low-alpine: to 1,400 m (4,500 ft).

HABITAT Often present but rarely abundant or conspicuous in damp alpine and valley tussock grasslands, herbfield and scrub. Var. *tenellum* prefers stony sites, especially river beds and moraine.

COLLECTED Upper Dart Valley, Mt Aspiring National Park, 1,010 m (3,300 ft). January 1968.

* Trisetum youngii Hook.f.
After Mr W. Young, Haast's assistant.

May be as tall as or taller than *T. antarcticum* but its broad flat leaves have long soft hairs and the flower stems and heads are usually more slender and longer than in *T. spicatum*.

It occurs on Mt Hikurangi, in ravines at the western base of Ruapehu and Ngauruhoe and on the Tararua Range in the North Island, but is more widespread in the wetter regions of the South Island. Being present in both the subalpine and low-alpine zones it may occur with one or both of the other species.

Genus **KOELERIA**
After G. L. Koeler, a German writer on grasses.

A rather large temperate zone genus, characterised by densely crowded spike-like flower heads containing 2–5 flowered, shining, compressed spikelets. Their flowering glumes have a very short awn.

The few native species have not yet been fully documented so that only a common one is shown.

Koeleria cheesemanii (Hack.) Petrie
After Mr T.F. Cheeseman, well-known botanist.

Its habit is similar to *Trisetum spicatum* but plants are slightly glaucous and covered in fine hairs. Flower heads are very dense but they lack the obvious awns of *Trisetum* – the flowering glume has only a short awn attached between the pair of teeth at its tip.

DISTRIBUTION North and South Islands: Mt Hikurangi; widespread in mountain regions of the South Island.

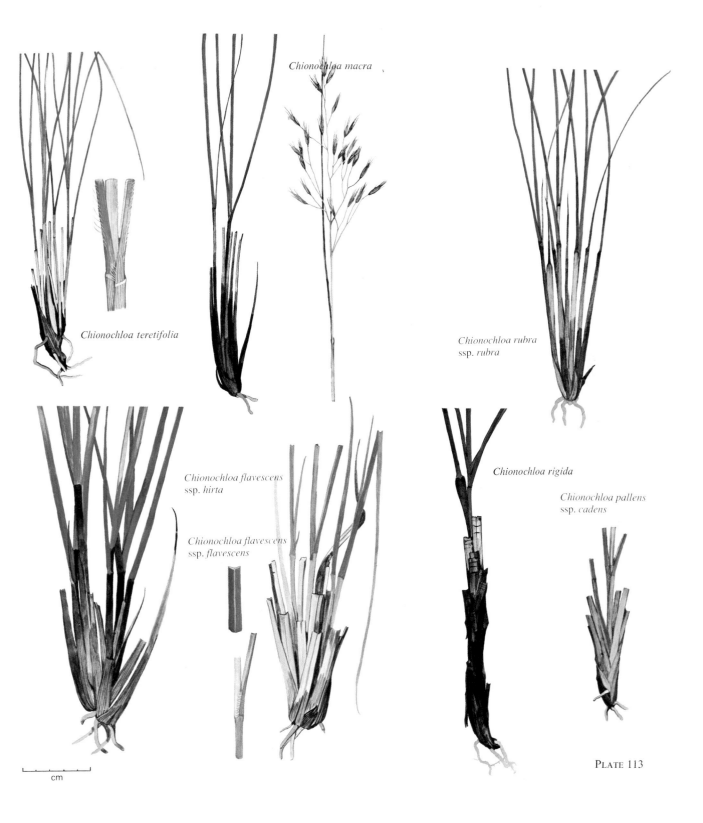

Chionochloa macra

Chionochloa teretifolia

Chionochloa rubra
ssp. *rubra*

Chionochloa flavescens
ssp. *hirta*

Chionochloa flavescens
ssp. *flavescens*

Chionochloa rigida

Chionochloa pallens
ssp. *cadens*

cm

PLATE 113

Low- to high-alpine: 900–2,000 m (3,000–6,500 ft).
HABITAT Usually on sunny rock outcrops but sometimes present on moraine and in open tussock grassland and herbfield.
COLLECTED Garvie Mountains, Central Otago, 1,220 m (4,000 ft). November 1970.

* ***Koeleria novo-zelandica*** Domin. is similar to *K. cheesemanii* but it may be taller (to 50 cm) with a narrower head in which the spikelets are often purplish-green. Its distribution and habitat preferences are also generally similar to *K. cheesemanii*.

Genus **CHIONOCHLOA** SNOW TUSSOCK; SNOWGRASS
"Snow-grass".

An Australasian genus of some 22 species which are concentrated in New Zealand. A recent comprehensive revision has recognised 16 indigenous alpine species, five of them with subspecies. Distributions range from local to widespread. The snow tussocks are the most prominent members of the low-alpine flora and give the vegetation much of its character.

Most have a tussock habit and their leaves have a hairy ligule. Flower characters are quite distinctive for the genus but rather uniform within it. Spikelets are large and contain several florets while the flowering glumes each have a conspicuous awn which is usually bent or twisted at the base. Vegetative features are much more variable and therefore have been used to recognise most of the species and subspecies. A limited amount of hybridism occurs but the following key should allow recognition of most alpine snow tussocks (for use of key see Glossary):

A	Leaves tightly rolled like a rush and often sharp-pointed:	B
AA	Leaves flat, loosely rolled or V-shaped in section, grass-like:	J
B	Old leaves breaking off at junction of sheath and blade:	C
BB	Old leaves persistent on plant:	H
C	Old leaves breaking off below the ligule with part of the sheath:	D
CC	Old leaves breaking off at the ligule:	G
D	Back of leaves and flower stalks distinctly hairy; on ultramafic outcrops; Nelson–Marlborough, to 1000 m:	*C. defracta*
DD	Back of leaves and flower stalks glabrous:	E
E	Old leaf sheaths distinctly coiled; on limestone bluffs; in Fiordland, to 1000 m:	*C. spiralis*
EE	Old leaf sheaths remaining straight, plants reddish:	F
F	Inner surface of leaf above ligule with conspicuous long hairs; Nelson–Westland, 600–1700 m (red tussock):	*C. rubra* ssp. *occulta*

FF	Inner surface of leaves above ligule without conspicuous hairs; N. Island volcanic mts, Marlborough, N. Canterbury, 550–1400 m (red tussock):	*C. rubra* ssp. *rubra*
G	Leaves obviously hairy, not needle-tipped, bases slimy; W. Southland–Fiordland, 300–1400 m:	*C. teretifolia*
GG	Leaves hairless, needle-tipped, bases not slimy; S. Westland–Fiordland., to 1200 m:	*C. acicularis*
H	Plants mat forming, leaves <20 cm long, not reddish; Nelson–N. Canterbury, 700–1700 m (carpet grass):	*C. australis*
HH	Plants erect, leaves >20 cm long, reddish; south of Nelson–N. Canterbury	I
I	Plants copper coloured; south from mid-Canterbury, to 1500 m (copper tussock):	*C. rubra* ssp. *cuprea*
II	Plants reddish, florets purple; N. Westland uplands, 450–950 m:	*C. juncea*
J	Old leaves breaking off at the base:	K
JJ	Old leaves persistent on the plant:	T
K	Leaf sheaths persistent after blades fall, leaf bases V-shaped in section:	L
KK	Leaf sheaths breaking into short chaffy segments after blades fall, leaf bases loosely rolled to flat in section:	R
L	Leaves soft, with distinct yellowish midrib; S. Island south of 43° 31', 1000–1900 m (mid-ribbed snow tussock):	*C. pallens* ssp. *cadens*
LL	Leaves stiff and sharp-tipped without yellowish midrib:	M
M	Flower heads purplish, small sparse tussocks with very conspicuous hairy ligules; Fiord., to 1400 m:	*C. ovata*
MM	Flower heads not purplish, tussocks usually dense, ligules not very conspicuous:	N
N	Plants confined to Stewart Island:	O
NN	Plants from South Island only:	P
O	Leaves stiff, erect with very sharp points, sheaths without hairs; Stewart Island, 700–970 m (curled snow tussock):	*C. crassiuscula* ssp. *crassiuscula*
OO	Leaves not stiff, erect or sharp-pointed, sheaths with many long hairs; Stewart Island, to 970 m:	*C. lanea*
P	Leaves curved to spirally coiled but not stiff or sharp-tipped; Southern Alps from 44° south, 1200–1600 m :	*C. vireta*

252

Chionochloa australis

Chionochloa ovata

Chionochloa oreophila

Chionochloa crassicula
ssp. *torta*

PLATE 114

cm

PP	Leaves stiff, curved to spirally coiled when dry or dead, sharp-tipped:	Q
Q	Long prostrate stems, leaves curved to slightly twisted; Southland — eastern Fiordland., 700–1400 m (curled snow tussock):	*C. crassiuscula* ssp. *directa*
QQ	Short upright stems, leaves twisting with tips curling when dry or dead; Southern Alps from Lewis Pass south, 600–1800 m (curled snow tussock):	*C. crassiuscula* ssp. *torta*
R	Leaves broad (to 10 mm), sheaths pale or purplish; Westland-Canterbury north to Tararua Ra., to 1500 m (broad-leaved snow tussock with 4 ssp.):	*C. flavescens*
RR	Leaves narrower (to 7 mm), sheaths dark brown at base; S. Island south of 43°:	S
S	Flower heads hairy only at base of branches; S. Island east of main divide, to 1600 m (narrow-leaved snow tussock):	*C. rigida* ssp. *rigida*
SS	Flower heads hairy: west of main divide; W. Southland, Stewart Island, 500–1450 m (narrow-leaved snow tussock):	*C. rigida* ssp. *amara*
T	Small mat-forming plants, leaves <15 cm long with pale shining sheaths; S. Island, wet mts, snow-banks, 1000–1850 m (snow-patch grass):	*C. oreophila*
TT	Tussock-forming plants without the above features combined:	U
U	Leaves soft, without yellowish midrib, sheaths dark brown often purplish and rounded; S. Island, east of main divide, 500–2000 m (slim snow tussock):	*C. macra*
UU	Leaves tough with conspicuous yellow midrib, sheaths pale and V-shaped:	V
V	Inner side of leaf blades with obvious long hairs; S. Island north of 43°S, 1100–1800 m (midribbed snow tussock):	*C. pallens* ssp. *pilosa*
VV	Inner side of leaf blades without hairs; N. Island and northern Marlborough-Nelson, 1100–1600 m (midribbed snow tussock):	*C. pallens* ssp. *pallens*

DISTRIBUTIONS AND HABITATS

Chionochloa juncea Zotov

"Junceus" — referring to the rounded, tightly-rolled, *Juncus*-like leaves.

South Island: confined to the coastal ranges north-east of Westport.

Subalpine to low-alpine: 600–1,100 m (2,000–3,500 ft).

A locally common tussock on the low coastal ranges.

Chionochloa spiralis Zotov

"Spiraled" — referring to the coiling of the leaf sheath on drying.

South Island: recorded only from isolated sites on limestone near tree line in Fiordland.

Chionochloa acicularis Zotov

"Acicular" — referring to the leaf tips.

South Island: confined to south-western Fiordland south of about Caswell Sound.

Lowland to low-alpine: to 1,200 m (4,000 ft).

Despite a limited distribution it is important in snow tussock-herbfield and usually the commonest snow tussock in forest openings and subalpine scrub.

Chionochloa teretifolia (Petrie) Zotov

"With rounded leaves".

South Island: confined to southern Fiordland and western Southland.

Low-alpine: 900–1,200 m (3,000–4,000 ft).

Usually on poorly drained, often peaty sites not far above the tree line. They glisten both in the sun and fog because of the many fine hairs on the leaves. The distinctive pattern of hairs, shown here, is from a cultivated plant collected from Borland Saddle, Hunter Mountains, Fiordland National Park, 1,040 m (3,400 ft).

Chionochloa rigida (Raoul) Zotov   NARROW-LEAVED SNOW TUSSOCK

"Rigid" — the leaves are somewhat rigid.

It extends from the Rakaia and Hokitika catchments southwards and on Banks Peninsula, and is usually the dominant snow tussock in these regions. Subspecies *rigida* occurs to the east of the main divide as far as Southland from the lowlands to low-alpine zone: to 1,400 m (4,600 ft), while ssp. *amara* occurs in the high rainfall regions along and west of the main divide and Stewart Island (Mt Anglem), mostly on poorly drained sites in the subalpine and low-alpine zones: to 1,450 m (4,800 ft).

COLLECTED Subspecies *rigida* from Old Man Range, Central Otago, 910 m (3,000 ft). December 1962. In the drawing one leaf has been pulled away to show the characteristic chestnut colour of the sheath.

Chionochloa flavescens Zotov   BROAD-LEAVED SNOW TUSSOCK

"Turning yellow" — perhaps referring to the seed head.

North and South Islands: Tararua Range; widespread along and near the South Island main divide as far south as the upper Waitaki and Clarke catchments.

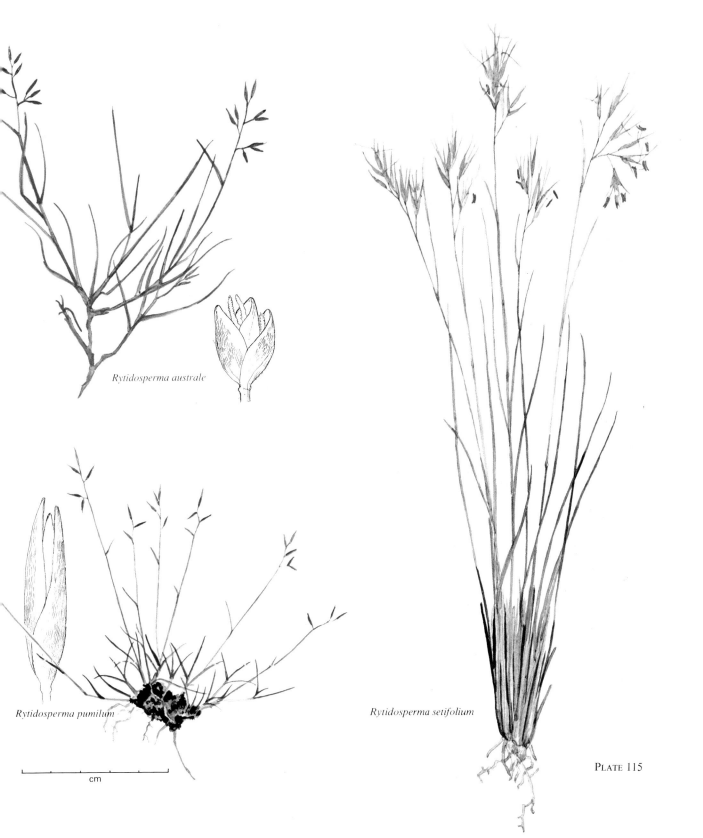

Rytidosperma australe

Rytidosperma pumilum

Rytidosperma setifolium

cm

PLATE 115

Chionochloa rubra Zotov — RED TUSSOCK
"Red" — most plants are distinctly reddish.

North, South and Stewart Islands: widespread and conspicuous on the volcanic mountains: in the South Island it is common on the mineral belt of Nelson–Marlborough but elsewhere is usually restricted to poorly drained often peaty valley floors, terraces or rolling slopes, mostly below the tree line.

Subspecies *rubra* is restricted to the North Island mountains, Marlborough and north Canterbury; ssp. *occulta* is limited to Nelson and to the west of the main divide south to the Cascade Plateau; while "copper tussock" ssp. *cuprea* occurs from the Waimakariri catchment southwards to Fiordland and Stewart Island.

Lowland to low-alpine: to 1,500 m (5,000 ft).

COLLECTED A cultivated plant of ssp. *rubra* from Mt Ruapehu, Tongariro National Park, *ca* 1,200 m (4,000 ft).

Chionochloa macra Zotov — SLIM SNOW TUSSOCK
"Slim" — referring to its common name.

South Island: widespread on the drier mountains of the interior from northern Marlborough to central Southland.

Montane to high-alpine: 500–1,900 m (1,500–6,500 ft).

It is usually associated with narrow-leaved snow tussock. North of the Rakaia Valley it is common over a wide altitudinal range but on the lower sites is usually restricted to cold shady slopes. Further south it is common only at higher altitudes, typically in a zone above the limits of *C. rigida*.

COLLECTED Rock & Pillar Range, Central Otago, 1,370 m (4,500 ft). December 1970.

Chionochloa pallens Zotov — MIDRIBBED SNOW TUSSOCK
"Pale" — referring to the leaf sheath.

North and South Islands: on the higher mountains of the North Island from the Raukumara Range southwards; widespread in the higher rainfall western regions of the South Island but with some eastern extensions from mid-Canterbury northwards.

Subspecies *pallens* with persistent leaf blades and only prickle teeth or pimples on the inner or lower surface of the blades, is confined to the North Island and northern Nelson–Marlborough; ssp. *pilosa* with persistent leaf blades and long hairs on the inner or lower leaf surface occurs between southern Nelson-Marlborough and the Whataroa-upper Rangitata catchments; and ssp. *cadens* with the old leaves breaking off at the base replaces ssp. *pilosa* further south.

Low-alpine: 1,100–1,800 m (3,500–6,000 ft).

From the Tararua Range southwards it is usually associated with broad-leaved snow tussock but in most areas it prefers better-drained or higher altitude sites than those occupied by *C. flavescens*.

COLLECTED Subspecies *pilosa* from Gertrude Valley, Darran Mountains, Fiordland National Park, 910 m (3,000 ft). January 1968.

Chionochloa crassiuscula (Kirk) Zotov — CURLED SNOW TUSSOCK
"Rather thick" — referring probably to the leaves

South and Stewart Islands: in the higher rainfall western mountains from about Lewis Pass southwards.

Subspecies *crassiuscula*, with very sharp pointed leaves, is confined to the higher peaks (above 700 m) of Stewart Island and was known previously as *C. pungens*; ssp. *torta* occurs throughout the species range in the South Island; while ssp. *directa* is confined to boggy sites in southern Southland–Fiordland.

Subalpine to low-alpine: 800–1,800 m (2,700–6,000 ft).

Typically it is the most important species near the upper limit of snow tussock-herbfield. On cold south slopes or seepage areas it may extend below the tree line.

COLLECTED Subspecies *torta* from upper Eyre Creek, Eyre Mountains, northern Southland, 1,370 m (4,500 ft).

Chionochloa australis (Buchan.) Zotov — CARPET GRASS
"Southern".

South Island: restricted to the mountains of Nelson, north-west Canterbury and north Westland almost as far south as Arthurs Pass.

Low- to high-alpine: 900–1,800 m (3,000–6,000 ft).

It usually carpets large areas with its dense sward and, being unpalatable, may increase at the expense of preferred species. Because stems and leaves lie down-hill, steep slopes, which it favours, may be very slippery to cross.

COLLECTED Near Lake Sylvester, Cobb Valley, north-western Nelson, 1,500 m (5,000 ft). January 1967.

Chionochloa oreophila (Petrie) Zotov — SNOW-PATCH GRASS
"Snow-loving".

South Island: widespread along and near the Southern Alps from Nelson to Fiordland.

Mostly high-alpine: 1,200–2,000 m (4,000–6,500 ft).

Usually common in snowbanks where it may form a complete turf; less important on stable sites in fellfield.

COLLECTED Cascade Saddle, upper Dart Valley, Mt Aspiring National Park, 1,680 m (5,500 ft). February 1970.

Chionochloa ovata (Buchan.) Zotov
"Ovate, egg-shaped" — referring to the shape of the flower head.

South Island: confined to the mountains of Fiordland and western Southland.

Low-alpine: 800–1,400 m (2,500–4,600 ft).

It may be locally common on wet or shaded sites in snow tussock–herbfield.

COLLECTED Secretary Island, Fiordland National Park, 1,070 m (3,500 ft). February 1967.

*__*Chionchloa defracta__* Connor, is confined to grassland and shrubland of ultramafic outcrops in Nelson and Marlborough, to 1,000 m.

*__*Chionochloa lanea__* Connor, occurs in boggy grassland and shrubland on Stewart Island, to 1,000 m.

*__*Chionochloa vireta__* Connor, occurs close to the main divide from south Canterbury to Fiordland, in low-alpine grasslands: 1,200–1,600 m (4,000–5,200 ft).

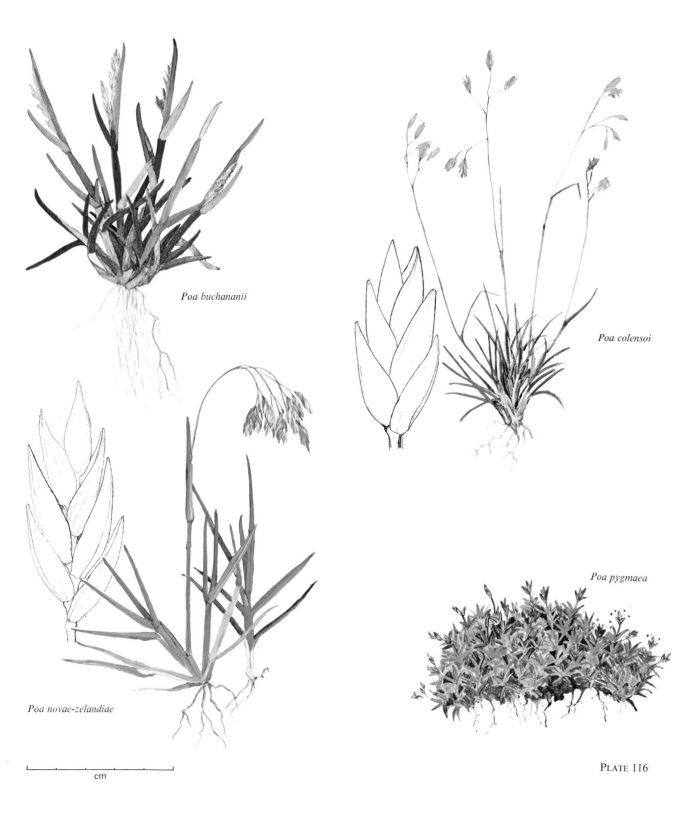

Poa buchananii

Poa colensoi

Poa novae-zelandiae

Poa pygmaea

cm

PLATE 116

Genus **RYTIDOSPERMA**

"Wrinkled seed" — a misnomer based on wrinkled insect larvae in the flowers of the specimen first described.

An Australasian genus with about 40 species. They are mostly small fine-leaved tussocks with prominent hairy ligules. Flower heads are loose and irregularly branched with large 4–8 flowered spikelets in which the outer pair of empty glumes almost completely encloses the florets. A prominent awn with a twisted base is attached between the pair of teeth at the tip of the flowering glume. Distinction between species is based largely on microscopic characters — distribution and length of hairs on the flowering glumes plus glume, anther and awn lengths — and therefore may not always be possible with certainty in the field.

Of the 27 species in New Zealand nine are naturalised from Australia, but the eight that may reach the alpine zone are all natives. Three that are both common and widespread are shown.

Rytidosperma setifolium (Hook.f.) Connor & Edgar BRISTLE TUSSOCK
"With slender leaves".

(= *Notodanthonia setifolia* (Hook.f.) Zotov)

Forms small pale-green to light-brown tussocks with glabrous, wiry leaves each with a prominent hairy ligule, and persistent sheaths.

Flower stems (5–40 cm long) exceed the leaves and have a small loose head in which the outer empty glumes are green-striped and the hairy florets, long awns and orange anthers are all prominent.

DISTRIBUTION North and South Islands: widespread in mountain regions throughout.

Lowland to high-alpine: to 1,700 m (5,500 ft).

HABITAT Typically on rock outcrops but sometimes present on moraine. In Marlborough, north Canterbury and locally elsewhere, it has become important in open depleted snow tussock grassland and herbfield.

COLLECTED Hooker Valley, Mt Cook National Park, 910 m (3,000 ft). January 1969.

Rytidosperma pumilum (Kirk) Clayton & Renvoize ex Connor & Edgar
"Very small".

(= *Erythranthera pumila* (Kirk) Zotov)

Wiry creeping stems are highly branched and mostly buried while the rolled bristle-like leaves are short with broad papery sheaths.

Flower stems (5–20 cm tall) exceed the leaves and the dark-green spikelets are distinctive with their 2–3 florets completely enclosed by the outer empty pair of dark glumes.

DISTRIBUTION South Island: widespread in the drier interior and eastern regions.

Mostly montane to high-alpine: 600–1,800 m (2,000–6,000 ft).

HABITAT Often present in the tussock grasslands and herbfields, sometimes becoming plentiful on open depleted sites. It extends into shallow snowbanks on well-drained slopes.

COLLECTED Rock & Pillar Range, Central Otago, 1,100 m (3,600 ft). April 1970.

Rytidosperma australe (Petrie) Clayton & Renvoize ex Connor & Edgar
"Southern".

(= *Erythranthera australis* (Petrie) Zotov)

The habit is similar to *R. pumilum* but the leaves may be flat. In the 2-4 flowered spikelets the pair of outer glumes are shorter and do not completely enclose the glabrous flowering glumes.

DISTRIBUTION North and South Islands: there are a few records from the main chain ranges of the North Island but it is most common east of the divide in the South Island.

Low- to high-alpine: 900–1,500 m (3,000–5,000 ft).

HABITAT On damp sites in tussock grassland and shallow snowbanks.

COLLECTED Rock & Pillar Range, Central Otago, 1,370 m (4,500 ft). January 1971.

Genus **POA**

"Fodder-grass".

A large genus of the temperate and cold regions. Many of the 500 or so species are highly variable, a feature that also applies to the 29 native mainland species recognised in a recent revision.

They have flat or rolled leaves with a translucent scaly ligule.

The spikelets are compressed and contain 2–8 florets. Flowering glumes are ridged or keeled along the back and have no awn but often there are tangled hairs at the base of the glumes.

About 21 native species reach the alpine zone. The following key should allow most alpine poas to be identified but for some features a good lens will be needed (for use of key see Glossary):

A	Old leaves breaking off at junction of sheath and blade	B
AA	Old leaves persistent on plant	E
B	Forms small greyish tufts, leaf tips curved, flower spikelets silky hairy	*P. maniototo*
BB	Plants bluish-green or light green, leaf tips narrowed to a point, spikelets not obviously hairy	C
C	Plants lax-leaved, forming light green turves, rhizomatous	*P. hesperia*
CC	Plants stiff-leaved, usually needle sharp, forming bluish-green turves or loose tussocks	D

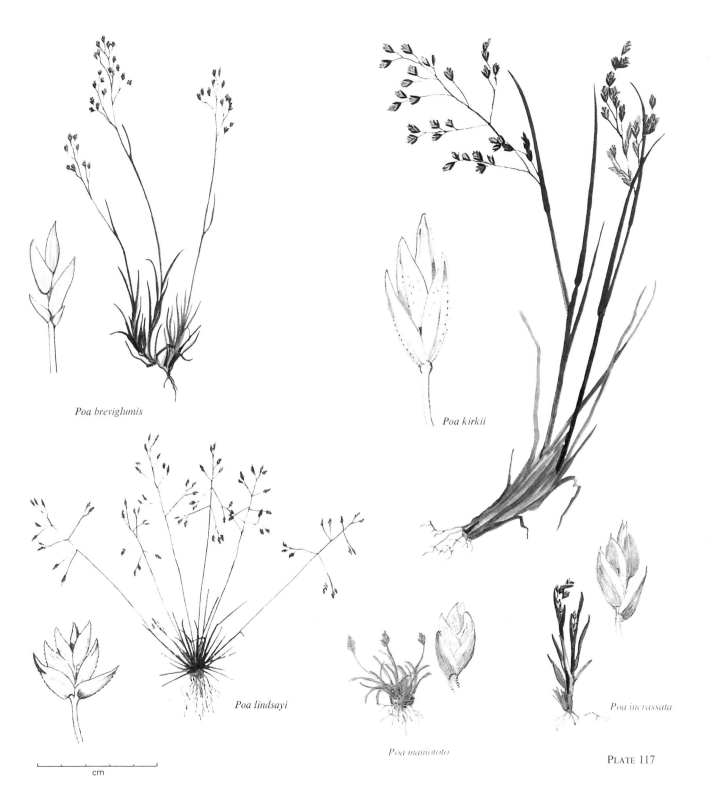

Poa breviglumis

Poa kirkii

Poa lindsayi

Poa maniototo

Poa incrassata

cm

PLATE 117

D	Loose tussocks 5–30 cm tall, flower heads barely overtopping the leaves	*P. colensoi*
DD	Plants rhizomatous, 10–20 cm tall, flower heads far overtopping the leaves	*P. acicularifolia*
E	Plants glaucous harsh and rigid, leaves in one plane; on loose debris or scree	*P. buchananii*
EE	Plants not as above	F
F	Mature flower heads very contracted	G
FF	Mature flower heads open or lax	I
G	Forming low cushions, flower heads <3 cm tall, brownish green, anthers >1 mm long; cushionfield plant	*P. pygmaea*
GG	Small tufted or stoloniferous plant, flower heads >3 cm tall, usually purplish tinged, anthers <1 mm long; from damp sites	H
H	Lemma of florets with hairs on the nerves (veins)	*P. senex*
HH	Lemma of florets without hairs on the nerves	*P. incrassata*
I	Plants bright green, leaves soft broad and flat, flower heads bright green to purplish green, nodding; mostly on damp rocks	J
II	Plants not as above	K
J	Leaf sheaths usually purplish, leaves 1-3 mm broad, florets sharp tipped	*P. novae-zelandiae*
JJ	Sheaths green to light brown, leaves 2–6 mm broad, florets blunt tipped	*P. subvestita*
K	Plants forming clumps or swards 15–40 cm tall, not tussock-forming; mostly Westland	*P. cockayneana*
KK	Plants smaller, or equal in height, but tussock-forming or tufted, not forming extensive swards	L
L	Spikelets with very small and unequal outer glumes, reaching < halfway up adjacent flowering glumes	*P. breviglumis*
LL	Outer pair of glumes longer, reaching > halfway up adjacent flowering glumes	M
M	Flowering glumes silky with short white hairs	N
MM	Flowering glumes glabrous or with hairs only on midnerve and/or in the tufts near base	O

N	Leaves grey-green or blue-green, rarely reddish, usually folded, flowering glumes silky hairy almost throughout	*P. lindsayi*
NN	Leaves light green, flat, flowering glumes silky hairy only in lower half	*P. tonsa*
O	Ligule on leaf ciliate across the top, 0.5–1 mm long	P
OO	Ligule smooth across the top, usually >1 mm long	Q
P	Leaves <1 mm wide and inrolled	*P. pusilla*
PP	Leaves >1 mm wide, flat or folded	*P. intrusa*
Q	Leaves rough on inner (upper) surface at least near the base, anthers 0.6–2.7 mm long	R
QQ	Leaves smooth on inner (upper) surface, anthers 0.2–0.7 mm long	T
R	Leaf sheaths rough, leaves 3–6 mm wide	*P. celsa*
RR	Leaf sheaths smooth, leaves 1–3 mm wide	S
S	Anthers >1.5 mm long	*P. dipsacea*
SS	Anthers 0.6–1 mm long	*P. kirkii*
T	Plants rhizomatous, flower heads 15–40 cm tall, branches below florets rough; Stewart Island	*P. aucklandica*
TT	Plants tufted or cushion-like to 15 cm tall, branches below florets smooth; South Island, along and west of Main Divide	*P. sublimis*

DISTRIBUTIONS AND HABITATS

Poa colensoi Hook.f.

After Rev. W. Colenso, early New Zealand botanist.

It varies from small tufts to tussocks and from 5 to 50 cm tall depending largely on altitude.

North, South and Stewart Islands: widespread in mountainous regions throughout.

Lowland to high-alpine: to 2,100 m (7,000 ft).

One of the most common grasses throughout the alpine zone with a very wide range of habitats. A tolerance of grazing has allowed it to persist and usually increase where pressure has been heavy.

COLLECTED Mt Brewster, Haast Pass, Mt Aspiring National Park, 1,830 m (6,000 ft). March 1968.

*Poa acicularifolia Buchan.

"Sharp-leaved".

South Island: apparently restricted to eastern Nelson, Marlborough and mid-Canterbury (Broken River basin) between the montane and

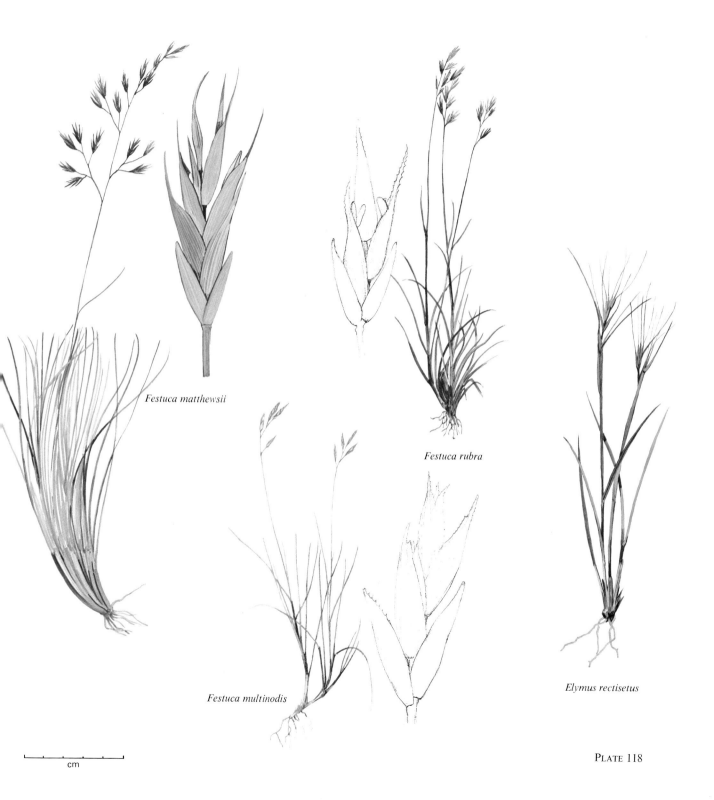

Festuca matthewsii

Festuca rubra

Festuca multinodis

Elymus rectisetus

cm

PLATE 118

low-alpine zones. Its compact glaucous patches, 5–15 cm across, may be confused with blue tussock (*P. colensoi*) but are best distinguished by the very sharp-tipped, short, rigid leaves and the hairy lower half of the flowering glumes. It occurs on ultramafic and limestone outcrops.

Poa lindsayi Hook.f.
After Dr L. Lindsay, British botanist who first collected it.

North and South Islands: local in the North Island but widespread east of the main divide to the south of Nelson in the South Island.

Lowland to low-alpine: to 1,500 m (5,000 ft).

Its small tufts usually colonise bare soil in depleted tussock grassland, sunny sites on rock outcrops, moraine, or occasionally scree. COLLECTED Old Man Range, Central Otago, 1,200 m (4,000 ft). December 1968.

* *Poa tonsa* Edgar
"Shaven" — refers to the glabrous flowering glumes that distinguishes it from the related *P. lindsayi*.

South Island: in the upper Awatere Valley (Shingle Ra.) of Marlborough and in Central Otago; in low-alpine tussock grasslands, including rock outcrops.

Poa pusilla Bergg.
"Very small".

North, South and Stewart Islands: it occupies wet open sites in mountain regions throughout, up to the low-alpine zone, to *ca* 1,500 m (5,000 ft).

Poa kirkii Buchan.
After Mr T. Kirk, early New Zealand botanist.

Its small tufts are quite variable, 10–45 cm tall. Leaves are flat or rolled, shorter than the flower stem, and the uppermost leaf sheath encloses much of the flower stem. Flower heads are lax, erect and brownish-, reddish-, or purplish-green.

North, South and Stewart Islands: Ruahine and Tararua Ranges; widespread in mountain regions of the South and Stewart Islands.

Montane to low-alpine: 700–1,500 m (2,000–5,000 ft).

Often common but inconspicuous in snow tussock grassland and herbfield. COLLECTED Mt Burns, Hunter Mountains, Fiordland National Park, 1,370 m (4,500 ft). January 1968.

Poa novae-zelandiae Hack.
Of New Zealand.

Plants are distinctive but may be confused with *P. subvestita*.

North, South and Stewart Islands: Mt Hikurangi, Tararua Range and the volcanic mountains; widespread in all but the driest areas of the South Island.

Subalpine to high-alpine: 800–2,100 m (2,500–7,000 ft).

Usually on rock ledges or crevices but it also colonises moist moraine and loose debris in fellfield. COLLECTED Mt Brewster, Haast Pass, Mt Aspiring National Park, 1,830 m (6,000 ft). March 1968.

* *Poa subvestita* (Hack.) Edgar
"Somewhat hairy" - referring to the fertile glumes of the florets.
(= *Poa novae-zelandiae* Hack. var. *subvestita* Hack.)

Similar to *P. novae-zelandiae* but plants are usually larger and with wider leaves and blunt-tipped rather than pointed florets. It occurs mainly along and west of the South Island main divide on shaded rocks in the montane to high-alpine zone: mostly 760–2,050 m (2,500–6,800 ft).

Poa buchananii Zotov
After Mr J. Buchanan, early New Zealand botanist.

South Island: widespread on the greywacke mountains, especially in the drier interior, from Nelson-Marlborough to north Otago.

Low- to high-alpine: 1,100–1,800 m (3,500–6,000 ft).

On screes and loose debris in fellfield. COLLECTED Mt Richmond, Two Thumb Range, south Canterbury; 1,520 m (5,000 ft). January 1969.

Poa pygmaea Buchan.
"Very small".

South Island: confined to a small area in Central Otago-Pisa Range, Dunstan Mountains, Mt Cardrona.

High-alpine: 1,500–1,900 m (5,000–6,500 ft).

Its dense cushions, 5–10 cm across, are common on exposed sites on the summit plateaux, less so in early snowbanks. COLLECTED Pisa Range, Central Otago, 1,830 m (6,000 ft). January 1970.

Poa incrassata Petrie
"Thickened" probably referring to the midrib of the floret.
(= *Poa exigua* Hook.f.)

South and Stewart Islands on the higher interior mountains of western and Central Otago to Fiordland and Stewart Island.

Low- to high-alpine: 800–1,900 m (2,650–6,500 ft).

Often a common if inconspicuous member of windswept tussock grassland, cushionfield, fellfield and early snowbanks. COLLECTED Old Man Range, Central Otago, 1,610 m (5,300 ft). December 1969.

* *Poa senex* Edgar
"Old man" — the locality, Old Man Range, where first collected.

South Island: known only from the Old Man and Pisa Ranges, Central Otago, in low- to high-alpine cushion bog and snowbank areas. Generally similar to *P. incrassata* and *P. sublimis*.

* *Poa sublimis* Edgar
"High or lofty" — referring to its elevation.

South Island: along and west of the main divide, in low- to high-alpine damp sites among rocks and in snowbanks.

Poa cockayneana Petrie
After Dr L. Cockayne, famous New Zealand botanist and pioneer ecologist.

South Island: largely confined to the subalpine and low-alpine zones in Westland, especially on avalanche chutes above and below the tree line. In south Westland it also colonises moraine.

Poa breviglumis Hook.f.
"Short-glumed" — referring to the outer pair of empty glumes in the spikelet.

North, South and Stewart Islands: widespread in mountain regions.
Mostly subalpine to high-alpine: 800–1,800 m (2,500–6,000 ft).
Often common in moist open or depleted tussock grassland or herbfield.
COLLECTED Blue Mountains, south Otago, 760 m (2,500 ft). December 1964.

Poa maniototo Petrie
"Maniototo" — from where the species was first described.

South Island: common locally in depleted tussockland and high-alpine communities on stony or well drained sites of the drier central regions; from lowland to high-alpine, to 1,600 m (5,250 ft).
COLLECTED Northern Dunstan Mountains, Central Otago, 1,730 m (5,600 ft). February 1985.

* Poa hesperia Edgar
"Western" — referring to its distribution.

South and Stewart Islands: along and close to the main divide from Westland to Fiordland; from subalpine to high-alpine, in snow tussock grassland and fellfield.

* Poa intrusa Edgar
"Thrust in" — referring to its central distribution and within that of the closely related P. kirkii.

South Island: Canterbury, Otago and northern Southland, mostly along and east of the main divide; subalpine to low-alpine, in tussock grassland. Distinguished from P. kirkii and P. celsa by the short and finely ciliate ligule.

* Poa celsa Edgar
"High, lofty" — referring to its elevation.

South Island: Nelson to north Westland, in low-alpine tussock grassland or on rock outcrops. It differs from the related P. kirkii, with which it sometimes occurs, in its larger size and longer anthers.

* Poa dipsacea Petrie
"Thirsty" — referring to its very wet habitat.

South Island: mainly Marlborough and Canterbury, rare in western Nelson; in low-alpine tussock grassland and herbfield, mostly in seepage areas and along streams. Its bright green smooth leaves and long anthers are distinctive.

* Poa aucklandica Petrie
From the Auckland Islands.

Subspecies rakiura Edgar is confined to Stewart Island, among rocks in snow tussock grassland on the summit of Mt Anglem at ca. 900 m (3,000 ft).

Genus FESTUCA
"A straw".

A large genus from the temperate and tropical mountain regions. Many features, including their habit, are similar to Poa but their flowering glumes are rounded on the back rather than keeled and are also sharp-tipped, usually with an obvious awn.

Of the five native mainland species, three reach the alpine zone.

Festuca matthewsii Cheesem.   ALPINE FESCUE TUSSOCK
After Mr H.J. Matthews, a forester and native plant enthusiast.

Small tufts or tussocks are dull glaucous with narrow, rolled, smooth leaves up to 30 cm long. Flower stems exceed the leaves and produce a lax head of flattened spikelets (1–1.5 cm long) in which each of the 5–7 flowering glumes is awned.
DISTRIBUTION South Island: widespread in mountain regions almost throughout.
Subalpine to low-alpine: 700–1,500 m (2,500–5,000 ft).
HABITAT Small tufts are common but inconspicuous in snow tussock-herbfield and valley grassland in the wet forested regions. On the run country of the drier interior and eastern mountains it forms distinct tussocks and these have increased at the expense of snow tussock, in response to burning and grazing, especially in south Canterbury and Central Otago. Their tussocks may be confused with the accompanying blue tussock, Poa colensoi, except when flower stems with the obvious awns are present.
COLLECTED Pisa Range, Central Otago, 910 m (3,000 ft). January 1967.

Festuca multinodis Petrie & Hack.
"Many-noded" — referring to the flower stem.

Its small tufts have rolled, bristle-like leaves and long, smooth, often purplish sheaths. Flower stems reach 10–20 cm in alpine areas with many leaves (10–12) especially near the base. The usually compact flower heads have 4–8-flowered spikelets, 6–9 mm long with a short to well-developed awn.
DISTRIBUTION North and South Islands: apparently confined to parts of the Wellington coastline; Banks Peninsula, the Awatere Valley and Central Otago in the South Island.
Coastal to high-alpine: to 1,400 m (4,500 ft).
HABITAT An inconspicuous member of snow tussock grassland and herbfield in Central Otago.
COLLECTED Rock & Pillar Range, Central Otago, 1,370 m (4,500 ft). February 1969.

Festuca rubra L.
"Red" — referring to the flower stems and leaf tips in some forms.

Stems are usually loosely tufted and bent or sometimes creeping at the base. Leaves are 8–15 cm long and bristle-like, but those on the flower stem are broader and partly flattened. Their sheaths are not deeply split as in *F. multinodis*. Flower heads are usually compact and erect or nodding, with pale-green to glaucous spikelets.

DISTRIBUTION North, South and Stewart Islands: widespread from East Cape and the upper Waikato River southwards.

Lowland to low-alpine: to 1,500 m (5,000 ft).

HABITAT Occurs sporadically in tussock grasslands and herbfield, on moraine and loose stony debris. A doubtfully native species.

COLLECTED By Professor G.T.S. Baylis, upper Copeland Valley, Westland National Park, 1,070 m (3,500 ft). January 1947.

Genus **ELYMUS**

From "Elymos" — Greek for millet.

A widespread genus with seven species occurring in New Zealand. Two of them reach the alpine zone.

Elymus solandri (Steud.) Connor BLUE WHEATGRASS

After Daniel Solander, botanist on Cook's first voyage to New Zealand.

(= *Elymus rectisetus* (Nees) Löve and Connor)

Highly variable but easily recognised by its pale-green to glaucous tufts and distinctive flower heads of up to 10 spikelets in which the 5–12 florets each have very long slender awns.

DISTRIBUTION North and South Islands: occurs throughout.

Lowland to low-alpine: to 1,500 m (5,000 ft).

HABITAT It ranges from tussock grassland and herbfield to loose mobile debris approaching scree but, being palatable, it is common only where grazing has been light or relaxed, or on inaccessible sites.

COLLECTED Hawkdun Range, north Otago, 1,460 m (4,800 ft). December 1969.

* *Elymus enysii* (Kirk) Löve and Connor

After Mr J.D. Enys, early Canterbury botanist.

Easily distinguished by the slender lax habit, thin flat leaves and narrow head with few (2–4) flowered spikelets that have only short awns up to 2 mm long.

It occupies flushes in subalpine and low-alpine grasslands of inland Nelson, Marlborough and Canterbury.

GLOSSARY

Alternate: arranged singly, not in opposite pairs.

Anther: the part of the stamen containing the pollen.

Aril: an appendage, often fleshy, on the outside of a seed.

Awn: a stiff, bristle-like projection especially on the glumes of grasses.

Axil: the upper angle between the leaf and stem.

Blade: the flattened part of an organ, especially a leaf.

Bract: a modified, often much reduced leaf, especially on a flower stem.

Calyx: the outer, usually green series of floral parts; consists of separate or joined sepals.

Capsule: a dry fruit formed from two or more fused carpels, which splits open when ripe.

Carpel: one unit of the female part of a flower; consists of a basal seed-bearing ovary joined to a receptive stigma by a usually stalk-like style.

Compound: composed of several similar parts, as opposed to simple.

Corolla: the usually showy series of floral parts; consists of separate or joined petals.

Crown: the area of the junction between root and stem.

Cushion plant: one with its shoots densely massed together and distinctly raised above the ground surface.

Endemic: native only to a particular country or region.

Flaccid: limp; not rigid.

Floret: a small flower, usually one of a cluster, as in the head of a daisy or the spikelet of grasses.

Frond: a leaf, especially of ferns.

Glabrous: without hairs.

Glandular hair: a hair tipped with a swollen gland.

Glaucous: of a distinctly bluish-green colour.

Glume: a small chaffy bract, especially in the flower heads of grasses, sedges and related groups; they may be either empty (sterile) or enclose a floret, (flowering glume).

Habit: the general appearance of a plant.

Indusium: an outgrowth that covers the sorus in many ferns.

Involucre: a group of bracts surrounding a flower head.

Keel: an obvious central ridge, as on a boat.

Key: as used in this book, select one of two alternatives, beginning with A or AA and then continue as directed by the letters until a species is named.

Lax: loosely arranged or widely spaced.

Leaflet: one section of a compound leaf.

Ligule: (in grasses) an appendage at the junction of the leaf blade with its sheath.

Linear: long and narrow with parallel margins.

Mat plant: one with its shoots densely massed together but not obviously raised above the ground surface.

Midrib: the main central vein of a leaf.

Node: a place on a stem where one or more leaves are attached.

Opposite: a pair of organs attached at the same level on opposite sides of an axis.

Ovary: the part of the flower containing the ovules and later the seeds (see carpel).

Pedicel: the stalk of a single flower in a compound head.

Petal: a separate member of the corolla.

Petiole: the stalk of a leaf.

Pinnate: with leaflets arranged regularly in two rows on either side of the stalk as in a feather (= once pinnate); twice-pinnate has the first order leaflets themselves pinnate; 3-pinnate has the second order leaflets themselves pinnate.

Pubescent: covered in short soft hairs.

Ray floret: strap-shaped florets that form a rim to the flower head in many members of the daisy family.

Rhizome: an underground, usually creeping stem.

Rootstock: a short, erect, underground stem.

Rosette: a group of organs radiating from a centre, especially many overlapping leaves more or less flattened against the ground.

Runner: a trailing stem which roots at the nodes.

Scale: a thin usually dry flap or leaf-like part.

Sepal: a separate member of the calyx.

Serrated: sharply toothed with the teeth pointing forward.

Sessile: without a stalk.

Simple: of one part; undivided (cf. compound).

Sinus: (in *Hebe*) a gap between the margins of the two leaves of an opposite pair that may be present in the bud before the pair of leaves separate. It occurs near the base and, if present, is seen between the unopened leaves in the terminal bud (see *H. odora*, Plate 92).

Sheath: a tubular envelope enclosing the stem, especially the lower part of the leaf in grasses and sedges.

Sorus (Sori): (in ferns) a cluster of sporangia.

Spikelet: a cluster of one or more florets in grasses, sedges and rushes.

Sporangium: (in ferns) a sac or other structure containing spores.

Stamen: the male or pollen-bearing organ of the flower; consists of an anther and its stalk.

Stigma: the part of the carpel which receives the pollen, usually at or near the tip of the style.

Stipule: scale-like or leaf-like appendage at the base of a petiole; usually paired.

Style: the more or less elongated part of the carpel between the ovary and stigma.

Sub-shrub: a semi-woody plant, usually herbaceous above and woody near the base.

Summer-green: dying back to underground parts in winter.

Tomentum: a dense covering of soft woolly hairs.

Trifoliate: having three leaflets.

Vascular plants: those with longitudinal strands of specialised conducting tissue; excludes algae, fungi, lichens, liverworts and mosses.

Whipcord: a shrub in which the leaves are reduced to scales that are close-set and pressed against the stem.

Whorl: an arrangement with similar organs arising from the same level.

INDEX

266

COMMON NAMES

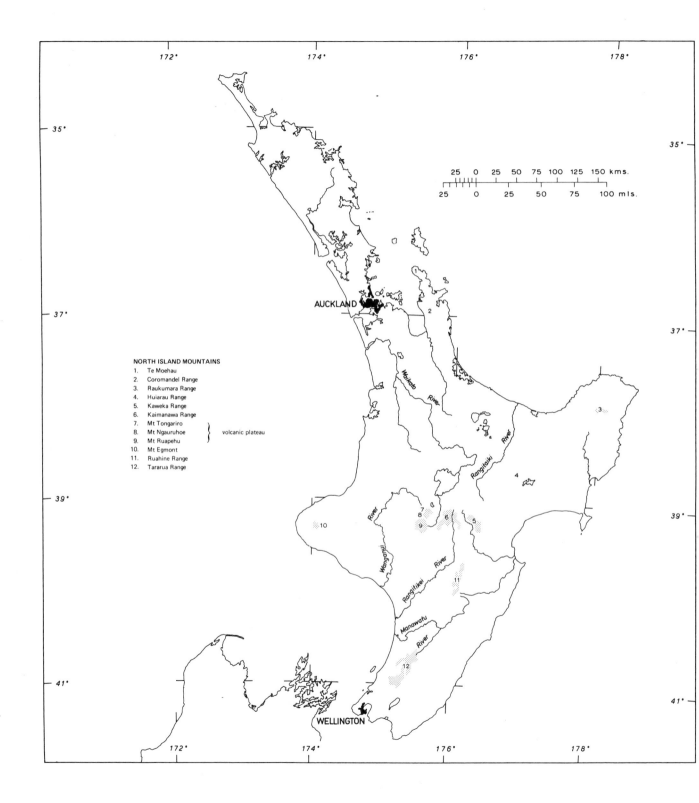

NORTH ISLAND MOUNTAINS
1. Te Moehau
2. Coromandel Range
3. Raukumara Range
4. Huiarau Range
5. Kaweka Range
6. Kaimanawa Range
7. Mt Tongariro
8. Mt Ngauruhoe
9. Mt Ruapehu
10. Mt Egmont
11. Ruahine Range
12. Tararua Range

} volcanic plateau